INVISIBLE MASTERS

RE-MAPPING THE TRANSNATIONAL

A Dartmouth Series in American Studies

SERIES EDITOR

Donald E. Pease
Avalon Foundation Chair of Humanities
Founding Director of the Futures of American Studies Institute
Dartmouth College

The emergence of Transnational American Studies in the wake of the Cold War marks the most significant reconfiguration of American Studies since its inception. The shock waves generated by a newly globalized world order demanded an understanding of America's embeddedness within global and local processes rather than scholarly reaffirmations of its splendid isolation. The series Re-Mapping the Transnational seeks to foster the cross-national dialogues needed to sustain the vitality of this emergent field. To advance a truly comparativist understanding of this scholarly endeavor, Dartmouth College Press welcomes monographs from scholars both inside and outside the United States.

For a complete list of books available in this series, see www.upne.com.

Elisabeth Ceppi, *Invisible Masters: Gender, Race, and the Economy of Service in Early New England*
Yael Ben-zvi, *Native Land Talk: Indigenous and Arrivant Rights Theories and the US Settler State*
Joanne Chassot, *Ghosts of the African Diaspora: Re-Visioning History, Memory, and Identity*
Samuele F. S. Pardini, *In the Name of the Mother: Italian Americans, African Americans, and Modernity from Booker T. Washington to Bruce Springsteen*
Sonja Schillings, *Enemies of All Humankind: Fictions of Legitimate Violence*
Günter H. Lenz, edited by Reinhard Isensee, Klaus J. Milich, Donald E. Pease, John Carlos Rowe, *A Critical History of the New American Studies, 1970–1990*
Helmbrecht Breinig, *Hemispheric Imaginations: North American Fictions of Latin America*
Jimmy Fazzino, *World Beats: Beat Generation Writing and the Worlding of U.S. Literature*
Zachary McCleod Hutchins, editor, *Community without Consent: New Perspectives on the Stamp Act*
Kate A. Baldwin, *The Racial Imaginary of the Cold War Kitchen: From Sokol'niki Park to Chicago's South Side*

ELISABETH CEPPI

INVISIBLE MASTERS

Gender, Race, and the Economy of Service in Early New England

DARTMOUTH COLLEGE PRESS
HANOVER, NEW HAMPSHIRE

Dartmouth College Press
An imprint of University Press of New England
www.upne.com

Manufactured in the United States of America
Typeset in Sabon by Integrated Publishing Solutions

Library of Congress Cataloging-in-Publication Data available upon request

Hardcover ISBN: 978-1-5126-0295-1
Paperback ISBN: 978-1-5126-0296-8
Ebook ISBN: 978-1-5126-0297-5

5 4 3 2 1

For Ben and Joel

From cradle to grave this problem of running order through chaos, direction through space, discipline through freedom, unity through multiplicity, has always been, and must always be, the task of education, as it is the moral of religion, philosophy, science, art, politics, and economy; but a boy's will is his life, and he dies when it is broken, as the colt dies in harness, taking a new nature in becoming tame. Rarely has the boy felt kindly towards his tamers. Between him and his master has always been war. Henry Adams never knew a boy of his generation to like a master, and the task of remaining on friendly terms with one's own family, in such a relation, was never easy.
—Henry Adams, *The Education of Henry Adams*

Perhaps this is one of the unfailing laws of progress in our being. Perhaps the Master of Life always rewards those who do their little faithfully by giving them some greater opportunity for faithfulness. Certainly, it is a comfort, wherever we are, to say to ourselves: —

"Thou camest not to thy place by accident,
It is the very place God meant for thee."

—Lucy Larcom, *A New England Girlhood*

CONTENTS

ACKNOWLEDGMENTS

THIS PROJECT BEGAN HALF my life ago, as an essay on Elizabeth Knapp that I wrote in my second term of graduate school at the University of Chicago, for a class taught by Janice Knight. She is the reason why this unlikely fascination with Puritans took such fierce hold on me. Laura Rigal, Janice Knight, Lauren Berlant, and the members of the Early American Cultures Workshop were brilliant and helpful readers of different revisions of the Knapp material and other chapters in my dissertation. I thank Lauren also for the gift of Samuel Sewall's diary, which has come in very handy. Clark Gilpin set the tone for a wonderfully collegial early Americanist cohort; among that group, I was especially lucky in the friendship of Shoshannah Cohen, Jonathan Field, and Jolynn Parker. My writing group partners, Jacqueline Stewart, Jennifer Peterson, and Leigh Anne Duck, offered keen feedback and camaraderie, as well as extraordinary patience when my "drafts" consisted primarily of block quotations from a decade's worth of laws in which the word "servant" appeared. Even from this distance, it is clear how much I learned from the people named above and Jon Aronoff, Jacqueline Cooper, Laura Demanski, Colin Johnson, Alison Landsberg, Greg Nosan, Katie Skeen, and Alicia Tomasian.

I have also been fortunate in the people who have made working at Portland State University (PSU) so rewarding. Peter Carafiol and Susan Danielson have been wonderful mentors and friends. A list of colleagues who contributed indirectly to this book's completion by inspiring, encouraging, and challenging me would be too long to be meaningful and yet would still leave people out. So instead I will thank those whose influence was more tangible: Susan Kirtley, Alastair Hunt, and Lee Medovoi, who invited me to present my work in progress in formal settings; the people who attended those presentations and offered critical feedback; and Sarah Ensor, Marie Lo, Jonathan Walker, and Leni Zumas, who wrote alongside me and were delightful company. I drafted chapter 5 at a Faculty Writing Retreat sponsored by the Office of Academic Innovation, and I thank the retreat's conveners, Janelle Voegele and Dannelle Stevens, and the other participants for making it such a productive experience. This book would have been very different if I had written it fresh out of graduate school, and that is in large part because of the insights I have gleaned from the experience of teaching my marvelous students, who have a knack for revealing new ways of seeing texts that I have read far too many times.

Over the years, the project has been funded by the Mellon Foundation, the Walter J. and Carol Blair Fellowship, the CBS Bicentennial Narrators Fellowship, the Fletcher Jones and Robert L. Middlekauff Fellowships at the Huntington Library, and two PSU Faculty Enhancement Grants. This support made it possible for me to conduct research at the Huntington Library, the American Antiquarian Society, and the Massachusetts Historical Society, and I thank the staffs of all those institutions—and of PSU's Millar Library and its interlibrary loan partner libraries—for their knowledge and assistance. The introduction and chapters 2 and 4 include material from articles previously published in *American Literature* and *LIT: Literature Interpretation Theory*; I am grateful for permission to use the material here, and for the opportunity to thank the anonymous reviewers whose suggestions greatly improved those essays.

I essentially started the project anew in 2009, after a term as English department chair and having my son, Benjamin. I researched, wrote, and revised the book over the next eight summers, mainly from home. For making a cluttered desk in a hot room feel like community, I thank Michelle Bobowick and Chuck Veneklase, Ronnie and Lili Boicourt, Mandi and Steve Hoyt-McBeth, Karl Kesel and Myrna Yoder, Trisha and Chris Mumm, Mark and Meghan Whitaker, all the kids, and especially our presiding spirit, Teri Rowan. Jasmin O'Neill has been my partner in pacing all over northeast Portland. Thanks to the incomparable Debra Gwartney and Barry Lopez for welcoming us so warmly each summer into the magical world of Finn Rock.

The book found its way to Dartmouth and the University Press of New England through a thread of advice and encouragement that connected Fredrika Teute to Lee Medovoi and finally to Donald Pease, and I will always be grateful for their support. Sarah Rivett provided wisdom at a key juncture. Jim Egan and an anonymous reviewer for the press offered the kind of incisive criticism that any author would hope for, and the final revision reflects my respect and admiration for their engagement with my work. Thank you to Richard Pult, Mary Garrett, Jeanne Ferris, and everyone at the press for giving my book a home.

My family circle expanded as the book took shape. Thanks to Joe and

Becce Bettridge; Marce and Matt Bettridge; Angella and Jason Jones; Sam Chambers and Rebecca Brown; Kim Evans and David LaRocca; Nathan Goldberg and Talia Gad; and cousins Jonah, Lydia, Anna, Sarah, Ruby, Star, and Stella for being such great in-laws. I especially appreciate Becce Bettridge for always being so open to the many things we can learn from each other.

It is a joy to thank those who have always been there for me. Rayna Kalas, Sam Puathasnanon, and Jennifer Yun are true friends. My brother Chris was my earliest best friend and is still both a dear one and a man I respect and love very much. Barbara August has always meant loving-kindness. I am lucky to have these people in my life: Alison Ceppi; Brian Ceppi; Allison, Cameron, and Ethan Ceppi; Ben and Penelope August; Natalie August; Billy August; Traci and Alexandra Hoffman; and Arlene Hoffman. Laura Ceppi, Robin Ceppi, and Joy Brown have given generously of love and support and made this all possible. Special thanks to my dear father, Michael Ceppi, for teaching me persistence.

While I began work on chapter 1, my son learned to crawl on the floor between piles of books with strange titles. Now that I am writing these last few words, he can throw a pretty darned good little fastball. Ben's big heart and interesting mind have been the best things about all of the days in between. For reasons I understand and others that may always remain mysterious, I wrote this book for my beautiful boy.

With grace and brilliance and kindnesses large and small, Joel Bettridge nestled this book into the life of our family, letting it be what it was and lending me his confidence in what it could become. Having Joel as my partner and Ben's dad is the great gift of my life. I started this project long before we met, but he has always been my ideal reader.

INVISIBLE MASTERS

INTRODUCTION: UNPROFITABLE SERVANTS

WHEN JOHN WINTHROP recorded the reasons why he would soon emigrate from England to Massachusetts, he reckoned the difference between them in servants. His accounting was both economic and spiritual. Winthrop calculated that as master of Groton Manor, he "spent three or four hundred pounds yearly" to maintain his "charge," but he anticipated living comfortably with only "seven or eight servants" in New England. He then considered a parable of a master with three servants. In the Gospel of Matthew, the master distributes eight talents among them: five to the first servant, two to the next, and to the third a single talent. The two "good and faithful servants" double their allotments and increase their master's wealth, but the "unprofitable servant" buries his lone talent and is brutally "cast . . . into outer darkness."[1] Winthrop read the allegory as a vocational tract: "if I should let pass this opportunity, that talent which God hath bestowed on me for public service were like to be buried."[2] He would not bury his talent in English soil. God called Winthrop to New England as a profitable servant, his peers chose him to be the Bay Colony's first governor, and he obeyed willingly. Eight servants embarked with their master on the *Arbella* in 1630.

Were they present when he exhorted his fellow passengers to remember the kind of servants God had chosen them to be? As they prepared to board, Winthrop delivered "A Model of Christian Charity," the lay sermon that contains his best-known contribution to American cultural history, his description of New England as a "city upon a hill." There he affirmed the community's common purpose in crossing the Atlantic: "to improve our lives to do more service to the Lord . . . to serve the Lord and work out our salvation under the power and purity of his holy ordinances."[3] Yet he warned that "if our hearts shall turn away, so that we will not obey, but shall be seduced, and worship other gods, our pleasures and profits, and serve them . . . we shall surely perish out of the good land whither we pass over this vast sea to possess it."[4] He echoes the classic refrain, "No man can serve two masters. . . . Ye cannot serve God and mammon."[5] This injunction is commonly understood to pit piety against profits, but Winthrop does not do that. "Mammon" constellates wealth, pride, and Satan under the sign of a tyrannical master. In the working out of salvation, "pleasures and profits" are moral when they serve God but become "mammon" when they are served as "other gods." Winthrop's stirring vision of his community's moral economy rests on the doctrine of one God, one Master.

Servants helped Winthrop improve his life and fulfill his calling to serve the commonwealth. Each of the eight servants who traveled with him from England increased his initial land grant by fifty acres. Before the decade was out, his household would also include Algonquian servants, chosen from among the prisoners, widows, and orphans of the Pequot War. He helped establish the trade network that connected New England and his own family's fortunes to the West Indies and Atlantic slavery.[6] Writing in his journal in the summer of 1638 as the master of Ten Hills Farm, Winthrop again reckoned the difference between Massachusetts and other British Atlantic colonies in servants. "Near all the lords" of the privy council "did favor this plantation," he marveled; even those "who savored not religion" were "amazed to see men of all conditions, rich and poor, servants and others, offering themselves so readily for New England, when, for furnishing of other plantations, they were forced to send about their stalls, and when they had gotten any, they were forced to keep them as prisoners from running away."[7] The governor had faith that the "city upon a hill" would thrive as a commercial venture because of its reputation as a good master.

The entwining of earthly servitude and mastery, the theology and typology of master and servant, and civic ideals of public service is no quirk of Winthrop's imagination. His example evokes a pervasive discourse that powerfully shaped how Puritans in New England understood the visible and invisible worlds and their place in them. Yet this discourse has generated almost no interpretive interest.[8] Perhaps the very ubiquity of service as a commonplace of Christian labor is the reason why it has not seemed worth probing Cotton Mather's premise that "the *Homage* which we owe unto the Heavenly Lord, is ordinarily described by *Metaphors* drawn from the *Service*, of an Earthly Master."[9] Yet these "Metaphors" reflected the complexity of covenant theology and resonated intimately with the variety of experiences involved in service as an institution.[10] As lived metaphors, master and servant signified multiple spiritual and moral types, and their plasticity made them ripe for use in a moral vocabulary that accommodated the decisions godly men made in response to the pressures and opportunities of the Atlantic economy—decisions that profoundly changed what it meant to serve earthly masters and what it meant to be one.

Invisible Masters rewrites the familiar narrative of the relationship between Puritan religious culture and New England's economic culture as a history of the primary discourse that connected them: service. Instead of interpreting the rhetoric of markets and money, it focuses on texts that capture friction between spiritual types of master and servant and traditional and enterprising practices of legal and institutional servitude: the enslavement of Native American prisoners of war and their families; the practice of binding out Puritan children; Atlantic slavery; debt servitude; and apprenticeship. In these productive conflicts, servants and their Christian masters created new types of master and servant that recalibrated traditional forms of obedience and authority and ideas about what counted as moral and spiritual labor. The book traces a genealogy of economic personality in these types as they press toward ideologies of mastery and service, attending to their meanings at particular cultural moments and tracking their transformations from the first generation of Puritan migration through the antebellum period.[11] Though the argument begins with the familiar figures of Puritan origins narratives and ends with Benjamin Franklin, it does not document an inevitable march toward a secular capitalist modernity. Rather, it participates in the project that Sarah Rivett has outlined for scholars of early American literature, "to construct new genealogies" from the evidence of "rhetorical forms that entwine the secular and the sacred."[12] The emerging concepts of mastery and service in this account include forms of piety (including a calling to be Christian masters of African and Native American servants and slaves); ideals of public service (including authorship) that conceive of "the public" in both secular and sacred terms; and the virtuous self-mastery of modern liberal subjectivity.

This book takes a literary critical approach to questions that scholars in other disciplines have posed about the role of master-servant relations in the history of capitalism. Legal and labor historians have charted the emergence of the modern employer-employee relationship and wage labor from the early modern Anglo-American law of master and servant, debating what that history implies about how "free" modern labor is.[13] More recently, scholarship in the "new" history of capitalism has examined the science of mastery on antebellum slave plantations as a model of capitalist management.[14] An exemplary contribution to that field, Bethany Moreton's *To Serve God and Wal-Mart*, shares this book's premise that Christian servanthood provides rich material for disturbing the equation of capitalism with secularization, along with the assumption that "master" translates into "manager" and "servant" into "worker." Moreton argues that the corporate Goliath thrived on a confluence of regional markets, broader economic conditions, and an "ideology of free enterprise as Christian service." This ideology united worker, manager, CEO, and shopper in a corporate culture where they "learned to revalue shopping as selfless service to family, and service in turn as a sacred calling. In this context, the salient identity became not citizen-consumer nor worker of the world, but Christian servant."[15] There is no straight line between Winthrop's ideal of "Christian servant" and Sam Walton's, but the connections between this project and Moreton's demonstrate that service can provide a framework for interdisciplinary conversations about the relationship between economic and religious culture across traditional regional and temporal boundaries.

This book joins revisionist approaches to early New England that collectively resist the determinism of free labor and secularization associated with Max Weber's *The Protestant Ethic and The Spirit of Capitalism*. The premise that New England's laborers were bound only by divine covenant and driven by "the inner compulsions of worldly asceticism" has grounded accounts of its exceptional economic culture.[16] Indeed, from an empirical standpoint, unfree labor was marginal to New England's economy, particularly in a comparative colonial context.[17] Counting servants, however, tells only part of the story, and several recent books have demonstrated the dependency of New England's commercial networks and household economies on servitude and slavery.[18] These works reconceive the exceptionalist narrative by focusing on New England as a unique culture of service among many in an Atlantic economy characterized by slippery distinctions between freedom and unfreedom that were increasingly racialized.[19] In Wendy Warren's bracing formulation, "messianic impulses alone could not and did not sustain New England; the Atlantic system required more."[20] Accounts of how men like Winthrop facilitated and profited from slavery and servitude add fresh urgency to familiar questions about the relationship between Puritanism and capitalism, but most have bracketed questions of theology, doctrine, and piety.[21] *Invisible Masters* considers legal and institutional servitude as part of a broader discourse of service that includes the spiritual economy, providing conceptual grounds of moral contest between those "messianic impulses" and the Atlantic system's "requirements." How did trade in and the willingness to profit from the labors of African and Native American servants transform the meanings of spiritual service? How did their understandings of themselves as God's servants affect how Puritans viewed those they served and those who served them?

To give these questions their due, we cannot treat New England slavery as still more proof that Puritans were hypocrites whose religion "explain[ed] away their greed."[22] To do so would ignore a substantial body of interdisciplinary scholarship that has created a more nuanced picture of how they reconciled piety with commerce.[23] The most compelling recent contribution to this literature, Mark Valeri's *Heavenly Merchandize*, depicts Massachusetts Bay ministers, merchants, and magistrates as conscious agents in the transition from a society with markets to a market society, working together to create a new "moral and cultural vocabulary" from the material practices, ideas, and rhetoric of their common piety."[24] Valeri shows how a market ethos developed within complex human relationships, not just in response to abstract forces and doctrines. In the lively religious culture he re-creates, ministers sought God's will in commercial success, and the phrase "pious merchant" was no oxymoron, even in the case of slave merchants. One can hardly imagine a more satisfying account of such exchanges among elite male peers, but this was not a society of equals. Puritan women and children, African Americans, and Native Americans did not just contribute to the New England economy but actively shaped its economic culture; and hierarchies of gender, race, rank, and age undergirded the moral ideas and rhetoric of the market order. How did elite men's relationships with their dependents shape their moral imagination? How was it shaped by their knowledge of themselves as God's servants in the spiritual economy? How did their wives and children, servants, and slaves contribute to that moral vocabulary?

Invisible Masters addresses these questions by focusing on the cultural economy of the household, interpreting narratives set in domestic spaces (including Mary Rowlandson's wilderness), household conduct instructions, laws, sermons, and personal writings that reveal how crucial the concepts of master and servant were to what was commonly called the household service of God. The household was not just the main physical site of labor for all who worked under English governance but the primary cultural and conceptual space where that work was sanctified and disciplined—not just made productive, but made meaningful.[25] To make the household both materially and spiritually profitable, all of its inmates, even the master of household, had to emulate servant personhood. Master and servant defined the changing threshold of the family and were portable forms of obedience and authority that moved among family, church, state, and market, all of them conceived of as extensions of household space. Embodying masterly authority whether or not they had servants, New England's magistrates, ministers, and merchants guarded the shifting boundary between private and public spaces.

The primary currency in the cultural economy of the household was obedience, in particular the complex concept of obedience at the heart of covenant theology.[26] Calvinists believed that God had made two covenants with man: his covenant with Adam, the covenant of works; and his covenant with Abraham, the covenant of grace. Humans are the sinful progeny of Adam's disobedience, but under the covenant of grace, God predestined some human beings—the "elect" or "saints"—for salvation by faith alone. The elect were bound to obey the moral law and to credit God's grace alone for their ability to do so. They searched their bodies, hearts, minds, and souls for signs that their obedience was evangelical (or "new"), the faithful labor of God's beloved, and not merely moral or "legal," a dutiful path to damnation; and they turned to another of the gospel's unprofitable servants as a means of telling the difference.[27]

"Lord, increase our faith," beseech the disciples in the fifth verse of Luke 17, and Jesus responds by asking them to imagine themselves as masters. He then poses some rhetorical questions. When your servant comes in weary from the field, do you invite him to sit down to his dinner, or do you greet him with a command: "Make ready wherewith I may sup . . . and serve me, till I have eaten and drunken; and afterward thou shalt eat and drink"?[28] Does the master "thank that servant because he did the things that were commanded him? I trow not." When he turns to the spiritual lesson in the last verse, Jesus asks the disciples to identify themselves as servants instead of as masters: "So likewise ye, when ye shall have done all those things which are commanded you, say, We are unprofitable servants: we have done that which was our duty to do." Puritan saints must obey the moral law, but they also must grasp with all their fallen faculties that doing so was, according to Calvin's commentary on the parable, "only paying what he owed."[29] Zealous pursuit of good works and manifestly godly comportment might be evidence only of "the pride of the flesh," and thus a hypocrite's labor. Earthly blessings—from material prosperity to the capacity to read or hear and be edified by the parable—were made possible by the work of the Holy Spirit and God's gift of grace, bestowed upon the elect despite their utter unworthiness for it. Luke 17:10 expressed such thankful obedience as perfectly as corrupt human language could manage to do.

The parable was a touchstone of piety throughout the colonial period, and a few iterations of it capture, in miniature, the arc that this book traces of New England's racializing economic culture. It was a source of contention between John Cotton and Thomas Shepard, two of the leading ministers of the founding generation. In sermons preached before and after they immigrated to New England in the early 1630s, Cotton emphasized "say" in verse 10, presenting it as a spiritually profitable meditation, a ready phrase the elect could internalize as a means of growing in grace and active faith; while Shepard warned his auditors that proclaiming oneself to be an "unprofitable servant" might just be the crutch of a hypocrite, a particularly dangerous form of legal obedience.[30] What conflicts might have resonated in the fall of 1708, when the wealthy Boston merchants Samuel Sewall and Andrew Belcher attended the Reverend Nehemiah Hobart's rendering of the parable, which Sewall thought he "preached excellently"?[31] Sewall was a jurist whose most enduring piece of writing is a 1701 abolitionist tract, *The Selling of Joseph*, in which he argues that "the extraordinary and comprehensive Benefit accruing to the Church of God, and to *Joseph* personally, did not rectify his brethrens [*sic*] Sale of him"; Belcher traded grain and was also among a "privileged class of slave-trading merchants."[32] Sixty years later, the Reverend Samson Occom returned from a two-and-a-half-year missionary trip to Britain, where he raised 12,000 pounds for his mentor Eleazar Wheelock's Moor's Indian Charity School and advocated for Mohegan land rights on behalf of his tribe. He soon learned that Wheelock was diverting the money to educate white children, and his long absence from home, combined with systematically low wages, had compounded his debts to Wheelock and other creditors.[33] Venting his frustration in a 1768 letter, Occom wrote, "that Debt I owe to Dr. Wheelock remains Still against I find my Family is very Chargable & I am [unfortunately] to Say he is unprofitable."[34] Occom turned Luke 17:10 into a critique of Wheelock's hypocrisy: a parable of the unprofitable master.[35] Like Winthrop, Occom had been given a talent for public service. This servant of the Lord increased his masters' wealth, but buried in debt, he could never be as profitable to his Master and his people as he longed to be.

Luke's unprofitable servant is an exemplum and Matthew's is a cautionary tale, but both versions exemplify the willing obedience to God the Master that was the primary virtue of Puritan economic and religious culture. In spiritual types of master and servant, the distinction between two kinds of covenant obedience also denoted virtuous and degraded relations to money and wealth: not just profits but also wages and prices, buying and selling, and debt and inheritance. Excavating the ancient roots of capitalism, the anthropologist David Graeber observes that the Christian narrative of redemption entwines a slavery-to-freedom story with the "language of the marketplace."[36] Types of master and servant tether worldly experience to this master plot. One place to see this clearly is in the rhetoric of vocation, the doctrine at the center of Max Weber's account of the Protestant ethic and its secularization. Indeed, Weber implies the significance of these types, citing the parable of the talents to explain his concepts of calling and asceticism.[37] A commonly cited scripture, or proof-text, of Puritan vocation was 1 Corinthians 7:20–24: "Let every man abide in the same calling wherein he was called. Art thou called *being* a servant? Care not for it, but if thou mayest be made free, use *it* rather. For he that is called in the Lord, *being* a servant, is the Lord's free man: likewise also he that is called *being* free, is Christ's servant. Ye are bought with a price; be not ye the servants of men." Servants who "care not" about their humble earthly station embody "Pauline indifference," the asceticism of the Christian everyperson in their callings. In his *Treatise of the Vocations or Callings of Men* (circa 1600), the eminent Puritan divine William Perkins explains that Christians in their vocations must continually strive to align their "general callings" as God's servants with their "particular callings," the earthly stations to which God appoints them. To continually "join both our callings together," he instructs his readers, Puritans should "consider the main end of our lives, and that is to serve God in the serving of men in the works of our callings."[38] The plasticity of the term "servant" as a sign of humble earthly labor and exalted spiritual labor holds the chiasmus together, sustaining the paradoxes of Protestant liberty: that freedom is service, and the price of redemption is a gift from God.

The Pauline counterpart to that faithful servant is the hypocrite "eye-servant." In Ephesians 6:5–9, Paul offers instructions to servants and their "masters according to the flesh." Servants must obey "with fear and trembling, in singleness of your heart, as unto Christ. Not with eye-service, as menpleasers, but as the servants of Christ, doing the will of God from the heart." Masters must also heed this injunction: "And, ye masters, do the same things unto them, forbearing threatening: knowing that your Master also is in heaven; neither is there respect of persons with him." These common injunctions against eye-service and hypocrisy are variations on the theme sounded by "ye cannot serve God and mammon." Alan Heimert and Andrew Delbanco have proposed that while Catholics asked what to do to be saved and Protestants asked how to know whether they were saved, the fundamental question for American Puritans was, "'What am I in the eyes of God?'"[39] The eyes of God were the eyes of a Master. All humans are naturally slaves to sin, but had God chosen them to be His servants?

This book treats this difference between two kinds of servants as a crucial Puritan division of labor, arguing that the concept of God the Master was more important to New England's economic culture than any particular doctrine. An extended passage from Cotton's *The Way of Life* provides a foundation for this argument. The sermon has been taken by Perry Miller and Stephen Innes to exemplify Puritan vocation, but Cotton preaches across doctrines, spiritualizing the qualities that Weber associated with secular vocation—diligence, asceticism, and a man's sense of duty to his wealth—as forms of covenant obedience.[40] The passage begins with the familiar chiasmus of vocation, "We live by faith in our vocations, in that faith, *in serving God, serves men, and in serving men, serves God:* The Apostle sweetly describes it in the calling of servants, *Eph. 6.5. to 8. Not with eye-service as men pleasers, but as the servants of Christ, doing the will of God from the heart.*"[41] Wage labor is mere legal obedience: "We wrought not for wages, nor for the praise of you, if so, wee [*sic*] had not been the servants of Christ." Hypocrites work for wages, while God's servants inherit the ability to be a man who "serves Christ in serving of men, [who] doth his work sincerely as in God's presence, and as one that hath an heavenly businesse in hand, and therefore comfortably as knowing God approves of his way and work."[42] We associate the work ethic with diligence, but Cotton does not warn about the dangers of idle hands. Instead, the peril is an eye-servant's diligence: "hast thou a Calling, and [are] never so diligent in it, it is but a *dead worke*, if thou want faith. . . . [I]f we can tell how to be eye-servants, it is but a dead worke, for want of faith."[43] To do "heavenly businesse," the elect must feel that they are always "in God's presence," working under their Master's eye, like servants who faithfully devote themselves to increasing a master's profits whether or not the master is there to see it.

Without taking Cotton and his peers as the creators of an exceptional capitalist morality, *Invisible Masters* traces the emergence of spiritual and secular vocations from the types in this passage. It tells the story of how this quintessential type of hypocrite—a man who forgets that he has a Master in heaven—becomes the ideal subject of liberal capitalism, a man capable of self-mastery. While this figure has been taken to epitomize secular modernity, it is not uniquely or exclusively secular.[44] Rather, it is one type of economic personality in an ideology of service in which multiple masters compete with God for moral authority. These multiple forms of moral obedience register the shifting balance between the secular and the sacred in economic culture. The eye of God the Master becomes both an internalized economic conscience and the eye of a public invested with the authority of a master, an entity to be served. But the self-mastering man might still imagine himself to be working under God's eye as well as in the public eye, perhaps conceiving of God as Father or Creator rather than Master.

Benjamin Franklin's *Autobiography* illustrates the dynamism of the secular and sacred in his version of vocation, his desire to "be serviceable to People in all Religions."[45] He twice repeats the primary doctrine of this "Creed": "the most acceptable Service of God is doing Good to Man."[46] Franklin reverses the terms of the chiasmus of orthodox vocation, converting man pleasing into a modern calling to public service, but God is not just a placeholder in his chiasmus. To Weber, Franklin epitomized secular vocation, but we might instead see him as creating a concept of God that provides moral authority both for what Tracy Fessenden has described as the "unmarked" Protestantism that stands for religion in American culture and the "post-Protestant secularism" that produced it.[47] Franklin faithfully served three masters: God, the public, and yes, most of all, himself. Though Franklin alters the balance between sacred and secular obedience, this is not Weber's secular vocation.

Unlike bifocals and the "long arm," a contraption for pulling books down from high shelves, this calling is not truly a Franklin invention. Rather, it is a particularly well-publicized moment in the genealogy that this book sketches, one that shows how Franklin's model of vocation emerges not just as an ideal of class mobility and independence for moral men of English descent, but also as a gendered and racialized ideology of dependence for those who served them. A century before Franklin, a sixteen-year-old servant named Elizabeth Knapp enacted lay public service by beseeching the townspeople at her bedside to make good use of their time, lest they fall under Satan's dominion as she had done. Mary Rowlandson recalled her longing while in captivity to have a Christian master instead of heathen ones. Cotton Mather set forth instructions for the particular calling of white Christian masters with black slaves, while the merchant Sarah Kemble Knight chided Connecticut farmers for allowing their slaves to eat from the common pot. Urging her husband to "Remember the Ladies" at the Continental Congress, Abigail

Adams declared her doctrine of companionate marriage: "That your Sex are Naturally Tyrannical is a Truth so thoroughly established as to admit of no dispute; but such of you as wish to be happy willingly give up the harsh title of Master for the more tender and endearing one of Friend."[48] Occom reminded the white ministers gathered at the execution of Moses Paul, a Wampanoag convicted of murdering a white man outside a tavern, how to serve the Lord: "to do the work the Lord Jesus Christ your blessed Lord and Master has set you about, not fearing the face of any man, nor seeking to please men, but your Master."[49] Like Franklin, Occom racializes an eye-servant's hypocrisy: for Franklin it becomes the economic conscience of a white man performing his self-mastery in the public eye; for Occom, it is a species of white pride expressed as an assumption of mastery over others, evinced by whites' habit of treating Native Americans—even ministers—as their servants. Dramatizing the play between visible and invisible masters, these instances map one cultural route by which modern ideologies of mastery and service came to be, and how they came to be bound to distinctions of gender, race, and class.

Perhaps surprisingly, the prodigal son is a critical figure in this history, and this book begins by explaining what his journey from profligate to penitent reveals about a central feature of the cultural economy of the Puritan household: the correlations between servants and children, and masters and fathers. In seventeenth-century New England, most servants were children, and many children, even those from elite families, spent time in service to a master. Children working at "the bark of their fathers' commands" made up a significant portion of the laboring population of colonial Massachusetts.[50] Christopher Tomlins has observed that labor law "not only was preoccupied with controlling youth," but "comprehensively mudd[ied] the distinction between *son* and *servant*," while Helena Wall attributes what she calls the "ambiguities of family" to the slippages between masters and fathers, and servants and children, which she links to the putting-out system.[51] But beyond noting its connection to the fifth commandment, scholars have not considered how this correlation resonated in the spiritual economy, where the saints knew themselves as both God's servants and his children.

Chapter 1, "The Child Who Serves: Household Obedience and the Public Authority of Masters," reads such "muddy distinctions" and "ambiguities" as evidence of the lived experience of the covenant dialectic in the governance of household, church, and state. I have described a version of the covenant dialectic in which "servant" was an exemplum, but in a second version, God distinguished his beloved children from mere servants. In Paul's allegory, two sons of Abraham signify the two covenants: the covenant of works was embodied by Ishmael, son of the bondwoman Hagar; and the covenant of grace by Isaac, son of the free-woman Sarah. The condition of the son followed that of the mother, so obedience to the moral law was the "obedience of servants," while evangelical obedience was the "obedience of sons."[52] Obeying like a son was evangelical or new obedience; obeying like a servant was hypocrisy. God's children would live forever in his household, while servants would be cast out, or turned out of doors, as the common phrase had it. Yet covenant sonship also posed the threat of libertinism; children of God might rest in the inheritance of grace, deeming themselves free from the moral law. And covenant servitude came with a promise: the reward of working toward the good of another, not the self. In the dialectic, God's children must internalize servitude as a curb on libertinism, and God's servants should internalize sonship as a curb on legalism. The covenant synthesis of "childe-like service" was the essence of evangelical obedience.[53]

Chapter 1 establishes the significance of the child who serves as a type of work for love for God's elect and of the servant turned out of doors as a type that spiritualizes the diligent labors of the damned as a source of spiritual and economic profit for the chosen few.[54] Reading a range of texts from the decade of the Great Migration (1630–40), the chapter argues that these types of covenant obedience were essential to the exchange between private and public forms of authority and shows how distinctions of gender, race, and rank shaped their various applications. I begin by describing how the servant-son and master-father analogies function in household governance manuals by Perkins and his student, the influential theologian William Ames, and establishing the meanings of these types in God's household by focusing on how three of the leading ministers, Cotton, Shepard, and Thomas Hooker, preached the doctrines of humiliation and adoption. In Luke 15:19, the verse known as the prodigal's petition, he expresses his willingness to be his father's hired servant. These ministers preached the prodigal's petition as a fitting expression of humiliation's ideal of child who serves, who has internalized God as both Master and Father. This ideal connects Christ to the prodigal, Native American war orphans, ministers-in-training at Harvard College, and a book of poems by Anne Bradstreet.

But this chapter also establishes the gendering and racialization of its countertypes: the licentious child who relies on his or her inheritance and the hypocritical servant who labors dutifully for the benefit of the family and then is turned out of doors. In these types, New England's ruling elite spiritualized the labor and wealth of those who might never be children of God, including the fathers of Pequot children who were sold into West Indian slavery and those who refused to serve their earthly fathers—like Anne Hutchinson and others of her faction who were banished to the wilderness, like Hagar and Ishmael. The book follows this gendering and racialization of public and private authority as it defines the relationships between earthly households and God's household; between private and public forms of piety; and between the earthly institutions of family, church, and state as elites adjusted the boundaries between them in a new market order.

Chapter 2, "Answering Back: Elizabeth Knapp's Demonic Possession and the Gender of Public Service," considers a spectacular instance in which humiliation's ideal of child service clashed with the institutional practice of binding children out as servants. The conflict centers on the governance of the tongue as crucial evidence of properly humbled labor. Servants of God, like earthly servants, were to hold their tongues before their Master and to submit themselves to his will; and the authority of ministers, masters, and magistrates in their callings was invested in their power over the speech of their dependents. In 1671, Satan seized control of the Reverend Samuel Willard's servant Elizabeth Knapp, ventriloquizing her in spectacular fashion. Knapp's case has been read as a portent of the Salem witchcraft cases and as an episode in the history of the class and gender politics of speech. This chapter considers the special role that the law of master and servant played in governing domestic and public speech. The child who serves as a lived metaphor of humiliation defined Knapp's relation to Willard, but it also provided the script for their gendered callings to public service: demonic possession and authorship. In Valeri's account, Willard works with his wealthy merchant congregants of the Old South Church to craft concepts of vocation for an evolving market ethos.[55] Reading Willard's 1672 narrative of Knapp's possession alongside the sermons he preached in Groton and, later, to Boston's elite at the Third Church, I present Knapp as Willard's partner in this venture, demonstrating her effect on his influential Halfway Covenant evangelism and preaching of market morality.

Mary Rowlandson's experience with ungodly masters also shaped Willard's moral rhetoric, as I discuss in Chapter 3, "Servant to a Christian: Mary Rowlandson's Captivity and the Racialization of Obedience." When Rowlandson renders her captivity as servitude and her captors as masters, she embodies the orthodox doctrine of vocation: the servant's calling. She spiritualizes her own labors in captivity as child service and presents her own son, Joseph, as a type of this ideal. Rowlandson's narrative was at the same time a vocational manual for increasingly racialized New England households in the aftermath of King Philip's War. Rowlandson's depiction of servitude and mastery across divides of gender, race, and religion taught Puritan men how to be good masters of the Native Americans they made into their servants as they expanded the legal culture of racialized servitude that would define postwar Native-Anglo relations, and serves as a model of a secularized form of moral obedience to be emulated by these children as they served such masters. She also spiritualizes male mastery in her negative portrayal of her native mistress Weetamoo, so different from her representation of Quinnopin as a kind master. Her narrative was an essential contribution to a broad cultural effort to convert practices previously deemed to be hypocrisy into a new kind of vocation: the ideal of white Christian men as masters who can compete with God the Master for moral authority.

Building upon the Rowlandson chapter and recent scholarship on New England slavery, Chapter 4, "Racial Vocation: New England's Calling to Slavery," focuses on the cultural work of reconciling white Christian mastery with the African slave trade. I argue that Puritan proslavery and abolitionist discourses worked together to further Rowlandson's project of converting practices formerly deemed to be hypocrisy into new callings of white masters and nonwhite servants, becoming a fully realized concept of racial vocation. My analysis focuses on the decade that framed the breaking of the Royal African Company's monopoly in 1698, and it discusses the making of racial vocation in the debate between Sewall and John Saffin, sermons and tracts by Cotton Mather, laws regulating servitude, and Knight's 1705–6 travel narrative. These texts racialize master and servant personhood, and in so doing they redefine the callings of merchants, ministers, and magistrates. Knight's public calling was a form of "deputy mastery" over racial and class others—as was authorship itself, even for abolitionist writers like Sewall. By reinterpreting secular vocation as an accommodation not just to commerce but also to slavery in particular, the chapter reconceptualizes it as a form of spiritualized white male mastery of others and themselves.

Chapter 5, "The Spirit of Mastery: Samson Occom, Benjamin Franklin, and Modern Hypocrisy," shows how the doctrines of racial vocation shaped the moral imaginations of two famous eighteenth-century sons of New England. Of course, Weber famously distilled from Franklin's writings the very essence of the capitalist spirit. Franklin was also the quintessential apprentice made good. In contrast, Occom was never bound by contract to any master, but he discovered that his calling to serve the Lord nevertheless bound him to an ideology of white mastery. This chapter juxtaposes Franklin's paradigmatic ideology of service as self-mastery and Occom's vision of spiritual and earthly service, showing how what it meant to "master" oneself and "serve" others was shaped by the racialization of legal and spiritual servitude and mastery and by their shared awareness of the public as a domain of white mastery. Both men offer post-Puritan versions of the prodigal, eye-servant, child who serves, and servant turned out of doors, adapted to the purposes of their public callings—including authorship.

The coda, "Serving the Plot," follows these types into the literary culture of antebellum New England, as they are transformed by the imaginations of Ralph Waldo Emerson, Margaret Fuller, Nathaniel Hawthorne, Frederick Douglass, the Native American minister and activist William Apess, Harriet Beecher Stowe, and Catharine M. Sedgwick. I conclude by considering some of the forms they take in our present economy of service.

Narratives of Puritans' influence on modern American culture frequently focus on how they transformed what it meant to save themselves, but they also transformed what it meant to serve themselves. In *Something for Nothing*, Jackson Lears charts the emergence of two main modern currents of American morality, both of which are derived from Calvinist theologies of grace: a "culture of control," whose hero is the self-made man who embodies a managerial and disciplinary ethos; and a "culture of chance," which is under the sway of the confidence man and the gambler. Lears recasts the "work ethic" as an "ethic of mastery" for the culture of control, arguing that it rises from the "growth of an Arminian emphasis on human beings' individual ability to save themselves" that "sanctioned self-help in secular as well as religious matters."[56] As this book argues, this "ethic" was forged within providential discourse not just as a will to master fate, but also as a will to master others—especially those deemed incapable of mastering themselves. This study of early New England reveals that ideals of service and mastery contain histories of masters and servants. Viewed this way, it seems all the more pressing to follow Lears's prompts to interrogate the morality of mastery and remain alive to the alternatives it works so hard to suppress.

[1]

THE CHILD WHO SERVES: HOUSEHOLD OBEDIENCE AND THE PUBLIC AUTHORITY OF MASTERS

Father, I have sinned against heaven, and before thee, and am no more worthy to be called thy son: make me as one of thy hired servants. —Luke 15:18–19

Methoughts I heard one calling, *Child!*
 And I reply'd, *My Lord.*
—George Herbert, "The Collar"

FEW PURITANS WASTED THEIR portions on harlots, but the parable of the prodigal son taught even the godliest among them to make "a right use" of their sins.[1] To grow in new obedience, the elect cultivated what John Cotton called a sense of "daily ungodlinesse," rooted in the knowledge that they were unworthy of their Father's mercy and love.[2] The parable's dramatic narrative of sin, repentance, and forgiveness patterned the routine rhythms of the life of sanctification. Iconic images of the son's prostration and the father's embrace were woven into the fabric of Elizabethan and Jacobean culture—literally, in the case of tapestries. Reformed evangelists would have considered prodigal plays and stained-glass window scenes as, at best, dangerous distractions from the word of God, but the parable provided them with powerful visual rhetoric that was a central feature of Protestant aesthetics and a shaping force of Protestant subjectivity throughout the British Atlantic.[3]

But the familiar postures also obscure an aspect of the parable that Puritans knew by heart: a pattern of exchanges between sonship and servitude, and fatherhood and mastery. After the prodigal squanders his portion, starvation compels him to bind himself as a servant to the "citizen"—who, instead of feeding him, sends him to feed swine. In this degraded condition, the prodigal compares himself to the servants in his father's household, "who have bread enough and to spare" (Luke 15:17). In Luke 15:18–19, he rehearses what he will say to his father when he returns, starting with a confession, "I have sinned against heaven, and before thee, And am no more worthy to be called thy son," and continuing with a petition, "make me as one of thy hired servants."[4] When the prodigal returns, his father spies him from afar and embraces and kisses him, the iconic gesture of mercy. The prodigal begins his confession, but his father stops him before the petition, commanding his servants to clothe, ornament, and prepare a feast for his restored son. The prodigal expresses his repentance as willingness to be his father's hired servant, and his father expresses his forgiveness by acting as a master to his servants and as a father to his son. In the Puritan literary imagination, faith enabled the elect to perceive the servant within the kneeling son and the master's command in the father's embrace. The parable thus allowed the faithful a glimpse of how God viewed them and how, by His grace, they might come to know themselves: as children who serve.

The child-servant and father-master analogies also organized the visible world, as a defining aspect of early New England's "legal culture of work" and the cultural economy of its households.[5] Servants and children were frequently conjoined as fraternal twins of dependent personhood, equated as the progeny of earthly fathers under the fifth commandment. "Children and servants" form a compound subject in laws regulating labor and discipline, household governance instructions, and sermons, and the phrase is sometimes modified by "rebellious and disobedient" (although parents were also cautioned to scrutinize even manifestly obedient children and servants for signs that they were mere "eye-servants" who obeyed to please men rather than God).[6] As noted in the introduction, most servants were children, and the routine practice of "putting out" children to live in other households meant that many children, even those from elite families, spent time in service.[7]

Another common version of the analogy positioned servants as outsiders who could entice children into disobedience. In this vein, we might recall that one of the lessons William Bradford drew from the case of Thomas Granger, a teenager who was hanged in Plymouth for committing buggery with "a mare, a cow, two goats, five sheep, two calves and a turkey," was "what care all ought to have what servants they bring into their families"; or the case John Winthrop recorded on board the *Arbella*, in which a servant "bargained with a child to sell him a box worth 3*d*. for three biscuits a day all the voyage, and had received about forty, and had sold them and many more to some other servants." For the dual transgressions of profiteering on subsistence goods and of initiating the child into immoral traffic, the enterprising servant was made an object of public discipline: "We caused his hands to be tied up to a bar, and hanged a basket with stones about his neck, and so he stood two hours."[8]

Scholars of New England labor, migration, household governance, and patriarchal authority have speculated about the cultural symbolism of the analogy but have neglected its theological dimensions. Studies of the covenant dialectic have paid careful attention to the social and institutional implications of its household tropes but have treated the correlation between childhood and servitude only in passing.[9] As a result, scholars have overlooked the significance of the child who serves as a lived metaphor that was vital to the Puritan project of building a commonwealth in the image of God's household. Across doctrines and earthly institutions, the dual master-father tempered the radical and individualistic implications of Puritan theology by defining both Christian liberty and Christian labor as willing obedience in a station of God's choosing.[10] When the prodigal rehearses his petition, expressing his repentance as willingness to be his father's hired servant, he exemplifies not only the properly humbled and repentant Puritan saint but also every man, woman, and child obediently at work in their household callings and public vocations.

This chapter examines the servant-child and master-father dialectics as a central structure in New England's economy of service, a cultural system in which the ideal of child-like service was both the means and end of spiritually profitable labor. As a discourse of lived obedience and authority, these dialectics defined the nature of consent in the saint's relationship to God and in the governance of household, church, and state. In one of the many fine studies of childhood in early Anglo-America, Holly Brewer has emphasized that childhood was a "metaphor for obedience and submission to church and kingdom."[11] I take to heart Brewer's insight that this trope "transcended metaphor" to become a "structure through which many people understood their world," but I would add that the servant-child and master-father analogies undergirded that structure, adding the element of willing service to the ideal of loving obedience. The child who serves was a portable type of consent to authority that was at once rational and affective, spiritual and worldly. Tracking its meanings reveals the important roles of master and servant in aligning household authority with public authority in New England.

This focus on the servant-child and master-father dialectics revises familiar accounts that have located conceptual roots of modern subjectivities in the culture of New England Puritanism. Scholarship on the Protestant ethic has commonly focused on particular doctrines, including following Max Weber's emphasis on vocation, but the concept of God as both Master and Father was more important than any particular doctrine to the story of how Puritans reconciled market logic and behavior with spiritual and moral ideals.[12] Cathy Matson has argued that "the most dynamic ways to conceptualize economic behavior" can be found in "the myriad intimate and public spaces where people coexisted, communicated, and constituted fleeting or enduring personal relationships out of mutually insistent needs."[13] Household obedience and authority were the primary expressions of Puritan "economic behavior" in such spaces and relationships, and the figures that embodied them were commonplaces in the moral vocabulary that spiritualized the market economy and the profits generated in it.

Centering the work ethic in the family also adds a new dimension to understandings of how a Lockean model of filiation based on voluntary consent emerged from the Filmerian patriarchal household—understandings that have focused on transformations of the meanings of parent, child, husband, and wife.[14] Yet the master-servant dyad marks the clearest difference between early modern households and the "affectionate" kinship model, which excludes it as a necessary internal structure. What happened to the kinds of obedience and authority invested in that dyad? This chapter addresses that question by considering master and servant as conceptual and rhetorical hinges between private forms of obedience and authority (the individual's relationship to God's household, the household service of God) and public ones (ministers and magistrates). All familial identities were defined dialectically with those of master and servant to spiritualize the earthly household, and private and public rituals of obedience were exercises in internalizing a master's will. The child who serves and its counterparts—the licentious child who refuses to serve and the hypocritical servant who works for wages only—would become the self-mastering liberal subject and the disinterested citizen who served the public, but they would also spiritualize the labors of those deemed incapable of mastering themselves, noncitizens whose value and virtue depended upon their willingness to serve men, whether from love or fear.

Servants, Sons, and the Household Service of God

The theological children and servants of the covenant were forged into lived metaphors in the works of the Puritan divines William Perkins and William Ames and animated by the preaching of their disciples, including three of the leading ministers who migrated to New England—Cotton, Thomas Hooker, and Thomas Shepard. These types emerged from two primary doctrines: humiliation and adoption. John Calvin called Christ's redemptive labors "the whole course of his obedience," which begins with his "humiliation": "from the time when he took on the form of a servant, he began to pay the price of liberation in order to redeem us."[15] A common proof-text of humiliation was Philippians 2:7–8: "He made himself of no reputation, and took upon him the form of a servant, and was made like unto men: and was found in shape as a man. He humbled himself, and became obedient unto death, even the death of the cross." Ames's exegesis distinguishes between Christ's "taking of human nature," which was "the action of God alone," and Christ's choice of the "condition of a servant which accompanied the taking of human nature." This division of labor makes humiliation a model of consent. Finding himself in the shape of a man, Christ willingly exchanges sonship for servitude, "humbl[ing] himself" and "mak[ing] himself obedient unto death."[16] "Obedience unto death" combined the grim reality of Puritan martyrdom and what Hooker called the "difficult worke" of humiliation, by which the soul must not only repent of sin but shun pride, to "see nothing in himself but all in and through Christ."[17]

The form of Christ's humiliation—his willing exchange of sonship for servitude—was a crucial aspect of the Protestant *imitatio Christi*, and public and private rituals of humiliation were a central occupation of Puritan piety.[18] Martyrdom and humiliation present two versions of obedient labor in one's place. Willingness to serve was a daily expression of faithful thankfulness for Christ's willingness to obey his Father unto death. Scholars have emphasized humiliation's rhetoric of "emptiness," of making the soul a vessel fit to receive grace.[19] But the rhetoric of servant self-making was essential to the many applications of the doctrine, including as a discourse of labor discipline and social hierarchy that reinforced vocation's imagery of spiritual labor as willing contentment with a servant's place.

The son and servant were also paired in the doctrine of adoption to promote willing service as an ideal. In humiliation, serving the Lord means shunning pride and cultivating the willingness to do whatever God wills, even if that means being a servant. In adoption, serving the Lord means knowing that you are a child of God, feeling his mercy and his love, but not resting in the inheritance of grace. Adoption is the process by which the Calvinist elect inherit God's covenant with Abraham. After God calls them out of sin in vocation, he "gives the faithful the dignity of sonship," taking them into his household as his children.[20] Common proof-texts of adoption depict an ontological divide between sonship and servitude. In John 8:35, sonship signifies permanent membership in a family and servitude a temporary status: "The servant abides not in the house forever but the son abides forever." Paul's allegory of the covenants, in Galatians 4:22–31, also stresses the inevitability and justice of the servant's being turned out of doors. The allegory presents Sarah and Isaac as types of evangelical obedience and Hagar and Ishmael as types of legal obedience. The elect were the children of the freewoman, not the children of the bondwoman, who would be cast out of God's household as Hagar and Ishmael were from Abraham's. But how could they discern whether they obeyed as a child or as a servant—who, however dutiful, would inevitably be turned out of doors? Critiquing Weber's emphasis on salvation anxiety as the source of the work ethic, Charles Cohen contends that the child working from love, instead of the servant working from fear, models the saint at work.[21] But in adoption, God's children do not shun servitude; they internalize it. Their knowledge of God as both Father and Master creates a dialectic of fear and love, wrath and mercy, that kept them from two paths to hell: the "dirty way" of sin and licentiousness, and the "clearer way," dutiful hypocrisy.[22]

An extended passage from Cotton's *Treatise of the Covenant of Grace* exemplifies how these servant-son types brought God's invisible work of redemption and conversion vividly to life. "It was much indeed for the Son of God to make himself a *servant*," Cotton observes, just before graphically describing the crucifixion: Christ "cr[ies] out, My soul is in an agony unto the very death, and through anguish thereof to sweat drops of blood . . . undergo[ing] the very pangs of *Hell* for our sins."[23] Like Ames, Cotton borrows the verb "to make" from Philippians 2:7, instead of Calvin's use of "taking on the form of a servant" and Paul's use of "being found in shape of" to describe Christ's labor in humiliation. In the grammar of the sentence, Christ's exchange of sonship for servitude is subordinate to the excruciating labors of his crucifixion, but the elect must own their unworthiness of both of these sacrifices to allow the Holy Spirit to bend their naturally prideful souls and hearts toward service. Christ freed man from the bondage of sin by exchanging divine sonship for human servitude, by "*taking* our nature upon him, and giving himself unto a state of *bondage*, from a state of liberty, to redeem us unto liberty from a state of bondage under the curse of the *Law* of God, even unto liberty from *sin*, and *death*, and *Satan*, and this *World*, and from the *indignation* of the most High: A wonderful deliverance!" (TCG 157).

Yet those genuinely humbled by Christ's sacrifice will find no assurance in that state, because "the soul knows not whether all this humiliation, which is wrought in him, came from the wrath or mercy of God" (TCG 159). If the Son as servant "wrought" this humiliation, Christ the restored Son makes it evidence of mercy, not wrath: "here is the special work of the *Son*, he doth *bring us back* again to the *Father*, and *reveals* what the Father hath done unto us." The Holy Spirit "doth *enlighten* the soul . . . to see what it is that the Lord hath done for him in mercy . . . whence the soul begins to see the *Fathers* [*sic*] *love*." This enlightened soul "now begins with some more hope, and liberty to call God *Father*" (159–60). What Cotton calls the "liberty to call God *Father*" is freedom from calling him Master, which is permitted by willingness to serve Him. God's children must understand that the covenant of grace frees them from "the terrors of the Law" (157), but not from the duty of obeying it.

Thus in adoption, the Holy Spirit infuses God's children with the "spirit of bondage," a reminder of being enslaved to sin and in "a state of *bondage*, before we be thus redeemed."[24] The spirit of bondage teaches the value of Christ's sacrifice: "The Lord will never so dishonour his own work," Cotton explains, "as to pay so great a price to work so great redemption, for those that never knew what it meant. nay, first he will teach them their *bondage*," instilling in them the knowledge that they were, and deserve to remain, "*the servant of sin*" (TCG 167). The freedom to serve God "cost[s] dear," he admonishes: "be not therefore servants to lusts and passions, to the world and to the Devil" (171).

God's children must take advantage of means of grace like prayers and attendance at sermons in the liberty of sonship, not as a servant's legal obedience. Later in the sermon, Cotton warns that "the children of gracious parents" might "*fall* from the Covenant of grace" by a "*self-confident cleaving* unto those gifts of grace, which by the Covenant they have received." Indeed, "they may grow so confident" that "they will not subject themselves unto the *righteousness of God* in Christ Jesus." If this happens, "the *Covenant of grace* is unto them turned into a *covenant of works*; they are now become the children of the *bond-woman*, and not the children of the *free-woman*" (TCG 224). Humiliation curbed the spiritual threat of "self-confident cleaving" to the inheritance of grace, and the spirit of adoption curbed the peril of "self-confident cleaving" to good works as evidence of justification. We can see how carefully Cotton calibrated the conditional and absolute elements of the covenant by attending to how he preached childhood and servitude, allowing his auditors not just to rationally grasp the perils of license and hypocrisy, but also to feel them. The child who serves resolved the conditional and absolute aspects of the covenant into an ideal of loving obedience.

Puritan conduct instructions applied this ideal of covenant obedience to the sphere of human action. The most exalted figure in vocation manuals was neither the ascetic minister nor the industrious tradesman, but the child who serves willingly and cheerfully. "A Christian is the freest of all men in the world," proclaims William Perkins in *A Treatise of the Vocations or Callings of Men*. "For in that respect he is the child of God in Christ, he is truly freed from hell, death and condemnation; yea and in part from sin and Satan and that in this life." "And yet," he adds, signaling the productive paradox of vocation, "he must be a servant unto every man."[25] The dual master-father unites God's household with earthly households: "God's church is his family and men that live therein are the children of God. He is the father and master of that family: therefore let this practice of earthly parents teach us, when we begin the actions of our calling, to go to our heavenly Father for his blessing" (WP 469). Servants and sons were uncanny doubles in God's household, not only of each other but also of the men, women, and children striving to obey both their heavenly "father and master" and their earthly rulers in their particular callings.

Christopher Tomlins has observed that "orthodox liberal discourses" about the early modern economy have obscured its household character, making labor "descriptively, conceptually, culturally" synonymous with the work of adult males outside the household.[26] One way to correct that perception is to historicize vocation as a discourse of household service that spiritualized dependency and entwined hierarchies of age, gender, and race with ideas of moral labor. Household governance manuals defined the particular callings of family members and simultaneously provided a script for the lived metaphors of covenant obedience, the general calling to child-like service. In the family, all people in their callings—fathers and sons, mothers and daughters, husbands and wives, and masters and servants—learned how to serve and profit "the father and master of that family," not themselves.

The Reformation's attacks on church authority increased the authority of masters of household for the spiritual educations and lives of their dependents, and the primary goal of the household service of God was to produce the kind of obedience that reconciled earthly profits with spiritual ones.[27] In this calling, men embodied three kinds of private authority. As Ames explains, "The power of the husband is moderated by a certain equality; the power of the master is for command alone; but the paternal power is a kind of mixture."[28] This strain of mastery within paternal power—the power to command obedience to the moral law—was a vital aspect of Puritan household governance that has been slighted in studies of New England patriarchal authority. The element of mastery is what qualifies the "certain equality" between marriage partners, and the husband's command over his wife also creates asymmetry along the "master-mistress" axis, as I discuss below in this chapter and in greater detail in chapter 3.[29]

The master of household must exercise his authority within its lawful limits, and the work of knowing when to treat children and servants equally and when to treat them differently was part of this discipline. Perkins and Ames offered instructions for this daily ritual of humiliation. In *Conscience with the Power and Cases Thereof*, Ames stresses the asymmetries between servitude and childhood, pronouncing outright that "servitude is much different from the state of a child."[30] While childhood is the preferred condition, the form of the comparison itself reinforces the dual nature of patriarchal authority and submission in earthly households and God's. God's child should internalize certain aspects of servitude. One role of servants in the household, Ames observes, is to help children stave off pride: "the condition of a Sonne tendeth chiefely to his owne proper good, not of his Father; but servitude doth aime directly at the good of the Master, and not of the Servant." Unlike childhood, servitude is a condition "undertaken by voluntary consent or punishment": while children are "not ordinarily enjoined [to do] any work," the servant is "bound to do all kind of worke."[31] The servant teaches the child the nature of voluntary consent to labor toward the "good" of the masterly father, not his "owne proper good." Ames concludes by affirming the affective superiority of childhood: "in all things, children are more tenderly and favourably to bee used then [*sic*] servants." In their callings, the servant teaches the child to know his father as a master, and the child teaches the servant to know his master as a father, to strive to be used "more tenderly and favourably," though he will remain a servant only. But they all learn that the fruits of their labors do not properly belong to them. Perkins distinguishes between two kinds of exemplary labor, the "dutiful obedience of children" and "faithful service of servants to masters" (WP 417). These phrases suggest the effect of the child on the servant and the effect of the servant on the child as different forms of dependence on the patriarch as father and master. "Dutiful obedience" registers the servant in the son, the internalized humiliation that counters the spiritual inheritance of grace; while "faithful service" suggests the son in the servant, the desire to work for love that characterizes those whose humble personhood is defined by obedient labor for another's profit.

The necessity of turning an incorrigible servant out of doors in adoption doctrine translated into the patriarch's duty to distinguish servants from sons as objects of discipline. Perkins cites John 8:35 to explain the patriarch's duty to censure his dependents for "faults." Whether servant or child is "the delinquent party," the patriarch "ought to proceed by private censure . . . sometimes by admonition, otherwhiles by correction and chastisement, according to the quality of the offence and the condition and state of the person." However, "when none of these means will do good, if the party be a servant, the master may and ought to remove him" (WP 438). A servant who has failed to properly internalize his master's will, and thus the moral law, shall be expelled from the family, while even incorrigible sons "abide ever." These instructions also teach the father-master to align his will with God's, governing his dependents from an awareness of himself as God's child and servant.[32] The father has no obligation or duty to love his servant, but he might nevertheless choose to do so. Like God, the earthly master can choose to treat servants temporarily like sons and sons like servants to maintain the dialectic of obedience. The incorrigible servant provides a particular opportunity for the father-master to exercise mercy and, in so doing, to remember how unworthy he is of God's mercy.

While the power to command took various forms, its purpose of producing children who serve marked a critical point of exchange between private authority and public authority. Ames divided the patriarch's "private authority" from the "public authority" of ministers and magistrates, and the boundary between father and master marked the transition between them.[33] Describing the "particular callings"—the earthly stations to which God appoints each Christian—Perkins provides a list of examples: "the calling of a magistrate, the calling of a minister, the calling of a master, of a father, of a child, of a servant, of a subject, or any other calling that is common to all" (WP 451). In the list, "master" is the hinge term as particular callings move from public (magistrate and minister) to private (father), from the law of the state and church to the law of the family, while "servant" marks the transition from private dependency to political subjection. M. Michelle Jarrett Morris has observed of the "flow" between household and state authority in the "little commonwealth" model that "remarkable power resided in the hands of fathers. New England colonial authorities both buttressed that authority and used it to make fathers magistrates in their own homes." As "courts and lawmakers affirmed the authority of male heads of household," so "fathers used that authority to further the goals of the body politic."[34] But it was as both master and father that the patriarch's authority extended beyond the sphere of his immediate family, and the "mixture" infused those public callings with household affections.

The household master put this theory into practice when he shepherded his dependents into the public space of the church. The Sabbath was a day of rest from menial labor, even for servants. Yet, as Perkins instructs his readers, the master of household had an important duty to perform: "To bring his family to the church or congregation on the Sabbath . . . that they may profit in knowledge and obedience" (WP 437). Perkins reminds masters that in bringing their families to participate in this sacrament, they are obeying the moral law: "For this very cause the fourth commandment is given first of all and principally to the master of the family, that he might see the Sabbath kept." If the master is to ensure that "knowledge and obedience" are yoked together for the spiritual profit of his dependents, he is also to know and obey the commandments of his divine Master. Faithful obedience circulates when the father-master crosses the threshold of his home having internalized his own subordinate relation to God, and when his dependents cross it having internalized the alignment of God's mastery with the household master's power to command obedience to the law. In the exchange between the family and the church as spaces of edification, the master of the family serves in loco parentis in relationship not just to God the Father, but also to public ministers.

Cotton's preaching on baptism exemplifies how child service facilitates the exchange between household and church authority, and between private and public forms of devotion. He uses an analogy to the routine practice of turning children out of doors into other households as servants to preach the paradox of baptism as a "conditional inherited right."[35] The practice of infant baptism and its relation to church membership was a locus of anxiety about the social and spiritual implications of the inheritance of grace.[36] In baptism, Cotton explains, man "[gives] himself unto the family of Christ, to become a servant to him" (WL 35–36). "By the Covenant children are borne to God, and by Baptisme admitted into his family," he affirms, but the child must also give his "consent, when he comes to years of discretion," to remain within it, and faith "so traines it [the child] up, as that it may not fail of its consent in due time." In his analogy, a period of servitude provides "training" in consent for baptized children and their parents. When parents "put their children into a good family, are you not wont to say to them, Now that you leave my house, see that you doe your Master faithfull service, please him, and you shall please me, but if you run from him, looke for no countenance from me?"

(388–89). Baptism does not license the children of the faithful to "run from" their obligation to serve God. They must stay in their appointed places to continue to grow in grace and faith. God's children of all ages must internalize a master's will when they cross the thresholds of earthly institutions.

In the realm of public authority as in the household, willing obedience was a duty of both superiors and inferiors. Superiors must align their commands with God's, for if they do not, Christian liberty required inferiors to disobey them. Ames describes the nature of obedience that "inferiors" owe to ministers and magistrates in their "public callings": "We must obey *In the Lord*, Eph. 6:1, 5; and *In the fear of God*, Col. 3:22."[37] Ames's scriptural citations invoke the servant-child dialectic: Ephesians 6:1 is Paul's version of the fifth commandment, stipulating that children must honor their parents "in the Lord"; while Ephesians 6:5 and Colossians 3:22 define the obedience of servants to masters, the mandate to avoid eye-service or hypocrisy. As they labor toward child-like service in their spiritual lives, Puritans must also know ministers and magistrates as fathers and masters, obeying them from love and fear. The legitimate authority of the individual to determine which commands might be "against the command of God" competes with these mandates of public obedience, but the master's command seemed to prevail over the father's embrace when conflicts over such authority were adjudicated—whether in public or in private.

Darren Staloff has observed the importance of lay consent to Bay Colony church and civil authority, and the correlations between childhood and servitude, and fatherhood and mastery, provided lived forms of that consent in spiritual and earthly life.[38] Ministers conducted rituals of humiliation in which children of God sought the experience of willing contentment to serve. The analogical scaffolding of household government reinforced the spiritual types. And magistrates shared the master's power to move children and servants over the thresholds of earthly institutions. "The Body of Liberties" (1641) codifies this cultural logic as it refers to civil authority. In the list of liberties, those of children are followed by those of servants, and after that come those of "foreigners and strangers," the category that includes the notorious prohibition against "bond slaverie" except in the case of "lawfull Captives taken in just warres, and such strangers as willingly selle themselves or are sold to us." After insisting that these slaves "shall have all the liberties and Christian usages which the law of god established in Israel concerning such persons doeth morally require," it concludes that "this exempts none from servitude who shall be Judged thereto by Authoritie."[39] An essential part of the magistrate's "Authoritie" was the power to make people servants. Magistrates, ministers, and fathers were thus empowered to enact on earth God's appointment of all humans to the servant's calling.

The ministerial vocation is a special instance of how the child-servant and master-father dialectics legitimated exchanges between private and public callings. In *Christian Oeconomy* Perkins reminds fathers that the church rather than the family should be their "first and principal care." Fathers should honor the calling "of their children which have the most pregnant wit and be endued with the best gifts" by having them "consecrated unto God and brought up in the study of the scriptures, to serve afterward in the ministry of the church" (WP 430). In *Conscience with the Power and Cases Thereof*, Ames's chapter on the "mutuall obligation between Ministers and their Flock" immediately follows his chapter on the obligations of masters to servants, which concludes with the mandate that the incorrigible servant should be turned out of doors.[40] In the logic of the transition, the master's authority over his saucy servant is transferred to the servant of the Lord. Ministers may be invested with masterly command, but they must not act as masters to their congregants. Ames proclaims that the minister's first duty is "to behave towards the Congregation as Servants, and not Lords. . . . Now they are Servants of God as their proper Lord."[41] As they emerge from their fathers' families into the public space of their employment, ministers must remember that they, too, have a Master in heaven.

In his preaching manual, *The Art of Prophesying*, Perkins offered ministers techniques for helping even the most righteous and holy children of God cultivate their inner servants. For these faithful Christians, preachers should propound "the law without the curse, whereby they may be taught to bring forth fruites of new obedience beseeming repentance." To explain how to craft "waies of Application" appropriate to such auditors, Perkins makes an analogy to household governance: "And as a father doth oftentimes set his yron rods that are appointed for the servants before the eyes of his sonnes, that they may be frayed: so the meditation of the curse is to be stirred up very often in the faithfull themselves, lest they should abuse the mercie of God to licencious living, and that they may be more fully humbled."[42] Perkins's analogy seems as blunt an instrument as the "yron rod." The fear of corporal punishment represents the "feeling of sinne," as Perkins puts it, a sense of deserving the wrath of God the Father.[43] The threat of corporal discipline should promote the spiritual discipline of humiliation. But the economy of fear in the passage is more complex than it seems. As Perkins's student Ames affirms, fear of punishment can inculcate obedience, but only if that fear is not "servile"—which is defined by having a "chiefe respect unto our own misery." Fear is only "laudable" and effectual when punishment "be respected only secondarily, and be fear'd especially for this cause that it separat's from God, and tend's to this end to make us more wary in waiting before God."[44] A fear of the rod would be servile, capable of instilling only legal obedience. To prompt evangelical obedience, Perkins's analogy must emphasize the fear of being separated from God the Father.

Perkins makes the fear in his analogy "laudable" when he specifies that the "yron rods" are those "appointed for the servants." The son should not fear the "yron rods" but rather being treated as his father's servant, a sign of separation from his father that takes the form of knowing him as a master. The son who knows his father as a master and has internalized his own resemblance to a servant is "more fully humbled" and thus prepared "to bring forth fruites of new obedience beseeming repentance."

Perkins's analogy extends to the minister-auditor relationship. The image of God the Father grounds the analogy between family discipline and preaching in the passage: ministers are masters and fathers, and auditors are sons and servants. By encouraging preachers to bring the "yron rods" meant for servants "before the eyes" of their auditors, Perkins also supplies them with an image of their ministerial calling as mastery. Attending sermons and reading conduct manuals, household masters and magistrates also learned how to wield such "yron rods" in their roles as dispensers of justice and keepers of law and order, and their children and servants learned to obey both them and God. In God's household, and the private and public spaces conceived of in its image, the correlation of fatherhood with mastery and childhood with servitude should keep God's children from "abus[ing] the mercie of God to licencious living." No biblical figure better embodied this ideal than one synonymous with licentiousness itself: the prodigal son.

The Prodigal Servant

Cotton and Hooker found in Luke 15:19, the prodigal's petition ("make me as one of thy hired servants"), rich material for preaching the spiritual work of humiliation as the foundation of a moral economy. Hooker takes the parable as his text for *The Soules Humiliation*, where the petition exemplifies the genuinely humble soul's "content[ment] to be at his fathers disposing" (SH 79).[45] Cotton uses the prodigal's awareness that he is unworthy of his father's mercy as a lesson in frugality: "It were, he thought, a shame to such a Father, to have such an unthrift to be his son, he had not the temper of a son in him, and now he would be content to be as an hired servant" (WL 310). The prodigal's conversion from wastrel to penitent is also his transformation from "unthrift" to a man with "the temper of a son," who understands his inheritance as a wage that he had not earned and that was not properly his to spend. The faithful man should strive to find contentment in "homely employment," undertaking it "freely" as a "work of his calling, *Luke 15.19. Make me one of thy hired servants*" (443).

Cotton's and Hooker's approaches to the prodigal's petition affirm the doctrinal and stylistic differences between them that scholars have long observed, but they also challenge a conventional way of understanding how those differences might relate to the Protestant ethic. Hooker and Shepard were preparationists who believed that God provided the elect with conditional faith that prepared their souls for the infusion of grace, and the two preached humiliation and contrition as stages in this exercise.[46] Many have insisted that the rationalized labor and managerial discipline of the work ethic emerged from the preparationists' breathtakingly slight gesture toward the sinner's agency in conversion and emphasis on the minister's authority to determine that it was not hypocrisy; and those who blame the work ethic on preparationism tend to champion Cotton and his doctrine of absolute free grace as a "constant brake" on capitalism.[47] Without slighting these differences or their social implications, I take these ministers' shared premises to provide more compelling evidence of the relationship of theology to Puritan market morality. Cotton agreed with Hooker that humiliation was "difficult worke," and that a primary discipline of all earthly callings was to know God as both Father and Master.

Both ministers translate "servant" into "drudge" to emphasize the prodigal's degradation and heighten the sincerity of his repentance. Cotton demeans the dutiful elder brother as a hypocrite who "if the Father crosse him, he so loures [scowls]" and "is apt to take offence for every occasion," while exalting the prodigal, who "would now be content to be an hired drudge" (WL 117). Hooker invokes a range of servant commonplaces when riffing on the petition, praising the prodigal as "a heart worth gold," who "doth not seeke to be his owne carver, and say, if I may be my fathers steward, and have some eminent place in the house, then I will go home," but instead "is content to be any thing, so his father will but receive him into his family, though it were but to be a drudge in the kitchen" (SH 79–80). Hooker plays on his auditors' familiarity with servant hierarchies: a particular calling as a "servant" might, in fact, be an "eminent place" as a steward, but the prodigal embraces the life of the lowly kitchen drudge.[48]

The prodigal as drudge is a household version of Christ as the washer of disciples' feet, and Cotton collates those images to spiritualize willingness to exchange a high social station for a low one. In *The Way of Life*, Cotton observes of the prodigal that "a man of his rank and breeding was not wonted to hired servile work, but the same faith that made him desirous to be in a calling, made him stoop to any work his calling led him to" (WL 443–44). A servant's conventional posture conveys the spiritual "stooping of the heart." As the passage proceeds, Cotton connects the prodigal's petition with Christ's humiliation and contentment to serve the disciples:

> *Phil. 2.5,7. Let the same minde bee in you that was in Christ Jesus, hee made himselfe of no reputation*; he stood not upon it, that he was borne of God, and equal to the most High, but he made himselfe a servant, and of no reputation, and so to serve God, and save men; and when his Father called him to it, he stooped to a very low employment, rose up from Supper, and girded himself with a Towell, and washed his Disciples feet, *John 13*. They thought it was a service too homely for him to doe, but he tells them, that even they ought thus to serve one another. So faith is ready to embrace any homely service his calling leads him to, which a carnall heart would blush to be seene in; a faithful heart is never squeamish in this case, for repentance will make a man revenge himself upon himself, in respect of the many homely services he hath done for Satan. (WL 444)

The performance of "homely services" in itself is not salvific, but faith allows the elect to emulate Jesus in the work of willingly making themselves "a servant, and of no reputation, and so to serve God." Christ's physical postures of humility—"stooped," "stood not," "washed his Disciples feet"—make the "faithful heart" a metonym for a laborer who understands that "there is no work too hard or too homely for him" (WL 444). These bodily gestures can help spiritual children know whether they are God's servants or hypocrites who continue remain "content to serve the Devil," to do his "base drudgery."

The spiritual discipline of "revenging himself upon himself" for homely services for Satan might suffice for Cotton's auditors, but perhaps not for Hooker's. The "Soule that is truly humbled with the sense of his owne vileness . . . saith, let mee be a miserable slave and imprisoned, let mee be a servant, and be brought to the heaviest hazards, I care not what I be, if the Lord will but receive mee to mercy" (SH 99). Here and in another passage he adds "I care not what I be" (80) to the prodigal's petition, creating a subtle aural collation with 1 Corinthians 7:21, a proof text of vocation: "Art thou called being a servant? care not for it: but if thou mayest be made free, use it rather." The plasticity of servant as a spiritual signifier for both "eminent" stewards and "miserable slaves" was essential to its use as a figure in a racializing labor culture that legitimated Puritan men's moral authority to determine which servants to treat like children and which to turn out of doors.

The soul that is willing to be God's slave is fit to live in his household forever as his child. Hooker emphasizes the petition as a threshold discourse, reveling in its performativity: "I confesse I doe deserve the worst, but if any man will once helpe me in, and but throw mee over the threshold, if I may but Scoure the Kettles, or doe any drudgery, I will never out again" (SH 98). The phrase "throw mee over the threshold" makes God's household into a vividly real domestic space for his auditors, but the prodigal's contentment to "Scoure the Kettles" is a metaphor for cheerful submission to authority across earthly institutions.

The "threshold" between the prodigal's father's household and the rest of the world is also the threshold between family and church, for the man who is called to "helpe in" the humbled soul is Hooker himself. The soul that is content to serve a father is also willing to submit to the minister's authority. Staloff notes that church covenants "obliged the congregant to privilege the speech acts of the ministers above all others" and cites Hooker's view that the laity was to "submit to the will of their clerical officers in almost every aspect of church business."[49] Hooker's preaching on the prodigal reinforces his social doctrine. He chides his auditors, perhaps especially those of high social rank: "You take it as a disgrace to be reprooved by a servant, or an inferiour, but the humble Soule, takes it whatsoever it is, and is willing to be reprooved by any" (SH 220). Hooker relishes his role as the prodigal, but he also plays the master-father to his congregants, enjoining them to humble themselves imaginatively in relation to his authority in particular.

While such admonitions have been taken as evidence of the authoritarian bent of Hooker's preparationism, Cotton also preaches the governance of the tongue as evidence of willing submission to authority, observing that the truly humble would "never open their mouthes to any arrogancy of spirit in doing any homely service" (WL 116). As a counter to such "arrogancy," he offers his auditors a meditation—a means of grace intended, as one believer put it, "to get these truths from thy head to thy heart."[50] Cotton translates the prodigal's imperative ("make me as one of thy hired servants") into a rhetorical question: "What drudgery can be too homely for me to doe for God?" (WL 444). Repeating this phrase to themselves or in company as they moved from the public duty of attendance on sermons to private forms of piety like closet devotions and household services, members of the laity internalized the minister's authority over the word of God as they made themselves children who serve.

Though no prodigal, John Winthrop's son Deane lived these tropes from Cotton's preaching. In a 1634 entry in his *Journal*, Winthrop recounts the fourteen-year-old's conversion experience.[51] The boy was "so wrought upon by the ministry of the word . . . as he could not be brought to apprehend any comfort in God, being much humbled and broken for his sins, (though he had been a dutiful child, and not given up to the lusts of youth)." For months he "went mourning and languishing daily," while "attending to the means, and not giving over prayer," until finally "he came at length to be freed from his temptations, and to find comfort in God's promises." After providing "good proof of his understanding in the things of God," Deane was "received into the congregation," and his father reports that "he went on cheerfully in a Christian course, falling daily to labor, as a servant." Deane's "cheerful" willingness to "labor, as a servant" gives his parents hope—if not assurance—that their son is also God's child. Winthrop immediately follows this conversion account by describing a dream in which he saw his children lying in bed with his wife "with crowns upon their heads," which his wife interpreted to mean that "God would take of her children to make them fellow heirs with Christ in his kingdom." But not all of Cotton's auditors hewed to this model of child-like service as readily as Deane Winthrop. Indeed, some of Cotton's adherents became notorious for failing to govern their tongues and humble themselves before public authority.

The Antinomian Controversy and the Gender of Mastery

Jonathan Beecher Field has critiqued the scholarly tendency to position the Antinomian Controversy as a "specific episode of crisis" in early New England history.[52] He urges that we could better grasp its significance by viewing it as an "artifact of print culture" and, like the daily tensions and conflicts it projects, a "literary, rather than historical, phenomenon."[53] The controversy evokes the very literariness of Puritan daily life, as conflicts over theology, doctrine, and authority were at the same time contests over the meanings of the lived metaphors of childhood and service, fatherhood and mastery. Abram Van Engen has recently framed it as a "contest in New England over who controlled the family—and how wide its affections went," offering a sensitive reading of the lived metaphors of father and child across multiple texts; but those metaphors of "paternal authority" were always shadowed by the figures of master and servant, even in texts that do not explicitly trade in the familiar analogies.[54] Anne Hutchinson's civil and church trials publicized the necessity of God's children to internalize him as both Father and Master, and the power of ministers and magistrates to determine whether their congregants were children who served or servants to be turned out of doors.

These lived metaphors of humiliation and adoption connected the theological debate that Michael Winship has aptly reconceived of as a "free grace" controversy to the gendered thresholds between private and public forms of authority.[55] In Elizabeth Maddock Dillon's ingenious reading, the trial transcripts provide evidence of gender as a discourse through which both Hutchinson and Winthrop articulate "proto liberal" notions of publicity and privacy, but we can also trace this history in the gendering of doctrinal discourse itself.[56] The concept of the public as a male master emerged alongside the gendering of hypocrisy and licentiousness, from the common premise that women could not be their own masters. Spiritually and socially, Hutchinson was both a child who would not consent to serve and an incorrigible servant who had to be turned out of doors. She was not just a Jezebel, as she has been so often characterized, but also an unrepentant prodigal and a Hagar.

The distinction between sons and servants preoccupied Shepard, both in his personal faith and in his evangelism. In his journal, Shepard recorded that it helped him see "how Legal righteousness makes us servants and how faith makes us sons. . . . [F]aith, renouncing all doing for the inheritance, immediately receives Christ who is his inheritance." Sounding his leitmotif, the dangers of resting in duties, Shepard mused that a man who "quiet[s] his conscience" by performing "some duties" is "under the stronger power of sin than before because he is now sheltered under the Law and thus still he is a servant and in bondage."[57] Shepard offered his auditors a compressed version of the prodigal's petition to suggest how they might know themselves as heirs whose souls are "fully satiated with" the "special love" Abraham reserved for the child "to whom he gave his inheritance and portion." The prodigal, Shepard explains, "did not know he should be received; but when he came, 'Make me a servant, if not a son, (saith he;) and his father hung about his neck,' etc.; So here" (PTV 612). Shepard adds "if not a son" to his shorthand petition, emphasizing servitude as provisional to sonship. The syntax of the sentence and the compression of the petition with the embrace emphasize the immanence of God's mercy and love ("and" in the sentence does a lot of work). Yet even in this condensed version, the prodigal's consent to serve determines the meaning of sonship and of the father's gesture as an expression of God's love.

The servant plays a crucial role: to make the son more "sonlike." Shepard teaches his auditors how to pray, preaching an allegory of a man who, like Abraham, has "a son and a servant." The servant prays in vain "for the inheritance or a part of it, of the portion of the son," unlike the faithful "praying and desiring from a sonlike spirit" (PTV 468). The servant will never inherit the son's portion. Yet the very futility of his prayers is spiritualized as a benefit for the covenant son, if only as a trope for both his regenerate and unregenerate auditors to grasp. The labor ideal for both son and servant is to work for the good of a superior being: for the son, God; for the servant, the son.

Shepard's obsession with this imagery may well have increased in response to Cotton's preaching of it, which may in some instances have responded to Shepard's.[58] In early 1636, he wrote Cotton a letter asking him to clarify several points about his doctrine of adoption, including "whether a Christian having once his sonship sealed to him by the spirit ever doubts again of God's love to him as a son, though he fall into diverse gross and scandalous sins."[59] Yes, Cotton replied, "a child of god sealed by the spirit falling into diverse gross, and scandalous sins may doubt again of gods love;" but, he concedes that "sons of god so sealed do more rarely fall into such sins . . . yet sometimes such as do so fall may yet retain or doubtless claim unto gods fatherly love." In Cotton's experience, God will "leave his sealed children some times to such renewed doubtings, the better to raise up their hearts rather to lay up all our joy in christ" (AC 31–32). However, Christians must not "build the signs of their Adoption upon [any] sanctification, But such as floweth from faith in christ jesus" (32). Any other sense of "holiness and righteousness, though it were as true as that of Adams in Innocency may be as his was a mortal seed . . . whereas the least seed of faith, and of that holiness which floweth from it, abideth for ever."

Shepard was not reassured by Cotton's response, and neither was the group of ministerial elders who soon wrote to Cotton, pressing him more vehemently on his readings of John 8 and Galatians 4. From these exchanges about how to distinguish the workings of Adam's mortal seed from Christ's redeeming seed in conversion, the Antinomian Controversy grew. In its aftermath, these men would take Hutchinson's "monstrous birth" as a sign that her doctrinal "errors" had been engendered by blighted seed (AC 214).

Had Cotton authorized such boldness? Following his reply to Shepard's queries discussed above, Cotton and the group of elders debated the proper exegesis of Galatians 4 in increasingly heated terms. Cotton's response had not allayed their concerns about his preaching of free grace and its influence on his prominent and influential lay followers. They wrote to ask sixteen questions, the thirteenth of which articulates the primary doctrinal issue: "Whether evidencing Justification by Sanctification, be a building [of] my Justification on my Sanctification: or a going on in a Covenant of Works" (AC 52). Not surprisingly, this question provokes the lengthiest response, including a protracted discussion of the allegory of the two covenants.

A man may find evidence of his justification in his faithful performance of duties and good works, Cotton explains, and yet not be "under a Covenant of Works," but "only sometimes go aside to a Covenant of Works" (AC 55). Abraham, who "had long waited for the promised Seed," was one type of such a man. Omitting Sarah's agency in prompting her husband to do so, Cotton observes that Abraham "was justified by believing the Free promise" but "turned aside to go into Hagar, (who was a Type of the Covenant of Works) for the hastening of his sight and fruition of the promised Seed." Thus, Cotton concludes, "sundry Children of Abraham . . . having been driven out of their Sins by a Spirit of Bondage, and finding a need of Christ, and their own insufficiency and unworthiness to receive him: do therefore seek and wait for him (by the mighty Power of God) in every Ordinance and Duty" (AC 55). Like Abraham, God's elect children might "go aside" to works and remain heirs, not hypocritical servants.

The elders were having none of it. The allegory only proves "that for any man to go aside to a Covenant of Works whereof you make Hagar to be a Type to seek to see the promised seed there, is to go aside to a Covenant of Works" (AC 74). Cotton's exegesis implies that all "doing or use-making of Works" is such legal obedience only, and the elders insisted that "to seek to see the Lords face by seeking to feel the Lords own Work in us, is not going aside to Hagar." They even objected to Cotton's "frequent urging the term of Works" itself, which "may seem to savour more strongly of Popish leaven than Protestant Doctrine doth imply." According to the elders, it is Cotton who preaches works righteousness, not the ministers whom his followers had accused of doing so.[60]

In his rejoinder, Cotton cheekily cites the proof-text that made Hagar "a type of a Covenant of Works Galatians 4" as he clarifies his position (AC 120). He did not intend to "beat men off from the use of holy duties or from seeking the face of God and sight of Justification by Christ in the use of them," but rather to "prevent a twofold and frequent abuse of the use of holy duties even in honest minds" (AC 121). Such abuse was like "Abraham's use of Hagar as a servant to Sarah to do the household duties of a Servant in the family," while a faithful seeking of God's face in such duties was like his "marriage fellowship with Hagar," his "expecting the promised seed by virtue of the promise in her loins." His reading genders and eroticizes the difference between two kinds of legal obedience, one whereby the child properly internalizes God as a master and one that is mere servitude. He cannot resist a final retort. "Not I but the Apostle saith, Hagar was a type of the Law or Covenant of Works," he says, citing Galatians 4 again, and this time noting the verses also (AC 131–32). They, not he, make good works into "causes" of assurance, offering as doctrine merely "an empty tautology" (AC 132) that "clothe[s] unwholesome and Popish doctrine with Protestant and wholesome words" (AC 134). Judging by this exchange, Cotton may well have inspired Hutchinson's irreverence as well as her doctrine.

The vitriol in these exchanges provides a glimpse of the terms of the larger conflict as it escalated. Theological questions about salvation and damnation acted out in the material world were matters of life and death, and violence was not just rhetorical. As the most powerful member of the "Hutchinson faction," Governor Henry Vane warned the Reverend Hugh Peter, an ally of his nemesis John Winthrop, "the light of the gospel brings a sword, and the children of the bondwoman would persecute those of the freewoman."[61] Who were God's children and who merely servants? John Wheelwright, Hutchinson's brother-in-law, preached a fast-day sermon exhorting the "children of God" to "have their swords redy, they must fight and fight with spirituall weapons."[62] Vane, Hutchinson, Wheelwright, and others saw themselves as the children of the free. Hutchinson's unwavering certainty of that spiritual identity would soon mean that she was no longer a free woman. At her trial, Puritan ministers and magistrates were not just public fathers, but master-fathers exercising their authority—their God-appointed obligation—to determine whether offenders would be punished as incorrigible children or as servants to be turned out of doors.[63]

Magistrates cited Hagar and Ishmael as types of banishment in the sedition trials of Wheelwright and William Aspinwall, the church deacon who had drafted a "bellicose" petition, signed by over sixty men, to protest Wheelwright's conviction.[64] Denouncing the "disturbance the seditious application of Mr. Wheelwright hath wrought among us," the General Court pronounced its sentence: "as *Cain*, *Hagar*, and *Ismael*, were expelled as troublers of the families, (which were then as commonwealths) so justice requires . . . that such disturbers should be put out from among us" (AC 254). Discerning that Wheelwright's "speech and behavior at present were more modest and submiss[iv]e, then [*sic*] formerly they had been," the court determined not to banish him but only to disenfranchise him (AC 259). Aspinwall did not exhibit such modesty. As he was about to be sentenced, he asked the court to "shew a rule in Scripture for banishment," but when it "answered as before, that Hagar and Ismael were banished for disturbance," Aspinwall pushed back. Abraham cast out Ishmael and his mother, but with bread that symbolized God's promise that Ishmael would found a nation. So, Aspinwall reasoned, "if a Father give a child a portion and sent him forth, it was not banishment." Winthrop recounts the exegetical triumph of the court's reply: "the Scripture calls it a casting out, not a sending forth; and one said further that he was not a childe worthy of such a portion" (AC 261). Unrepentant to the last, Aspinwall was banished. Yet the condemned and the court agreed on his proper type: Aspinwall is Ishmael, not Hagar. Justice demands that he be cast out as a servant, but not that he be feminized.

In both the civil trial and the church trial that followed it, Hutchinson's male examiners showed her what Perkins had called the "yron rods intended for the servant" in their public attempts to humble her. Addressing Hutchinson at the opening of the civil proceeding in November 1637, Winthrop explains that she has been "called here as . . . one of those that have troubled the peace of the commonwealth and the churches," a "woman that hath had a great share in the promoting and divulging of those opinions that are the causes of this trouble," by "maintain[ing] a meeting and assembly in your house that hath been condemned by the general assembly as a thing not tolerable nor comely in the sight of God nor fitting for your sex" (AC 312). She has persisted in her "erroneous way" despite being "cried down," and so she has been summoned to allow the court to "reduce you that so you may become a profitable member here among us." She may yet be reclaimed as a child of church and commonwealth, but only if she demonstrates willing obedience to their authority.

It immediately becomes apparent that she will not do so. Winthrop opens by accusing her of breaking the law by "countenancing" Wheelwright and the other "parties in this faction," who are actual "transgressors of the law" (AC 313). Hutchinson asks which law they have transgressed, and Winthrop invokes the fifth commandment, "honor thy father and thy mother," as "the law of God and of the state." They proceed to debate each other, with Winthrop insisting that she has dishonored her earthly "fathers of the commonwealth" and Hutchinson parrying that her proper "fear of the Lord" gives her the liberty to resist earthly parents who "will not give me leave" to obey him (AC 314). By "countenancing" the seditious parties, Winthrop insists, she has "put honor upon them," a charge that she refutes: "I may put honor upon them as the children of God and as they do honor the Lord." Rather than continuing to debate these lived metaphors of liberty and obedience, Winthrop sputters, "We do not mean to discourse with those of your sex but only this . . . you do dishonor us."[65] Hutchinson "acknowledge[s] no such thing neither do I think that I ever put any dishonor upon you." From the court's perspective, Hutchinson's very denial proves Winthrop's charge. She has perverted the household service of God, "call[ing] a company together from their callings to come to be taught of you" (AC 315). Not only does she refuse to obey the magistrates, but she appropriates the master-father's authority to "call" people across the thresholds of church, family, and state—an authority that Winthrop reasserts, admonishing her that "we do not call you to teach the court but to lay open yourself."

Hutchinson not only continues to deny the magistrates as her fathers "in the Lord," but she also likens herself to them. Later in the trial, Hutchinson provides an account of her conversion, including her lived experience of Abraham's family drama. In one of her most damning admissions, she says that God allowed her to "see which was the clear ministry and which the wrong" by "the voice of his own spirit to my soul," and when pressed how she knew it was God's voice, she asks, "How did Abraham know that it was God that bid him offer his son, being a breach of the sixth commandment?" (AC 336–37). When Deputy Governor Thomas Dudley replies, "By an immediate voice," she responds, "So to me by an immediate revelation" (AC 337). Her dangerous likening herself to Abraham reinforces her dangerous licentiousness, and she repeats this gesture even as she apparently attempts to walk back from her characterization of the "voice" as a "revelation." She explains that the "voice" had "shewed me what he would do for me and the rest of his servants." But as so many of God's children are wont to do, she "did presently like

Abraham run to Hagar." Cotton had taught her that God's children did so, as a way of waiting for the promise of grace, and she conforms to that narrative, noting that "after that he did let me see the atheism of my own heart, for which I begged of the Lord that it might not remain." Yet her assertion exposes the obvious gender and sexual friction in the type. Just how much assurance should one of God's female children have? A year later, she heard the voice again, and "since that time I have been confident of what he hath revealed unto me" (AC 337). Having internalized what it is to be Hagar spiritually, her assurance should be that of Sarah, or perhaps Isaac, but not of Abraham.

Only the court was a man with "a son and a servant," and with the authority to act as Abraham and the liberty to move between the spiritual types and their social applications. All but three of her examiners in court raised their hands when asked by the governor whether it "be the mind of the court that she shall be banished out of our liberties and imprisoned till she be sent away" (AC 347). She would be the bondwoman after all.

Yet the rulers had not finished teaching Hutchinson her bondage. The church trial held in March 1638 was, as several of her examiners noted, a ritual of "humiliation" designed to demonstrate her continued unwillingness to serve them, and to give Cotton a chance to publicly renounce her and return to the fold.[66] Cotton addresses Hutchinson as a woman whom God had endowed "with good parts and gifts fit to instruct your Children and Servants and to be helpful to your husband in the Government of the family" and also "a sharp apprehension, a ready utterance and ability to express yourself in the Cause of God" (AC 371). Cotton thus invokes her calling as a mistress of household, and makes it clear that this office is not equal to that of a master of household, as her proper role is to "be helpful to" her husband in his role as family master, not to usurp it. Household mastery is exchangeable with public authority only for men. Hutchinson presumed to call herself to a man's vocation, misunderstanding the purpose for which God had granted her these gifts. Her doctrines were unsound, but even if they had been borrowed word-for-word from Shepard, the fact that she had assumed a public office would have "conveyed the poison of your unsound principles into the hearts of many which it may be will never be reduced again." Cotton expresses confidence that God has willed their treatment of her, for it is "just with God thus to abase you . . . for the Lord looketh upon all the children of pride and delights to abase them and bring them low" (AC 372). Shepard certainly shared that delight. Perhaps piqued by Cotton's measured praise, Shepard chimes in to admonish her, "lest the Crown should be set on her Head in the day of her Humiliation" (AC 373). Hutchinson protests, "It was never in my heart to slight any man but only that man should be kept in his own place and not set in the Room of God" (AC 377). Men are the proper rulers of the boundary between their "own place" and "the Room of God."

They are also to determine the boundary between what is in her heart and her public speech, finding themselves "not satisfied" that her statements amount to genuine repentance. They condemn the "Misgovernment of this Woman's Tongue," a "great Cause of this Disorder" that must be tamed lest she "go on still in seducing to seduce and in deceiving to deceive and in lying to lie and in condemning Authority and Magistracy still to condemn" (AC 384 and 385). Even Cotton chimes in: "I see this pride of Heart is not healed but is working still" (AC 386). Shepard argues that excommunication is required, for "to drop a Lie . . . and to maintain a Lie: and to do it in a day of Humiliation, and in the sight of God, and such a Congregation as this is" offends "the Honor of God and the honor of this Church to bear with patience so gross an offender" (AC 386–87). John Wilson concludes that "though she hath made some show of Repentance yet it doth not seem to be cordial and sincere" (AC 387). Hutchinson was excommunicated, turned into a spiritual, social, and physical Hagar.[67]

Hutchinson had not been reformed into "a profitable member here among us," but she would still be profitable as a type of child who would not serve and of a servant turned out of doors. In *Parable of the Ten Virgins*, a sermon series preached over the course of four years during the controversy and in its wake, Shepard made her a powerful emblem of libertinism and hypocrisy, one that brought the promises and perils of the inheritance of grace harrowingly to life. He both harnesses the fear that God's children could become mere servants and celebrates the profitability of such hypocrites, especially wealthy and powerful merchants like the Hutchinsons.[68]

To warn those who might, like Hutchinson, mistake Christian liberty for individual freedom, Shepard presents a variation on the "world turned upside down," in which the familiar trope of masters being forced to serve their servants is intertwined with the horror of spiritual children becoming servants:[69] "When the children of kings and peers, of princes, shall be made to come at the call of their grooms and kitchen boys, if ever they stood before the face of princes, they will count this a heavy thralldom and bondage; so, if ever you stood before the God of the whole earth, you will account it a heavy bondage to have a heart sometime for and sometime not for the Lord" (PTV 265). The exemplary humility of

Puritan subjectivity is conveyed by Shepard's injunction to ask the faithful to identify themselves not just as children, but the children of kings and princes. Shepard's variation on the commonplace of the servant on top as an emblem of social and spiritual disorder adds the additional curb on liberty provided by asking adults to identify themselves spiritually as children who are "standing before" their social superiors, whether at home, in church, or—God forbid—in court. Shepard sets his topsy-turvy scene in an aristocratic household quite unlike the middling status of most Puritan households. If libertinism carries the threat of instant social reversal of the kind experienced by Hutchinson and some of her followers, Christian liberty is spiritually (and perhaps socially and economically) aspirational.[70]

Shepard seems to allude directly to Hutchinson in passages that explain why God would allow hypocrites to reside with saints in his Church. God might particularly love wealthy hypocrites, those who can be "very serviceable to his church, and so to Christ . . . both in regard of outward means of subsistence, and also with edifying gifts." Outwardly prosperous but spiritual servants, they are "like carriers that carry another's money and wealth to him, and then turns [*sic*] them out of doors" (PTV 188). God loves both his children and these servants, manifesting a "double love" to men (79). "Some he loves as servants," Shepard clarifies, "that as we hire some men to do our work, and give them meat and wages, and then turn them out of doors, or let them go." His analogy spiritualizes the labor of masters who fulfill their duties to their servants, who "give them meat and wages" though they will have to content themselves with earthly compensation only. Sometimes God even "hires wicked men" to work for "his sons and saints," either "giving them reward in this life, or hopes of reward hereafter, and when the work is done, and use made of their gifts, graces, spirits, then turns them out of doors. . . . Hagar and Ishmael cast out; Sarah and Isaac stay in the family." Shepard delights in making the merchant into a servant, humbling Hutchinson and her family as they would not do themselves. He affirms that the ministers and magistrates had fulfilled God's will in turning Hutchinson out of doors.

In another passage, Shepard transforms the hypocritical "foolish virgins" of the parable into servants: "thus it was with these foolish virgins; they were only servants in the house, no true spouse or sons, and were foolish at best, and had not the spirits of sons, but had their lusts; never were espoused savingly to the Lord Jesus himself, nor laid up all their hope in him, but were foolish" (PTV 469). The alliteration of "servant," "spouse," and "sons" finesses the gender slippage in the analogy, as does the association of baseness and foolishness with servants. Ivy Schweitzer has observed the cultural significance of the trope of all Puritans as spiritually feminized "'Bride[s] of Christ,'" but as Shepard's passage reveals, that trope was intertwined with those of the servant-son and master-father, complicating the gendering of the soul.[71] Men could be "brides," but perhaps wives and mothers, as Hutchinson's fate would indicate, would do well to consider themselves servants, not true sons.

How did the events affect Cotton's household doctrine? In a passage from *The Covenant of God's Free Grace*, a sermon preached to lament the failure of the children of First Church's founders to become full members, Cotton presents David's "transitory, disordered, unsettled" family as "a pattern for all houses," observing that "no house walks according to their callings . . . there was a sure Covenant, though his house was fleeting and unstable, yet there was an everlasting Covenant."[72] Echoing his preaching on baptism, Cotton correlates servants with children to preach the conditions of "a sure Covenant" and to ground the analogy between God's household, earthly households, and church membership. Here, however, the servant is an "apprentice," which heightens the experiential realism of the covenant as contract, and thus of its conditional aspect.[73] Cotton explains that an "apprentice must serve seven years before he can become a free man," while "the child of God is made free that first day that he gives up himself to God." But how does the child "give himself up to God"? By understanding that he is "made free" to serve God, as apprentices serve men: "though thou be a *servant* to another man, yet art thou the *Lord's free man*, 1 Corinthians 7:22. If we can but content ourselves to be the Lord's servants, we shall be his freemen."[74] This is the sole condition of the absolute covenant, the obligation of God's children to serve him. Cotton exhorts "every man and woman" to "labour specially to shroud and shelter themselves under this Covenant, that they may be kept sure in all disorders" and never "give over labouring for it."[75] Perhaps the fate of his Antinomian followers led him to stress the need for God's children to internalize the authority of earthly masters.[76] An apprentice's term of service is seven years, but the child of God serves for life.

Children, Servants, and Slaves

In his preface to Winthrop's *Short Story*, Thomas Weld assured his English audience that Hutchinson, the New England Hagar, had founded no nations of Familists in Rhode Island. Her deformed fetus was not the only proof. Weld tied the spread of her erroneous opinions to deteriorating family government, observing "loose and degenerate . . . practices," like "no prayer in their families, no Sabbath, insufferable pride, frequent and hideous lying" (AC 216). These private sins also took public forms: "manifest Pride, contempt of authority, neglecting to feare the Church" (AC 217). Since the punishment suits the sin in divine justice, God commissioned Native Americans to slay Hutchinson's entire family, even heightening their savagery. Weld proclaims that "the Indians in those parts" had never before committed "the like outrage upon any one family, or families, and therefore God's hand is the more apparently seen herein" (AC 218). Such savagery was contained, he reassured his readers: "two Sagamores (or Indian Princes) with all their men, women, and children, have voluntarily submitted themselves to the will and law of our God, with expressed desires to be taught the same; and have for that end put themselves under our government" (AC 219). Hutchinson may have refused to serve Puritan master-fathers, but New England's natives—indeed, even their monarchs—would serve them, and willingly. Needless to say, Weld's model of "voluntary submission" misrepresented the usual means by which they had been brought under English government.

The Pequot War, waged during the events of the Antinomian Controversy and involving many of the same principal actors, launched the cycle of war, captivity, servitude, and enslavement that defined Anglo-Native relations in New England and the Atlantic world. Native American children had already become the servants of English masters; one, Pawtucket John Sassamon, joined his master when he fought against the Pequots and claimed as his own bride one of the captives. But after the war, improvised and local instances would begin to harden into policy. Throughout the colonial period, Anglo-Native wars would produce innovative forms of service and mastery as captives were brought under Puritan governance as objects of conversion from heathen to Christian, from criminal to slave, and from prisoner of war to household laborer. New England colonists did not wage war just to claim Native American land, but also to harness native labor, fueling their own economy and those of English colonies throughout the Atlantic. They drew upon scriptural precedent that permitted slavery in the case of prisoners of war to legitimate selling Pequot captives, mostly male combatants, as slaves to the West Indies; in return for them, the first recorded shipment of African slaves arrived on New England shores. The Body of Liberties would enshrine this practice as the legitimate power of magistrates to make children into servants and men into slaves.

Though Narragansett allies, and some Englishmen, questioned whether chattel slavery was just punishment for Pequot captives, English victors sought to "acquire women and children—and men and boys—to employ as household servants and to use as a commodity in regional and trade networks."[77] Efforts to convert to Christianity captives who were permitted to remain on their native soil were nearly always undertaken within a master-servant relationship, as a means of instilling obedience to English laws and the men who embodied them. Some masters and ministers earnestly sought to convert native child servants and their servant mothers into children who serve.

Yet they were primarily viewed through the same spiritual lens as the one Shepard trained on Hutchinson: as instrumental hypocrites, servants who will be turned out of doors. As God allowed Hutchinson into the church and state to profit his true children, he would allow Puritan householders to profit from the labors of men, women, and children who might only ever work "for wages only, and fear of the whip, who shalt not only abide in God's house as sons shall do."[78] Puritan household governance had always insisted that the master of household was responsible for the spiritual education of his children and servants, teaching them how to obey God. But in the case of Native American servants, it might be enough for them to obey the moral law only, as embodied by their earthly masters.[79] Not all profitable members of the New England economy would be saved, but all must serve. This book will trace the continued development of innovative types of spiritual and secular callings from the concept of instrumental hypocrisy as Puritan elites participated in the racialization of servitude as an institution.

Acting as translator between the English and Narragansetts in the negotiations about how to divide Pequot spoils, Roger Williams warned that enslavement was both unscriptural and bad policy, for their native allies were keenly aware that, in their need for labor, Englishmen would also seek to enslave them. Nonetheless, Williams claimed a Pequot boy for himself, the "little one with the red about his neck." Though in his 1643 treatise *Key into the Language of America,* he would tout the Narragansett as morally and spiritually superior to English hypocrites, he also "serve[d] as a conduit for recovering runaways in subsequent decades, and knowingly returned captives to abusive households, content to offer general admonishments to good care."[80]

The *Key* provides further evidence of his role in instilling a sense of English mastery into Narragansett fathers and their children. In his observations about the family in chapter 5, he laments the "extreme *affection*" that fathers have for their children, which "together with want of *learning*, makes their children sawcie, bold, and undutifull."[81] He then recounts a scene that echoes the setting of Perkins's doctrine of the "yron rod." As a guest in one Narragansett home, he requests a drink of water, and "the *father* bid his sonne (of some 8. yeeres of age)" to "fetch" it, but "the *boy* refused, and would not stir." Williams advises the father, "I would correct my *child*, if he should so disobey me." Thus prompted, the father "took up a sticke, the *boy* another, and flew at his *father*." At Williams's encouragement, "the poore *father* made him smart a little, throw down his stick, and run for *water*, and the *father* confessed the benefit of correction, and the evill of their too indulgent *affections*." Williams shows both the father and his son the "yron rods appointed for the servants," but as for their final "confession," perhaps they both just wished to turn the man and his advice, however politely, out of doors.

In the next chapter, "Of the Family and businesse of the House," Williams affirms that Narragansett households indeed have a concept of turning out of doors, including the following translations:

Nissawhócunck ewò.	*He puts me out of doores.*
Kussawhoki?	*Do you put mee out of doores?*
Kussawhocowóog.	*Put them forth.*
Tawhítch kussawhokiêan?	*Why do you put mee out?*
Sáwwhush, Sawhèke.	*Goe forth.*[82]

He associates Native American men's authority to move people over the threshold with a racialized work ethic, concluding with the observation that "many of them naturally Princes, or else industrious persons, are rich; and the poore amongst them will say, they want nothing." Rich and poor remain in their proper places. Williams takes these shared ideas of authority, obedience, and social hierarchy as the basis for a common concept of vocation, which he reinforces in the poem that concludes the chapter:

English and Indians busie are,
In parts of their abode:
Yet both stand idle, till God's call
Set them to worke for God. Mat. 20.7.[83]

Williams's scripture is the parable of the laborers in the vineyard, which concludes with Jesus telling the disciples, "whosoever will be chief among you, let him be your servant: even as the Son of man came not to be ministered unto, but to minister" (Matthew 20:27–28).

Williams himself had been turned out of doors, banished by the Bay

Colony's public masters for failing to submit himself to their governance. Field has reminded us that the *Key* functioned as political propaganda for an audience of English imperialists and was part of Williams's successful "political campaign to preserve Providence Plantations from the Bay Colony's territorial ambitions."[84] In what Field characterizes as an "apology" for Williams's "progress demonstrated in the *Key*," Bay Colony leaders produced *New England's First Fruits*, an account of their own (in reality, paltry) success at the "Conversion of some, Conviction of divers, Preparation of Sundry of the Indians."[85] While scholarly attention has focused on this part of the text, it has neglected the second, "Of the progresse of Learning, in the Colledge at Cambridge in Massachusetts Bay."[86] *First Fruits* presents a diptych of children who serve, and the division between the two parts might be taken to represent a gendered and racialized division of labor.

The first part tells of Sagamore John, dying of smallpox, who "committed his onely Child," a son, to the Reverend John Wilson "*to learne to know their God when I am dead*."[87] It celebrates those "*Indians* Children, Boyes and Girles we have received into our houses, who are long since civilized, and in subjection to us" who can read English, and who "pray in secret, and are much in love with us, and cannot indure to returne any more to the Indians." Some of them are even so "inquisitive after God and his wayes" and "industrious in their Calling," that they "much complaine of other servants idleness, and reprove them." One can imagine masters reproving incorrigible white servants by repeating the natives' disdain for their work ethic. Not all have become native children who serve, like these boys and girls, but there was hope for at least one more. A boy who ran away after being publicly punished "for some misdemeanour" believed that "God so followed him, that of his owne accord he returned home, rendred himselfe to Justice, and was willing to submit himselfe, though he might have escaped." In his willing submission to the moral law and the public masters who embody it, he demonstrated himself to be a fit member of godly households—if not, at least not yet, of God's.

Meanwhile, in the second part, New England's gifted sons are training to become servants of the Lord. Here, there are no girls. The account describes the worthy men chosen as schoolmasters, who, along with "twelve Overseers" (six magistrates and six ministers), "are to see that every one be diligent and proficient in his proper place."[88] Unlike in the first part, no exemplary youths are celebrated. Instead, what follows are a list of rules, punishments for infractions of them, and "the times and order of their Studies": a code of mastery.[89] These children, too, are learning to serve.

In *Prodigals and Pilgrims*, Jay Fliegelman tracks the servant-son imagery of adoption into the revolutionary period. "As republicanism transformed men into kindred 'sons of liberty' and subjects into citizens," he explains, "God's embrace and divine adoption made servants sons and prodigals pilgrims. The image of the liberated son embraced by a new parent stood in 1776 at the heart of evangelical Christianity and Revolutionary ideology. The two liberties and two redeemed sonships were ultimately one."[90] What begins as a servant and a son in Puritan discourse becomes the "two redeemed sonships" of secular and sacred republican virtue, the citizen and the pilgrim. But the servant's master doesn't just disappear; he takes ideological forms for the citizen-pilgrims who are Lockean versions of the child who serves. One form is the public, the disinterested citizen's only earthly master. Another is the internalized self-command that allows men the liberty to call God Father. The freedom of the son's inheritance, with its requirement of working for love, would become freedom from working with one's hands—the liberty to exchange manual labor for public service, as in the case of that famous prodigal, Benjamin Franklin. White male children, even apprentices like Franklin, would become more sonlike in their capacity to internalize God the Master, master themselves, and perhaps become masters of others. But the servant transformed into a son is just one strand of the cultural history of political authority, for the redemption of the two sons also relied upon the conversion of some servants into slaves.[91]

And how might republican womanhood have emerged from the ways God's female children lived out these types? Some evidence is provided in the conversion narrative of the widow Ann Errington, one of Shepard's Newtowne congregants. Shepard preached that sometimes "the Lord behaves towards" his sons "for some time, and for special reasons, as unto 'servants,' exercising them with many fears."[92] Perhaps it is no wonder, then, that Errington poignantly recounts a quandary presented by a particular Sabbath sermon. "I thought I was not humbled," she confesses. "And in [the] latter end [of] that sermon there was obedience of sons and servants then I thought—would I know? And I thought Lord gave me a willing heart, etc. And they that have sons can cry—Abba—Father, and so have some [place to] stay and I wished I had a place in the wilderness to mourn."[93] Even though it may just be an error of transcription, the gender shift in "they that have sons" versus they who are sons suggests one way women might have faithfully adjusted themselves to this imagery—or perhaps how Shepard suggested they do so. They were to imagine themselves to be Hagar, while striving to be Sarah; knowing themselves as mothers but also as children who submit to their Father's will. Perhaps Errington also speaks as the mother of the prodigal would have, had she been granted an existence.

The history of early American literature provides another example. The best-known child who serves from this period is not a person, but a book of poems written by Anne Bradstreet, the dutiful daughter of one of Hutchinson's examiners and the faithful wife of another. Seeking evidence of Puritan "proto-liberalism," Dillon identifies a premise that Hutchinson shared with those who condemned her: "the relocation of authority away from divinely ordained identity to an individualized and internalized relation to God (and/or natural law)."[94] In Bradstreet's case, this premise might have operated to legitimate female publicity within the traditional parameters of women's callings. Bradstreet's writing had never interfered with her duties as a good wife and mother, as her brother-in-law, John Woodbridge, assured readers in the "Epistle to the Reader" that prefaced the first edition of *The Tenth Muse*. These brilliant and accomplished poems "are the fruit but of some few hours, curtailed from her sleep and other refreshments," and they had never seduced her away from "her exact diligence in her place, and discrete managing of her family occasions."[95] Bradstreet employed the conceit of authorship as motherhood to humbly traverse the boundary between household and the transatlantic literary marketplace. In "The Author to Her Book" (1678), the author apostrophizes her work as "thou ill-formed offspring of my feeble brain," a "rambling brat" whose "blemishes" and "defects" include uneven (metrical) feet; despite her best efforts, she laments, "still thou run'st more hobbling than is meet." Referring to those who might wonder how such a creature came to "roam" in public, the speaker advises, "If for thy father asked, say thou hadst none." The final couplet makes publicity a matter of necessity:

> And for thy mother, she alas is poor,
> Which caused her thus to send thee out of door.[96]

This gentlewoman rhetorically humbles herself, speaking as a mother compelled by poverty to put her child out to service. Bradstreet borrows men's authority to turn servants out of doors to negotiate the perils of elite public womanhood: her book may "roam," but she remains in her proper place, the home. She faithfully honed her craft and her calling, having internalized the public as a master with the power to criticize, correct, and condemn—something Hutchinson was unwilling to do.

As they sought to be covenant sons, did women sometimes internalize the authority of Satan instead of God? The next chapter turns to the case of Elizabeth Knapp, a sixteen-year-old whose father turned her out of doors to live as a servant in the household of the town's minister. Soon afterward she become a very public figure in her spectacular struggle with the Devil inside her. Errington pondered how she could know whether she obeyed as a son or a servant, concluding that she could obey as a mother who wished that she had "a place in the wilderness to mourn." Knapp's place in the wilderness to mourn was a servant's calling. By enlisting her master as her hired hand, she would make it into a public vocation.

[2]

ANSWERING BACK: ELIZABETH KNAPP'S DEMONIC POSSESSION AND THE GENDER OF PUBLIC SERVICE

I will take heed to my ways, that I sin not with my tongue: I will keep my mouth with a bridle, while the wicked is before me. —Psalm 39:1

THE REVEREND SAMUEL WILLARD is famous again. In a *New York Times* blog post, "How Puritans Turned Capitalist," Willard epitomizes those inevitably "dour Puritan preachers" who "embraced markets as a moral good three and a half centuries ago," marking "a watershed in the formation of the American economy and the national character."[1] Willard owes this fresh publicity to Mark Valeri, whose important book, *Heavenly Merchandize: How Religion Shaped Commerce in Puritan America*, borrowed its title from a sermon that Willard preached in the 1680s from his pulpit at the Third Church, whose congregation included the most powerful merchant families of Puritan Boston. Valeri accords Willard a prominent role in his book, as a shaper of innovative concepts of vocation that reconciled piety with participation in increasingly complex forms of commerce. Together with the second- and third-generation merchant and magistrate elite, Willard helped make "service to the public good" into New England's "economic vocation."[2]

Willard first came to public attention as a formidable adversary of Satan. In the summer of 1671, sixteen-year-old Elizabeth Knapp was bound out to Willard as a servant in his household. That fall, she was seized by verbal fits and strange bodily contortions that made her ungovernable. Flailing in the throes of her affliction, Knapp was "violent in bodily motions, leapings, strainings, and strange agitations, scarce to be held in bounds by the strength of three or four."[3] She produced "sudden shrieks" (BA 422) and "roarings and screamings" (423); she "barked like a dog and bleated like a calf" and "imitat[ed] the crowing of a cock" (426 and 434). After consulting with a physician who rejected natural causes for her condition, Willard offered a diagnosis of demonic possession. As minister and master, Willard was charged with bringing Knapp's voice and body back in bounds. Called into battle with Satan, he wielded all the weapons at his disposal: the word of God, prayer, counsel, preaching, and the pen.

Willard found his first reading public when Massachusetts ministers consumed his 1672 narrative letter detailing the dramatic events. Such narratives were meant, as John Demos points out, to "reduce the Devil's influence by holding him up to public scrutiny," but the narrative also held Willard up to public scrutiny, gaining him the attention of Boston elders like Increase Mather.[4] Knapp's possession also occasioned Willard's first published sermon, *Useful Instructions for a Professing People in a Time of Great Security and Degeneracy* (1673), preached to his congregation in the aftermath of the event. Five years later, Willard was installed at the Third Church, where his experience with Knapp would continue to provide "useful instructions" for his vocation. During the Salem witchcraft trials, Willard published a pamphlet denouncing the admission of spectral evidence, and Thomas Brattle, a fellow critic of the trials, credited Willard's wisdom to his earlier treatment of "the Groton woman," a metonym for the "afflicted persons" at Salem—many of whom were, like Knapp, servants who accused more prominent neighbors of being witches.[5] Willard would succeed Mather as acting head of Harvard College—assuming Mather's position, in the words of one scholar, as "the symbolic leader of the New England clergy."[6]

The scant but ingenious interpretations of Knapp's possession concur with Brattle that her experience is most clearly legible when read retrospectively through the lens of Salem. Scholars have considered Knapp's servitude primarily as a self-evident sign of her marginal social status, which they see as a cause of her affliction.[7] In this, they take Knapp at her word. In Willard's account, she explains that the Devil "appeared to her" because "her condition displeased her, her labor was burdensome to her" (BA 431). But she also depicts servitude as an effect, not just a cause, of her satanic relations. She confesses to Willard the contractual obligations of the Devil's pact: "the term of time agreed upon with him was for seven years—one year she was to be faithful in his service, and then the other six he would serve her and make her a witch" (429). The battle between God, Satan, and Willard over Knapp's body and soul is a battle of masters.

Knapp's possession is a drama of consent that turns on the question of whom she will she serve, God or the Devil, Willard or herself? In this, Knapp is like all other Puritan earthly and spiritual children, striving against man's natural bondage to sin, Satan, and self and laboring toward willing consent to serve their Father. Knapp, Willard, and Satan publicize the routine spiritual labor of willing obedience to the covenant of grace. In particular, they make visible and audible the primary tangible sign of this invisible labor: the governance of the tongue.

As Jane Kamensky has brilliantly demonstrated, the governance of speech was a significant occupation of Puritan culture.[8] By ventriloquizing Knapp, the Devil exposes the critical role of the law of master and servant in governing the tongue. Knapp's possession reveals how service connects the governance of the tongue to work discipline, particularly in discourses of vocation and humiliation. In the doctrine of vocation, the soul is to hear and heed the voice of God calling it out of bondage to sin to serve Him. The discourse of humiliation identifies not answering back and being open to reproof and reproach as the primary traits that earthly and spiritual children and servants should evince. The internalization of mastery in vocation and humiliation entailed not just passive submission to patriarchal authority but also an active, ongoing process of imaginative self-making. As Leigh Eric Schmidt has observed, "the very obediences of devout hearing" follow a model of "submission that is, at the same time, an expansive reimagining of the subject."[9] Knapp's demonic possession enacts such a "reimagining" of the primary lived metaphor of covenant obedience: the child who serves.

In his history of literary servant conventions, Bruce Robbins describes dialogue between masters and servants as "a toleration of 'answering back,' a temporary, conventional suspension of the master's expectation of obedient silence and of his power to enforce it."[10] Robbins explicitly detaches his analysis of servants in literature from the history of actual servants, but "answering back" links conventional master-servant dialogue in literature to the particular calling of servants elaborated in laws and household tracts. If Puritan New England was, as Jeffrey Richards has put it, "a theater on a hill," then in a sense all speech was master-servant dialogue.[11]

Service connects the labors of Knapp's barks and bleats to the developing discourse of market morality to which Willard gave voice. Though they are increasingly part of New England's labor and social history, children, women, servants, slaves, non-Puritans, and other so-called strangers remain mostly absent from accounts of "how Puritans turned capitalist."[12] Valeri deepens our understanding of ministers, merchants, and magistrates as partners in the promotion of New England as a commercial venture, but he presents New England's economic culture as a series of transactions among elite men. However, Knapp and Willard were bound to each other. Reading the governance of the tongue as their common calling reveals economic vocation as the shared production of elite men and the women, children, and servants that God appointed them to govern.

Knapp's and Willard's callings to govern their tongues also connect New England economic culture to its literary history. The law of the master governed the social relationships in which rhetoric circulated and was spiritualized, whether in the form of speech, writing, or print: speaker-auditor and author-reader relationships were forms of master-servant relationships. The making of public service as a vocation also marked the development of authorship from the minister's vocation. The minister's sermonic authority invested authorship with the household master's authority—indeed, his moral and spiritual obligation—to command. Knapp did not have a pulpit, but her command performance drew her public to her bedside, where she offered them profitable services as well as demonic spectacles and thus enacted a form of public service that remained within the domestic sphere.[13] In a history of New England female authorship as a form of domestic public service that includes such lights as Anne Bradstreet, Mary Rowlandson, Hannah Webster Foster, Phillis Wheatley, Catharine Sedgwick, and Harriet Beecher Stowe, we might well inscribe the name of a woman who needed Satan's help to sign her own.

The Law of the Master and the Governance of the Tongue

Like the members of all households in Puritan New England, those in the Knapp and Willard households were bound to govern their tongues. In Puritan household governance manuals, a critical proof-text of the servant's particular calling was Titus 2:9: "Exhort servants to be obedient unto their own masters, and to please them well in all things, not answering again." In *Christian Oeconomy*, William Perkins collates it with Ephesians 6:5–7 and Colossians 3:22, which define hypocrisy as "eye-service," conflating the visible and audible signs of evangelical obedience. The servant "must take heed that he do not his master's business negligently, or for fashion sake, or with eye-service as a man-pleaser," Perkins instructs, "that in case of rebuke or controlment he answer not again."[14] A servant was to hear the voice of God in her master's lawful commands and reprimands and invisibly serve God by visibly and silently serving men.

In this, the earthly servant doing his "master's business" and God's business, not answering back to God's commands, modeled covenant obedience for even the most elite Puritans. Thomas Hooker cites Titus 2:9 to preach humiliation, admonishing his auditors: "That sturdy and peevish heart, let it be humbled, and your untoward and rebellious heart be brought into subjection; and you servants, Tit. 2:9, not answer your masters again; and you little ones, be not sturdy against your parents and disobedient unto their commands."[15] Although it contains one injunction to all of the elect and another for servants and children in particular, the sentence implies an analogy between the "sturdy and peevish heart" that must open itself to being humbled and the "sturdy" tongues of children and servants. Hooker does not just tell the elect to humble themselves; he gives them means to do so, inviting them to imagine themselves as servants and children who can govern their tongues as an exercise in shunning pride and cultivating obedience.

The servant holding her tongue before her master modeled lay submission to ministerial authority as it shuttled between the public and private service of God. In church, Hooker explains, the minister presents his auditors with portable mediations on pride that allow them to "humble your selves in secret, and say, this is my proud reason, my proud heart, and this is my proud carriage, it is I that would not submit to the command of Gods Word. And let every servant come in, and say, this is my proud heart, my Master, and my Mistris may not speake, but I give word for word: this is my fault" (SH 167). The properly humbled heed the master's authority over the word: those who have submitted to "the command of God's Word" will not "give word for word." By asking his auditors to repent as servants who have violated Titus 2:9, Hooker translates his instructions from church to family, from congregation to individual heart, and from hearing to speech. Hooker as a servant of God is also the vehicle of God's mastery, "the command of God's word." By not answering back to his commands, the spiritual child proves that she has internalized consent to God the Master as a condition of public service.

Puritan legal identities were public forms of domestic identities that both required and evinced the capacity to govern the tongue. Laws concerning the education of children were introduced by a preamble that established two premises: the first affirms that "the good Education of Children is of Singular behoofe and benefit to any Common-wealth"; the second laments that "many Parents and Masters are too indulgent and negligent of their duty in that kind."[16] To counter such "indulgence" and "negligence," the law orders "that the Select men of every Town . . . shall have a vigilant eye over their brethren and neighbours," not letting them "suffer so much barbarism in any of their families." In this role, selectmen embody a public form of God the Master, whose "vigilant eye" watches all—children and servants, and parents and masters alike.

Puritan children were trained to understand divine and positive law, language, and labor within the master-servant relationship. "Masters of families" must "endeavour to teach, by themselves or others, their Children and Apprentices, so much learning, as may enable them perfectly to read the English tongue, and knowledge of the Capital lawes"; once a week "at the least" they must "catechise their children and servants in the Grounds and Principles of Religion," or at minimum teach them "some short orthodox catechism without book, that they may be able to answer unto the questions, that shall be propounded to them . . . by their parents or masters or any of the Select men."[17] The law encodes a ready exchange between the authority of the "parents or masters" and "any of the Select men." Male public service was rooted in the legal obligation of the household master to teach his dependents to hold their tongues and to learn the English tongue.

Like Perkins's depiction of the servant's particular calling, the law yokes together the governance of the tongue with vocation. The final mandate of the law is "that all Parents and Masters do breed and bring up their children and apprentices in some honest lawfull Calling, Labour or imployment . . . profitable for themselves and the Common-wealth, if they will not or cannot train them up in learning, to fit them for higher imployments."[18] The law distinguishes between types of earthly labor: "Calling," "Labour," and "imployment" suggest greater and lesser degrees of spiritual value, with "higher imployments" reserved for those who can be "trained in learning"—a premodern division between mental and menial labor. But it also spiritualizes the "profitable" exchange between the labor of individual bodies and the corporate body. What makes these different forms of labor "lawfull" is the master, who ties profits to obedience. Masters must keep an eye on not just their children's tongues, but also their own purses: the law stipulated a penalty of "twenty shillings for each neglect therein." Whether masters neglect this duty and pay the penalty or dutifully fulfill it, the "Common-wealth" will profit from the labor of the child who serves and who lives this spiritual exemplum into adulthood in his or her calling.[19]

Laws governing "Children and Youth" also governed Puritan fathers, masters, and magistrates, who were meant to demonstrate that they were fit for spiritual childhood by showing that they had properly internalized the law of God the Master—that is, the obligation to serve. If the family patriarch proved to inadequately embody divine and positive law, the state would supply a public servant to act as a surrogate master. Selectmen who found "masters of families" negligent of their duty, "whereby children and servants become rude, stubborn, and unruly," were authorized, "with the help of two Magistrates, or the next County court," to "take such children or apprentices from them, and place them with some masters for years, (boyes till they come to twenty one, and girles eighteen years of age compleat)."[20] These state-appointed masters "will more strictly look unto, and force them to submit unto Government . . . if by fair meanes and former instructions they will not be drawn unto it." Presenting "fair means" as the primary tactic to instill obedience and "force" as a last resort, the laws echo the covenant dialectic of obedience in which the child's fear of being treated as a servant should elicit willingness to serve from love. If these children are not successfully compelled "by fair means" to consent to "submit unto Government," they will be "forced" to submit by masters who "will more strictly look unto" the governance of the tongue.[21]

The role of masters and town selectmen to keep a "vigilant eye" on the tongues of children and servants affected the Knapp and Willard families. In January 1670, in Watertown (where many of the original settlers of Groton—including the Knapp family—had lived), town selectmen were appointed to "speak with" Elizabeth's uncle William Knapp about his fourteen-year-old daughter, also named Elizabeth, specifically about her "Education" and "also being kept under restraint and Government."[22] On October 24, 1671, less than a week before the onset of Knapp's affliction, a man named Thomas Smyth appeared before the selectmen in Watertown and acknowledged that William Knapp's daughter, who had been bound out to him, "had not been so well attended in matter of Learning as she should have been" and promised to be more careful "that she shall be Learned in the knowledge of reading the English tongue."[23] Without suggesting a causal relationship between the two events (however tempting it might be to do so), I contend that the coincidence of the cousins' shared problems with the governance of the tongue nevertheless illuminates the extraordinary experience of Elizabeth Knapp of Groton.

Town records do not document the arrangement by which Knapp was bound out. The putting-out system used informal agreements, so it is possible that she was not bound out under the specific law mentioned above. But in Willard's narrative, Knapp testifies to her own unruliness, "complain[ing] against herself of many sins, disobedience to parents, neglect of attendance upon ordinances, attempts to murder herself and others" (BA 425). These sins would certainly seem to suggest sufficient rudeness and stubbornness to require a master who would "more strictly look unto" her. Was Knapp was bound out because her father, James Knapp, was an inadequate master of household? If so, he was in a bind: He was serving as one of the town selectmen when his daughter was bound out to Willard.[24] Knapp's inability to master his daughter and the resultant necessity of binding her out to a master more "vigilant" than himself suggested his failure as a family governor.[25] Yet as a selectman, he was supposed to embody an exemplary public form of household mastery.

Knapp was one of the men who "enterchangeably set our hands" with Willard in 1665 to ratify his seven-year contract to serve the Lord by serving Groton, at a rate of 60 pounds per annum.[26] Did James Knapp join hands with Willard to bind his daughter out as a servant in the minister's household? Or, as the lack of documentary evidence might suggest, did they make an informal oral agreement to force her to "submit unto Government"? Why did Knapp consent to bind out his daughter? Did Elizabeth consent to being bound out?[27]

Several aspects of Knapp's demonic possession suggest that she was answering back to the law of the master that bound her to Willard. The first is the timing of the episode. Knapp had consorted with Satan for five years before he entered her body, making his presence known to her when she lived at Lancaster, when "he presented himself and desired of her blood, and she would have done it but wanted [lacked] a knife" (BA 427). The Evil One followed her to Groton. Before she became Willard's servant, she received religious instruction at his house, and after lessons she would wait until darkness fell to "have [Satan's] company home" (424). After Knapp moved into the Willard household, Satan then "presented her a book, written with blood, of covenants made by others with him" and urged her to sign it. Knapp had always been related to Satan by blood, but she began to conceive of blood as a medium of legal, contractual consent only after she was bound out to Willard. Satan—the invisible master inside her—is the form the law takes during her possession.

Perhaps compensating for the failures of her father and master, Satan provides Knapp with instruction in the English tongue. In her clearest confession of ratifying the covenant, she presents it as an image of lawful master-servant relations, of mutual consent and mutual labor in the teaching of literacy. She both insists that "the Devil's quarrel with her was because she would not seal a covenant" (BA 426) and recalls that Satan assisted her in enabling her to sign her own name: he "demanded of her some of her blood, which she forthwith consented to, and with a knife cut her finger. He caught the blood in his hand and then told her she must write her name in his book. She answered [that] she could not write; but he told her he would direct her hand and then took a little sharpened stick and dipped it in the blood and put it into her hand and guided it, and she wrote her name with his help" (429). While the Devil's book is a commonplace of witchcraft culture, it resonates in this instance with the laws that specify the household master's duty to teach literacy to his children and servants.

Like the law, the satanic covenant links the acquisition of literacy with consent to masterly authority. Satan reverses the disciplinary trajectory of the laws, which resort to "force" only if "fair means" fail to compel "submi[ssion] unto Government." The Devil begins with force; he "demands" her blood and she "consents," cutting her own finger. He insists that "she must write" her name in his book, but when she "answer[s]" that she cannot write, Satan hardly behaves like a tyrant. Rather, he acts as a good master should, "directing" and "guiding" her until she can "[write] her name with his help"—thus enabling her to determine the relationship between her body, language, and labor. The Devil cuts her finger, catches her blood "in his hand," tells her he will "direct her hand," and places a writing implement (a "sharpened stick") into her hand. The blood and the hand are traditional metonyms of kinship and service. When Knapp "answer[s]" Satan that she cannot write and he responds with "fair means" to win her consent, he acts more like the father than the master in the covenant dialectic of obedience. He also makes her more like her own father, whose signature ratified Willard's seven-year contract, and who was very likely to have been among the townsmen who voted, two weeks before the onset of his daughter's fits, to continue to pay Willard 65 pounds annually through the final year of his contract—the rate at which it was settled in 1669.[28]

The law required household masters to impart "knowledge of the Capital lawes," and Knapp's possession seems shaped by her familiarity with them, especially crimes involving speech.[29] Knapp seems acutely aware that demonic possession, unlike witchcraft, is not a capital crime. As Kamensky explains, because "the possessed were not thought to speak for themselves," they did not "bear ultimate responsibility for the wounds their words caused. Indeed, when understood as diabolic ventriloquy, the utterances of the possessed became perverse proofs of their innocence."[30] Knapp tells Willard that she "feared [that] if she were a witch she should be discovered and brought to a shameful end, which was many times a trouble on her spirits," and she recounts that the Devil had goaded her to accuse others of witchcraft, explaining that "he had in their likeness or resemblance tormented her, persuading her that it was they—that they bore her a spleen, but he loved her and would free her from them—and pressed on her to endeavor to bring them forth to the censure of the law" (BA 430).

Witchcraft is not the only capital crime that Satan's mastery permits her to skirt. At sixteen, Knapp was old enough to be executed as a "rebellious son," the possible legal punishment for a child who "refused to hearken to 'the voyce of his Father, or the voyce of his Mother.'"[31] Satan speaking through Knapp denounces both Knapp's father and Willard as "rogues," one of his preferred "reviling terms." In one memorable sentence, he rails against James Knapp and another townsman, "calling them rogues, charging them for folly in going to hear a black rogue who told them nothing but a parcel of lies and deceived them" (BA 432). What Satan-in-Knapp "calls" James Knapp and Willard rails against their public employments. While "rogue" has come to signify villainy in general, it was also used to describe servants in particular.[32] By calling the two men "rogues," Satan deems them to be servants, not masters. Elizabeth Knapp borrows mastery from Satan to challenge the domestic underpinnings of the identities of Willard and her father as masters and selectmen, their identities under the law.

The fact that Satan's preferred verbal target is Willard rather than her father also evokes Knapp's awareness of the "censure of the law." Unlike verbal attacks on natural fathers, rebellions of speech against metaphorical fathers were not capital crimes. Knapp seems careful in other ways to define her relationship to the fifth commandment's chain of earthly fathers. Willard records that in one of Knapp's murmuring speeches, "one morning she said 'God is a father,' the next morning 'God is my father'" (BA 426). Even these affirmations of God's authority subvert earthly patriarchal authority. Knapp's shift from a general article to a possessive pronoun in the two phrases at once severs the analogy that likens Willard, her earthly master, to a father and displaces her natural father. The gendered identities in the law also give her a kind of freedom to call herself something other than child or servant. In one instance, Satan-in-Knapp denies being the Devil, saying, "I am not Satan; I am a pretty black boy [and] this is my pretty girl" (433). "Boy" and "girl," though socially marked by gender and age, were not particular callings as were "child" and "servant." But "boy" and "girl" were the identities in the law that determined the length of service for bound-out children: girls had to serve until the age of eighteen, and boys until the age of twenty-one. In this speech, Knapp translates the law into a kind of liberty, claiming a gendered identity that is not a domestic calling. She owns herself to be both "boy" and "girl" in a way that she does not own herself to be a servant or daughter, enacting a form of gendered self-governance. And as we have seen, Satan allows her to call James Knapp and Willard something other than father and master.

During her possession, Knapp appropriates the legal authority of public servants to move children across the thresholds of their natural families. She is the one who summons men across the boundaries between public and private vocations, "call[ing]" James Knapp and a neighbor away "from the meeting" (BA 432) to attend to her. In her power to move her male governors across thresholds, she can reclaim her father as a father and Willard as a minister. During the possession, Knapp is moved back home to her natural family. Her consent may not have been required to bind her out, but Satan enables her to restore herself to her father's household as a daughter and to bring her father along with her. She also brings Willard into the household, frequently commanding him to attend to her after she is "removed home" (425) to her father's house in midnarrative. As someone possessed by a demon, Knapp no longer labors invisibly and silently as a servant to enable Willard's ministerial labor; instead, she visibly and audibly demands his labor. Willard repeatedly comes to her home when he is, as he notes parenthetically in one instance, "being desired to be present" (428). Willard recounts that at one juncture Knapp "sent for me in haste at noon. Coming to her, she immediately with tears told me that she had belied the Devil . . . that the most of the apparitions she had spoken of were but fancies" (431). Willard compresses the space between Knapp's demand for his presence and his appearance at her side. Even as Knapp commands Willard in these instances, she allows him to exercise a crucial aspect of his vocation for which he would be renowned throughout his career: personal visitation.[33] In addition, she engages his authorial calling, his ability to leave a written record of his history of diligence in his calling.

Willard's authorial power also shaped Knapp's public calling. His manuscript preserves his servant's speech and the voice of Satan channeled through her. Knapp's father took pen to paper to hire Willard as Groton's servant of the Lord. When Willard did the same to narrate Elizabeth Knapp's demonic possession, he became her hired hand.[34]

Yet Willard's authorial power also allowed him to answer back as a master to his servant and to Satan's attempt to master both of them. By rejecting Knapp's irrational speech, Willard resists being hailed as her servant. After Knapp "cried out of a witch appearing in a strange manner in [the] form of a dog downward, with a woman's head" who disappears up the chimney, Willard declines to affirm that the mark of "something" in the chimney was in fact a dog's paw (BA 428). When Knapp "professed that the most of the apparitions she had spoken of were but fancies, as images represented in a dream," and "called God to witness to her assertion," Willard "told her I would willingly hope the best and believe what I had any good grounds to apprehend," but only if "she would tell a more methodical relation than the former" (431). Willard's pastoral authority to determine whether her speech is sufficiently "methodical" is an extension of his authority as her master and minister to govern her tongue. His mastery defines his calling to author his own "methodical relation" of Knapp's case.

"I . . . Saw Her Tongue": Reason, Consent, and Household Mastery

The urgent question of whether or not Knapp actually put her hand to the Devil's book dominates the narrative. Willard repeatedly expresses his "suspicion of the truth" of her account of the blood pact (BA 426 and 431). When Willard "pressed [her] to declare whether she had not consented to a covenant with the Devil," Knapp contradicts her vivid account of the scene of ratification: "she with solemn assertions denied it" (424). Willard takes a skeptical approach to Knapp's alternating confessions and denials, explaining that her "declarations have been so contradictory, one to another, that we know not what to make of them; and her condition is such as administers many doubts" (436). After weighing Knapp's contradictory testimony, Willard concludes with a question instead of an answer: "Whether she have covenanted with the Devil or no? I think this is a case unanswerable." Knapp's "contradictory declarations" keep the question of her written consent alive in the realm of speech, as does Willard's deference to God's ultimately mysterious will. By concluding that the case is "unanswerable," Willard is, in effect, not answering back to the command of his heavenly Master.

Like Brattle, scholars have touted Willard's skepticism toward Knapp's satanic covenant as it influenced his public vocation during the events at Salem.[35] But no one has tied it to his status as Knapp's master. The "reason" that defines Willard's response to Knapp is power articulated in the register of household mastery.[36] Willard's scientific method, his preaching of vocation and humiliation, and his authorship of the narrative were all invested with his authority as a household master to govern the hearing and speech of his dependents.

As the narrative opens, Willard positions himself not as a minister battling a demoniac, but as a master upholding his duty to keep a "vigilant eye" on his servant's speech. In the two weeks before her condition fully revealed itself, he noted "a strange change in her countenance" (BA 422). The "poor and miserable object," he explains, "was observed to carry herself in a strange and unwonted manner," and when questioned about her behavior, would "burst forth into immoderate and extravagant laughter." This laughter is a kind of answering back, but its spiritual meaning is not yet clear. In his role as family governor, Willard "diverse times inquired how she did, and she always answered well." Her dutiful response, in its incongruity with her verbal transgressions, actually stokes Willard's suspicions; as he puts it, it "made me wonder." What makes Willard "wonder" is the pressure Knapp has already put on the meaning of "answering well"—that is, obediently. As this expository paragraph ends, Knapp is not a threat to her superior, just an annoyance: the familiar figure of the verbally unruly servant. Willard thus uses the commonplaces of servant misbehavior to generate narrative suspense, setting the stage for the entrance of the Prince of Darkness and the "tragedy" that "began to unfold itself."

In a drama marked by shocking verbal conflict, one quiet scene portends Satan's power to disturb the alignment of visible and audible obedience. Satan does not command Knapp to serve him; he first uses "fair means," trying to win her consent by offering to serve her. But when Knapp refuses, Satan demonstrates his terrible power over her by performing the servant girl's labor invisibly. As Willard duly reports, Knapp asserts that Satan offered "to bring her in chips for the fire, [and] she refused; but when she came in she saw them lie by the fireside, and was afraid" (BA 428). The Devil's nefarious miracle of firewood answers back to Knapp's refusal; "fair means" fail to compel obedience, so he resorts to scare tactics. But in the visible realm, Satan's service registers as Knapp's answering back to Willard. Willard recalls the moment: "I, sitting by the fire, spoke to her to lay them on, and she turned away in an unwonted manner." Knapp's answering back to Willard takes the form of a silent gesture, "turning away in an unwonted manner" from her master. Willard does not record his reaction at that moment of her refusal, but in the narrative it works with "answering well" to increase his "wonder" about his servant. Demonic discourse translates Knapp's resistance of Willard's lawful command into an instance of Christian liberty—resistance to Satan's unlawful commands.

Willard writes a "tragedy," but Knapp's behavior resonates with Robbins's account of the comic servant's "functional deafness," the "habitual lapses into incomplete awareness" that "[free] her speech, allow[ing] her to comment against the grain instead of responding submissively."[37] Satan's mastery of her body effectively puts Knapp in such a condition of "incomplete awareness," permitting her to "comment against the grain." Willard notes that he finds Knapp in a "sottish and stupid kind of frame" (BA 427), and he reports that later, though she could speak, she was "in a case sad enough, her tears dried up and senses stupefied" (430).

In demonic discourse, the compulsory silence of obedient servitude becomes speechlessness, a sign of affliction. Knapp describes her periods of speechlessness as her tongue's extreme toil against constraint: "when she was taken speechless, she feared as if a string was tied about the roots of her tongue and reached down into her vitals and pulled her tongue down—and then most when she strove to speak" (BA 434). Knapp parodies the orthodox internalization of the master's power over the English tongue, imagining that her master physically governs it, ventriloquizing her.

Knapp's hands work with her tongue to perform speechlessness. Willard recounts an early episode in the narrative: "In the evening a little before she went to bed, [while] sitting by the fire she cried out, 'Oh, my legs!' and clapped her hand on them. Immediately [she cried out], 'Oh, my breast!' and removed her hands thither. And forthwith, 'Oh, I am strangled,' and put her hands on her throat" (BA 422). As they move from leg to breast to throat, Knapp's hands register Satan's invisible assaults. They also mediate between the verbal and the corporeal as they follow the cues of her voice over her body (particularly telling is the choking gesture that accompanies her peculiar ability to proclaim her own strangulation). Hands are the standard synecdoche of laboring bodies. Thus, as Knapp's hands draw attention to her master's invisible power over her, they also draw attention to her body as a laboring body. By working with her tongue to parody silence as a sign of servant obedience, Knapp's hands perform a different kind of productive labor, the labor of sign production.[38]

Scholars taking a psychoanalytic approach to these events have shared Willard's focus on Knapp's tongue as a primary site of contention in the narrative, reading it as a somatic expression of psychic resistance to the law of the father.[39] But the law of the master also governed her tongue.

Robbins observes of Samuel Richardson's heroine Pamela that "few literary servants have had every nuance of their every word scrutinized with such care," but Willard gives Mr. B a run for his money.[40] Though Willard has not witnessed many of the events he recounts, he emphasizes his personal witness of the mechanics of Knapp's speech to "countermand this apprehension" of those who doubt that "the devil did really speak in her": "First, the manner of expression I diligently observed and [I] could not perceive any organ, any instrument of speech . . . to have any motion at all. Yea, her mouth was sometimes shut without opening, sometimes open without shutting or moving; and then both I and others saw her tongue (as it used to be when she was in some fits, when speechless) turned up circularly to the roof of her mouth" (BA 435). Denied the use of her tongue as an organ of speech, perhaps deprived of instruction in the "English tongue," Knapp nevertheless makes it a powerful organ of signification, a visual sign of answering back to her masters, both visible and invisible.

As the laws would prescribe in the case of such a servant, her disobedience becomes a matter of public concern. At one point, Knapp's "tongue was for many hours together drawn into a semicircle up to the roof of her mouth, and not to be removed (for some tried with the fingers to do it)" (BA 426). Knapp's unruly tongue is a site of struggle between internalized self-governance and the need for external, public governance. When the public intrudes its fingers into her mouth, it literalizes its power over her speech. The willful labors of Knapp's tongue finally convince a skeptical Willard of the veracity of her symptoms, to answer in the affirmative the question of "whether she might properly be called a demoniac" (432). The Devil "began (as the persons with her testify) by drawing her tongue out of her mouth most frightfully to an extraordinary length and greatness and [making] many amazing postures of her body." At the end of the narrative, Willard focuses on Knapp's lips and her formation of "the labial letters, diverse of which were used by her viz. B, M, P—which cannot be naturally expressed without motion of the lips [and] which must needs come within our ken if observed—were uttered without any such motion. If she had used only linguals, gutturals, etc., the matter might have been more suspicious" (435). Willard links these corporeal evidences to proper social and spiritual relations when he turns to the content of Knapp's demonic speech, observing that Knapp had never violated the mandates of Titus 2:9: "the reviling terms then used were such as she never used before nor since in all this time of her being thus taken. Yea, [she] hath been always observed to speak respectfully concerning me." Defining her speech relation to him, Willard deems Knapp a demoniac, not a saucy servant.

Satanic Impertinence: Master-Servant Dialogue

Satan, however, is a saucebox who elicits impertinence from his verbal antagonists. Willard scripts several passages of direct dialogue with Satan that resonate uncannily with Robbins's account of theatrical master-servant dialogue. Robbins discusses various conventions of servant "impertinence" in such dialogues (repeating or echoing the master, misdirection, and flattery), kinds of comic speech that fluster rather than flout the master's assumption of power over the servant.[41] The echoing that Robbins sees as characteristic of servants' impertinence in comic dialogue (it would also be characteristic in novels) also characterizes the catechism, a ritualized form of spiritual speech regulated by the master-servant relationship. Indeed, catechism is a version of master-servant dialogue, ripe for subversion or creating an environment that expands the limits of what the servant can say, if not on her own behalf. The satanic dialogues in Willard's narrative can be read as a diabolic version of the master's responsibility for catechizing his servants.

Knapp impertinently answers back to Satan when his vehement pressing to sign the covenant a second time fails to secure her consent. He then uses "fair means" (the master's tactic of verbal persuasion), pointing out that "she had done it already, and what further damage would it be to do it again, for she was his sure enough" (BA 430). She echoes the Devil with the kind of impertinence that Robbins associates with master-servant dialogue, retorting that she "had done it already, and if she were his sure enough, what need [had] he to desire any more of her." Satan doesn't take kindly to his saucy servant's refusal and resorts to "force": "he struck her the first night, [and] again more violently the second." Though Satan punishes her impertinence, her endurance of the punishment functions as an instance of Christian liberty, because the Devil's commands are by definition unlawful. Yet because her discontent invited Satan's commerce with her, she also doubles as an image of the dangers of impertinent answering back, or insufficiently humbled speech.

Right after she recounts the dialogue, Knapp humbles herself properly in relation to her minister's traditional authority over spiritual speech. Willard strives to offer her means of grace in the form of shared prayers: "I therefore (as God helped) applied it to her and asked her whether she desired not prayers with and for her" (BA 430). Knapp "assented with earnestness, and in prayer seemed to bewail the sin, as God helped," and "afterward declared a desire to rely on the power and mercy of God in Christ." In the mutual work of humiliation between Knapp and Willard, she properly "declares" her desire to put herself at God's disposal, to "rely on the power and mercy of God in Christ," while he twice repeats "as God helped" to suggest the proper alignment of his own labors with God's will.

Willard also writes himself a scene of master-servant dialogue with Satan, focusing on the answering, replying, and rejoining that comprise his battle with the Evil One. The dialogue commences with Satan's verbal abuse: "He then again called me a great black rogue. I challenged him to make it appear [so]; but all the answer was, 'You tell the people a company of lies.' I reflected on myself, and could not but magnify the goodness of God not to suffer Satan to bespatter the names of his people with those sins which He Himself hath pardoned in the blood of Christ" (BA 432). Willard's pause for self-reflection and to "magnify the goodness of God" functions as a sort of spiritual aside, with God and his audience of ministerial peers and superiors in mind. "Bespatter" vividly evokes the physical act of utterance, conjuring the dual image of Satan-in-Knapp spitting while denouncing "the names of [God's] people" and the blood shed by Christ in his work of redemption.

Willard then responds by echoing Satan, turning his accusation against himself: "I answered, 'Satan, thou art a liar and a deceiver, and God will vindicate His own truth one day'" (BA 432). Following Willard's impertinence, Satan tries misdirection: "He answered nothing directly, but said, 'I am not Satan; I am a pretty black boy [and] this is my pretty girl. I have been here a great while'" (432–33). "Blackness" connects Satan's apparent misdirection to his "directed" speech when it resumes. Willard says that he "sat still and answered nothing to these expressions," but when Satan "directed himself to me again—[saying] 'Oh! You black rogue, I do not love you'—I replied, 'Through God's grace I hate thee.' He rejoined, 'But you had better love me'" (433). Knapp and Satan compel Willard to shape his speech in relation to his heavenly Master, and God answers by granting his servant the gracious ability to parry Satan's "not love" with the more forceful "hate."

But Satan's ultimate rejoinder provokes "great consternation" about the exchange in "some of the company there present," emboldening them to engage in direct dialogue with Satan. Willard's account of the lay-Satan dialogues dramatizes his assumption of mastery over spiritual speech, but it also reveals that the townspeople do not obey him as readily as a good master might expect his servants to do. Indeed, reading these passages within the broader context of Willard's employment in Groton reveals the complexity of master and servant as lived metaphors of labor relations and of the balance between lay and ministerial authority.

In his relation to the town, Willard was both master and servant. Spiritualized as a "solemn Engagement," Willard's covenant with Groton was a special form of a master-servant contract.[42] Laws codified the legal obligations owed by masters to "servants that have served diligently and faithfully to the benefit of their masters [for] Seven years," stipulating that such servants "shall not be sent away empty."[43] Willard's contract provided that he would not be "sent away empty": after seven years of diligent and faithful service he would be granted the minister's house and land.[44] Willard's contract codified the mutual labors of the minister and the town as a shared economic vocation. In addition to money, the minister's remuneration consisted of the fruits of the townspeople's manual labors. Each family was to contribute a share of Willard's salary in rye, pork, or "merchantable corne at price current." The "mowing . . . and fetching of hay" for him were stipulated as part of his salary, and townsmen were to "cut and Cart to his house and there to Cord for him the aforesaid 30 cord of wood at five shilling[s] per cord."[45] The relationship between town and minister is legible as a master-servant relationship, but one in which each party might claim the master position in a given instance. From a contractual standpoint, the townspeople were Willard's masters, but from the angle of the division between mental and menial labor, he was their master, since their labors granted him some respite from the labor of maintaining his household and enabled him to write and deliver sermons and provide pastoral care. The relationship between Willard and the townspeople of Groton suggests that we should not simply translate "master" as "employer" and "servant" as "employee" when considering the emergence of class from rank, or of a capitalist division of labor from the household.[46]

The conditions of Willard's employment were contentious. Townspeople were chronically delinquent in meeting their contractual obligations to him. In 1669, two men were chosen "to see that Mr. Willard have maintenance duely and truly paid to him."[47] The following year, a meeting of the selectmen insisted that "every inhabitant of the town shall pay their due and full proportion to our reverend pastor . . . according to the agreement" and that the inhabitants "are to bring in their accounts to the Deacon or to the men chosen for that end within the time prefixed or else they shall be accounted delinquents."[48] The threat of delinquency did not alleviate the necessity for the town to insist again in 1671 that the town's sergeants "shall see that Mr. Willards pay shall be brought in and faithfully payd to him according to the agreement of the towne."[49] Willard's wage for faithful service was to be "faithfully payd"—on time and in full.

The narrative suggests how these ongoing conflicts over Willard's compensation played out in a power struggle over the governance of speech. When the townspeople attempt to combat Satan, Willard does not approve: "Others put on boldness to speak to him, at which I was displeased and advised them to see their call clear, fearing lest by his policy and [the] many apish expressions he used he might insinuate himself and raise in them a fearlessness of spirit of him" (BA 433). The townspeople's "boldness to speak" and Satan's "apish expressions" alike evince a tenuous balance of divine versus demonic power, prompting Willard's "displeasure."

Willard responds to this challenge to his authority by assuming a master's relation to their speech, offering his own counsel: "I seeing little good to be done by discourse, and questioning many things in my mind concerning it, I desired the company to join in prayer unto God" (BA 433). But as the group "were kneeled down" in prayer, Satan cries out, "with a voice louder than before," "'Hold your tongue, hold your tongue; get you gone, you black rogue; what are you going to do; you have nothing to do with me.'" God silences Satan, but the intermission is only temporary. Upon cessation of the prayers, Satan "began afresh, using the former expressions—at which some ventured to speak to him, though I think imprudently." The company does not heed his counsel, and its members seem to Willard to be venturing all too close to the disobedience that left Knapp so vulnerable to the Devil's attacks.

Some people in the company then enter into a treacherous dialogue with Satan in which they seem to encroach upon on Willard's authority over spiritual speech: "One told him [that] God had him in chains; he replied, 'For all my chains, I can knock thee on the head when I please.' He said he would carry her away that night, [and] another answered, 'But God is stronger than thou.' He presently rejoined, 'That's a lie, I am stronger than God'—at which blasphemy I again advised them to be wary of speaking, counselled them to get serious persons to watch with her, and left her, commending her to God" (BA 433). Satan's rejoinders take the form of impertinent echoing, the servant's answering back. Willard's counsel is that of a master regulating between two types of disobedient speech—Satan's overt "blasphemy" and the company's "imprudence"—and Willard cautions the others to "be wary of speaking," to hold their tongues. His mastery is expressed instead in the humble gesture of "commending her to God," which is also a reproach to the impertinent speech of his congregants. The townspeople should not "give word for word," as Hooker put it, but should remain silent in their places, quietly but actively cultivating submission to God's word.

Public Confessions and Profitable Services

Knapp also addresses the townspeople as auditors who should hold their tongues and heed her counsel, repeatedly insisting on confessing to a group of laypeople rather than to Willard alone. As Willard notes when he questions her about the covenant, he "found her not so forward to confess, as she had been to others" (BA 429). Robbins's account of how the public emerges from theatrical master-servant dialogue helps us see Knapp's confessions as "public service." In master-servant dialogue, Robbins argues, the "servant voice" often "project[s] itself out of dialogue and into monologue—into a monologue, however, that is at once audience-directed and self-assertive. . . . [T]he general aesthetic authority for the servant's self-assertion [derives] from the audience, a second and sovereign master."[50] Knapp talks over the head of her earthly master and appeals to a higher authority: the audience as God. She gestures toward a secularized version of a public by conceiving of her primary audience (her "second and sovereign master") as the laypeople she beckons to attend to her rather than Willard or God.

In their content as well as their form, Knapp's confessions are directed toward the public good. To Demos, Knapp's desire for an audience is evidence of narcissism and "exhibitionism," but what she performs before them is disinterested public service, voicing a lesson in humble economic personhood.[51] Lay counsel and discipline had always been an essential aspect of Puritan culture, and in Boston new institutions like watch societies and voluntary societies drew upon this tradition to enlist private citizens "to promote economic reform."[52] As Valeri notes, such institutions "offered public-spirited individuals the opportunity to fulfill what [Cotton] Mather described as the calling of the good rich man: to spread moral exhortation, give counsel to neighbors, educate the poor, fund works projects, and provide alms."[53] Knapp's case suggests that the category of "public-spirited individuals" was not the exclusive domain of elite men. Demonic possession might be the calling of the disobedient poor young woman whose public authority to provide moral discipline, like that of elite men, was rooted in the internalization of household mastery.

As I discuss above, Satan does allow Knapp to answer back to hierarchical social relations, but Knapp's performance of resistance to orthodoxy also productively performs lay moral authority. In one "large confession in the presence of many," Knapp explains that Satan "had oftentimes appeared to her, presenting the treaty of a covenant and proffering largely to her—viz. such things as suited her youthful fancy, [like] money, silks, fine clothes, ease from labor, to show her the whole world, etc." (BA 423). The temptations of worldliness (given her frontier-town upbringing, it's hard not to read "the whole world" as Boston) might be particularly dangerous to a "youthful fancy," but they also threatened spiritual children: in Boston, Willard "admonished merchants against addiction to high style."[54] Knapp admonishes her listeners to "use [their] time better than she had done" (427) and "declare[s] against herself her unprofitable life she had led, and how justly God had thus permitted Satan to handle her" (428).

In her confessions, Knapp both articulates and enacts her own "useful instructions" in properly profitable spiritual speech. In one of her confessions, she conceives of speech as something to be "made use of," saying "that she had rather continue so speechless than have her speech and make no better use of it than formerly she had" (BA 434). In one instance when "her speech was restored to her," Willard observes that "she expressed a great seeming sense of her state. Many bitter tears, sighings, sobbings, complainings she uttered, bewailing of many sins aforementioned, begging prayers, and in the hour of prayer expressing much affection" (426–27). Willard's words denote a category of humble spiritual speech—sighings, sobbings, complainings, bewailing, and begging—that counter the prideful speech of her satanic utterances.

Willard uses "counsel," a word connoting private pastoral conference, to describe Knapp's audience-directed confessions.[55] Before her audience, Knapp "complained of a hard heart, counselled some to beware of sin for that had brought her to this, bewailed that so many prayers had been put up for her and [that] she [was] still so hard-hearted and no more good wrought upon her" (BA 432). But she remains silent when asked to give her own consent to spiritual labors: "being asked whether she were willing to repent, [she] shaked her head and said nothing." Knapp's refusal to answer, or affirm her willingness to repent, might be seen as answering back or disobedience, but it might also suggest a properly orthodox reverence for public confession. As long as she remains "hard-hearted," such an affirmation would be hypocrisy, a legal confession only. When her public answers back to her, "advis[ing] her also to bethink herself of making her peace," Knapp replies, "It is too late for me" (427). Though she sees herself as a lost cause, she acknowledges the spiritual labors on her behalf, noting that "so much pains were taken with her," though they "did no good." By enjoining the community to come together in service on her behalf while denying their ability to save her, Knapp performs a disinterested public service. If the townspeople heed her admonitions to serve God in serving her, their labors will be profitable regardless of her eternal fate.

The voice of the demoniac was still ringing in the ears of Groton's townspeople when they went to church in the aftermath of the episode. The maidservant and the minister had warned them to be more humble in their speech and hearing, and there is economic evidence that their counsel was heeded. Satan's was evidently not the only voice in Groton deriding Willard's services. In *Useful Instructions*, Willard laments the degradation of the "Office of the Ministry" as one of the "disorders" that led Satan to Groton: "doubtless the low esteem of this great Work appearing by too many evident symptoms, is one thing for which God is now pleading with us."[56] Willard warns that "Gods ministers may pity and pray for you, yea will; but God will not suffer his own glory thus to be trampled upon, nor his Servants thus to be abused" (UI 58). These "abuses" are verbal and economic: ministers are "despised, their Office questioned, their Authority cast off, and trampled upon, their persons undervalued and vilified, their comfortable Supply and Maintenance neglected" (UI 75). After the narrative, Groton's properly humbled servants renewed their commitment to Willard's services. In 1670, Willard received his first raise in five years, to 65 pounds, but in October 1672, the townspeople "by vote declared that Mr. Willard shall have for this present year eighty pound."[57] His salary remained at 80 pounds for the three years he stayed at Groton.

Willard exerted a master's command over Groton's lay speech, but he also shows an acute awareness that his audience included his social superiors, especially those "important Bostonians" whose ranks he would soon join. Demos points out Knapp's desire to be taken to Boston "for special presentation to an assembly of ministers," characterizing Boston "as the biggest stage that New England could offer her, and its clergymen . . . the most distinguished of potential reviewers."[58] God, of course, called Willard instead of Knapp to Boston, perhaps because he approved of Willard's deference to those "distinguished reviewers." At the conclusion of Willard's narrative, Knapp remains plagued by fits and speechlessness, and Willard remarks that "concerning which state of hers I shall suspend my own judgement and willingly leave it to the censure of those that are more learned, aged and judicious" (BA 435). Willard performs his consent, noting that he "shall suspend my own judgement" and submit "willingly" to the censuring authority of his earthly superiors. This deference is, in effect, another note in the range of his master-servant speech.

And it is this note that defines his authorial vocation as service to the Lord. Ultimately, Willard submits to the providential will of his divine Master: "what to make of these things I at present know not, but am waiting till God (if He sees meet) wind up the story and make a more clear discovery" (BA 431). Like Knapp, he does not just submit but performs submission; his deference is a way of not answering back to his divine Master.[59] Thus Willard frames his own authorial vocation as submission to God the author. Willard might write the conclusion of the narrative, but only God knows how the story ends.

Knapp would not write her own ending. At the end of the narrative, though she is not cured, Willard notes that "through God's goodness," she is "so abated in violence that now one person can as well rule her as formerly four or five" (BA 434). Soon, that "one person" would be her husband. Two years after the conclusion of the narrative, when Knapp was "18 years of age compleat"—the age of liberty under the law that likely bound her to Willard—Knapp entered into a marriage covenant, giving her hand to Samuel Scripture.[60] She obediently fulfilled the terms of the covenant by bearing five children; converting household service to childbearing, of course, only tied labor more emphatically to her body.[61] Knapp could not durably embody the private authority of household mastery that upheld public service as a labor ideal. But she did borrow it, for a time, in the form of Satan's masculine mastery. Following her marriage, Knapp receded into archival silence; there is no evidence that she answered back to her particular callings to motherhood and wifehood as she had to her servant's calling. Because non-elite women's lives tend to be preserved only when they strayed out of bounds, we might conclude that Knapp had learned to govern her tongue, at least enough that any mutterings could be resolved privately.

Lip Service

Yet Knapp would continue to speak through Willard. *Useful Instructions*, the sermon he preached in the aftermath of the episode, demonstrates her lasting effect on Willard's preaching of economic vocation. Willard's text, Jeremiah 7:12, presents Knapp's possession as providential punishment for Groton's "hypocritical services." Jeremiah 7 laments Judah's polluted commerce in speech and spiritual deafness. The people of Judah "trust in lying words, that cannot profit" and "swear falsely," rendering themselves deaf to God's voice calling them out of sin. "Obey my voice, and I will be your God, and ye shall be my people," God promised Judah's fathers, but they will not heed God's command: "they hearkened not, nor inclined their ear." Nor, God warns his messenger Jeremiah, will they heed his authority: "they will not hearken to thee: that shalt also call unto them; but they will not answer thee" (Jeremiah 7:11).

In Willard's sermonic version of Knapp's experience, she is not a witch or a demoniac, but an ordinary hypocrite who hearkens to neither her earthly nor her heavenly master. Like the formal elements of Knapp's possession, Willard's sermon trades in the orthodox imagery of hypocrisy as lip service that tethered economic imagery—of profits, greed, wages, robbery—to the law of the master. The "words, that cannot profit" are the products of labors undertaken for false masters, Satan and the self, instead of God, family, church, and state. Duties performed "not from a right principle; Grace, which onely can do any thing acceptably to God," pose even greater spiritual danger than outright disobedience (UI 67). When hypocrites pay lip service to God, they speak in the Devil's voice.

Through Jeremiah, God asks, "Is this house, which is called by my name, become a den of robbers . . . ?" Polluted commerce in speech violates economic vocation. In Willard's doctrine, legal obedience is spiritual property crime: "Hypocritical service is no better than robbery, pretended service to God" (UI 8). Indulging their "greedy desires" for sin, hypocrites "rob" God "*of that glory which is due to his name*, who requires hearty service" and "robs himself of all the good which he should otherwise get by his service, if it were done in sincerity." Willard warns that such hypocrites "shall be found the greatest self-Cheaters in the end" (9). When God's servants rob him of his proper measure of glory, they steal from themselves. Sincere service, the fundamental virtue of the Puritan vocation as both the means and end of spiritual labor, requires the elect to internalize God as Master. Viewed through the lens of the covenant dialectic, crimes against trade are a servant's violations against a master's authority, the form of patriarchal power that circulates between Groton as "house," the Knapp family, Willard's house, and houses of God.

Knapp's possession has exposed the corruption of pride at the root of Groton's earthly blessings, expounding the doctrine that "a people in the very height of outward prosperity, may be very near to ruine and destruction" (UI 62). "Oh how laborious Christians should we be, how sedulous in the work of God," Willard laments. "Oh how much of our time here have we wasted away . . . in that which profits not" (UI 64). He depicts Groton as a miniature of New England exceptionalism: "None in the world ever enjoyed a happier advantage to serve God in, then [*sic*] we have done for so long a season in this Wilderness, wherein we have enjoyed peace, and the liberties of the Gospel, liberty to be as good as we will, and all encouragements to serve God, but oh how much we have been wasting away unprofitably, in Contentions, and busie Wranglings about matters of an inferiour consideration, about our worldly Cares and Perplexities, &c. We have used but little care to redeem those precious hours from those encompassing vanities which beset us" (UI 64). Willard here takes his cues from Knapp's confessions, revealing their shared understanding of obedience—the "liberty to be as good as we will . . . to serve God"—as the basis of economic morality. The townspeople of Groton and, by extension, the New England community of saints have grievously neglected their obligations as God's chosen people by "wasting away unprofitably in Contentions and busie Wranglings . . . those precious hours" that God has granted them to labor in his service. As audible evidence of inadequate humiliation, "Contentions and busie Wranglings" are both the cause and effect of unprofitable labor.

Willard preaches that Knapp's affliction should prompt all of God's servants "to see whether our services and enquiries have not been hypocritical; whether or no we have not drawn *near to God with our lips, whiles* [*sic*] *our hearts have been far from him*" (UI 67). Your earthly superiors "may [be] put off with fine words and fair pretences, but not so God: hath not God made it to appear that he will not be mocked by us? We have offered up to him hypocritical services, and accordingly we have been paid" (68). Providential affliction is wages for "the greatest sin"—hypocritical services in the form of "fine words" and "mockery."

The way to regenerate a community debased by unruly traffic in speech is to engage it in the project of laboring to humble the tongues of its members so they can hear God's voice calling them to serve him. When Willard exhorts his auditors to make a "thorough work at home," searching for evidence of hypocritical or legal services masquerading as service to God, "home" refers to the heart of the individual believer as well as the family, church, and town. Individuals must be prepared to "take the shame" of sin instead of blaming others: "if while thou art standing before God, asking him by whom, and for what he is provoked? if he answer, *Thou art the man*, for these and those things he is provoked and offended; why, now *lay thy mouth in the dust*, reply not against him"

(UI 71). Willard immediately links this exhortation to market morality: "If the Command laid upon you be never so cross, be ready and willing to obey it." God might command a "proud heart" to "fling away" "a sin which hath brought thee in a great deal of profit, credit, or the like." But "the great *Searcher of hearts*" will expose such "profitable" sin as unprofitable service. Willard enjoins his auditors to labor to humble such proud hearts, so that they can stand before their Master "able in some measure sincerely to say, *Speak Lord, thy Servant heareth, Command me what thou wilt, I am ready to obey and follow thee.*" God's voice calling the elect out of sin and hypocritical services is a master's voice, and the elect should respond as humble servants, not answering back to his lawful commands, even if that means "flinging away" earthly profits.

Families as well as individual sinners are too quick to censure and blame others for afflictions instead of humbling themselves. Willard urges the Knapp family to examine why God singled them out for affliction, to "try what is the meaning of his [being] so severe in coming out against them, that they may learn to sit in silence, and justifie him" (UI 30). But he also warns the town's other families that heaping scorn upon the Knapp family in particular is not profitable labor. Parents must not simply give their children "some flighty reproofs for their sins" (74) but should "hold your Parental Authority over them, keep them within their bounds, you had better hear their hard thoughts of you now, then [*sic*] see them made vassals of Satan" (38–39). When parents discipline their children's speech, "mak[ing] use of that authority which God hath put into your hands," they should also discipline their own, by humbly "commend[ing] the success to God" (74). Children, in turn, must understand that they serve God when they obey their parents: "Learn to obey your Parents in all their lawful Commands, and that in obedience unto God . . . if you disobey and displease your Parents in it, be sure you lay yourselves open to Satan" (40). All the members of a household living under English law could practice consent to church and state authority by learning how to govern their speech and hearing.

Groton's properly humbled and obedient children should heed their parents' commands, and Groton's "children of disobedience" of all ages should respect ministerial authority. Willard admonishes the town's youth against spiritual deafness: "you have been often counselled and admonished in the House of God, yea earnestly and compassionately intreated to devote your young time to God, to give up the prime of your years to him; but you have slighted and disregarded such Counsels and Calls" (UI 36). Children in particular should not disregard Willard's ear-

tration fall upon the people, especially if persons in Office and Place do . . . endeavour to rectifie and amend them, but are overpowered" (77). The counterpoint to anarchy is humiliation, or continued dependence on the authority of ministers and magistrates. The voice of God must rule the voice of the people through the voices of his public servants.

While the overt mockery of Satan's speaking in Knapp might seem to pose the greatest threat to Groton's spiritual well-being, in his sermon Willard singles out Knapp's own voice and her contradictory confessions as he laments the use of confessions as a legalist crutch by hypocrites. Willard warns his Groton auditors against legal confessions: "If you only *confess*, it is but half a Fast, you must *forsake* too" (UI 79). God must have a "thorough Repentance": "You must repent of all your sins, that is, all universally, and all particularly, as he comes to discover them to you, you must be sure hide none under your tongue, spare none, but bring them all forth and confess them before God." Knapp's possession should warn all of Groton's people that if they try to hide sins under their tongues, God might grant Satan the liberty to publicize those sins against their will. God the Master authorizes the public speech of the demoniac as of the preacher.

Halfway Covenants

As an emblem of hypocritical confessions in *Useful Instructions*, Knapp inaugurated Willard's fame as a preacher of covenant renewal under Halfway Covenant measures. Whether viewed by scholars and Puritans themselves as a humane accommodation of orthodoxy to the world or the lamentable capitulation of orthodoxy to the world, the Halfway Covenant has been taken to mark a crucial moment in the secularization of Puritan piety that accompanied the growth of New England commerce.[64] Willard's sermon strongly suggests that the people of Groton had already adopted the Halfway Covenant measures or at least that he had advocated that they do so.[65] Willard may be alluding to the Halfway Covenant and the education laws cited above as joint ventures in the spiritual edification of youth when he refers in his sermon to the "many endeavours used by Church and Common-wealth for the instruction of Youth in the Ways of God" and observes that "there should be answerable improvement made" (UI 37). One of the ways in which spiritual and earthly children could demonstrate such "answerable improvement" was by not answering back to the lawful commands of their parents and masters and to the public form of these masters, the church and commonwealth.

Like the law, the forms of public childhood created by the Halfway Covenant reveal Knapp's demonic possession as a vocation. As institutionalized at Boston's Third Church, the synod's recommendations created a new category of church membership and spiritual childhood: "children of the church," who were "baptized children who had 'owned the covenant' and were striving for but had not yet attained the status of full members."[66] The Halfway Covenant's "children of the church" were an innovation with respect to church membership—the phrase denoted a category of virtuous elite public semiregeneracy. But this new form of public childhood was a variation on the traditional lived metaphor of ideal covenant personhood: the child of God who inherits the gracious ability to serve him. These baptized children must not rest in their covenant inheritance but must understand baptism as providing access to the means of growing in consent to serve the Lord. As Willard preached, God's covenant subjects must be "altogether at his command, and fully engaged in his service . . . you are not to be at your own dispose, but he must dispose of you, and you stand engaged to take all well, whatsoever it be that he shall call you unto."[67] As public forms of the servant-child dialectic of obedience, the demoniac, the child of the church, and the child bound out to service alike promoted the Puritan labor ideal.

While the Halfway Covenant measures preserved and perhaps even underscored the sanctity of public conversion testimonies for full membership, they also created opportunities for "halfway" members to publicly declare their obedience to the covenant. Baptized children could be brought to publicly own or affirm the covenant, a ritual of consent that was understood as a step toward conversion and full membership status. In these covenant renewal rituals, the "children of the church" publicly performed their ability to govern their tongues as evidence of growing in consent to serve God, to worship and obey him. Willard was renowned for conducting them.[68]

These confessions might have marked a halfway point between unregeneracy and church membership, but they were not to be half-hearted. Willard presented covenant participants with the threat of hypocritical confessions, warning, "you should not be like the Nightingale, a voice and nothing else."[69] In a sermon preached following a covenant renewal ritual, Willard exhorts the participants: "You have now declared, and promised, that you will not rise up against the command, nor call it a hard saying, but will receive the word at the mouth of the Lord, and his Servants, and will do accordingly: that you will not murmur at, or rise up against his providential disposure of you, but if he afflict you, cut you short, and carry you through diverse trials, and great exercises, you will submit to his hand, and be content that he shall be your Leader."[70] In the covenant work of humiliation, willing silence is a sign of contentment in being at God's disposal: public confessors have promised not to call the "commands" of God and ministers "hard sayings" and that they "will not murmure" or answer back to them. If his children fail to keep this obligation of the covenant, God will bring them "under that sharp censure which was given of Israel of old . . . *They flatter'd him with their mouth, and lyed to him with their tongues*. . . . God himself will declare against you, as he did against that hypocritical Generation, Isa. 29.13. *This People honoreth me with their lips, but their heart is far away from me*."[71] Knapp publicized the threat of hypocritical speech as a precursor not just of Salem's witches and their accusers, but also of Willard's "children of the church" under the Halfway Covenant.

Halfway Covenant measures illuminate one of the curious features of Knapp's battle with the Devil: his desire to have her sign his covenant twice. Even when Knapp admits to having signed the covenant, the Devil presents her with the opportunity to heighten the drama of verbal consent. She says that she signed the covenant, after which "the Devil show[ed] her hell and the damned," which makes her think better of her contract (BA 429). Satan then begins pressing her to sign it a second time, "to give him more of her blood and set her hand again to his book" (430). This account essentially seems to nullify her previous confession of having signed it, leaving her hovering in her halfway state: "partly through promises, partly by threatenings, he brought her at last to a promise that she would sometime do it; after which he left not incessantly to urge her to the performance of it." But Knapp will not give her consent to sign the covenant a second time, managing to "put it off" despite Satan's use of force, "pressing her with vehemence." Knapp's single signature echoes baptism's function as a covenant seal under the terms of the Halfway Covenant, expressing consent to the terms of the covenant but not, in itself, fulfilling them; while the ongoing verbal struggle over the second signature resonates with rituals of covenant renewal, in which the "children of the church" reaffirm their commitment to continue to labor toward consent in the form of the public testimony of conversion. Satan's refusal to take a single signature as sufficiently binding suggests the snares of legalism under the Halfway Covenant—no number of rote expressions of consent will ratify the terms of the covenant, yet one must continue to labor toward conversion.

At the Third Church, Willard's ambivalence about Knapp's satanic covenant would resolve itself into an emphatic exhortation on covenant consent. Willard formulated a script that covenant renewal participants could use to counter Satan's persuasions: "When Satan, or any of his Instruments at any time seek to . . . perswade you to joyne with them in any vain and sinful deed . . . say, shall I do this thing, who have covenanted with God against it? no, my word is past, yea I have sworn against this disloyalty, I have chosen the Lord, and my hand is to it."[72] Knapp's "promise that she would sometime do it"—that is, reaffirm a covenant that she has already signed—resembles the covenant affirmations of the halfway "children of the church," who promise that they will continue to labor toward public testimony of regeneration and attainment of full membership status. "You are bound to God and His Work, and are not to be for Sin and Satan," Willard exhorts. "The thought of the Covenant should be a dayly monitour to quicken and excite you to your Duty. Do not esteem the Covenant a snare to you, as some do. . . . [I]t is God's goodness to you that He hath [been] pleased to take you so near Him, only let it be your care to walk worthy of his Vocation."[73]

Knapp "walked worthy" of her vocation as a demoniac, calling on her people to humble themselves. The "great business" (UI 42) of humiliation and spiritual reform is the vocation of the people of Groton and New England: "every ones business . . . in his place," whether that "place" is "private" or "public." Willard encourages those in "a *Private Capacity*" who "cannot actively influence the Publick so as to mend it" to ask themselves, "may we not mend one?"[74] If "every one would do that which is to be done at home in this regard, it would surely Contribute not a little to a general *Reformation*: and we may by an holy exemplary Conversation, and earnest Prayers to God, help forward this work."[75] Knapp converted her domestic vocation, her "Private Capacity," into a capacity to "actively influence the Publick"; in her own voice and in Willard's public speech, she makes herself an agent of "mending" more than one, of extending "that which is to be done at home" into the public realm. From this perspective, Knapp seems less like a witch and more like an embodiment of republican wife and motherhood, and of sentimental authorship.

The governance of the tongue might be the shared labor of elite men, public and private, but as Willard put it, those in "a *Publick station*" were "advantaged peculiarly to put forward such a work" in print.[76] Willard perceived publication as a form of public service, a means of augmenting spiritual profits for servants of the Lord. In the preface to *The Child's Portion*, a treatise on the doctrine of adoption in which he argues that "the dutiful Child loves that his father should be calling for his service,"[77]

Willard explains his hopes for the print version: "Of the following Sermons, I shall only say thus much: They were (through grace) profitable to some in the preaching, whose desire and hopes of their being further profitable, if Printed, gave occasion to the Publication of them."[78] He concludes by "earnestly request[ing]" his readers to pray "that the Author may be serviceable in his generation, to the glory of God, and good of Souls." He signs himself "By your Servant in and for Christ, S.W."

Serving the Boston Public

Willard's performance in the Groton pulpit was a dress rehearsal for his preaching of humiliation at Boston's Third Church. "God hath now for a long time been calling us aloud to *REFORMATION*," Willard lamented. "How many years since he put it into the mouths of his Servants to complain of the Degenerating of this People. . . . But our ears have been sealed."[79] This complaint had been in Willard's mouth for at least twenty years. To reform, God's covenant people have "bound themselves to yield obedience to all his commands; promised that *all that the Lord shall speak unto them, they will do it*. Now God hath given them his Orders, according to which he expects that they should regulate themselves."[80] As evidence of obedience, Willard singles out the heart and tongue for special metonymic significance, observing: "Every faculty and member owes Obedience to the Will of God. We have our hearts to look after, and keep with diligence for God and His Glory. . . . Our tongue to order and keep within bounds, which must be well looked after, Psal. 39.1."[81] The image of the "tongue" as something to be "well looked after"—by its possessor and the public—connects the body of Willard's Groton maidservant to the bodies of his elite "children of the church" as subjects and objects of the labors of covenant renewal.

Such evangelical hearing and speech was the essence of economic vocation. In *Heavenly Merchandize*, Willard echoes his familiar refrain: "we are exceeding dull and hard of hearing and learning these things."[82]

> *Incline your ear, and come unto me; hear and your souls shall live*: and this is an hard work, which requires labour. God doth not ordinarily in these days reveal his mind to his people in dreams, to be sure not in his house where they are called to hear him speaking to them: it would be a rediculous [*sic*] thing to find men sleeping in the market place and at market; and yet how many such sights doth this heavenly mart present us withal? As if men expected visions instead of instructions; and there must also be an

> attentive ear, and that accompanied with a mind intent upon the present business: he that brings his body to the House of God, and leaves his heart behind him . . . is like to make but a poor purchase of it.[83]

"Let the drowsy beware" might be the caveat emptor of the "heavenly mart." Willard's analogy between church and market moves both ways. The ear that is "attentive" to God's instructions in church will also be shrewd about buying and selling. People with such ears will be wary of Satan's "broachers of false wares, his Merchants that have *the ballances of fraud* in their hands, who with a great deal of falsehood and cousinage [cozenage], and *with many fair speeches, deceive the hearts of the simple*."[84] The "present business" simultaneously evokes the active "market place" and the work of humiliation that promotes obedience and submission to authority across private and public institutions. A renewal of evangelical hearing is also a renewal of the ministerial vocation; it is the voice of God's messengers that his people must heed. Evangelical hearing is market savvy. The church and market align as spaces where men properly serve God.

Preaching humiliation (and thus the need for reliance on ministerial authority) was one way to retain a balance of power between ministers and their powerful congregants, even as ministers helped valorize the merchant as having a particular ability to channel wealth toward the benefit of the church and community—even, if only incidentally, toward the minister himself.[85] In contrast to the wrangling over country pay that Willard had endured at Groton, the Third Church "maintained the ministers as richly as anywhere in New England."[86] In addition to a good salary, church members voted to pay 200 pounds as a college fund for Willard's children and an additional 136 pounds "in money or plate" as a trust for Willard's wife, Eunice Tyng Willard, to show their "gratitude for 'the Faithfull and Painfull Labours of the Reverend Mr. Samuel Willard in the work of the Ministry among Us . . . being sensible of the Obligation we lye under both to God and him, for so great a blessing.'"[87] As Mark Peterson observes, by freeing Third Church ministers like Willard from "the constant worry over money matters that plagued many New England ministers," these resources enabled them to "[compile] a remarkable record of service not just to their own church but to the religious culture of Boston as a whole."[88]

Like Knapp's possession, Willard's death in 1707 would be presented as a "publick Judgment" that should prompt God's people to attend carefully to their Master's voice. In his funeral sermon, Ebenezer Pemberton warned that "God's Voice herein is loud to Sinners that have been

Deaf to the *Charms* of this *Wise Charmer*," and those that fail to heed it "will be sealed up unto Ruin, and all the Reproofs and Counsels of his Servant will be heavy items to Inflame their Reckoning."[89] Third Church members—including the Boston chandler Josiah Franklin and his son James, a printer—were listening. Eighteen years after Willard's death, these members raised the funds necessary to publish *A Compleat Body of Divinity*, a collection of 225 of Willard's sermons on the Westminster Catechism that was the "largest and most expensive book published in North America at the time."[90] Willard had baptized Benjamin, the youngest son of Josiah Franklin; this "child of the church" would become the most famous American of his time and would be held up in our time (whether for praise or for scorn) as the epitome of secular vocation. In Willard's biography as in American cultural history, Elizabeth Knapp is connected to Benjamin Franklin, two bound-out children whose resistance to their appointed masters provided a template for public service. As Knapp had done, Franklin would improvise new forms of service from the scriptural and legal obligations between masters and servants.

For a while, one of Willard's books kept hidden the first edition of a text more famous in American literary history than any of Willard's works. In her reconstruction of the publication history of Mary Rowlandson's captivity narrative, Kathryn Zabelle Derounian notes of the 1682 Boston edition of that narrative that although no complete copies are extant, approximately one-tenth of the text has been recovered "from waste sheets used as lining papers in two separate copies of Samuel Willard's *Covenant-Keeping*," a collection of his revival sermons.[91]

Knapp occasioned the first literary intersection of Willard and Rowlandson. During her affliction she asked to be attended by Rowlandson's husband, Joseph, minister of the neighboring town of Lancaster—where the Knapp family had lived before moving to Groton. Especially given Rowlandson's involvement in the case, it is likely that a copy of Willard's narrative passed through his hands. When the Knapps lived in Lancaster, they would have attended Rowlandson's church and interacted regularly with his wife.

Like Elizabeth Knapp, Mary Rowlandson was called to be a servant in the wilderness and converted that experience into a form of public service.[92] Unlike Knapp, Rowlandson authored her own servant's place, remaining obediently within God's household during her captivity and after it. In that domestic public calling, as I discuss in the next chapter, she would change what it meant to serve God and Puritan masters, creating new types of properly humbled handmaidens and profitable hypocrites for a racializing culture of servitude.

[3]

SERVANT TO A CHRISTIAN: MARY ROWLANDSON'S CAPTIVITY AND THE RACIALIZATION OF OBEDIENCE

Those that will not serve God, shall serve a worse Master.
—Samuel Willard, *Mercy Magnified on a Penitent Prodigal*

It was but the other day that if I had had the world, I would have given it for my Freedom, or to have been a Servant to a Christian.
—Mary Rowlandson, *The Sovereignty and Goodness of God*

MARY ROWLANDSON WROTE OF a wilderness thick with masters. "I thought of being sold to my Husband, as my master spake," she laments in the Thirteenth Remove of her captivity narrative, "but in stead of that, my master himself was gone, and I left behind."[1] After Rowlandson helps a sick and freezing "*English* Youth" to a fire, his master's daughter comes after her and is then accused of trying to run away with him (SG 90). Briefly reunited with her son, Joseph, she finds him "almost overcome with lice" and asks his master's permission to "comb his head, and look over him" (90). She then "bid him go into the Wigwams" to seek food, but because he "tarried too long," his master "beat him, and then sold him" to a new master "who told me he loved him: and he should not want. So his master carried him away, & I never saw him afterward, till I saw him at *Pascataqua* in *Portsmouth*" (90–91). What is being held captive like for Rowlandson? Typologically, it is like being *Judea capta* (Israel held captive in Babylon) and Lot's wife and Job. But as even this brief synopsis demonstrates, it is also like being a servant in an uncanny household, at the beck of masters whose power is at once familiar and profoundly unsettling.

Rowlandson's rendering of her captivity as servitude and her Algonquian captors as masters is a kind of domestic fiction.[2] Neal Salisbury observes that though she "adopt[s] . . . the terminology of English servitude—'master,' 'mistress,' and 'servant'—to describe her position in Quinnopin's household," Rowlandson "was not a servant in the English sense but instead an adopted member of Quinnopin's household, whose status was highly ambiguous."[3] In the disparity between her rhetorical adoption of servitude and her "adopted" status among the natives, Salisbury registers Rowlandson's authorial labor, not her failures as an ethnographer. As Mitchell Robert Breitwieser observes, "in both living and writing, Rowlandson seems to have been lifted out of ordinary wifeliness and to have been given a *vocation*."[4] By exchanging captivity for servitude, Rowlandson not only gives herself a calling, but she also embodies orthodox vocation: as Paul exhorts, "Art thou called being a servant? Care not for it: but if thou mayest be made free, use it rather."[5]

It would, of course, be a stretch to argue that Rowlandson exemplifies the ideal of Pauline indifference: of "car[ing] not" for her earthly condition. As Increase Mather (writing under the pseudonym of Ter Amicum) puts it in his preface, it is a "strange and amazing dispensation" for her to be called to serve Algonquian masters.[6] Rowlandson's struggle to obey masters who are particularly "strange and amazing" instruments of God's will is an extreme version of the routine covenant dialectic in which Puritan saints knew themselves to be God's children and cultivated the willingness to serve him. In captivity, Rowlandson is a Christian child bound out to non-Christian masters, willing herself to serve them across cultural and religious divides. Breitwieser identifies Rowlandson's "hatred for the Indian *as master*," but even "hatred" signifies a strain of willing obedience—the orientation not only of her labor, but also of her heart and spirit, toward the law of the master.[7]

Like God, her native masters, and her ministerial sponsors, scholars have valued Rowlandson for her labor. As a transitional figure bearing Puritan New England toward modernity as a proto-feminist, proto-capitalist, and proto-individual, and as the epitome of Puritan piety, Rowlandson has shouldered a substantial share of cultural work.[8] The range of recent critical concerns and approaches offers testimony to the richness and complexity of Rowlandson's narrative and its significant place in New England's literary and cultural history, but it has also privileged her resistance to orthodoxy, whether conscious or unconscious, as evidence of her modernity.[9] Rowlandson does not resist orthodoxy; instead, she embodies the productive forms of resistance entailed by orthodoxy. The tensions that readers have perceived between the corporate narrative and the experiential realism of captivity are evidence of productive frictions that generated modern ideologies of service and mastery from the law of master and servant.[10] Rowlandson labors toward modernity by obediently carrying the burdens imposed by God and her native masters until "the skin was off [her] back" (SG 87). When she promotes willing obedience as both the means of being "made free" and the proper expression of that freedom, she teaches Puritans how to heed their callings to rebuild their homes, churches, society, and economy in the aftermath of a devastating war.

She also teaches them how to be masters to the hundreds of Algonquian people, especially women and children, who were bound out in increasing numbers and in enterprising ways to English households after the war.[11] English magistrates sentenced direct combatants and their families to be servants and slaves in New England and throughout the Atlantic world. As they had done with the Pequot, these rulers intended not only to impose justice and subjection on their vanquished enemies but to profit from their labor, directing the captives' energies toward rebuilding the society and economy that had destroyed theirs. Jill Lepore powerfully juxtaposes her chapter on Mary Rowlandson to another chapter on Algonquian slavery under the rubric of "Bondage" to lift the "nearly complete veil" that Rowlandson's narrative "has unwittingly placed over the experiences of bondage endured by Algonquian Indians during King Philip's War."[12] If Rowlandson's captivity does occlude the experience of Algonquian bondage, both during and after the war, it does so by rendering it symbolically, as allegory.

In its depiction of servitude and mastery across a religious and cultural divide, Rowlandson's captivity narrative offers postwar governance instructions for Puritan households as they accommodated two related cultural changes: the "surge in Indian servitude [that] reworked local understandings of race" and the division of labor in conversion efforts, in which missions focused on free natives and households on legal servants.[13] Both changes had the effect of secularizing and racializing the household, as religious instruction in families was primarily intended to make Native Americans productive and moral subjects of English law, if not professed and professing Christians. Native converts, after all, had proved to be hypocrites at best, and double agents at worst. In her vocation as servant to the heathen, Rowlandson exemplifies moral obedience for native children who will be asked to serve masters across a cultural and religious divide—to be "servants to a Christian," not Christian servants. In turn, Quinnopin and Weetamoo provide models to be either emulated or shunned by Puritan men who were bound to act as Christian masters to their servants but not to labor to convert them into children of God. By providing cultural and conceptual grounding for the conversion of hypocrisy into innovative callings, Rowlandson's representation of captivity as servitude and of her captors as masters constitutes her primary gesture toward modern personhood. What is captivity like for Rowlandson? It is like being the prodigal son, whose bondage to a heathen master teaches him how to serve his father.

The Prodigal's Humiliation

Given the traffic of masters in the Thirteenth Remove, it is fitting that Rowlandson concludes that part of her narrative by speaking as the prodigal son. From the first pulpits built in New England, John Cotton, Thomas Hooker, and Thomas Shepard preached the prodigal's petition ("make me as one of thy hired servants") as a meditation in humiliation, and the prodigal's plea remained a powerful refrain in the postwar jeremiads, with their insistent calls for New England to humble itself.[14] As scholars have observed, jeremiads frequently lamented worldliness and the decline of piety, but their calls for spiritual renewal also reconciled piety with commerce.[15] Service was a crucial concept in sustaining this paradox, as Rowlandson's use of the prodigal reveals.

When Rowlandson confesses as the prodigal, she skirts the parable's explicit mentions of servitude and mastery and seems to stage her slant relation to the type.[16] The prodigal confesses twice: the first time in Luke 15:18, when he rehearses the confession to himself, followed by the petition; and the second time in verse 21, when he actually utters the confession to his father, who cuts him off before he can make his petition. Rowlandson chooses verse 21:

> On the Sabbath-dayes, I could look upon the Sun and think how People were going to the house of God, to have their souls refresht, & then home, and their bodies also: but I was destitute of both; and might say as the poor Prodigal, *he would fain have filled his belly with the husks that the Swine did eat, and no man gave unto him*, Luke 15.16. For I must say with him, *Father, I have sinned against Heaven and in thy sight*, ver. 21. I remembered how on the night before & after the Sabbath, when my Family was about me, and Relations and Neighbours with us, we could pray and sing, and then refresh our bodies with the good creatures of God; and then have a comfortable Bed to ly down on: but in stead of all this, I had only a little Swill for the body and then, like a Swine, must ly down on the ground. I cannot express to man the sorrow that lay upon my Spirit, the Lord knows it. (SG 91)

Unlike the prodigal, Rowlandson is not accepted as a son after uttering the confession. Instead, she recalls family gatherings on "the night before & after the Sabbath," when people would gather to "pray and sing, and then refresh [their] bodies with the good creatures of God; and then have a comfortable Bed to ly down on." Rowlandson's memory of singing and eating the "good creatures of God" certainly evokes the feasting of the prodigal, but her cherished memory signals the painful deferral of redemption to an uncertain time in the future. Rowlandson is left with the husks: as the next remove opens, instead of feasting, she famines on crumbs of moldy cake "so dry and hard, that it was like little flints" (93).

Critics have sensed anger and resentment in Rowlandson's confession, but none have considered the affective implications of her omission of the petition—that is, her choice of verse 21 instead of verse 18. If Rowlandson's contemporary readers and ministerial sponsors discerned a trace of resentment in her confession, or even if that confession just seemed rote, it would have signified legal obedience or hypocrisy, raising the danger of lip service: not resistance to orthodoxy but conventional pride.[17] Rowlandson has no need to rehearse the petition because she lived it—and in writing, relived it. She has not just been taken captive by natives but has made herself their hired servant, and in so doing has demonstrated her willingness to serve her Father and can confess as a true penitent. Indeed, because her original readers would have had the petition in mind to help them interpret her use of the type, Rowlandson does not so much elide it as engage the reader's imagination in the work of internalizing it.[18] Offering a sincere public confession near the midpoint of her "conversion" narrative, Rowlandson, like Elizabeth Knapp in her demonic possession, allegorizes the Halfway Covenant renewal rituals (public confessions of consent to serve God) performed by the "children" of Samuel Willard's Third Church, whose members "adopted" the Rowlandson family after her restoration.[19] Rowlandson's continued estrangement from her Father signals that the work of humiliation (of knowing oneself as God's child and internalizing his mastery) is never done. To paraphrase Susan Howe, both what Rowlandson does say and what she does not say as the prodigal make her a living meditation on humiliation.[20]

The orthodox form of resistance in Rowlandson's performance of the prodigal also characterizes other moments in the narrative that critics have read as evidence of resistance to orthodoxy. When Rowlandson's typologies do not quite fit her experience, when she expresses wonder at the providential failures of the English army and God's preservation of the heathen, and when she calls her native mistress insolent, Rowlandson exemplifies the difficult labor of humiliation, of disavowing pride and self-sovereignty and living the dialectic of obedience as a genuine penitent rather than a dutiful hypocrite. The minister's wife does not just feed swine; she becomes swine. Yet even this experience of debasement might be insufficient to cast out pride.

That is certainly the position that Samuel Willard takes in his 1684 jeremiad, *Mercy Magnified on a Penitent Prodigal*. Willard, whose home and church in Groton had been destroyed by a raid during the war, describes God's providential "publick rebukes" of his prideful children as "Wilderness Tryals."[21] The sermon connects Rowlandson's humiliation as the prodigal to New England's economic vocation. Indeed, Willard's preaching of the parable evokes her captivity so vividly that the prodigal sometimes seems to be a type of Rowlandson, not the other way around: "Think not worse of God or his ways because of the afflictions you meet withal," Willard exhorts, "but be willing to wait on him through all: . . . believe that he can take away the affliction: and believe that he will sanctifie it to you: and resolve with *Job, that though he slay you, you will trust in him*" (MM 269). As Cotton and Hooker did, Willard offers the prodigal's petition to his auditors as a meditation on humiliation: "It will be a truth for ever that you have committed things worthy of death, and are not worthy to be called sons and daughters of God, an hyred servants place is too good for you" (259). When God's children "shake off" their obligation to serve their Father, "God righteously provides him cruel and Tyrannical Lords, that shal bear rule over him" (109). For the prodigal as for Mary Rowlandson, these "cruel and Tyrannical Lords" took the form of foreign masters; indeed, like the prodigal's master, King Philip kept swine.[22]

Willard invokes swine keeping to preach market morality as an application of the parable, deriding the "world of men, . . . one courting his pleasures, another chasing after honours, a third heaping up wealth . . . unto any of which (in a true judgment) keeping of swine is a noble and honourable imployment" (MM 117). This quest for outward prosperity is the service of Satan, and the jeremidic turn to spiritual renewal is toward the "better Master" (121). As Willard exhorts his audience, "if thou wilt come to him he will give thee a better service, an *high-calling*; he will give thee a clean and not a dirty service, thou shalt be a freeman and no longer a slave, it shall be a Glory for thee to serve him" (121). The prodigal and Rowlandson exemplify the sinner's willingness to "come to" God by accepting "a dirty service." Rowlandson might be deprived the comforts of a father's embrace, but she continues to labor toward "an *high-calling*," striving to "be a freeman and no longer a slave," by obeying her earthly masters. Traversing the wilderness as a servant, Rowlandson is a prodigal mother; she works outside the home but is sanctioned to do so because her labors, both spiritual and social, are directed toward masters (including her readers). She embodies motherhood as a form of domestic public service.[23]

My Master, My Child

Critics have focused on the uncertain tenor of Rowlandson's restoration to her Puritan home at the conclusion of the narrative, but she also remakes her family—and the Puritan family—during her captivity.[24] Servitude binds the captive mother and her captive children to God's household and to each other as they are bound to their native masters. Michelle Burnham has observed that while Rowlandson is captive, her "maternity is not erased so much as it is held in suspension."[25] Rowlandson's relationship to mastery both holds her motherhood in suspension and makes the stasis productive. In Puritan household ideology, the female head of household was wife, mother, and mistress, and scholars have noted the whiplash in Rowlandson's conversion from mistress of a Native American servant to a servant of native masters. But Rowlandson's exchange of motherhood and wifehood for servitude is more complicated than the status reversal of "mistress to maid."[26]

In her wilderness household, Rowlandson's positions as wife and mother are no longer aligned with her position as mistress; instead, she is displaced to the servant-child axis. The captive Rowlandson exercises motherhood primarily in relation to masters, not children, fathers, or husbands. Abram Van Engen has argued that Rowlandson's narrative "points readers toward a basic underlying feature of later sentimental novels: the better sphere beyond politics centered on the mother and her home."[27] I concur with his claim, but by omitting the master-servant dyad from his account of Puritan family affections, Van Engen minimizes the differences between patriarchal households and modern ones and misses a critical conceptual source of Rowlandson's innovations. Rowlandson's mother-servant dialectic provides a model of motherhood as a gendered ideology of service that would uphold the woman-centered home of sentimental fiction and republican virtue—one in which, as Abigail and John Adams teased each other, men who seek domestic happiness "willingly give up the harsh title of Master for the more tender and endearing one of Friend" and men "have only the Name of Masters," at least in relation to their wives and children.[28]

Rowlandson makes herself a servant in emotionally wrenching scenes that position her between her children and her masters. She first refers to herself as a servant in describing her inability to comfort her dying daughter, Sarah. Herself wounded, holding her "poor wounded child in [her] lap which moaned night and day," Rowlandson can offer her daughter "nothing to revive the body, or cheer the spirits of her" (SG 74). Instead, her captors offer threats: "sometimes one Indian would come and tell me in one hour, that your *Master* will knock your Child in the head, and then a second, and then a third, your *Master* will quickly knock your child in the head" (74). She presents the repeated taunt that her master will knock Sarah on the head (is it really a threat or a promise of a mercy killing?) as an instance of native cruelty, but it also activates a dialectic of love and fear as motives for obedience. The dialectic is sustained by the repetition of "your *Master* . . . your Child," a brutal meditation on a mother's willing acceptance of her place as servant to the heathen. As a good Puritan, of course, Rowlandson must do the work of seeing her native "Master" as an instrument of God's will in taking her child. This devastating moment—which converts her sense of maternal powerlessness and grief into service to God, and makes her understand that she is both mother and servant—expresses the dire affliction of captivity and the routine emotional work of covenant subjectivity.[29]

Sarah's death marks the moment in which "your Master" becomes "my master," Rowlandson's first rhetorical acceptance of her place as Quinnopin's servant. In its immediate aftermath, she relates that "they sent for me home to my Master's Wigwam (by my Master in this writing, must be understood *Quanopin* . . . not that he first took me, but I was sold to him by another *Narhaganset Indian*, who took me when first I came out of the Garison)" (SG 75). This passage evokes Rowlandson's making herself into a servant in two ways: by the repetition of "my Master" in the sentence and by her parenthetical naming of Quinnopin, rather than the native who "first took" her captive, as her master, with her pause distinguishing being taken captive and sold to Quinnopin as a servant.

Rowlandson describes Sarah's burial as a moment of willing obedience to her appointed earthly masters and God the Master. She says, "I went to take up my dead child in my arms to carry it with me, but they bid me let it alone: there was no resisting, but goe I must and leave it" (SG 75). Rowlandson offers no resistance to their collective "bidding," and her child is given a wilderness burial. "At my master's *wigwam*," Rowlandson longs to "look after my dead child" (75); her maternity is not buried along with her child but displaced, defined in relation to a heathen master of household. "There I left that Child in the Wilderness," Rowlandson observes in one of the most powerful moments of the narrative, "and must commit it, and my self also in this Wilderness-condition, to him who is above all." The repetition of "I must," referring both to the future and the present, evokes at once the master's power to command and the ongoing emotional and psychological work of willing obedience, the spiritual work of committing herself and her child to their dual "Wilderness-conditions": Rowlandson's servitude and her daughter's unhallowed grave. The spiritual work of her narrative is to remember that God "is above all," a phrase that stresses God's sovereignty as the supreme legitimate power—above Rowlandson's maternal pride, her sense that her child belongs to her, and the power of mastery that God has granted to "cruel and Tyrannical Lords" to rebuke her for those feelings.

Rowlandson's willing acceptance of her servant condition and her obedience to Quinnopin allow her to exercise her maternity as a "liberty" from servitude. In the Ninth Remove, Rowlandson learns that her son is nearby and obediently "asked liberty to go and see him." Her masters "bade me go, and away I went," but she gets lost along the way, "traveling over Hills and through Swamps, and could not find the way to him" (SG 84). Lost in the wilderness, Rowlandson pauses to "admire at the wonderfull power and goodness of God" in keeping her safe and helping her find her way "homeward again"—that is, toward Quinnopin: "I turned homeward again, and met with my master, he shewed me the way to my Son" (84). God directs her to her master, but it is her master who directs her to her son. The parallelism of "my master . . . my son" evokes both her pain at being separated from her son and the balm that obedience provides her as she seeks to read her suffering as evidence of God's will.

Her son's masters also permit sonship as a liberty. When Joseph's master goes to "assault and burn *Medfield*," Rowlandson notes that "his dame brought him to see me. I took this to be some gracious answer to my earnest and unfeigned desire" (SG 76). The family drama here takes precedence over the national drama—she wants to see her son, even if her ability to do so means that another English town and other Christian families are being ravaged by war. She writes a narrative of her conversion from prideful mother to humble mother and servant, which parallels the one she pens for her sister at the beginning of the narrative when she lifts the sister's body tenderly from the threshold of the garrison and places her hopefully in God's household as his servant. Rowlandson's internalization of mastery carries her motherhood across the threshold, into the public space of the wilderness and of the narrative.

Rowlandson also wills herself to obey native masters who withhold from her the liberty of seeing her children and other family members. When native masters refuse to allow her to mother, they provide the kind of psychological and emotional resistance necessary to make her obedience evangelical. In the Twentieth Remove, Rowlandson discovers that her daughter is "now about a mile off," and she "earnestly desired them to let me go and see them: yea, I intreated, begged, and perswaded them, but to let me see my Daughter; and yet so hard hearted were they, that they would not suffer it. They made use of their tyrannical power whilst they had it: but through the Lord's wonderful mercy, their time was now but short" (SG 102). Pamela Lougheed has argued that moments of "Indian malice" in Rowlandson's narrative indicate the incursion of a dangerous liberalism into English culture.[30] Because the cruel Indian trope in such passages doubles as a tyrannical master trope, Lougheed's insight suggests how servant obedience and masterly authority become liberal ideology. "Tyrannical" signifies illegitimate power, as when a master assumes the prerogatives of a king. In patriarchal theory, a household master's power was analogous to that of both father and king, but from Rowlandson's perspective, the analogy holds only for white Christian masters. Her characterization of their power as "tyrannical" does not just invoke captivity as a version of the world turned upside down—it also racializes mastery and, along with it, the nature of her obedience. "The Lord's wonderful mercy" might not prompt native masters to permit her to embrace her daughter, but it does present the promise that he would shortly reinstate the racial regime in which Puritan men are the rightful bearers of a master's power.

Bound Out and Bound In

Rowlandson speaks as the prodigal mother, but she also speaks as the mother of the prodigal might have done, contemplating her lost child in bondage to a foreign citizen. The presence of her starving son in the Thirteenth Remove haunts Rowlandson's typological identification with the prodigal son. As a woman servant, not a man with servants, Rowlandson cannot occupy the position of the father in the parable: she has no fatted calf and no power to restore her son to his rightful and comfortable place in a family. But she can, however inadvertently, direct him toward a new master, one who assures her that "he loved him: and he should not want"—a master less like the foreign citizen and more like the prodigal's father, whose servants have "bread enough, and to spare" (Luke 15:17). Her captivity experience replays an experience common to Puritan parents who could not provide for their children and placed them as servants in other families.[31] Joseph's mother cannot provide for him, so she binds him out. The servant-child and father-master lived metaphors of the dialectic of obedience crossed the metaphysical divide in the putting-out system.

The spiritual meanings of binding out—as exemplum and rebuke, as promise and threat—shape Rowlandson's narrative. In a sermon preached to the Dorchester congregation on a day of humiliation in the aftermath of King Philip's War, Increase Mather presents putting out as a model of the spiritual labor of covenant renewal, especially for children. Mather explains that "when men visibly, and Explicitly bind themselves and their Children to Christ, they cannot bind them to a better Master."[32] He reminds second-generation Puritan parents that when they "renewed their Covenant with the Lord," that covenant included their children: "their *little ones* also did *enter into Covenant*."[33] Mather warns, "We know (my Brethren) what Pharaoh did yield unto, *goe now yee that are men and serve the Lord*, but as for your *little ones*, not so, they shall not be ingaged to serve God with you. Let not any of us be like unto him."[34]

Rowlandson's narrative offers spiritual and social discipline to children who must learn to serve. In the scenes of their mutual spiritual labor, Rowlandson and her son embody Mather's covenant ideal of earthly parents and children as God's spiritual children, exercising the opportunity he has provided with his gift of grace to serve him. To sustain the dialectic of obedience in captivity, Rowlandson and her son use the primary means God provides for them—a Bible and resistance to heathen masters. In the Eighth Remove, Rowlandson encounters Joseph, and together they "[bemoan] our dolefull condition," their estrangement from the comforts of home (SG 81). As earthly parents and children should do, they read scripture together: "I asked him whether he would read; he told me, he earnestly desired it, I gave him my Bible, and he lighted upon that comfortable Scripture . . . *I shall not dy but live, and declare the works of the Lord*" (82). This scene makes the wilderness into a spiritualized domestic space, depicting mutually obedient parent-child callings.

Joseph exemplifies obedient spiritual labor. Later in the same remove, Rowlandson observes him "lying flat upon the ground: I asked him how he could sleep so? He answered me, *That he was not asleep, but at Prayer*; and lay so, that they might not observe what he was doing" (SG 83). His "Prayer" is framed explicitly as resistance to his native masters; he mimes sleeping "that they might not observe what he was doing." Evading the surveillance of earthly masters to do God's work, Joseph's "sleeping prayers" refigure the trope of eye-service—serving man but not God, or hypocrisy. He insists on a divide between his earthly masters and God the Master; he has learned how to accept his earthly place or calling to serve God, not Satan, in serving the heathen. Thus, as I will elaborate below, his behavior serves as a counterpoint to Rowlandson's depictions of Praying Indians as racial eye-servants who appear to be doing God's work but are really serving their own ends, and Satan's.

Rowlandson also regresses in the passage. She initially misreads her son the way he desires to be misread by his masters, dramatizing herself as a spiritual child learning this lesson in covenant servitude with her natural son. She pauses to offer her own prayer in response: "I pray God he may remember these things now he is returned in safety" (SG 83). Her prayer translates the lessons of evangelical obedience from Joseph's place "lying flat upon the ground" in captivity to his place "in safety." Rowlandson's echoing prayer is that the extraordinary experience of servitude to heathens becomes a spiritual meditation for her child, and that his extraordinary example becomes a lesson for other Puritan children.

If Mather depicts binding out as both covenant promise and covenant obligation, in *Mercy Magnified*, Willard presents it as covenant threat. Jeremiads frequently invoked the commonplace of children's rebellion against authority as an index of disorder, as Willard does when he rails against the prodigal as a "Rebellious child" who must learn diligent service (MM 60).[35] According to Willard, the sinner's choice to serve "cruel and Tyrannical Lords" is both "necessary" and "voluntary": "the very nature of sin . . . is a relinquishing of the service of God and enslaving a man's self to Satan" (MM 113). Having willfully chosen not to serve God, man will necessarily be put in the position to serve Satan. The trope of hunger explains this paradox. The prodigal, Willard observes, binds himself out to the citizen because he is starving: "when he had spent all, and there was no friend to relieve him, what could he now do? He saw no other way, but either he must bind himself out or starve." In a kind of contractual realism, Willard uses an analogy to the master-servant relation to convey the spiritual peril of such service: "As a servant expects (at least) food and raiment for his work, so the sinner hopes to get quiet and settlement in the service of Satan" (114). "Let this humble thee," he urges, "to think that thou hast given Satan that possession of thy heart, that thou hast indented with him, and joined thy self to him" (MM 115–16). Willard's exegesis of the case of the prodigal suggests that we read Rowlandson's starvation, in its spiritual and social senses, as conceptually linked to the servant-child dialectic and, through it, to the racialization of obedience.[36]

Like the prodigal, Rowlandson is starving, and her citation of verse 16 provides grounds for her identification with him. She binds herself and her children out to "worse masters" under conditions of necessity and labors to discipline her will, to accept her physical and emotional reality as evidence of divine justice. In her hunger, Rowlandson is a mother, a fictive widow with insufficient resources whose children have been bound out, and is herself a bound-out child.

The connections between starvation and servitude illuminate one of the most vividly transgressive moments in the narrative, Rowlandson's famous contest with an English child for a bite of boiled horse hoof. The scene's evocation of the putting-out system becomes clear when we expand the interpretive context to include the scenes that frame the passage, scenes of the natives as tyrannical masters who deprive her of family and food. Rowlandson reports a visit with her niece and explains, "I would have tarried that night with her but they that owned her would not suffer it" (SG 95). Denied time with her family, as the scene unfolds, Rowlandson's hunger draws her first to one wigwam, where "they were boyling corn and Beans, which was a lovely sight to see, but I could not get a taste thereof," (95–96) and then to another,

> where there were two of the *English Children*; the *Squaw* was boyling *Horses feet*, then she cut me off a little piece, and gave one of the *English Children* a piece also. Being very hungry I had quickly eat up mine, but the Child could not bite it, it was so tough and sinewy, but lay sucking, gnawing, chewing and slobbering of it in the mouth and hand, then I took it of the Child, and ate it myself, and savory it was to my taste. Then I may say as *Job Chap.* 6.7, *The things that my soul refused to touch are as my sorrowful meat.* Thus the Lord made that pleasant refreshing, which another time would have been an abomination. (96)

Rowlandson associates Job's situation with social types of servitude. Immediately after this exegesis, Rowlandson returns "home to my mistresses *Wigwam*," only to be admonished: "they told me I disgraced my master with begging, and if I did so any more, they would knock me in the head. I told them, they had as good knock me in the head as starve me to death." Though she provides no explicit scriptural reference to spiritualize this moment, Rowlandson plays out the tensions between necessary and voluntary servitude, the prodigal's paradox of binding himself out because he is starving to a master who starves him. Rowlandson, accused of "disgracing" her native masters with "begging," is certainly humiliated, but because her master is both heathen and a woman, her resistance is not really disobedience but an orthodox resistance to serving Satan. Her indignation at her native masters is coherent only as racial prejudice, since it denies the context of a war in which scarce labor or provisions required for survival might conflict with everyday morality. Saucily echoing her mistress's "knock me in the head," Rowlandson evokes the uncanny resemblance between captive servitude and the routine frictions of master-servant relations in Puritan New England.

The Master They Served

In depicting natives as tyrannical masters who starve her, Rowlandson appeals to earthly as well as divine justice. Her resistance to her native captors enacts what Lawrence Towner has called "servant protest," diverse legal and extralegal challenges to Puritan masters.[37] Many variations of native cruelty that Rowlandson describes are specific violations of Puritan laws and customs governing Puritan masters, who were bound to provide their servants with adequate clothing, comfort in sickness, rest on the Sabbath, and spiritual education, and to be moderate in punishments and requirements of labor. If Rowlandson's native masters largely failed to meet this standard in wartime, so did many Puritan masters in times of peace.[38]

The Puritan tradition of Christian liberty provided scriptural grounding for resisting tyrannical masters. In hierarchical earthly relations, the inferior's obedience "should always be bounded by the limits of power possessed by the superior," instructed William Ames. "Therefore we must not obey men in things which are against the command of God."[39] Even for servants, "obedience must not be blind." Earthly masters were to moderate their commands according to divine law, and inferiors "ought to inquire . . . as to whether the precept be lawful, fitting, and obligatory"; if not, they must refuse it. If the superior punishes the inferior for disobeying such a command, "then the enduring of the punishment wrongfully inflicted counts for and has the force of obedience." It is from this perspective that Christ's resistance to Roman law constituted his ultimate obedience to his God's will: martyrdom is Christian liberty, a model of being "obedient unto death."[40] Rowlandson's resistant servitude recalibrates the balance between the moral and the spiritual in Puritan household ideology by racializing the distinction between obeying man and obeying God, and the capacity to determine the difference and act upon it.

Willard's exegesis of the prodigal illuminates how Rowlandson's "servant protest" racializes Christian liberty. Willard asserts a distinction between "bodily" and "spiritual" valences of the prodigal's service to the citizen: "this bondage is not bodily so much as spiritual; it is an enslaving or binding of the soul to his service" (MM 113–14). "He is now at Satan's beck, and ready to hearken to, and attend every hint from him, to come and go at his pleasure" (114). Obedience becomes evidence of degradation: the prodigal is "ready and forward to do all Satan's commands, let them be what they will; he refuseth none, though never so base; if he sends him into the field *to keep swine*, he goes readily, and willingly about his business, so sordid and slavish a spirit hath he gotten." From a spiritual standpoint, service to foreign masters requires disobedience—outright refusal of commands or at least unwilling obedience. Whether Rowlandson endures punishment for disobeying her native masters or wills herself to obey them, she embodies Christian liberty. Her racial difference from her masters tightens the connection between spiritual liberty and moral obedience for Rowlandson, but it might also legitimately relax it for native women and children whose foreign masters are Englishmen.

Rowlandson depicts several instances in which her captors do not share their scanty provisions with her as failures of native mastery. For example, in the Fifth Remove, Rowlandson observes that "because of my wound, I was somewhat favored in my load; I carried only my knitting work and two quarts of parched meal: Being very faint I asked my mistriss to give me one spoonfull of the meal, but she would not give me a taste" (SG 79). Her hunger registers protest against masters who, like the prodigal's foreign master, choose to starve her. Just after this she explains that she "hardly ate anything" when first taken captive, then tried to eat but found it "very hard to get down their filthy trash," but by the third week "I could think how formerly my stomach would turn against this or that, and I could starve and die before I could eat such things, yet they were sweet and savory to my taste." Her transgressions of English dietary conventions can be read a conversion narrative, her body and spirit accommodating themselves to a master's will.

Rowlandson's masters often ask her to work on the Sabbath. Immediately after her mistress refuses her the spoonful of meal, Rowlandson notes that she had been "knitting a pair of white cotton stockins for my mistress: and had not yet wrought upon a Sabbath day" (SG 79). This Sabbath, however, her masters "bade me go to work." When Rowlandson protests that "it was the Sabbath-day, and desired them to let me rest," adding, "I would do as much more tomorrow," her captors reply that "they would break my face." Rowlandson narrates this moment as a Christian servant whose master violates laws governing Christian mastery. Thus, her resistance to authority—specifically, an injunction to work—is justified. Rowlandson makes it clear that her request for liberty from work is not a violation of work discipline when she expresses her willingness to work "as much more tomorrow."

Rowlandson's heathen masters expect her to be obedient, to do her share of the work of maintaining the community without answering back, and not to flee into the woods, and they punish her for violations of these duties. But she depicts their threats and punishments as immoderate correction under English law. At the conclusion of the Twelfth Remove, she notes that "I went with a good load at my back (for they when they went, though but a little way, would carry all their trumpery with them) I told them the skin was off my back, but I had no other comforting answer from them than this, *That it would be no matter if my head were off too*" (SG 87). Rowlandson refuses to "carry. . . their trumpery" and to govern her tongue, but according to Puritan justice, those should not be capital crimes.

From Rowlandson's perspective, however, it is a capital crime merely for natives to be masters to Christian servants, as her depiction of the fate of her sister's master suggests. As Rowlandson recounts in the Twentieth Remove, her sister "desired her master to let her come and see me, and he was willing to it, and would go with her" (SG 101). But on her way "he overtook her, and began to rant as if he had been mad; and made her go back again in the Rain; so that I never saw her till I saw her in *Charlestown*" (101–2). Rowlandson concludes with the statement that "the Lord requited many of their ill doings, for this *Indian* her master, was hanged afterward at *Boston*" (102). Like so many male native combatants, including Rowlandson's own master, Quinnopin, he was certainly hanged for his role in the war, but Rowlandson's inclusion of the epithet "her master" adds tyranny to the charges against him.[41] Presenting his treatment of his servant as testimony against him, Rowlandson translates war crimes into crimes against domesticity relevant to postwar Puritan culture. The equation of mastery with white Christian men is a form of divine and earthly justice.

Though Rowlandson routinely refers to the natives as devils, and though missionaries commonly conceived of the heathens as slaves to sin and Satan, Rowlandson invokes the commonplace of the natives as servants of the Devil only once, and her use of this wholly unsurprising trope is more complicated than it might seem.[42] In the Nineteenth Remove, Rowlandson describes the role of Tom Nepenomp and Peter Tatatiqunca, pro-English Christian Nipmucks who worked with John Hoar in negotiating for her release.[43] As she reports, they had brought her a pound of tobacco, which she "quickly gave away" (SG 97). When one of the Nipmucks asks her for a pipe, she has none to give. "Then," she explains, "began he to rant and threaten. I told him when my Husband came I would give him some: *Hang him Rogue (sayes he) I will knock out his brains, if he comes here*. . . . So unstable and like mad men they were" (97). After this encounter, Rowlandson decides not to send for her husband to redeem her, because "*there was little more trust to them than to the master they served*" (97). The single use of this orthodox trope describes converted natives, not her native masters; the phrase becomes part of her critique of Praying Indians as hypocrites, eye-servants who are going through the motions of devotion but are serving Satan, not God. Rowlandson's obedience to her native masters might not be service to a Christian, but neither is it service to Satan. In her depiction of the Praying Indians, Rowlandson racializes the distinction between legal and evangelical obedience; only whites, it seems, can serve the Lord in serving men.

Indeed, Rowlandson separates her obedient servant labor from depictions of the natives' demonic comportment. Shortly after the passage above, she embarks upon a lengthy catalogue of the offenses of Praying Indians and a description of warriors returning from their victory at Sudbury: "They came home on a Sabbath day, and the *Powaw* that kneeled upon the *Deer-skin* came home (I may say, without abuse) as black as the Devil" (SG 101). This detail immediately follows: "When my master came home, he came to me and bid me make a shirt for his *Papoos*, of a holland-laced Pillowbeer." Rowlandson labors at the bidding of her master, who, like the "Powaw . . . as black as the Devil," has returned from slaughtering Englishmen—and on the Sabbath, no less—but she does not seem anxious about obeying his command. Despite Quinnopin's proximity to the Devil, Rowlandson's service to him seems spiritually and morally unremarkable, or at least it is not explicitly spiritualized or justified with a scriptural citation. Her obedient labor for Quinnopin suggests a model of earthly servitude across the racial divide, a form of moral obedience that is not hypocrisy.

Rowlandson's secularized model of obedient service to Quinnopin valorizes white Christian masters, but it also enforces the traditional English hierarchy between male and female masters. As critics have noted, Rowlandson treats her female masters—particularly Weetamoo, a powerful sachem—with particular scorn. Teresa Toulouse argues that the dual threats of Indianization and feminization expose anxieties about fatherly authority among second-generation Puritan men.[44] Rowlandson's representations of Weetamoo as mistress specifically target the masterly aspect of fatherly authority by feminizing violations of Christian mastery.

One of the most commented-on moments in the narrative is Rowlandson's most resentful commentary on Weetamoo as mistress. She describes the scene one Sabbath morning as the group prepares to travel:

> My mistriss, before we went, was gone to the burial of a *Papoos*, and returning, she found me sitting and reading in my Bible; she snatched it hastily out of my hand, and threw it out of doors; I ran out and catch it up, and put it into my pocket, and never let her see it afterward. Then they packed up their things to be gone, and gave me my load: I complained it was too heavy, whereupon she gave me a slap in the face, and bade me go; I lifted up my heart to God, hoping the Redemption was not far off: and the rather because their insolency grew worse and worse. (SG 86)

Weetamoo commands her to work on the Sabbath, gives her a "load" that is "too heavy," and literally throws the Bible away. Christian liberty and Puritan law based on it would not just permit but would obligate Rowlandson to resist the commands of such a flagrantly bad master. Critics have focused on the way the scene registers Rowlandson's indignation at her status reversal. Rowlandson's experience as a Puritan mistress, and as the daughter of a prominent man and the wife of a minister, certainly would have given her a sense of superiority over others, but it would also have taught her that a mistress is not a master.

Another of her skirmishes with Weetamoo reinforces this point. In the Thirteenth Remove, Rowlandson contends with two female masters:

> As I was sitting once in the *Wigwam* here, *Philips* Maid came in with the Child in her arms, and asked me to give her a piece of my Apron, to make a flap for it, I told her I would not: then my Mistress bade me give it, but still I said no: the maid told me if I would not give her a piece, she would tear a piece off it: I told her I would tear her Coat then, with that my Mistriss rises up, and takes up a stick big enough to have killed me, and struck at me with it, but I stepped out, and she struck the stick into the Mat of the Wigwam. But while she was pulling of it out I ran to the Maid and gave her all my Apron, and so that storm went over. (SG 89)

Like the one above, this scene evokes both Christian liberty and servant protest. Rowlandson seems justified in her sauciness because Weetamoo and Philip's maid, both as women and as heathens, have no legitimate authority to command her. Yet her refusal provokes the threat of immoderate correction, of being beaten with a "stick big enough to have killed" her. The threat of excessive violence works; fear compels Rowlandson to obey. But the scene also suggests that a mistress with a giant stick still does not equal a master; the stick is a supplement only. From Rowlandson's perspective, even the powerful Weetamoo lacks the power to restore her as the prodigal's father or Quinnopin can: mistresses are doubly removed from fatherly authority, which makes them more likely to act as tyrants. Rowlandson's frequent use of a collective "they" rather than "she" when referring to her mistresses, even to a single mistress, also extends the ideology of mastery beyond its embodiment by particular masters. The use of the gender-neutral "they" allows her critique of her native mistresses to function as a corrective to Puritan masters. Her representations of Weetamoo enjoin Puritan masters to treat their servants as Christian men should, translating the affective dimensions of racialized household obedience for an economy in flux.

The Price of Redemption

Critics who have historicized and theorized Rowlandson's economic activity in the narrative have focused on it as a form of independence from the traditional household economy. Burnham argues that Rowlandson's "efforts to contribute her earnings to the household of her Indian master gradually diminish, and her economic activity takes on an increasing autonomy," shifting from "goodwife" to "independent producer-exchanger."[45] But, as Burnham concedes, any "economic independence" that Rowlandson gleans in captivity offers only a "temporary escape from patriarchal subordination," so that captivity is both an "inscription of Puritan patriarchal law and an escape from it."[46] While Rowlandson's economic activity might gesture toward capitalism and liberal subjectivity, it remains within the bounds of patriarchal domesticity. She does not labor outside the household economy but "inscribes" herself within "Puritan patriarchal law" by rendering her captors as masters. Rowlandson understands that money will redeem her from captivity, but in the narrative as in conversion doctrine, the price of redemption is defined in relation to obedience. As a servant, Rowlandson obediently directs her economic activities toward the profit of her multiple masters—her native captors, New England, her readers, and God. By obeying her native masters and striving to obey God in so doing, Rowlandson becomes a type of the "unprofitable servant" in Luke 17:10, who knows he can never repay his debt to God but labors from the certainty that he must repay it.

In captivity as in Puritan society, Rowlandson has a labor relation to her household, in which the affective bonds are economic ones. Rowlandson labors for her masters' good, not her own. In the Eighth Remove, she reports, "Philip *spake to me to make a shirt for his boy, which I did, for which he gave me a shilling*" (SG 83). We might read the shilling as a wage or a price, but in either case, Rowlandson knows that it belongs to her master: "I *offered the money to my master, but he bade me keep it; and with it I bought a piece of Horse flesh.*" The verbs that mark these transactions suggest that Rowlandson exchanges a kind of voluntary employment for Philip for compulsory servant labor; Philip "speaks" to her while her master "bids" her to keep the shilling. The horse flesh is not a direct reward of her labor for Philip, but rather for Rowlandson's obedience in offering the money to her master, who acts as a good master in letting her keep it. When Rowlandson obeys her native masters, she obeys the terms of exchange and respects the value of property, making her labor both materially profitable and spiritually unprofitable.

Arguing that Rowlandson's economic modernity is expressed primarily in the money form rather than commodity exchange, Nan Goodman contrasts Rowlandson's "commodity-based exchanges, which are replete with the vocabulary of revulsion or pleasure," with "the neutrality and future orientation that accompanies her transactions with money."[47] Goodman offers a fascinating reading of the passage in which Rowlandson is given a piece of bear meat for making a shirt, and a quart of peas for a pair of stockings as evidence of her proto-monetized, impersonal self; but Rowlandson's economic personhood is also expressed in the aftermath, when she cooks a pea-and-bear pottage for a dinner party: "I boyled my Pease and Bear together, and invited my master and mistress to dinner, but the proud Gossip, because I served them both in one Dish, would eat nothing, except one bit that he gave her upon the point of his knife" (SG 83). Rowlandson wants to convert the fruits of her labors into the affect of shared mastery, the pleasure of service among peers, but Weetamoo and Quinnopin rebuff her. "I served them both in one Dish" seems to express both her hopeful intention for the meal and perhaps, given the outcome, a brutal revenge fantasy. Rowlandson might not brim with affect here, but the sting is clear—especially when she refers to her mistress as a "proud Gossip." The point of the knife with which Quinnopin feeds Weetamoo wounds Rowlandson's own pride. In the affective economy of captivity, Rowlandson remains in her masters' debt.

This disappointment does not stifle Rowlandson's desire to please her masters, as we see when Rowlandson's country pay takes the form of a knife. After she corners a "sorry Indian" who has failed to pay her for a shirt, he finally makes good on his end of the bargain: "if I would make another shirt, for a *Papoos* not yet born, he would give me a knife, which he did when I had done it" (SG 84). A knife-wielding Rowlandson returns to the wigwam but does not provide a precedent for Hannah Dustan, who would kill and scalp her captors during King William's War.[48] Instead, she reports, "I carried the knife in, and my master asked me to give it him, and I was not a little glad that I had any thing that they would accept of, and be pleased with." Rowlandson's "gladness" at "pleasing" her master with the knife demonstrates not just obedience, but also the proper emotional framework of willing obedience. The very specific knife becomes "any thing" that would please her masters. Rowlandson's domestic and authorial labor converts fear—the threat of violence of master against servant as well as of servant against master—into child-like service, even when serving strangers who cannot be metaphorical fathers to her.

Rowlandson equates buying and selling with affect directed toward a master, even when she is the object of exchange. Like her motherhood, Rowlandson's wifehood is also held in suspension by mastery. Preparing to travel "*upon a Sabbath-day-morning*," Rowlandson reports, "I asked my master whither he would sell me to my husband." Quinnopin answers, "Nux [yes]," "which did much rejoyce my spirit" (SG 86). The prospect of being sold is cause for rejoicing. The exchange of "my master" for "my husband" generates positive affect associated with a male master's power to dispose of her body.

Her experience also demonstrates that the kindness of individual masters is no substitute for freedom. The affective marketplace is volatile: "Sometimes I met with favour, and sometimes with nothing but frowns," she observes, dragging herself in exhaustion from wigwam to wigwam (SG 85). Rowlandson must continually work to locate herself emotionally and psychologically in relation to her masters and the labor she performs for them, and this affective work is precisely the aspect of vocation that encompasses both its spiritual and secularized forms.

Rowlandson embodies vocation in relation to Weetamoo's volatility in particular, encountering primarily frowns. But in a stolen moment of favor, she finds herself "not a little glad" to understand her value to her mistress when another of Quinnopin's wives wishes to claim her: "The *Squaw* laid a Mat under me, and a good Rugg over me; the first time I had any such kindness shewed me. I understood that *Wettimore* thought that if she should let me go and serve with the old *Squaw*, she would be in danger to loose, not only my service, but the redemption pay also"

(SG 97). Goodman reads "redemption pay" as evidence that Rowlandson's version of exchange shifts from a barter economy and an understanding of herself as a commodity to the impersonality of the money form.[49] She stresses how money-based transactions inflect Rowlandson's changing economic personality, but here—as elsewhere in the narrative—the primary medium of exchange is service: Weetamoo fears the loss of both Rowlandson's service and the redemption pay. The equation of service and redemption pay may or may not express why Weetmoo values Rowlandson, but it definitely illuminates how Rowlandson understands Weetamoo's reckoning. The phrase "my service, but the redemption pay also" forms a kind of chiasmus with Rowlandson's concluding meditation, "freedom, or servant to a Christian." Both allude to the productive paradox of the calling: "He that is called in the Lord, being a servant, is the Lord's free man: likewise also he that is called being free, is Christ's servant. Ye are bought with a price, be not ye the servants of men. Brethren, let every man wherein he is called, therein abide with God" (1 Corinthians 7:22–24). Viewed through the lens of vocation, "redemption pay" evokes not just money but an exchange of masters, the freedom to serve God in one's appointed place. If this moment does capture Rowlandson's articulation of an evolving market morality, it takes the form of a doctrine of servant obedience and demonstrates her belief that the profit she generates does not properly belong to her.

Standing Still

To fulfill her vocation, Rowlandson must remain in her servant's place and "therein abide with God." Rowlandson literally stays in place. She does not avail herself of perhaps the most common form of extralegal servant protest—running away.[50] Indeed, she presents multiple instances in which she counsels others against running away and refuses to do so herself. And these moments, rather than scenes of monetary exchange or barter, provide the clearest evidence of Rowlandson's economic personhood. As Ames had instructed a previous generation of Puritans, "Servants owe to their Masters subjection as well as honour; And therefore, they ought not to runne away from their Masters: because this were the same, as to take away another man's proper goods; and so no lesse unlawfull then [*sic*] very Theft."[51] In Rowlandson's resistance to running away, she respects and values herself as the property of an earthly master (understanding the loss not only of the redemption pay but also of her service) and willingly obeys her captivity as a calling.

Vocation and martyrdom are two versions of obedient service to God in one's appointed place. In the narrative, Rowlandson repeatedly associates the martyr Goodwife Joslin with counsels against running away, translating her gruesome fate into a lesson in daily obedience.[32] At the end of the Third Remove, before separating from a group of child captives, Rowlandson "*asked them whether they were earnest with God for deliverance*; they told me they did as they were able, and it was some comfort to me, that the Lord stirred up *Children to look to him*" (SG 77). Immediately after this she counsels Joslin, pregnant and cradling her toddler, not to run away from her masters. Rowlandson first offers practical, self-interested reasons for Joslin to stay put, saying, "I wisht her not to run away by any means, for we were near *thirty miles* from any *English Town*, and she very big with Child." But Rowlandson also points out to Joslin the spiritual and communal benefit of remaining in her place, citing Psalm 27, "Wait on the Lord, Be of good courage, and he shall strengthen thine Heart, wait I say on the Lord." Rowlandson's counsel to the children to be "earnest with God for deliverance" and her advice to Joslin demonstrate the spiritual value of submission to a master's will in contrast to the false liberty of running away.

We cannot know what might have happened to Joslin and her offspring had they successfully escaped into the wilderness, but her "sad end" reinforces Rowlandson's admonition against running away. As the Fourth Remove opens, Rowlandson diverges from her immediate experience to report her second-hand account of Joslin's fate. Her captors, Rowlandson recounts, "stript her naked, and set her in the midst of them; and when they had sung and danced about her (in their hellish manner) as long as they pleased they knockt her on the head, and the child in her arms with her: when they had done that they made a fire and put them both into it, and told the other Children that were with them that if they attempted to go home, they would serve them in like manner: The Children said she did not shed one tear, but prayed all the while" (SG 78). By positioning these servant children as direct witnesses of the scene, Rowlandson frames it as a specific injunction for children to labor spiritually by standing still, a lesson that they learn both from Joslin's martyrdom and from their native masters. In the register of savage cruelty, the natives repeat to the captive children Rowlandson's warning to Joslin about not running away. The grim threat that natives would "serve" attempted runaways as they served Joslin perverts service as an ideal. But the wording also invokes the servant-child dialectic, in which the fear of being treated like a servant should prompt children to serve from love. Because they both love God and fear him, his children should remain obediently their places.

Rowlandson depicts herself as a spiritual child who serves in her own refusal to run away. In the Thirteenth Remove, Rowlandson describes her encounter with "an *English* Youth in this place, one *John Gilberd* of *Springfield*," whom she finds wounded and "lying without dorse [outdoors], upon the ground"(SG 89). Unlike Rowlandson's son earlier in the narrative, the boy is dying, not feigning sleep so he can pray. After Rowlandson coaxes Gilberd to come near a fire, his master's daughter comes and asks Rowlandson where she had taken him. Rowlandson leads Gilberd's mistress to him, but upon returning to her own home she finds that it had been "noised about, that I was running away and getting the *English* youth, along with me; that as soon as I came in they began to rant and domineer: asking me where I had been, and what I had been doing? and saying they would knock him on the head" (90). She assures her masters that they are mistaken in their suspicions: "I told them I had been seeing the *English Youth*, and that I would not run away, they told me I lyed, and taking up a Hatchet, they came to me, and said they would knock me down if I stirred out again; and so confined me to the *Wigwam*." She likens her situation to David's "*great strait*": "If I keep in, I must dy with hunger, and if I go out, I must be knockt in the head." Then the Lord's mercy comes to her in the form of a man who brings her "a pair of stockings that were too big for him, and he would have me ravel them out, and knit them fit for him. I shewed myself willing, and bade him ask my mistriss if I might go along with him a little way; she said yes, I might, but I was not a little refresht with that news, that I had my liberty again." Instead of running away when confronted by the threat of the hatchet, Rowlandson proves her trustworthiness by offering her obedient labor, and she is rewarded by being granted the "liberty" of limited mobility: the ability to "go along . . . a little way" with the Indian whose stockings Rowlandson tailors (and who also offers her some groundnuts to eat).

As Rowlandson awaits her redemption in the final remove, a native couple tempts her one last time to run away: "In my travels an *Indian* came to me, and told me, if I were willing, he and his *Squaw* would run away, and go home along with me: I told him *No*: I was not willing to run away, but desired to wait Gods time, that I might go home quietly, and without fear. And now God hath granted me my desire" (SG 107). When Rowlandson affirms that she is "not willing to run away," she expresses the alignment of her will and God's with the law of the master and experiences her self-command as legitimate. That internalized command is both rational and affective, and her obedience earns her not just redemption but God's fulfillment of her "desire" to go home "without fear." She pleases her native masters, God the Master, and the master inside her, and this obedience is more valuable to her than what she would deem the immoral liberty of violent resistance or running away.

A Good Master Well Served

Rowlandson does not seem to find it hard to resist running away from Quinnopin. In the Nineteenth Remove, Philip holds out dual promises to Rowlandson. "Two weeks more and you shal be Mistress again," he predicts, equating redemption with gendered mastery instead of wife or motherhood (SG 96). When she asks "if he spake true?" he reassures her, "Yes, *and quickly you shall come to your master again*." The echoing phrases "Mistress again" and "master again" reveal an emotional equivalence between Rowlandson's imminent restoration and the more immediate prospect of Quinnopin's return after a three-week absence. The reunion scene that follows is one of the most sustained moments of physical and emotional revival in the narrative.

> After many weary steps we came to *Wachuset*, where he was: and glad I was to see him. He asked me, *When I washt me?* I told him not this month, then he fetcht me some water himself, and bid me wash, and gave me the Glass to see how I lookt; and bid his *Squaw* give me something to eat: so she gave me a mess of Beans and meat, and a little Ground-nut Cake. I was wonderfully revived with this favor shewed me, *Psal.* 106.46, *He made them also to be pittied of all those that carried them Captives.* (96)

Psalm 106 firmly places this moment in the history of Judea capta, but Quinnopin's care seems to exceed a reading of him as an instrument of God's pity: it does not entirely account for Rowlandson's "glad I was to see him." The master labors in this scene to revive his servant: "he fetcht me some water himself." The passage registers obedience as comfort when Quinnopin "bid[s]" her to wash and his squaw to feed her: a version of the prodigal's father bidding his servants to feed and clothe his son. As Steven Neuwirth observes, "the woman looking at the woman in the 'glass' sees herself through her master's eyes—as property."[53] But she seems to see her reflected self as subject rather than object. The affective dimension of their relation is expressed in the detail about the mirror:

"he gave me the glass to see how I lookt." One can imagine the mirroring of her initial pleasure to see him in the glimpse he allows of her own fresh reflection.

Rowlandson's representation of Quinnopin as a good master is, of course, a reminder that God works in mysterious ways: she is "wonderfully" revived by "this favor," not his favor. Rowlandson's description of Quinnopin's labor as "this favor" evokes the prodigal's petition as an expression of true repentance. According to Willard's exegesis of "make me as one of thy hired servants," the prodigal both "desires admission into his fathers family, under his favour and care" and "submits to be disposed of as he sees meet, and will not repine, but account it a favour" (MM 248). Rowlandson will remain a servant and not a child in Quinnopin's household, but by citing the psalm and obediently accounting her master's care a "favor," she performs the work of humiliation required for reinstatement in God's household.

By crediting God rather than Quinnopin with her revival, Rowlandson also racializes the dialectic of obedience. Quinnopin is a master who can never be a father to her. Indeed, her insistence that he was a good master might also contain the threat that he acted as a husband to her; immediately after the bathing scene, which comes near the conclusion of the narrative, Rowlandson observes that "my master had three *Squaws*" (SG 96). Like the Praying Indians, who might worship and live under English governance but cannot, according to Rowlandson, ever be Christians, Quinnopin's mastery might fulfill Christian mandates, but he can never be a Christian master: he can serve God only unwittingly, if not unwillingly. Quinnopin's good mastery and Rowlandson's obedient servitude to good and tyrannical masters combine to produce postwar versions of Puritan household governance and work discipline that were at once familiar and innovative, grounded in a racialized dialectic of obedience.

Mistress Again

At the end of Rowlandson's narrative, her family—and the Puritan family in general—is neither what it had been nor what it would become. Philip is no prophet: Rowlandson's restoration does not make her "mistress again." Nor are her wifehood and motherhood fully restored. "I met with my dear Husband," she writes, "but the thoughts of our dear Children, one being dead, and the other we could not tell where, abated our comfort each to other" (SG 108). Rather, as she wearily recounts, using the singular pronoun despite her husband's presence, "in that poor, and destressed, and beggerly condition I was received in, I was kindly entertained in severall Houses." Her description evokes hospitality, Christian charity, and perhaps the experience of a child being bound out to a kindly Christian household: "Mr. *Thomas Shepard* of *Charlestown* received us into his house, where we continued eleven weeks; and a Father and Mother they were to us." Shepard and his wife were roughly the same age as Mary and Joseph Rowlandson.[54] While Rowlandson's place in the Shepard household is provisional, it nevertheless finally admits her to a family governed by a Christian man who can embrace her as a father, not just as a master.

"Instead of the Husk, we have the fatted Calf," she affirms, in a tone more muted than celebratory, at the conclusion of the narrative, presenting the deferred feast of the prodigal in the context of recounting memories of being "in the midst of thousands of enemies, & nothing but death before me" that haunt her insomniac "night season" (SG 111). Even after her restoration, she seems to have given herself the elder brother's portion of the fatted calf, not the prodigal's. Restored but not "mistress again," unable to fully accept a father's or husband's embrace, clutching the memory of holding her dead daughter before leaving her to a resting place in the wilderness, Rowlandson puts pressure on the boundaries of the Puritan family from within rather than from without.

In the haunting concluding paragraph of the narrative, Rowlandson meditates on the social and spiritual meanings of her experience.

> Affliction I wanted, and affliction I had, full measure (I thought), pressed down and running over; yet I see, when God calls a Person to any thing, and through never so many difficulties, yet He is fully able to carry them through and make them see, and say they have been gainers thereby. . . . If trouble from smaller matters begin to arise in me, I have something at hand to check myself with, and say, why am I troubled? It was but the other day that if I had had the world, I would have given it for my freedom, or to have been a Servant to a Christian. I have learned to look beyond present and smaller troubles, and to be quieted under them. As *Moses* said, *Exod.* 14.13. *Stand still and see the Salvation of the Lord.* (SG 112)

Critics have observed that Rowlandson's equivocation, "freedom, or . . . a Servant to a Christian," seems a wary expression of the contrast between past captivity and present redemption. Breitweiser asks, "Is the redemption an emancipation and a compensation, or a favorable exchange of masters that leaves the abjection of servitude intact?"[55] I follow Breitweiser in focusing on Rowlandson's expression of redemption as a "favorable exchange of masters," but I depart from his sense that her phrase implicitly criticizes orthodoxy and patriarchy.

In its allusion to the price of redemption, its equation of freedom with servitude, and its concluding affirmation of "standing still" as obedience to God's will, Rowlandson's equivocation expresses that she has internalized God the Master even in the form of her heathen masters, so that she can embody the paradox of Christian liberty and the dialectic of Puritan work discipline. Presenting "freedom" as equivalent to being a "servant to a Christian," Rowlandson finally articulates a version of the prodigal's petition, "make me as one of thy hired servants." She presents her version as a meditation in willing obedience, "something at hand to check myself with" in the work of shunning worldliness and self-sovereignty. As a public servant, she offers this phrase as a meditation to her readers as well. Willingly obeying her heathen masters, she learned how to serve her Father. Noting that God "calls a Person to any thing," Rowlandson demonstrates how the concept of vocation produces the kind of impersonality that Goodman associates with a monetized self. The Puritan everyperson is God's servant.[56]

But God did not create all servants and masters equal. Rowlandson's equivocation genders and racializes the dialectic of obedience and the household and public callings whose spiritual and moral value were determined by it. Rowlandson's willingness to be "servant to a Christian" is a desire to be a Christian servant, to serve God in serving men—which is the productive paradox of vocation. But the phrase also redefines what it means to be servant to a Christian, to be a Christian master, and to be God's child. Rowlandson's syntax inverts Paul's, emphasizing the particular calling of "servant to a Christian," rather than the freedom of Christian service. Her equation of "Christian" with "master" supersedes Quinnopin's particularity as a good heathen master. Though Quinnopin provided Rowlandson with succor and care, she would rather take her chances with a Christian master interchangeable with any other. She would serve such masters in their private and public forms, equating the domestic service of wives, mothers, and daughters with liberty for white Christian women.

Teaching women how to spiritualize dependency, heathen masters might be exchangeable with Christian masters, but the asymmetries between them also map an ideology of racial dependency. Only white men can legitimately be masters and internalize their own mastery, not just God's. The self-mastering white man who is free to contract with other equally independent individuals has been taken to exemplify modern personhood, but the legal and ideological servants of such men are, in their very inequality, equally modern.

"These Children Shall Serve"

In the immediate aftermath of King Philip's War, Native American women and children were bound out in increasing numbers to such Christian masters. Hundreds of Native Americans, including Philip's nine-year-old son, were transported on slave ships to the West Indies.[57] Puritan magistrates also expanded customary practices that made vulnerability to forced labor the defining condition of life for the Algonquians who were permitted to remain on their native soil, particularly women and children.[58] Though the Puritan missionary effort had long been undertaken in earnest by only a few ministers and members of the elite, the war would mark a decisive move away from conversion and toward servitude as the governing model of Native-Anglo relations. Efforts to "Christianize" native servants were primarily oriented toward making them moral and reliable workers, inculcating the behaviors of "temperance, industry, sexual continence, and family prayer" that, outside the context of conversion, could signify only legal obedience—the obedience of servants, not of sons.[59] For native servants, particularly children, it would be enough to obey Christian masters; they need not learn to obey God in so doing.

In August 1676, Daniel Gookin, the superintendent of Christian Indians for the Bay Colony, bound out thirty-one native children. Salisbury signals the significance of this act as part of the interpretive context for Rowlandson's narrative by including Gookin's "A Memorandum of Indian Children put Forth into Service to the English" among the documents in his edition of Rowlandson's narrative. Gookin insisted that, like Elizabeth Knapp and other Puritan children, these "children bee religiously educated & taught to read the English tounge [tongue]."[60] He proposed ("humbly," of course) that the General Court of the Bay Colony "set the time these children shall serve; & if not less than till they come to 20 yeares of age. unto which those that had relations seemed willing."[61] Finally, he asked that "the Court lay som penalty upon them if they runne away before the time expire & on their parents or kindred that shall entice or harborr & conceale them if they should runne away." Gookin himself would become the master of an eight-year-old boy, Joshua, and a six-year-old girl, "daughter to the widow quinshiske."[62] Though sincere in advocating leniency, Gookin presents religious education and literacy as ways to achieve earthly obedience rather than conversion. Above all, like

Rowlandson, he believes that these native children must not run away from their masters. When she chooses not to run away, Rowlandson acts as the kind of servant that Puritans wanted their children to be, but also as the kind of servant they wanted Native American children to be after the war—submissive to masters who worshipped different gods.

Reading Rowlandson's concluding passage alongside Gookin's memorandum reveals her narrative's use in reconciling this secularized master-servant labor with spiritualized work discipline for all New Englanders.[63] Rowlandson's use of "servant to a Christian" as a reminder to "stand still" in obedience to her divine Master is aligned with the project of keeping Native American children in their proper place and obedient to Puritan authority, in the form of their direct masters and the General Court as agent of divine law. Rowlandson's obedience to her nonwhite, non-Christian masters marks a transition toward a modern ideology of mastery, not just to the rule of particular masters.

In turn, her representations of her captors as masters provide conduct instructions for Puritan masters of non-Christian servants, who should continue to obey God in their particular callings as masters. Rowlandson might endorse the project of making conversion secondary to servitude, but she calls Puritan masters to reform their behavior toward their servants that might too closely resemble actions that Rowlandson had attributed to native tyranny. I do not want to overstate this point: Puritan masters would still have been obligated to moderate punishments and allow their servants to rest on the Sabbath—something Rowlandson's native masters fail to do. Yet by emphasizing these violations of Christian comportment, Rowlandson warns Christian men of the danger that leniency toward converting servants poses to their own callings as masters. In short, Puritan masters should treat their Indian servants as Quinnopin had treated her, not as Weetamoo had.

Rowlandson also reminded Puritan fathers and children that they must continue to know themselves as God's servants, even as the culture increasingly empowered them as masters. Daniel Hoar—the son of John Hoar, one of the agents who negotiated Rowlandson's redemption—was convicted of murdering Christian native women and children living under Gookin's governance at Concord. Daniel Hoar petitioned the General Court "for relief from his murder sentence," saying that "your poor Petitioner hath lived as a servant unto his father all his days and hath gathered nothing for him self save his clothes."[64] Hoar's petition for clemency evokes the prodigal's petition; it is framed as a kind of servant protest. Puritan fathers should treat their sons as good masters, not tyrannical masters, would. But the sons must labor to obey the law of the master, even if that is embodied inadequately by their natural fathers.

Multiple forms of modern economic personhood would emerge from the distinction between the obedience of the child, who works for love, and the obedience of the servant, who works from fear. Serving from love remained an ideal for English sons and their fathers, for whom spiritualized labor in one's place provided a model of socioeconomic mobility and public liberty. English daughters and their mothers could also be children who served, so long as their labors, even extrafamilial ones, were properly conceived of as domestic and directed toward the good of men. For New England natives, laboring for masters who were no longer obligated to treat them as God's potential children, diligence and obedience were to be signs of submission to the laws of men. All New Englanders would learn to obey the ideology of white male mastery. Rowlandson's wilderness service to heathens—as much as the labors of Puritan New England's ministers, merchants, craftsmen, farmers, and fishermen—helped create Benjamin Franklin's world, which David Waldstreicher has recently described as "runaway America," a world of servants, slaves, and masters.[65]

It was long thought that Mary Rowlandson died shortly after her husband, Joseph, in 1678. However, thanks to the sleuthing of David L. Greene, we now know that she was twice widowed: she married Samuel Talcott and died as Mary Talcott in January 1711.[66] Greene resurrected Rowlandson on the evidence of a strange court case.[67] In 1707, Mary Rowlandson Talcott appeared in court to provide a fifty-pound surety that her son, Joseph, would answer allegations that he had gotten his brother-in-law drunk and sold him as an indentured servant into Virginia. The prodigal brother-in-law, it seems, returned to the Puritan fathers with an accusation instead of a confession on his lips. Protesting against the policy of enslaving Native Americans, the missionary John Eliot warned that "to sell soules for money seemeth to me a dangerous merchandize."[68] A generation later, Samuel Sewall would take this line of argument in his abolitionist tract "The Selling of Joseph," in which he lamented Puritan New England's participation in the African slave trade. Rowlandson and her prodigal son created racialized concepts of household obedience and public callings that would continue to be adjusted to meet the opportunities that black servants provided their Christian masters.

[4]

RACIAL VOCATION: NEW ENGLAND'S CALLING TO SLAVERY

Evil must not be done, that good may come of it.
—Samuel Sewall, "The Selling of Joseph"

You may *Spiritualize* the most *Earthly Business* in the World, by a Chymistry that shall fetch *Heavenly Thoughts out* of it. These *Thoughts* you may Turn into *Prayers*, even while you are at your *Business*. And you may *Dart* up your *Prayers to the Heavens*, notwithstanding what you are doing on *Earth*.
—Cotton Mather, *A Christian at His Calling*

IN JUNE 1700, a week before "The Selling of Joseph" was printed in Boston, Samuel Sewall pondered how the tract that now holds a privileged place in the history of Anglo-American abolitionism came to be. In his diary, he wrote that he had been "long and much dissatisfied with the Trade of fetching Negros from Guinea," even feeling "a strong Inclination to Write something about it"—"but," he added, "it wore off."[1] Instead, he followed an inclination to read Paul Bayne's commentary on Ephesians, in particular the passages in which, a century before Sewall's quandary, the Puritan divine affirmed the legality of perpetual servitude and casually equated that "slavish" form of servitude with the English enslavement of "Blackmores."[2] After reading this work, Sewall "began to be uneasy that I had so long neglected doing any thing." Other Bostonians were publicly "doing things" about slavery: some petitioned the Bay Colony's General Court "for the freeing a Negro and his wife, who were unjustly held in Bondage"; a committee proposed "a Law that all Importers of Negros shall pay 40s [shillings] *per* head, to discourage the bringing of them"; and Cotton Mather "resolve[d] to publish a sheet to exhort Masters to labor their Conversion." Sewall heard God's voice in these works of men, beckoning him out of his "long neglect" to act. The entry concludes with his expression of "hope that I was call'd of God to Write this Apology for them; Let his Blessing accompany the same." By finally fulfilling his "Inclination to Write," the judge and merchant added a new occupation to his calling to public service: abolitionist author.[3]

In that role, Sewall has long been positioned as an exceptional figure, a man ahead of his time.[4] But his diary entry also points to an assumption that he shared with people who opposed his view that buying and selling Africans and holding them in perpetual bondage was immoral: that slavery was embedded in New England's culture of vocation. Traditional discourses of faithful service and hypocrisy provided the conceptual and moral grounds of contest about the morality of African slavery, and master and servant embodied those concepts. When Sewall consulted a tradition of Puritan thought about the legality of slavery, he read conduct instructions for masters and servants. Both the passages from Bayne and others from William Ames's *Conscience with the Power and Cases Thereof* that frame Sewall's tract were drawn from guidelines for these particular callings, which also applied to all Puritans in their general callings to serve God.[5] In his 1696 conduct manual, Cotton Mather intoned the familiar warning: "*Ye cannot Serve God and Mammon*. Thus, ye cannot Serve the Lord Jesus Christ, and Serve the *World*, the *Flesh*, and the *Devil*."[6] Traditionally, serving both God and the flesh was hypocrisy, an abuse of Christian liberty and a perversion of vocation.

But as Mary Rowlandson's captivity narrative reveals, the racialization of servitude began to convert some kinds of hypocrisy into new callings: servant to a Christian as distinguished from servant of Christ. African slavery fueled that process. The work of Puritan magistrates who read and wrote petitions and motions; Puritan ministers who produced sermons and "sheets"; Puritan merchants who ran slave ships; Puritan masters who commanded enslaved peoples; enslaved peoples sold into Puritan slavery; and the women, children, and white servants in the households where all lived together—was all of this business the service of the Lord or the service of mammon? Had Puritans made the two masters into one?

A wave of recent scholarship, building upon the pioneering work of Lorenzo Greene and others, has demonstrated the inseparability of racial slavery and New England commerce.[7] As William Pettigrew observes, "slavery and the slave trade were not the relics of a traditional, precapitalist society; they were the distillate expressions of modern society's dynamic founding moments."[8] New Englanders fostered the simultaneous expansion of slavery and capitalism, as well as the emergence of modern racial ideologies alongside cultural and political concepts of modern liberty. This understanding of slavery's significance to New England's economic culture also compels us to reinterpret its most famous (or infamous) contribution to modernity—the secular vocation of the Protestant ethic. As a range of texts written in the decades around the turn from the seventeenth century to the eighteenth reveal, the work ethic was a racial vocation. It emerged, in both secular and sacred forms, from the pressures that slavery exerted on traditional distinctions between moral and spiritual obedience, and between hypocrisy and faithful service.

The decade that bracketed Sewall's pamphlet provides rich evidence of such "distillate expressions" of New England modernity, as Puritans adjusted their moral culture to accommodate the most fearful commerce the world has ever known. Blacks never accounted for more than 2–3 percent of the population of New England throughout the colonial period, but the breaking of the Royal African Company monopoly in 1698 created new and lucrative opportunities for New England merchants to traffic in enslaved African and West Indian men, women, and children.[9] In "The Selling of Joseph," Sewall explains one reason why his intervention seemed so urgent: "the Numerousness of Slaves at this day in the Province, and the Uneasiness of them under their Slavery."[10] Laws register the cultural effects of this "Numerousness." Beginning in the 1680s, rulers created a separate slave code: laws governing servants became increasingly racially marked, especially in the use of the racial triad "Negro, molotto [mulatto], or Indian."[11] As they passed laws that marked nonwhites as separate legal persons from whites, magistrates also produced new forms of white legal personhood in laws that continued the tradition of referring to "servants or children" without a racial designation.[12] The legal distinction between "servants and children" and "servants and slaves" was one expression of a broader racialization of Puritan moral and religious culture. Sewall's tract captures a particularly fraught moment in the racialization of servitude as a legal institution, but also of traditional spiritual types of faithful service and hypocrisy: the ideal of the child who serves and its counterparts, the eye-servant and the servant turned out of doors.

The cultural work of reconciling Christian mastery with African slavery produced new versions of vocation, racializing not only the household callings of masters and fathers and of children and servants, but also public callings exalted as service to New England—the ministry, the magistracy, commerce as a way of generating wealth for the godly community, and authorship. In 1706, Cotton Mather would finally publish the "sheet" Sewall mentioned in his diary, *The Negro Christianized*[13]—governance instructions designed exclusively for masters of black slaves.

Puritan New England made the "two masters" into one, in part by creating three kinds of white master: one to govern white servants, another to govern black slaves, and a third to govern themselves.

Eye-Servants and Praying Masters

Transformations to the figure of the eye-servant hypocrite were essential to this cultural work. Ames and Bayne exemplify the tradition of citing Paul's injunctions against eye-service in conduct instructions for both masters and servants, warning them to work for the good of their heavenly Master in their callings. The obedience that servants owe to "their Masters in the Lord," Ames insists, "should not guide it selfe with an eye upon the knowledge of Men, but of God; nor should it aime chiefely at the reward to bee receiv'd from Men, but from God."[14] Bayne decries eye service as "outward service which goeth no further then [*sic*] that a man can take knowledge of," doing "the outward thing onely, though with a morall honest meaning, Gods will as well as mans work."[15] Christians should take their inward psychological, emotional, and spiritual experience of the fear of God as evidence of their Master's presence and will. Doing the "outward thing onely, though with a morall honest meaning," is hypocrisy. The fear of God is the internalization of the moral law—the premise, not the proper end, of spiritually profitable labor.

Masters are prone to a particular kind of eye-service: acting as tyrants instead of masters. Ames stipulates that God has granted masters only a "limited Dominion" over their servants, "whereof they are to give account to God, as the common Master of them, as well as their Servants."[16] Bayne agrees with Ames's point but not with his point of view, choosing to share a subject position with masters who must "avoid all crabbed and cruell dealing in our Calling over" servants, remembering that "*We have a Master*, &c" to "prevent the deceitfull thoughts which we might fancie with our selves" (that is, the sin of pride).[17] Masters, like their servants, must strive in all their endeavors to keep "God in their sight."[18] Though warning against worldliness, these instructions to masters render God's justice in economic terms, with Ames referring to spiritual rewards and Bayne depicting God as "a Master who will keepe an Audit with them, and pay them their due."[19]

Bayne adds a second definition of eye-service to Ames's exegesis, one that provided a conceptual pathway for reconciling Christian mastery and racial slavery. This second kind of hypocrite obeys only when his earthly master is present. "Further then [*sic*] his master can thus see him, he will do nothing, and he careth not what lewd part he commit, if it shall not come to his masters knowledge," he explains.[20] "All such servants even as the first, before God, are not sound hearted, but these second eye servants are full of the most damnable hypocrisy." As the passage continues, Bayne uses a discourse of whiteness to illustrate this "vice to be taxed in servants." "The world is full of such Camelions as can shew any colour white, that can look with all countenances," he laments, "but they cannot shew such a face as commeth from a white sincere heart, they are deepely gone in eye service." He depicts two kinds of obedience (one outward and one inward) as two kinds of whiteness (one visible and one invisible). The "most damnable" hypocrites can mimic exterior whiteness, but they do not have "white sincere hearts." The capacity to internalize God's will defined vocation; the failure to do so was hypocrisy. This strand of deceptively white "damnable hypocrisy" would be crucial to spiritualizing the calling of Puritan "masters in the flesh" who sought to profit from the labors of their nonwhite, non-Christian servants.

In contrast to the counterfeit whiteness of "damnable hypocrisy," the first kind of eye-service—doing the "outward thing onely, though with a morall honest meaning"—would become a lawful kind of eye-service essential to racial vocation, instrumental hypocrisy. In racial vocation, the eye-servant may lack the capacity to willingly obey God and earthly masters at the same time, but he or she can obey earthly masters. Such servants might inflame their master's tendency to become a tyrant, but resisting that urge spiritualizes his calling. Both the nonwhite servant who obeys the moral law in the form of his earthly master and the master who labors to produce servants who obey him would embody versions of instrumental hypocrisy as racial vocation. Masters could serve God by acting as a model of earthly mastery and spiritual service for their white servants to emulate and aspire to, and as a model of earthly mastery worthy to be obeyed by their black slaves. The slave trade made Puritan masters into chameleons who could show different colors of white adjusted to the color of their servants' skin, not the color of their hearts.

Mather's *A Good Master Well Served* demonstrates how these spiritualized hypocrites adjusted Puritan morality and household culture to New England's commerce in racialized bound labor.[21] The sermon opens by citing traditional proof-texts of eye-service (Ephesians 6:5–8 and Colossians 3:22–25), and they provide Mather with his primary refrain: masters and servants must remember their common Master in heaven (GM 4, 22, 33, and 38). Even the structure of the sermon racializes this central trope: for most of his fifty-five-page "brief discourse," the term "servant" is racially unmarked, but in the final three pages, Mather directly addresses the "Scores of Slaves, the poor Blacks" of New England. We can track the making of racial vocation in the differences between these sections. The very existence of separate instructions for black servants not only distinguishes them from white servants but also modifies a central premise of the earlier instructions: that those for earthly servants apply equally to their masters as servants of God. By racializing the callings of master and servant, the sermon racializes vocation itself.

"Like master, like man" is not just a commonplace of literary servitude, but the premise of Puritan vocation in the first section of Mather's sermon. Their common Master appoints them to remind them of their likeness to each other as a spur to willing obedience and a curb against the strains of hypocrisy most associated with their stations: for masters, the tendency to be tyrants; for servants, to work only when they are watched. In modern vocation, the concept of God the Master coexists with a concept of virtuous self-mastery exercised under the public eye. By keeping an eye on each other, masters and servants learn to obey a Master who is invisible not because he resides in a sphere beyond human perception but because he resides within them.

Masters and servants teach each other to internalize God's mastery by serving as a moral watch within the household, surrogates for the public eye. Servants can be God's eyewitnesses. As Mather warns, "Woful, Rueful, will be the Condemnation of those *Prayerless Masters*, whose unhappy *Servants*, must bring in this Testimony before the Judgment Seat of God. . . . *Masters*, Consider of these Things in the Fear of God" (GM 19). The master serves as the public eye for servants as well, even when they attend "private meetings." Mather issues a "very particular Warning" to servants who "frequent the *Private Meetings* of *Young People*, to Pray, and Sing, and Repeat Sermons, and Confer with one another" (32). Though he lauds the "*Real Blessings*, unto the Neighbourhood" of such meetings, he warns servants not to use their attendance to justify insubordination. Servants must not do anything to "give your *Masters* (or *Mistresses*) any just cause for this Reflection," that their servants have become "more *slothful*, and more *saucy*, and that their *Business* is more neglected." Such servants are "but so many *Impious Hypocrites. Wo to you, Servants, Hypocrites*, if you make your *Private Meetings* the Incentives or Occasions of any *Wickedness*."

But masters could also be "Impious Hypocrites." The curse of Ham was one of the primary scriptural justifications for holding Africans in bondage, but in Mather's exegesis, it provides a warning against eye-service for masters.[22] Masters "do a little bear the Image of *God*, in that *Government*, which you have over your *Servants*," so they must "see to it, That you be not yourselves the *Servants* of the *worst Masters* in the World" (GM 7). If a master is "Commanded always by the *Devil*" and the "*Earthly Sensual Devilish* Inclinations of his own Heart," he threatens not only his own spiritual fate but also his servant's: "how lamentably Cursed then will you try to make your Servants, if their Master must be a Servant of the Devil." Mather offers a meditation to curb this hypocrisy: "let every *Master* say, *The Lord of Heaven shall be my Master*" (8). The spiritual exercise of internalizing both God as Master and their own status as captains of their servants' souls teaches masters how to "see to . . . [them]selves."

Servants provide visible evidence that their masters are God's servants, not the Devil's, so masters should take particular care when choosing whose fates they will govern. When Mather refers to the earthly labor market, hypocrisy becomes not just his theme, but the premise of his tract. "It is true, and, alas, that it is true!" Mather wails, "there is too much Scarcity of *Godly Servants*, to afford a *Choice*, unto us all; but if we can't have *Godly Servants*, yet let it not be our *Choice*, to have *Servants*, that shall be noted for any visible and notorious *Ungodliness*" (GM 9). Mather's lament about servant disobedience, while hardly unique, is remarkable for its resignation in positing an acceptable space between "Godly Servants" and servants who are at least not "visibly Ungodly." When Mather asks masters at least to try not to choose servants "that shall be noted for any visible and notorious Ungodliness," he concedes that some forms of hypocrisy are acceptable; and his recommendation to avoid visibly and notoriously ungodly servants grants Puritan masters the liberty and authority of their moral sense in a market where godly servants are a scarce commodity. Masters were free to employ the kind of moral and honest eye-servant who had long epitomized Puritan hypocrisy, so long as they at least attempted not to choose any visibly "damnable hypocrites" in the servant population.

This decision is in the self-interest of masters, for their servants are visible, bodily signs of their masters' spiritual and moral state, and the public is watching. Mather warns that "our own Disobedience unto God, is often Chastised in the *Disobedience*, and the Misbehavior, of our *Servants*" (GM 8). Meanwhile, the bodies of hale and well-fed servants demonstrate that their masters have not violated their callings. "Be a *Master*, but be not a *Tyrant*," Mather instructs his audience: "Let not your *Servants* have their *Lives* Embittered, their *Healths* Impaired, their

Bodies Macerated, by your Tyranny" (12). If a servant's body does bear the marks of a master's discipline, the wounds should suggest appropriately moderate correction, not a tyrant's lash. Servants' bodies should demonstrate their masters' capacity for self-governance.

So should his servant's occupations. In both the earthly and spiritual dimensions of their relationship, masters should imagine their servants as future masters and strive to provide a model of the good master that servants should wish to become. Mather urges his audience to "faithfully . . . *Teach* your Servants the *Work* of that Calling, for the learning whereof, any of them are bound unto you. While you use them for *Servants*, you must so use them, that in Time they may come to be *Masters*" (GM 12). "Send not your *Servants* upon the Devil's Business," Mather warns. "Make not your *Servants*, the Tools of any Wickedness. . . . [S]how that you would not have the *Conscience* of a Servant in any thing Imposed on" (11). He urges masters to hide any morally dubious elements of their trades from their servants: "If there be any *Mystery of Iniquity* in any of your Trades, don't let your *Servants* understand any of *Them*. Show them not any Subtile and Shuffling *Tricks*, which belong to the Arts of *Cheating*" (13). Masters should not engage in any activities that they would feel obliged to conceal from their servants. Nor should masters let fear of competing with their former servants in the marketplace compel them to hide "any Ingenious or Significant part of your *Trade*, out of any Covetous, Envious, Undermining purposes. . . .Those Masters, who by letting their Servants go away Unfurnished with the *Skill* of their *Trades*, do necessitate them unto the Second Service of *Journey men*, [and] are Guilty of a great Iniquity!" (12–13). Masters' obligations to their servants form a moral guide for valuing the "Ingenious" and laudable aspects of their earthly business and avoiding the "Subtile and Shuffling Tricks" of "the Arts of Cheating."

Spiritually, masters should strive to be like Abraham, a "Praying Master" who was particularly adept at training servants to become "the *Servants* of God" (GM 19). As Mather puts it, "a *Praying* Master, like *Abraham*, will be very like to have Servants, like unto himself." Such masters understand that they are never isolated from God's sight or hearing—or from the eyes and ears of their servants. "The *Secret Prayers* of those *Masters*," Mather explains, "fetch the *Spirit* of God from Heaven, on almost all that Live with them. Thus ought, *Masters* to Pray; and in the hearing of their *Servants* too, they ought thus to Pray." Mather presents overheard prayer as a kind of salutary eavesdropping: God listens from above and the servant from below.

If earthly masters are watched and heard from above and below, servants must imagine themselves under the constant gaze of two masters as they strive toward the ideal of child-like service. "Let your *Obedience* to your *Masters* (and *Mistresses*) while you are *Servants* be such, as will manifest that you are the *Obedient Children of God*," Mather instructs (GM 38). "You are the *Animate, Separate, Active Instruments* of other men. *Servants*, your *Tongues*, your *Hands*, your *Feet*, are your *Masters*, and they should move according to the Will of your *Masters*." This image of a body moving according to another's will might seem an odd metaphor for consent, but Mather depicts this hollowing out of the will as instrumental, a way for servants learn to manifest child-like obedience "while [they] are *Servants*." Internalizing God as a Master is both the means and the end of the willing service of vocation, and the failure to do so is hypocrisy. "If you are those *Eye-servants*, who will Obey your *Masters* no longer than their *Eye* is upon you, know it," Mather warns, "the *Eye* of the All seeing and Almighty God, is upon you, to Condemn you, for this *Disobedience*."

Faithful servants will "Imitate [their] *Masters* in all their Laudable *Properties* and *Practices*," but this ideal depends on their capacity to willingly obey only "good masters," those who never forget their own Master in heaven (GM 37). Mather asks servants: "Have you discerned, that your *Masters* are *Praying* Men, *Honest* Men, *Laborious* Men, Men that *Walk with God*, and Men every way *Conscientious*?" "Learn of such *Masters*," Mather harangues them, "or else your *Masters* will rise up as terrible *Witnesses* against you, in the Day of Gods pleading with you." Mather entrusts servants to "discern" that their masters are not just "*Praying* Men" who go through the motions of outward service, but "Men that *Walk with God*," who are in "every way *Conscientious*." Even his command that servants "imitate" their masters requires their active spiritual and moral engagement and insight, not just rote obedience.

Servants may even lawfully disobey a master's commands if they do not accord with God's will. Mather instructs servants: "Your *Obedience* unto your *Masters*, is to be Limited by that caution, in Col. 3.22. *Servants, Obey in all Things, your Masters, according to the Flesh, in singleness of Heart, fearing of God*" (GM 39–40). A servant's refusal of a master's unlawful commands enacts the broader principle of Christian liberty, a daily exercise of the imitatio Christi: "If your *Masters* put you upon the doing of any thing, that is contrary to the *Fear of God*, then, in the *Fear of God*, forbear to *Obey*; rather *Suffer* than *Obey*" (40). Ungodly masters who "will have you to *Cheat*, or *Lye*, or Profane the *Sabbaths*" provide an opportunity for servants to "*Obey God rather than man*; there is that prohibition for you, in 1 Cor. 7.23 *Be not the Servants of men*." Even ungodly masters can provide servants with the opportunity to develop the moral conscience required for self governance and to become earthly masters.

Servants were also to imitate Christ in their callings through their willing contentment to accept a humble earthly station; shunning pride is the primary spiritual labor of all of God's servants. Mather exhorts servants with "Proud Hearts" (GM 35) to humble themselves by modeling themselves on Christ: "Wear *Humility*, as a *Badge*, of your being *Servants*, unto that Blessed Lord, who once *took on Himself the Form of a Servant*" (36). A properly humbled servant will labor "cheerfully," no matter how degraded the work or meager the earthly compensation: "Truly, the meanest *Work* that you have to do, in your *Service*, though it be in the *Stable*, or the *Kitchen*, you may thus render very Glorious . . . with such a Consideration as this, *Though it be a mean Thing that my Master, or my Mistress will have me to do, yet it is the Will of the Lord Jesus Christ that I should now do it; & therefore I will do it cheerfully*" (34). Whether elbow deep in crusty pots or knee deep in stable mire, a servant should thank God the Master for the capacity to obey cheerfully.

Mather insists that masters should pay any wages owed to their servants by contract, but he also tells servants to "care not" whether their wages are sufficient: "It may be, you'll have Little *Pay* from any man, for what you do. Yea, but the Lord Jesus Christ will be your *Pay master*: *He* will Grant you Everlasting Recompences, in that blissful World, where not the Least Thing that has been done for the Lord, shall ever be forgotten!" (GM 35). This lesson applies to both earthly servants and all Christians as servants of the Lord: "*John* said unto *Servants, Be content with your Wages*; and *Paul* said, unto the Servants of the Lord Jesus Christ; *Be content with such things as you have*." Mather continues: "Whatever may be your *Portion* here, prove your *Godliness*, by your *Contentment* with your *Portion*. If your Carnal Appetites are not in all things gratified, Meditate, *Servants must not be Choosers; My Glorious Master, see it not fit for me to have these Little Things; and why should I murmur?*" (29). Servants who are not "Choosers" but are content with the portions doled out by visible and invisible masters exemplify the asceticism of the calling and its ideal of working for love.

Mather explicitly deputizes such properly humbled servants to speak as their master's moral consciences. He provides a script for playing the role of a "Servant worth Gold" (GM 46) to a visibly ungodly master, one who (in a vivid Matherian description) has "a Vice like some Leprosie cleaving unto him":

> Syr, I pray, that you would give me Leave to do the part of a true Servant in this one thing; I perceive your Prosperity is very much Endangered by some Temptations, whereof it would be well, if you were more aware. . . . You know Syr, What the Word of God speaks, about the Families that call not on His Name; You know Syr, What the Word of God speaks about those that sit with vain persons; You know 'tis said, Swear not at all; and 'tis said, Be not Drunk with Wine, wherein is Excess. You'l Excuse my Freedome with you, Syr, and Believe that I desire nothing in this World, more than your Prosperity. (GM 47–48)

Mather both empowers servants as agents of their masters' salvation and keeps them in their proper places. "If thy *Master*, be not a *Monster*," Mather assures them, "he'll thank thee for such a *Representation*: and, *What knowest thou, O Servant, but thou mayst Save thy Master*?" (48). The godly servant demonstrates his potential as a master not just in what he says, but in how he says it: properly deferential, properly in his place, gently reminding his master what he already "knows," politely requesting "Freedome" from him. As the godly servant "desire[s] nothing in this World, more than" his master's "Prosperity," so servants of God should likewise direct their gazes and their labors toward the "Prosperity" of their heavenly master. Godly masters, in turn, obey in "fear and trembling" by striving not for earthly prosperity but for the reward of producing faithful servants "like unto themselves."

For those servants who internalize the moral law of the master, a glorious future awaits. Mather encourages servants to imagine themselves as future masters: "Consider with your selves, *Were I my self a Master, or a Mistress, what sort of a Servant would I desire*? So, *Servant*, go thy way, and be thy self *Such* a Servant" (GM 51). Instructing servants how to be the kind of servant God called them to be, Mather encourages them to imagine the kind of servant they would want to have. "Behave your selves Vertuously" during your term of service, Mather exhorts them, and "how meanly soever you may *fare*, you shall have the *Continual Feast* of a Good Conscience in you." This "Good Conscience" will be the basis of future public credit: "When your Time is out, it is likely that *God* will multiply his Blessings upon you; *Men* will Respect you, Employ you, Value you." Better still, "when *Time shall be no more*," Christ will "set open for you, the Doors of His *Heavenly Fathers* House, to which you shall be welcomed with a, *Well done, Good and Faithful Servant, Enter into Joy*."

When Mather turns to address black servants, it becomes clear that while the possibility of heavenly rewards remains open to them, the promise of earthly advancement and the liberty of self-mastery is available only to white servants. The spiritual "likeness" between masters and servants, a shared capacity to internalize the moral law of God the Master, turns out to be whiteness. Even white servants with black hearts and consciences might become earthly masters, however dire their eternal fate. The long opening section of Mather's sermon suggests how differences of rank and ethnicity, and differences between those who owe wages and those who should virtuously accept whatever wage is on offer, emerge from master-servant discourse. But these distinctions are subsumed in racial difference at the end of the sermon. The nature of consent is itself racialized, with orderliness and submission to earthly masters stressed for racial others and the ability to cultivate a "Good Conscience" and master oneself held out to white servants alone—indeed, equated with whiteness.

Mather may leave "Blacks" for the end of his vocational treatise, but the section on black servants clearly punctuates his earlier instructions—and in typical Mather fashion, he finishes with an exclamation point: "Give Ear, ye pittied *Blacks*, Give Ear!" (GM 53). Thus commences Mather's exhortation to the "scores of Slaves" present in his congregation. The section on blacks might be brief, but it does critical work, explicitly calibrating the callings of masters and servants to meet the spiritual and moral demands of African slavery. We can track the racialization of these callings and the doctrines they signify in the differences between these passages and the rest of the sermon.

The word "slave" appears only four times in the first fifty-two pages, and in none of these instances does it refer to black servants. Rather, each time it signifies spiritual abjection, the degradation of unregeneracy: the difference between a hypocrite's dutiful path to hell and that of a sinner. Mather urges servants to strive toward conversion, exhorting them to "Renounce, and, Forsake, the Service of those *Invisible Masters*, a *Slavery* to whom, is inconsistent, with the *Service* of the Lord Jesus Christ" (GM 22). After admonishing them not to run away from even the most abusive masters, he gives servants an exception: "But yet, for those *Invisible Masters*, I mean, those *Tempters*, and those *Tempers*, which Enslave your Souls, in a Distance from God . . . *Run Away from those Hellish Taskmasters*!" (4). Mather asks them to consider how fortunate they are to be servants to a Protestant, not the slaves of a Muslim or Catholic: "I tell you, a Turkish, or a Spanish *Slavery*, is not a thousandth part so miserable, as the Accursed Slavery of your Souls, to the *Invisible Destroyers* of your Souls" (23). While obviously trying to terrify unregenerate servants, he also reassures them that they can free themselves from this "Accursed Slavery," goading them with a question he intends to be rhetorical: "But will you at length take a Course, for your own Deliverance, O *Wretched Servants, that you are*?"

Mather provides a map for this "Course," a script for the unregenerates who seek to convert spiritual slavery into consent to willingly serve Christ. He even occupies the rhetorical position of a spiritual slave, modeling rhetorical humility before the Lord: "I am willing to abandon all the Corrupt Interests of this present Evil World. . . . I am willing that the Lord Jesus Christ, the only Mediator, should . . . do all that for me which he does for all his Chosen. . . . I am Willing, in Gratitude unto the Lord Jesus Christ, for my Salvation freely Purchased and Applied by Him, to Serve him, in Constant Endeavors. . . . Unto all of this I am Willing" (GM 27). All of this "willing" testifies to a capacity for "*Thankful Obedience*," for being "kept and helpt by the Power of that Grace" working through Mather's mediation as servant of the Lord to free sinners from spiritual slavery.

But when he addresses black servants, Mather's point of view remains firmly aligned with that of the master, racializing his calling to serve the Lord as minister and as author along with the master's. He maps the spiritual abjection and moral incapacity of invisible slavery onto black bodies. Mather typologizes African slaves as "Ethiopians," citing Psalm 68.31: "Ethiopia shall soon stretch out her Hands unto God." In Mather's rendering, this text is vocational: "even those poor Black *Hands* of yours, the Lord calleth for them. Lift those *Hands* of yours in *Petitions* to the Lord; *Pray* constantly, as well as you can, *That the Lord would make you Servants unto Himself, and Pardon you, and Accept you, and Save you, thro' Jesus Christ for ever*" (GM 53). Mather expresses his racialized version of the work ethic when he urges "*Swarthy* People" to use their hands and their mouths to "*Pray* constantly, as well as you can," and to "*Vow* solemnly as well as you can, *That you will be the servants of the Lord, by the Help of His Grace, as long as you Live*." All Christians in their vocations should labor incessantly against their inability to save themselves, but blacks seem to Mather to suffer from a particular incapacity.[23]

White servants must choose whether to serve themselves or to master themselves by serving God and their earthly masters at once. In contrast, black servants should focus primarily on obeying their earthly masters. We can see this in the different ways Mather warns against running away.

When admonishing white servants not to "*Unlawfully* Desert the Service, wherein the Good Hand of God has fixed them," he frames this as an issue of consent and of practice in spiritual obedience: "If sinners entice thee to Run away, Consent thou not" (GM 24). But in the final section of his sermon, consent is less a spiritual than a moral discipline. Mather includes "running away" in a list of infractions that associate disobedience with the color of their skin: "And be sure, that you never *Stretch forth your Hands*, unto any Evil; alwayes *Keep your Hands from doing any Evil*; do not by Fornication, by Drunkenness, by Stealing, by Lying, by Running away, make yourselves infinitely *Blacker* than you are already" (53). Mather's formulation implies that however much they display visible godliness, black servants cannot entirely free themselves from the sinful connotations ascribed here to the color of their skin.

In the earlier section of the sermon, Mather empowers God's spiritual servants to pursue a course for their own deliverance. He does grant black slaves the capacity to be saved, but he minimizes their agency in the process. "You are better *Fed,* & better *Clothed*, & better *Managed* by far, than you would be, if you were your *Own men*," Mather chides his black listeners. "All that now remains for you, is to become first the *Good Servants of the Lord Jesus Christ*, & then, of those that have purchased you" (GM 53). Although Mather puts spiritual service "first," the syntax of the sentence and broader context complicate that priority. The spiritual, psychological, and emotional work required to become "Good Servants of the Lord" is framed by the agency of those who "manage" and "have purchased" them. Black servants require external supervision: the "management" of a white master or any white capable of embodying the ideology of mastery—here, "those that have purchased you." In this passage, Mather puts the master's obligation to his servants in the passive voice, displacing actual masters from the subject position into a category of invisible and pervasive agency. Mather uses the grammar of white mastery as ideology, expressed as Mather's point of view. Masters of black servants vie more competitively with God the Master for moral and spiritual authority than do masters of white servants.

Slaves should take a more passive "Course" to become the servants and children of God. "Put yourselves into the *Hands* of the Lord Jesus Christ," Mather commands them: "Be willing that the Lord Jesus Christ should make you *His Own*. And then, for the sake of the Lord Jesus Christ, be Good *Servants*, unto those that own you; Do for your *Masters*, and your *Mistresses*, all the *Service* that you can; and be orderly in every thing" (GM 53–54). Though Mather affirms that slaves should "be willing that the Lord Jesus Christ should make you *His Own*," he emphasizes earthly service, the obedience they owe "unto those that own" them. As does the section as a whole, this passage calls on masters to internalize their own mastery along with God's by calling their slaves to be "be orderly in every thing," obeying the moral law embodied by their masters for "the sake of the Lord." At the same time, Mather implies that such masters may be content to have servants who try as hard as they can to please them.

At the end of the sermon, Mather racializes the rewards that the future might hold for obedient servants. He stretches the concept of Pauline indifference, telling black servants to care not whether they "are Fed among the *Dogs*, with the *Orts* [scraps] of our Tables," because if they obey their earthly masters for Christ's sake they shall "at length, Ly down unto a *Feast* with *Abraham* himself, in the Heaven of the Blessed. Been't you Discouraged; it will be but a *Little*, a *Little*, a *Little* While, and all your pains will End in Everlasting Joyes" (GM 54). This is a far cry from the promise of earthly employment that Mather holds out for servants who do not tax their consciences and God's mercy in hypocrisy. Mather does affirm that these slaves have souls and might well be admitted into God's household. Yet even in heaven, it seems, black slaves will remain at their master's feet, "Ly[ing] down unto a Feast with Abraham" instead of with the dogs as at their earthly master's table.

Mather also racializes the threat of damnation for disobedience, immediately following his promise of a heavenly feast with a caveat: "But if you will not be such Orderly *Servants*, 'tis a terrible thing that I have to say unto you" (54):

> All the *Sorrows* that you see in this World, are but the *Beginnings of Sorrows*, and Little *Emblems* of the *Sorrows* that remain for you in another. Do you meet with *Hunger* here? You shall there be *Hungry and hardly bestead* [placed] for ever. Does the *Heat* Oppress you here? You shall there be *Tormented in a Flame* hotter than that of Brimstone for ever. Does the *Cold* afflict you here? You shall there have *Gnashing of Teeth* for ever? Do you here sometimes want your *Sleep*? There you shall *not Rest*, neither *Day nor Night*, for ever? Are you *Beaten* here? Why, the *Devil* will be your *Overseer*; and you'l be Weltring under intollerable Blows and Wounds, World without End. (GM 54)

Mather threatens both masters and servants with images of hell in the earlier section of his sermon (GM 45). But here he intends the fear of eternal damnation to produce a more passive kind of obedience in servants who will not be "Orderly." Like Rowlandson's captivity narrative, this passage racializes willing obedience to masters who are monsters, as well as the concept of Christian liberty. The servants in the earlier passages were deputized to chide and reform their masters and also permitted to disobey those whose commands were unlawful. It is unclear whether black servants are being punished for the disobedience of their masters, but Mather does not present them with the option of legitimate disobedience.

The passage racializes not just the servant's calling, but also the master's. The belief that black slaves innately and uniquely incite their masters to act as tyrants is a key doctrine of racial vocation. Not only does Mather refrain from threatening such monster masters with their servant's capacity to testify against them to God, but he does not even directly testify against them himself. Nowhere here does he enjoin masters to remember their Master in heaven as a curb against tyranny. Instead, black slaves bear the threat of damnation for visibly and notoriously ungodly white masters who make their lives a hell on earth.

For whites, vocation's promotion of spiritualized labor in one's place became a discourse of social mobility. If white servants stay in their places spiritually and socially, showing that they can internalize the moral law, they might well become future masters. Unlike the servants of the previous section, these "pittied Blacks" "have so little cause to desire your being any other than *Slaves* as you are, & where you are, that it would soon make you miserable to be otherwise" (GM 52–53). Blacks can make themselves God's children, but they do not even have "cause to desire" earthly liberty. Every one of the elect is called to be a servant of God, and they must humble themselves before their heavenly Master. In contrast, black slaves must learn how to be content with the providential humility that is inextricable from the color of their skin, "as you are & where you are." Black slaves may become the servants of God, but even if they do so, unlike white servants they cannot gain the liberty to be their own masters.

Mather concludes his sermon with the only direct address to masters in the section addressed to black servants: "*Masters*, These poor *Negroes* will hardly mind what I say; I pray, do you *Repeat* it unto them" (GM 55). In this command to masters, "I pray" marks polite deference between peers, linking Mather and the masters in common superiority to the "poor Negroes" rather than marking a site of mutual labor between masters and servants, or servants and children. Mather's language racializes his earlier discussions of prayers as a source of shared spiritual edification and emulation between masters and servants. "Like master, like man" breaks down along racial lines. Like Rowlandson's Praying Indians, "poor Negroes" might be taught to pray, and even to serve God in so doing, but they cannot entirely escape the taint of hypocrisy that shadows such visible godliness. The most laudable spiritual expression for black servants is to obey white Christians.

At the same time, Mather's praying masters bolster their vocations even if their servants' prayers can only ever signify laudable hypocrisy. Whether or not blacks have the capacity to serve God in serving men, they must try as hard as they can; whether masters ever have an orderly, much less a Christian, black servant, they must try as hard as they can to produce one. For masters, both current and aspirational, this is the work ethic: the spiritualization of labor against resistance and in the absence of a guaranteed reward.

Praying Merchants: The Lex Mercatoria and Sarah Kemble Knight's Moral Watch

The calling of praying masters modeled the calling of Christian merchants, who would be asked to internalize God the Master in ideological forms that muted the connotation of external compulsion. Mark Valeri characterizes *A Christian at his Calling* as Mather's "most thorough statement on secular vocation," observing that it "correlated moral obligation, providential order, spiritual felicity, commercial knowledge, and market profits" and redefined the merchant's calling by setting "profitability as the chief standard for vocational choice."[24] An element of its "secularity" is its promotion of ideological forms of God the Master. As in *A Good Master*, Mather here emphasizes obedience as the primary virtue of vocation, admonishing men to "Let *Obedience* to GOD, be the *Spring*, and the *Strain* of all your *Business*."[25] Yet he only twice explicitly invokes God the Master, the primary embodiment of authority in traditional discourses of vocation.[26] Instead, Mather preserves the concept of God the Master in the tract's leitmotif: "Be thou in the Fear of the Lord, all the Day long."[27] Instead of the external constraints of a master's command, the "Fear of God" presses toward moral self-restraint: "The *Fear of God* must Lay upon us, a *Restraint* from all *Profanity*, and from all *Dishonesty*, and from all *Intemperance*, and from every thing that plainly violates the Laws of God, and this *All the Day Long*."[28]

While he does not explicitly cite Ephesians 6:5–6 or 6:9, Mather alludes to these passages throughout the tract, exhorting his readers to continually cultivate the fear of God by remembering that God's eye is always upon them: "We should at no Time in the *Day*, utterly Forget, that the *Eye of God* is upon us, but *Set the Lord always before us, All the Day Long*. The *Fear of God* will place a man, as under the *Eye of God*."[29] When a man "*Works* at his Calling, and Act[s] in his *Occupation* with an Eye to God, Act[s] as under the Eye of *God*," he need not be constantly reminded of his obligations to God the Master but has the liberty to "follow his *Occupation*."[30]

In *Lex Mercatoria*, another conduct manual for godly merchants, Mather suggests another way that the eyes of God the Master instill economic morality in modern vocation: they become the public. Stressing honesty as a key virtue of the merchant's calling, Mather decries "false dealers": "The Holy *Angels* of God, look upon our *dealings*; and it would be an admirable thing if we could always behave our selves, as before those *Flaming Eyes*, the Holy *Angels* of God. But, what, if our Neighbours did so too? We read, *A Thief is Ashamed, when he is found*. We should be *Afraid* of those *dealings* whereof we should be *Ashamed*, if we *are found*."[31] When Mather includes fear along with the shame of being seen by the "*Flaming Eyes*" of God's angels and those of their neighbors, he presents merchants with new metaphors for their internalized economic conscience. He even renders caveat emptor as a version of eye-service: "It is not enough to say, *Caveat Emptor; Let the Buyer look to himself*! But it must be said, *Let the Seller also look to it, that he don't Oppress the Buyer*."[32] Buyers and sellers show that their moral view aligns with God's and the neighborly watch when each "look[s] to himself" in moral commerce. In the context of a decade that produced a new flurry of racial codes, both legal and cultural, even vocational tracts like this that do not overtly discuss Africans or Native Americans should be understood as equating with whiteness a Christian's capacity to "look to himself" in his earthly business.[33]

The travel narrative of the Boston merchant Sarah Kemble Knight dramatizes the alignment of the merchant's and the master's ethos in the moral vernacular of New England's racializing service economy. In 1704–5, Knight traveled from Boston to New York to settle a relative's estate, recording her experiences in a journal often touted as an early example of secular New England writing. Knight has been taken to embody the shift from "Puritan to Yankee," to speak on behalf of the development of New England's commercial morality as it eclipsed traditional Christian piety.[34] But Knight's point of view synthesizes that of the merchant with that of Mather's Christian master, called to govern those deemed incapable of governing themselves: women, enslaved blacks, and Native Americans, as well as white male farmers and magistrates who have failed to internalize their mastery over these others. Knight's journal is vernacular Puritan merchant literature, a vocational tract for commercial economic morality, and its existence demonstrates that women participated in the history of reconciling spirit and commerce that Valeri deems the domain of "men of commerce."[35]

The journey from Boston to New York confronts Knight with the dual terrors of physical hardship and being a buyer in a seller's market.[36] Traveling along a relatively undeveloped route, Knight cannot choose among various inns for the best quality or haggle for the best price. Her guides, hosts, and hostesses are not servants, and she is not their master; rather, they provide services for which Knight is a paying customer. By writing about her experience, Knight can assert her self-command as a merchant and as a woman traveling with male guides who do not quite function as surrogate patriarchs.

The logic of racial vocation connects her point of view, her narrative voice, and her selection of detail, and she dramatizes its doctrines in her extended depiction of New Haven, Connecticut, as Boston's moral uncanny double. Though "they are Govern'd by the same Laws as wee in Boston, (or little differing,) . . . and many of them good, Sociable people, and I hope Religious too," the inhabitants of New Haven are "a little too much Independant in their principals [*sic*]."[37] The independence of the people seems to her an improper diversion of their principles from moral law, particularly laws that increasingly defined the moral order as white male mastery over nonwhite servants.

With characteristic hyperbole, she depicts the Native Americans of New Haven as "the most salvage [savage] of all the salvages of that kind that I had ever Seen."[38] Among their transgressions against civility, she decries that they are "Govern'd by Laws of their own making," including the ability to divorce "on the least dislike or fickle humour" by "saying *stand away* to one another"; that they "mourn for their Dead by blacking their faces, and cutting their hair, after an Awkerd and frightfull manner"; and, of course, that "they trade most for Rum, for which they'd hazzard their very lives; and the English fit them Generally as well by seasoning it plentifully with water." These "English" are dishonest dealers, but the joke is at the expense of the Native Americans. Knight views neither group as her peers.

Perhaps their greatest offense, though, is that they "give the title of merchant to every trader; who Rate their Goods according to the time and spetia [specie] they pay in."[39] Not all "traders" can embody the merchant's calling, meriting the "title of merchant." Knight satirizes one scene of commerce: "Now, when the buyer comes to ask for a comodity, sometimes before the merchant answers that he has it, he sais, *is Your pay redy*? Perhaps the Chap Reply's Yes: what do You pay in? say's the merchant. The buyer having answered, then the price is set." She concludes, "It seems a very Intricate way of trade and what Lex Mercatoria had not thought of."[40] If, as Mather defines it, the *lex mercatoria* (the body of laws governing trade) is above all a code of honesty, Knight's very irreverence spiritualizes her vocation, demonstrating that she merits "the title of merchant" and is superior to those who engage in this "very Intricate way of trade."

Mistaking a trader for a merchant violates the lex mercatoria, and so does mistaking a black slave for a white human. After observing that the region offers a surplus of oysters and that family life there seems comfortable, Knight offers the following commentary on master-slave relations in New Haven: "But too indulgent (especially the farmers) to their slaves, suffering too great familiarity from them, permitting them to sit at Table and eat with them (as they say, to save time), and into the dish goes the black hoof as freely as the white hand."[41] From her perspective, not even the most diligent businessman should cite efficiency as a reason for "freely" mingling "the black hoof" and "the white hand."

Immediately following her denunciation of the New Haven farmers' leniency, Knight recounts a legal case that demonstrates the moral and financial risk of misperceiving the slave as human.

> They told me that there was a farmer lived nere the Town where I lodgd who had some difference with his slave, concerning something the master had promised him and did not punctualy perform; which caused some hard words between them; But at length they put the matter to Arbitration and Bound themselves to stand the award of such as they named—which done, the Arbitrators Having heard the Allegations of both parties, Order the master to pay 40s [shillings] to black face, and acknowledge his fault. And so the matter ended: the poor master very honestly standing to the award.[42]

Suggesting that these magistrates are guilty of a miscarriage of racial and economic justice, Knight clearly identifies with the "poor master" who "very honestly" honors his obligation to "pay 40s to black face, and acknowledge his fault." These magistrates are not just inadequate embodiments of the law, they are also unfair dealers. When she satirizes the masters, magistrates, and farmers of New Haven, Knight embodies the merchant's version of racial vocation. By affirming her faith that servants belong at their masters' feet, not mingling their hands in the same dish, she also exemplifies the self-mastery that licenses the godly merchant to conduct her business as she sees fit.[43]

The journal concludes with a passage that departs from its dominant tone and expresses Knight's gratitude for her safe homecoming after a five months' absence. "I cannot fully express my Joy and Satisfaction," she writes, "But desire sincearly to adore my Great Benefactor for thus graciously carrying forth and returning in safety his unworthy handmaid."[44] Because they read the rest of the narrative as secular, critics have suggested that this ending may not be entirely sincere or is at least incongruous.[45] Rather, it captures the play of multiple masters that defines modern vocation: the coexistence of God the Master with more ideological forms, like God the Benefactor. Knight demonstrates that single complex woman could have internalized various forms of moral and spiritual authority, and in idiosyncratic ways. Here, she is the Lord's "unworthy handmaid," a commonplace that spiritualizes her private and public callings by enacting humble self-command. Elsewhere in the narrative, her internalized mastery is expressed in her tone of wry superiority over unfair dealers, racial others, and whites who do not fully inhabit their calling to govern those others or themselves.

Knight's remarks about the "poor master" of "black face" give us a good idea of her opinion of a famous case in which a slave successfully sued his master, one that took place not in the backwater of New Haven but in her very own "safe home."[46] In 1694, a Boston merchant and jurist named John Saffin entered into a contract of indenture with a man named Adam.[47] The terms of Adam's indenture were fairly standard, requiring seven years of faithful service: "Provided that the said Adam my Servant do in the mean time go on chearfully quietly and Industriously . . . and doe behave and abear himself as an Honest true and faithfull Servant ought to do during the Tearm of Seven Years as aforesaid."[48] The stipulation of working cheerfully codifies the traditional discourse of humiliation, of the patient and cheerful acceptance of a servant's place. In Adam's case, this ideal of covenant labor became a discourse of racial inequality, a legal basis upon which white masters like Saffin might claim authority to convert their black servants into slaves.

Saffin at once availed himself of his right to trade or sell Adam's labor for the duration of the seven-year contract. "Out of meer kindness to and for the Encouragement of my negro man Adam to go on cheerfully in his Business," Saffin placed him into the "Custody, Service and command" of

Thomas Shepard, Saffin's tenant on Boundfield Farm, in Bristol.[49] Adam had to cheerfully serve not just one but two earthly masters. At the end of the seven-year term, in March 1701, Saffin claimed that Adam had not behaved according to the terms of the contract and ordered him to go to Swansea to serve a different master. Adam not only refused to go, but he also took the opportunity to sue for his freedom.

Appearing before the General Court (whose members included Sewall), Saffin argued that Adam had not fulfilled his contractual obligations to be "chearful, "quiet," "Industrious," "Honest," "true," and "faithfull." Instead, as Shepard had testified in a sworn statement from 1699, Adam had been "a very disobedient Turbulent outragious and unruly servant these many years."[50] The court found for Adam, contending that his behavior had substantially complied with the terms of the indenture. Even if Adam had not been a model faithful servant, the court argued, a perfect compliance should not be expected, since "there was much to be allowed to the behaviour of Negroes, who are so ignorant, rude and brutish."[51] Saffin sought to ground his claim to bind Adam perpetually in his failure to work cheerfully; though the court ruled against Saffin, they treated Adam as evidence of "the behaviour of Negroes"—specifically, their incapacity to comply perfectly with a master's will, much less God's will. In racial vocation, white masters must will themselves to be content in the knowledge that their black slaves might not be able to serve them cheerfully. The white master's capacity to do so was deemed morally and spiritually equivalent to a black servant's ability to be seen to serve his master cheerfully.

Household Hypocrisy and the Sewall-Saffin Dialectic

In court on opposite sides in Adam's case, and in the public world governed by Boston's worthy gentlemen, Samuel Sewall and John Saffin were antagonists. Their dueling pamphlets, "The Selling of Joseph" and "A Brief and Candid Reply,"[52] have been taken to represent an early debate or dialogue in the history of Anglo-American abolitionist and apologist literature, but both men express emerging forms of racism when they disagree about whether, how, and why God made Africans inferior to Europeans, and whether that inferiority legitimated enslaving Africans. Racism is also built into the very form of the exchange. Their "debate" was a dialectic of hypocrisy and vocation that generated a synthesis: the public white master. Sewall and Saffin embodied that role differently, but they shared its point of view.

Could African slavery be reconciled with Christian mastery? Sewall argued that it could not: slavery made Puritan masters into Bayne's "damnable hypocrites," "deepely gone in eye-service." Slavery tempts masters to "connive at the Fornification [*sic*] of their Slaves, lest they should be obliged to find them Wives, or pay there [their] Fine." Indeed, "it seems to be practically pleaded that they might be Lawless." When Sewall observes that "'tis thought much of, that the Law should have Satisfaction for their Thefts, and other Immoralities," the pronouns blur the immoralities of master and slave. Sewall does not just testify against individual masters but also implicitly charges merchants with crimes against morality, lamenting the "horrible . . . Uncleanness, Mortality, if not Murder, that the Ships are guilty of that bring great Crouds of these miserable Men, and Women." Even the guiltiest "Ships" cannot go to hell, but those who profit from their voyages can, and they threaten to drag New England down with them. Passages like this render as understatement his observation, "*Holiness to the Lord*, is more rarely engraven upon this sort of Servitude."[53] Sewall's visual metaphor echoes Mather's concerns about servants as physical signs of their master's spiritual states. By referring to "Servitude" instead of servants, Sewall points to a systemic problem, extending concerns about the callings of particular masters to New England's place in the world of Atlantic commerce. "It may be a question whether all the Benefit received by *Negro* Slaves, will balance the Accompt of Cash laid out upon them," he explains, and he later expresses this idea more emphatically: "Evil must not be done, that good may come of it. The extraordinary and comprehensive Benefit accruing to the Church of God, and to *Joseph* personally, did not rectify his brethrens Sale of him."[54] Slavery is "evil," such "damnable hypocrisy" that no economic benefit can redeem it, but Sewall focuses on its effect on masters, not just the enslaved. His argument combines the moral logic of minister, magistrate, and merchant under the sign of the good master.

Saffin counters that God has called "the "People of God in all Ages" to be masters of "Bond men, Women and Children."[55] These servants and slaves were "commonly kept by holy and good men, and improved in Service," he observes. "Therefore by the Command of God, *Lev.* 25.44, and their venerable Example, we may keep Bond men, and use them in our Service still; yet with all candour, moderation, and Christian prudence, according to their state and condition consonant to the Word of God." Saffin's "we" characterizes New England, not just legal masters, as a good master. Though he refers to "the times of the Gospel," Saffin's rendering stresses the moral law. The "holy and good men" permitted to "keep

Bond men" need not convert them to "improve" them "in Service." God requires the good men only to "use" enslaved peoples "with all candour, moderation, and Christian prudence." Indeed, Saffin intends the rhetoric of his own "candid" pamphlet to exemplify the virtuous "candour" of the Christian master.

The notorious poem that immediately follows this passage might raise the question of whether Saffin exemplifies "moderation," however. He concludes his tract with "The Negroes Character":

> Cowardly and cruel are those *Blacks* Innate,
> Prone to Revenge, Imp of inveterate hate.
> He that exasperates them, soon espies
> Mischief and Murder in their very eyes.
> Libidinous, Deceitful, False and Rude,
> The spume Issue of Ingratitude.
> The Premises consider'd, all may tell,
> How near good *Joseph* they are parallel.[56]

The poem makes it hard to take Saffin at his word when he suggests that these particular "Bond men" are capable of being "improved in Service." Yet because it immediately follows his affirmation that slave holding is legal for good masters, we should take pains to read it as congruent with that position and not, as it might seem to us, hypocritical.

The belief that converting blacks was either extremely difficult or impossible was a doctrine of Sewall's and Saffin's racial vocation. White masters could at best expect orderly comportment, not the willing obedience of the calling, from their servants. By dramatizing the extreme futility of even trying to make such servants orderly, the poem spiritualizes the master's calling to "improve" them.

The poem's tone and point of view also promote racial vocation. The second couplet depicts a version of eye-service, a moral staring down that aligns the speaker's privileged insight into the "Innate" qualities of blacks with the eye of a master. The poem invites "all" to share this perspective of one who "espies / Mischief and Murder in their very eyes." The specific qualities that the master-speaker deems "innate" to "Blacks"—they are "Libidinous, Deceitful, False and Rude"—disqualify them from fulfilling the mandate of "candor" required of lawful masters. Whether or not Saffin's readers sanction his views about race and slavery, they share his presumed position as a white master. The cool irony of the final couplet, which mocks Sewall's likening of slaves to Joseph, seems a counterpoint to the slaves' "inveterate hate"; it combines a master's exemplary "candor" with "moderation" in a tone of self-command. Black slaves signify their own degradation, not that of their masters. To Saffin, slavery promotes market morality, precisely because slaves themselves "innately" violate it. The fact that he chooses a poem as the proper form for expressing these ideas suggests the broad cultural value of attempting to master such intractably unwilling servants. Saffin might not ever produce an obedient African slave, but he successfully produces an ideal of virtuous and disinterested labor, that of white mastery as public service.

In depicting black slaves as inherent eye-servants, Sewall is not Saffin's antagonist, but his partner. Sewall affirms the public premise that few if any blacks are capable of governing themselves: "Few can endure to hear of a Negro's being made free, and indeed they can seldom use their freedom well; yet their continual aspiring after their forbidden Liberty, renders them Unwilling Servants."[57] Unlike white servants, black slaves only "seldom use their freedom well" and rarely embody vocation's ideal of willing service. It is difficult to tell whether Sewall finds fault with blacks who "continually aspire" to attain their "forbidden Liberty," but he clearly locates that "Liberty" on earth, referring to "a Negro's being made free" by men—masters and magistrates like Saffin and himself—not by God. Slavery threatens the kind of invisible liberty that God grants to at least some of the slaves' masters. "For men obstinately to persist in holding their Neighbors and Brethren under the Rigor of perpetual Bondage," Sewall avers, "seems to be no proper way of gaining Assurance that God has given them Spiritual Freedom."[58] In these contrasting definitions of freedom, Sewall racializes the dialectic of obedience. Vocation encourages men to continual spiritual self-examination as a "proper way of gaining Assurance that God has given them Spiritual Freedom," while hypocrisy is an improper, prideful resting in such "Assurance."

Sewall's alternative to the "damnable hypocrisy" of slavery is to promote the contractual white mastery of white servants. "And all things considered," he notes, "it would conduce more to the Welfare of the Province, to have White Servants for a Term of Years, than to have Slaves for Life."[59] In response, Saffin mocks Sewall for "mak[ing] a large Discourse" to prove such an obvious point: that keeping white rather than black servants "conduceth most to the welfare and benefit of this Province" and that "white men . . . are in many respects to be preferred before Blacks; who doubts that?"[60] In fact, Saffin shrewdly argues, white servitude might be even more unscriptural than African slavery: "If it should be unlawful to deprive them that are lawful Captives, or Bondmen of their Liberty for Life being Heathens; it seems to be more unlawful to deprive our Brethren, of our own or other Christian Nations of the Liberty, (though but for a time) by binding them to Serve some Seven, Ten, Fifteen, and some Twenty Years."[61] Sewall and Saffin agree that the skin color of the servant determines the "lawfulness" of his or her labor and the spiritual value of its economic "benefit" not just for individual masters, but also for the economic vocation of "this Province" and "other Christian Nations."[62] By associating white servants with the consent to contract, Sewall's argument against holding black people as slaves promotes an ideal of white self-mastery that is compatible with slaveholding.

Sewall's and Saffin's shared vision of virtuous white mastery as the basis of New England's economic culture emerged from the household version of conversion discourse in which the child who serves signified faithful obedience and the servant was a hypocrite who provided wealth and labor for the godly but would be turned out of doors from God's household.[63] Mather's *A Good Master* establishes how this spiritual imagery translates into the racialization of earthly households. His statement that "Our *Servants* are most of them, yet in their *Youth*" (GM 30) is a demographic fact with social and spiritual implications. The edifying "likeness" of masters and servants in Mather's first section also presumes the likeness of servants and children, and of masters and fathers. Masters to such servants "indeed should be *Fathers* unto" them. Mather advises his audience that "You should give your *Servants* reason to testifie concerning you, *That man has been a Father to me, as long as I have Lived with him*" (10). Servants, in turn, must "Let your *Obedience* to your *Masters (and Mistresses)* while you are *Servants* be such, as will manifest that you are the *Obedient Children of God*" (38). The phrase "while you are *Servants*" suggests that earthly servitude is just a temporary status for those who can exchange service for both earthly mastery and spiritual childhood.

Indeed, Mather urges servants to conceive of themselves as potential spiritual fathers to their masters' children. "This would be a wondrous Thing indeed," he encourages servants, "if the Children of those, with whom you dwell, may have cause for ever to say, *Blessed be God, for sending such a Servant into my Father's House; God has made that Servant a Father (or a Mother) to my Soul; Had it not been for what I saw and heard of that Servant, I might have been undone Eternally*" (GM 46). By thinking of themselves as spiritual parents to their masters' children, servants learn not just to become masters, but to become the kind of masters who will act as fathers to their servants. In this developmental model, a servant's becoming a master is identical with a child's becoming an adult, one who fulfills his calling by remaining spiritually a child who serves.

The separate instructions for black servants detach them not just from the category of servant but also from that of children. In his concluding section, Mather elides the possibility of earthly liberty for black servants, both by separating them from the servants who are "yet in their Youth" and by affirming that they can, in fact, join the household of God: "So, though your *Skins* are of the color of the *Night*, yet your *Souls* will be washed *White* in the *Blood of the Lamb*: and be Entitled unto an *Inheritance in Light*: Though you are in *Slavery* to men, yet you shall be the *Free-men* of the Lord, the *Children* of God" (GM 54). Like the servants in the first section, black servants should obey their masters to manifest their obedience to God the Father, but they will remain "in Slavery to men"—at once nonchildren and perpetual children, people whom Mather does not represent as parents, either earthly or spiritual, actual or potential. The servant turned out of doors will reside ever as a slave in Christian households, while the child who serves has liberty to govern his own household.

Sewall and Saffin agree with Mather and each other that black slaves, even earthly children, are not children when they distinguish between a master's obligations to white servants and those to nonwhite servants. Sewall alludes to turning out of doors to racialize a distinction between children and servants in earthly households and as a discourse of spiritual hypocrisy. Arguing that white servants are a more godly source of labor than black slaves, Sewall alludes to laws that prohibited blacks from serving in the militia: "As many Negro men as there are among us, so many empty places there are in our Bands, and the places taken up of Men that might make Husbands for our Daughters. And the Sons and Daughters of *New England* would become more like *Jacob*, and *Rachel*, if this Slavery were thrust quite out of doors."[64] In Sewall's version of household hypocrisy, "servant" becomes "slavery" and "turning out" becomes "thrust out," conveying his sense of moral and spiritual urgency and the fact that his primary concern is not for the bodies and souls of enslaved peoples but about the effect of "slavery" on New England's economic vocation. Such hypocrisy becomes a kind of genetic mutation in the reproduction of the cultural economy of the household.

While Saffin does not explicitly cite Ames directly as Sewall does, Ames might well have provided Saffin authority for his counterargument. Ames's chapter on the mutual obligations of masters and servants distinguishes childhood as a "natural" condition from servitude, which is "either undertaken by voluntary consent, or else imposed by way of punishment."[65] "In all things," Ames insists, "Children are more tenderly and favorably to bee used then [*sic*] servants."[66] Saffin uses a version of this argument to dispute Sewall's point that because all men are the sons of Adam, they have equal title to liberty. While Saffin affirms the premise that "all Mankind are the Sons and Daughters of *Adam*, and the Creatures of God," he denies Sewall's conclusion and says that Christians are "Exhorted *to do good unto all, but especially to them who are of the Household of Faith, Gal. 6.10*."[67] "I may love my Servant well, but my Son better," Saffin adds, drawing the threshold of God's household on the line between servants and sons. The two different kinds of love that a master of household has for children and servants signify two different kinds of authority, and masters obey God when they honor the difference. Saffin translates a master's disobedience of God's mandate to love servants and children differently into the social sphere as a faux pas, concluding that "it would be a violation of common prudence, and a breach of good manners, to treat a Prince like a Peasant."

Saffin felt that he, in fact, had been treated like a peasant. His poetic rendering of blacks as "the spume Issue of Ingratitude" connects his status as a master of African slaves with his status as a public servant. In his notebook, Saffin complained, "They that Rule in the Comonwealth are Expos'd to the Ingratitude of the people the [*sic*] Govern."[68] Such "Ingratitude" abides in "peoples hearts" across ranks, "from the Prince to the peasant." Saffin then offers a kind of natural history of "ingratitude" as "the most hatefull, and basest of all Vices, and the most opposite to Naturall Equity. None but men are capable of Ingrattitude its [*sic*] never found amongst bruit [brute] Beasts." Magistrates and masters share the burdens of governing prideful subjects. In this sense, at least, Saffin affirms that blacks are not "Beasts," though he would deem outrageous the notion that God might call them to "Rule in the Commonwealth."

Such rulers also racialized the offices in which free blacks could serve the commonwealth. Though his master and Boston magistrates agreed that he lacked the capacity to govern himself, once he was turned out of doors, Saffin's "unwilling servant" Adam would do his part to strengthen the commonwealth in the ways permitted to "Negroes." As Sewall mentions, militia service was restricted to whites. Blacks had been specifically included in the militia in 1652, but in 1656 Massachusetts reversed that policy, excluding Native Americans and "Negroes" from training.[69] A 1707 act barring "free Negroes" from militia training required them instead "to do service on the highways and in cleaning the streets, etc., as an equivalent."[70] Militia service is not equivalent to "service on the highways" as a form of public service. Free blacks were denied the same modes of "serviceability" as white servants, and their service was restricted to manual labor that would quite literally enable mobility for other New Englanders. The name "Adam Saffin" appears on a June 18, 1711, list of thirty-three "Free Negroes" required to work "faithfully & diligently" on "cleansing & Repairing the High wayes and other Services of this Towne."[71] Adam's legal freedom had been restored, but he continued to bear the name of the master who had schemed to deny it to him. Slavery redrew the boundaries of the household along racial lines, transforming public callings, private callings, and the types of legitimate obedience and authority that connected them.

Fathers of Children, Masters of Slaves

According to Mather, Sewall was guilty of the kind of "ingratitude" that Saffin grumbled about, and like Saffin, both Mather and Sewall associated that base trait with "Negroes." A series of entries in Sewall's diary from October 1701 describes a heated exchange between Sewall and Mather, who was incensed that Sewall had cast a vote that effectively ousted Increase Mather, Cotton's father, as president of Harvard.[72]

> October 20. Mr. Cotton Mather came to Mr. Wilkins's shop, and there talked very sharply against me as if I had used his father worse than a Neger; spake so loud that people in the street might hear him. Then went and told Sam, That one pleaded much for Negros, and he had used his father worse than a Negro. . . .
>
> October 9. I sent Mr. Increase Mather a Hanch of very good Venison; I hope in that I did not treat him as a Negro.
>
> October 22. 1701. I, with Major Walley and Capt. Saml Checkly, speak with Mr. Cotton Mather at Mr. Wilkins's. I expostulated with him from 1 Tim. 5.1. Rebuke not an elder. He said he had consider'd that: I told him of his book of the Law of Kindness for the Tongue, whether this were correspondent with that. Whether correspondent with Christ's Rule: He said, having spoken to me before there was not need to speak to me again; and so justified his reviling me behind my back. Charg'd the Council with Lying, Hypocrisy, Tricks, and I know not what all. . . .
>
> Thorsday October 23. Mr. Increase Mather said at Mr. Wilkins's, If I am a Servant of Jesus Christ, some great Judgment will fall on Capt. Sewall, or his family.[73]

Sewall casts this dispute between famous Puritan families in the household terms of racial vocation. The "Negro" racializes the callings of fathers and children, particularly when they turn themselves out of doors, moving between the public ("in the shop," "in the street," and in printed "pleading") and the private realms. The final diary entry turns the charge of hypocrisy back on Increase Mather (and, by association, Cotton Mather, who picked the fight), decrying his violation of the rule of "Kindness for the Tongue." It is presumably ungodly for "a Servant of Jesus Christ" to wish that a "great Judgment" would befall Sewall "or his family." Even in the Puritan vernacular, the "Negro" makes the callings of fathers, sons, and public "servants of Jesus Christ" a calling of whiteness.

This exchange captures how the "Negro" pressed Puritan families toward a modern model of voluntary filiation. The master of household who governs the family as a little commonwealth would become more emphatically a father to his children; a husband to his wife; an employer, employee, or public servant of white men; and a master of nonwhites. Cotton Mather's household governance instructions from the period show how ideological forms of master and servant emerged as racial slavery transformed familial callings. The traditional spiritual and earthly ideal of willing obedience embodied by the child who serves a master-father persisted. In *A Family Well Ordered*, Mather retains the premise "that our *Servants* are in some sort likewise our *Children*."[74] He even reassures childless men that they can fulfill their paternal obligations if they have servants: "A considerable part of what is to be done for our *Children*, I pray, *Masters*, Think . . . whether nothing of This may be done for your *Servants*."[75]

What makes servants and children socially and spiritually exchangeable both in themselves and as objects of labor for Puritan men is that both are distinguished from "Slaves." In working to "bring your *Children* to the Fear of God," Mather insists, "let not your *Authority* be strained with such *Harshness*, and *Fierceness*, as may discourage" them.[76] "To treat our *Children* like *Slaves*, and with such Rigour, that they shall always *Tremble* and *Abhor* to come into our presence, *This* will be very unlike to our *Heavenly Father*," he notes. Unlike the authority of the master of a slave, the father's authority "should be so Tempered with Kindness, and Meekness, and Loving Tenderness, that our Children may *Fear* us with *Delight*, and see that we *Love* them, with as much *Delight*."[77] Unlike "slaves" who "Tremble and Abhor," children and servants like them who learn to fear their fathers "with Delight" can serve God in their callings, to "know . . . the God of thy Father, and Serve Him with a perfect heart, and with a willing mind."[78] Slavery as distinguished from service thus creates a more affectionate model of parent-child relations, one that still insists on the father's authority to command his children's obedience but as a father, not as a master.

As godly heads of household, men necessarily serve the public, even if their business is confined to the family. Mather touts the governance of a "Well-regulated Family" as an "opportunity" to be almost "*Incomprehensibly* Serviceable."[79] Lisa Wilson observes that the concept of serviceableness defines the labor of adult men in colonial New England and connects it to vocation.[80] Mather's vocational tracts show how it emerges as an ideological form of mastery from the father-master and child-servant dialectic. But the traditional dialectic also kept men of business tethered to their role as household managers. In *A Christian at His Calling*, Mather appeals to men as master-fathers with spiritual obligations to their dependents: "While we are at the *Table*, and on other *Opportunities*, *All the Day Long*, we may watch to drop upon our *Children* and our *Servants*, those things that may be Highly Edifying unto them. . . . To *Do Good All the Day Long, is to Fear God All the Day long!*"[81] Alongside the traditional master-father, Mather presented the "master" strand of patriarchal authority in different guises. In *Youth under a Good Conduct*, Mather renders as "guidance" the aspect of paternal authority traditionally associated with mastery—the power to command obedience to the moral law: "Whenever they make sure of the Great GOD for their *Father*, from this Time, they will put themselves under the *Guidance* of such a Father. A *Father* is to be a *Guide* unto His Children; and it becomes them to refer themselves unto his *Guidance*."[82] Children must learn how to willingly accept a father's guidance as training in guiding themselves: "If *Young* Persons be not better *Guided*, than they can *Guide* themselves, they will never know that way."[83] This course in self-guidance is the domestic version of working under the fear of God in their callings, invoking the authority—but not the person—of a master to promote self-governance.

A White Master Well Served

A decade after *A Good Master Well Served* appeared, Mather published a tract dedicated entirely to the particular calling of mastery over black slaves. No less a vocational tract than *A Christian at his Calling*, *The Negro Christianized* "correlated moral obligation, providential order, spiritual felicity, commercial knowledge, and market profits," as Valeri put it; and one way it did so was by creating a kind of a master who need not think of himself as a father to his servants.[84] While *A Good Master Well Served* presumes that servants are children, *The Negro Chris-*

tianized singles out enslaved children as an exceptional type of enslaved person. "Sometimes *Negro-Children* are cast into our *Families*," Mather observes, lauding the "Christian *Master* or *Mistress*" who "will with all due Solemnity, Engage to bring up those Children in Christianity, and to do their best that they shall be the Servants of JESUS CHRIST" (NC 44). These children are "Negro" first and "Children" second, and the hyphen makes them the kind of children who have masters, not fathers. Mather hedges by suggesting that enslaved children are "cast into" families, as if by lot. He seeks to manage the moral and spiritual risks of men's determination to buy and sell human beings, while providing authority for men to think of themselves as masters of others' spiritual fates, not just their own.[85]

In the traditional covenant dialectic, masters are interchangeable with fathers, as servants are with children. Children who did not consent to serve their fathers, and masters who did not act as fathers to their servants, were hypocrites. In *The Negro Christianized*, the detachment of a master's authority over his slave from a father's authority over his child is not hypocrisy, but rather a new kind of calling, one aligned with a merchant's morality. "Pray, deal faithfully," Mather cautions. "Householder, art thou a *Christian*?" (NC 11). This was not a rhetorical question.

Mather sounds the conventional "Admonition" to masters, citing Ephesians 5:9 and urging them to "confess, That the God of Heaven is your *Master*" (NC 4), after which he immediately repeats the injunction (4–5). Those called to be Christian masters of "Negro" servants seem to need that double reminder, for such servants test a master's capacity not to succumb to tyranny: "If your *Negroes* do not comply with your *Commands*, into what Anger, what Language, Perhaps into a misbecoming *Fury*, are you transported?" (4). Mather sympathizes with the master's exasperation but nevertheless insists that masters "attend unto the *Commands* of your more Absolute *Master*; and they are His *Commands* concerning your *Negroes* too." Their callings oblige them to at least attempt to make slaves Christians: "You deny your *Master in Heaven*, if you do nothing to bring your *Servants* unto the Knowledge and Service of that glorious *Master*" (5). Masters of black slaves must redouble their efforts to resist the temptations of earthly tyranny and spiritual hypocrisy. "Christian" and "master" must be bound together in this calling, to spiritualize both the labors of particular Christian masters and the equation of Christianity with mastery.

"Things look very *Black* upon us," Mather laments, decrying the damnable effect of hypocritical masters on New England's economic vocation

(NC 17). Masters have "expected and exacted Revenues of profit" from the enslaved but have done little if anything "to save them from their Blindness and Baseness, and that the Great GOD might have Revenues of glory from them." "Alas, if you have not thought and car'd and *Watched for the Souls* of your Negroes, as *they that must give an Account*," Mather warns, "You will give up your *Account* with *Grief*." New England masters have even more obligation to "Watch" for the souls of the enslaved, given their residence in the spiritual metropole, exceptional among the slaveholding and slave-trading "*Skirts*, the outborders, the Colonies and Plantations of the *English nation*."

If slavery's threat of hypocrisy seemed ever more pressing, it also presented an even more powerful opportunity to reconcile service to God with earthly commerce. In the conclusion of *A Good Master Well Served*, Mather turns a master's obligation to pray with and for his servants into rhetoric that cements his bond of whiteness with masters. In *The Negro Christianized*, the master's obligation to be a praying master to his slaves is no in-joke but a required course in converting hypocrisy into vocation. A Christian "dost *Pray* for thy *Servants*, that they may become the *Servants* of the Lord Jesus Christ, and the *Children* of God. . . . What! *Pray* for this; and yet never *do* any thing for it! It is impossible, or, such *Praying*, is but *Mocking* of God?" (NC 12). This master who pays lip service to his slaves' salvation inverts the ideal of the praying master. Reprising his use of the master and monster near-rhyme from *A Good Master Well Served*, Mather drives home the distinction between a Christian master's calling and the lip service of a hypocrite: "Suppose that Language were heard from the mouth of a Master concerning a Servant; *If I can have the Labour of the Slave, that's all I care for: Let his Soul go and be damned, for all me!* would not every Christian say, This were Language for the Mouth of a *Devil*, rather than for the Mouth of a *Christian*! Would not every Christian cry out, *Let him not be call'd a Master, but a Monster that shall speak so*!" (NC 13). The voices of "every Christian" raised together to condemn the master-monster is the voice of a public speaking as the moral watch, with the power to "call" a master a monster.

Christian masters of slaves "do good" by training their servants for membership in God's household, not future parenthood or earthly employment. Mather offers a different reading than Saffin offered of Galatians 6:10, emphasizing not the "command" but the "*Opportunity*, to *Do Good* unto our *Servants*, who are of our *own Household*; certainly, we may do something to *make them Good*, and bring them to be of the *Household of Faith*" (NC 6). As in *A Good Master Well Served*, Mather's promise of spiritual childhood for "Negroes" spiritualizes white men's authority to deprive them of earthly liberty and economic justice. "Your *Negroes* are immediately Raised unto an astonishing Felicity, when you have *Christianized* them," he explains. "Though they remain your *Servants*, yet they are become the *Children* of God. Tho' they are to enjoy no *Earthly Goods*, but the small Allowance that your Justice and Bounty shall see proper for them, yet they are become the *Heirs* of God" (19). Masters should focus their labors on making slaves good children and servants of God, not on training them to become earthly parents or masters of household. In so doing, masters internalize not just God the Master but their own mastery, their earthly role as dispensers of "Justice and Bounty."

Mather blurs the master's agency to save his slaves with God's providential power of election: "How agreeable would it be, if a Religious Master or Mistress thus attended, would now think with themselves: *Who can but tell that this Poor Creature may belong to the Election of God! Who can tell, but that God may have sent this Poor Creature into my Hands, that so One of the Elect may by my means be Called*" (NC 3). In *A Good Master Well Served*, Mather tells black servants that God has called their "Black hands." Here, he tells masters that God has delivered slaves into their "Hands." When Mather grants that the master may have the "means" to enable his slaves to "be Called," he encourages him to own himself as a spiritual, not just an earthly, master.

A "Negro Christianized" is not the same as a Christian Negro. Admonishing masters to "Christianize" their slaves, Mather stresses the benefit of making them more obedient. Masters who "have instituted their *Servants* in Christian Piety, will even in this life have a sensible *Recompence*," he affirms (NC 20). The "more *Serviceable*, and Obedient and obliging Behaviour of their Servants unto them, will be a sensible & a notable *Recompence*" (20–21). The morality of minister and merchant align with that of the master.[86] Dismissing conversion as a ground for earthly liberty, Mather instead insists that instruction in Christian piety will make slaves more contented in their place. He reassures masters: "Were your *Servants* well tinged with the Spirit of *Christianity*, it would render them exceeding *Dutiful* unto their *Masters*, exceeding *Patient* under their *Masters*, exceeding faithful in their Business, and afraid of speaking or doing any thing that may justly displease you" (21). He depicts the "Spirit of Christianity" as a medium of moral obedience; those with callings work in the fear of God, but slaves will labor in the fear of their masters, "afraid of speaking or doing any thing that may justly displease" them.

Though Mather reminds masters that they have a Master in Heaven to keep them from acting like tyrants to their slaves, he also appeals to them as their own eye-masters. Masters can "see" that their slaves' "*Ungospelized Souls* are in danger of an Eternal *Banishment* from the *Favour* and the *City* of God" (NC 12) and can also "see how laboriously, how obsequiously your *Negros* apply themselves, to serve you, to content you, to enrich you" (13–14). Mather threatens masters who are not prompted by these sights to Christianize their slaves, gothicizing hypocrisy to instill the fear of God in them: "Neighbors, you have such a sight, in all your Negroes, as long as they are left a People of no understanding." He continues: "The uninstructed *Negroes* about your houses, appear like so many *Ghosts* and *Spectres*. You may, without being Fanciful, imagine that like so many Murdered *Ghosts*, they look very Ghastly upon you, and summon you to co-answer before the Tribunal of God, for suffering them to perish in their miserable Circumstances" (16). In the gothic version of eye-service, not just God but the slaves themselves act invisibly on their master's moral conscience. The souls of "uninstructed" slaves haunt Puritan houses like ghosts, threatening their masters with eternal damnation. The labor of "instructing" them should make them content to reside and labor permanently in their master's house.

These eternal children and permanent servants should become objects of spiritual labor for the white members of Puritan households, training them in their vocations. Masters of household "who cannot themselves *Personally* so well attend the *Instruction* of the *Negroes*, may employ and reward those that shall do it for them" (NC 28–29). Mather suggests that "*Children* may help the *Negroes*, to Learn the *Catechism*, or their well-instructed and well-disposed *English Servants* may do it: And they should be *Rewarded* by the *Masters* when they do it" (29). For "Children" and the "English Servants" who resemble them, the enslaved person in the house provides an opportunity to equate the reward of pleasing a master with earthly rewards, and to practice occupying the position of a master. The white English servant occupying the role of questioner in the catechism to an enslaved "Negro" epitomizes racial vocation. White children and English servants learn to internalize their mastery over blacks as their own capacity for self-governance.

The labor of Christianizing should not be entirely delegated to children and English servants. For adult men who are already masters, particularly those whose employments increasingly drew them away from their households, "Negroes" should keep them mindful of their obligations to the spiritual lives of their household dependents: "Tis fit for the *Master* also *Personally* to enquire into the progress which his *Negroes* make in *Christianity*, and not leave it *Entierly* [*sic*] to the management of others" (NC 29). The phrase echoes Mather's remark to black slaves in *A Good Master Well Served* that they are "better managed" by their masters than they would be if they were their "own men." These passages suggest how the particular calling of white men as masters of black slaves was homogenized into a concept of white "management" of racial others that emerged alongside models of affectionate fatherhood in which English servants counted as children.

The master's effort to "Christianize" black servants is a form of instrumental hypocrisy that spiritualizes the profit produced by slaves, whether or not they ever become the children and servants of the Lord. Like Sewall and Saffin, Mather offers a theory of innate racial inferiority that doubles as a discourse of vocation: "Indeed, their *Stupidity* is a *Discouragement*. It may seem, unto as little purpose, to *Teach*, as to *wash an Aethiopian*. But the greater their *Stupidity*, the greater must be our *Application*. If we can't learn them so much as we *Would*, let us learn them as much as we *Can*" (NC 25). Mather encourages white men to spiritualize their mastery over the bodies of others as a form of labor discipline: "the greater must be our *Application*." Whether or not it produces that elusive and paradoxical being, a black Christian slave, the master's labor shall not be unprofitable. Mather urges masters to "consider the incomparable *Benefits* that would follow upon your *Endeavours* to *Christianize* your *Negroes*, and bring them to a share with your selves in the *Benefits* of the Heavenly *Inheritance*" (18). The master's "care and cost about the cultivation of your *Negroes*" might "be laid out upon such a stony and Barren soul, that you can see no Fruit of it, yet it is not all thrown away." The "blessed God" is watching and "will approve and reward what you have done" (18–19). The labor of "Christianizing" African servants may or may not result in their salvation—only God knows if it will—but the effort spiritualizes the master's vocation and New England's economic vocation.

Mather's characterization of Onesimus, a runaway servant converted by Paul and returned to his master, exemplifies his version of racial vocation. "Onesimus" means "serviceable" or "useful," which Mather renders as "profitable" both here and in *A Good Master Well Served* (GM 9). Paul's experience with Onesimus should reassure masters "who use their *Negroes* with most of *Christianity*" that they "will find themselves no losers by it" (NC 22). Onesimus was not just a servant, Mather observes, but "doubtless a *Slave*," a "poor *Slave*, on whose behalf a great Apostle of God was more than a little concerned; yea, one Book in our Bible was

Written on his behalf!" Paul converted Onesimus and returned him to his master Philemon: "When he was *Christianized*, it was presently said unto his *Masters*, Philem. 11. *In time past he was unprofitable to thee, but now he will be profitable*." Mather equates "Negro servant" with "slave" and reads Onesimus not as born again but "Christianized." These adjustments make New England masters into both Paul and Philemon: agents of a servant's conversion and his masters. The slave's "profitability" becomes a kind of just wage for masters who can serve both God and mammon.

Mather bestowed the name Onesimus upon his own slave, purchased by "Some Gentlemen of our Church" for "between forty and fifty pounds" and "cast into" Mather's family by his congregation in December 1706. Mather's history with the Onesimus that God called to serve him also directs us not to read profitable service in narrowly economic terms. In his diary Mather vowed, "with the Help of the Lord, that I would use the best Endeavours to make him a Servant of Christ, and also be more serviceable than ever to a Flock, which laies me under such obligations."[87] Mather imagines that Onesimus will allow him to be a more profitable servant to his congregants. Though Mather's "Endeavours" never succeeded in converting his slave, Onesimus did help make his master more serviceable.[88] Mather famously promoted the use of a smallpox inoculation whose efficacy he trusted based on the eyewitness testimony of Onesimus, who had been vaccinated in Africa.[89]

Mather, Sewall, Saffin, and Knight helped develop new forms of serviceability from the master-servant relationship, including a concept of authorship rooted in the premise that the public was a white master. Technologies of print expanded access to this form of public moral and spiritual authority and created new markets for it. The profitability of the print medium was not lost on Mather. At the beginning of *A Good Master Well Served*, he explains that he was prompted to preach the sermon after considering "the many Complaints which Families in all places made, of their wanting such a *Blessing*" as a good servant, and he decided to publish it, "just as it was uttered unto my own Congregation," so "I might in this matter, be a *Servant* unto the Lord Jesus Christ, and the Souls of my Neighbors, both the *Bond* & the *Free*, in Him" (GM 2). Print allows Mather to extend his sphere of influence beyond his immediate congregation to a community of "Neighbors" that could include anyone with access to his book and the capacity to read or hear. Mather's publication of his instructions for masters and servants is profitable as service to God and a form of public mastery.

The next chapter examines how the private and public callings of racial vocation shaped Benjamin Franklin's and Samson Occom's conceptions of authorship and serviceability. A woman who was their peer in cultural fame, the revolutionary poet Phillis Wheatley, was called to answer back in print to New England's white eye-masters.[90] Wheatley's poetry served the public cause of abolishing slavery and exposing the presumptions of innate African inferiority and white mastery embedded in the very concept of publicity. In "On Being Brought from Africa to America," she evinces a keen eye and ear for public opinion as a form of public mastery:

> Some view our sable race with scornful eye
> "Their color is a diabolic dye."[91]

Saffin's final couplet ironizes the very concept of a black Christian, but Wheatley speaks with moral authority as a black Christian herself, exposing the hypocrisy of evangelicals who would equate dark skin with intractably black souls:

> Remember, *Christians, Negros* black as *Cain*
> May be refin'd and join th' angelic train.

Her master, John Wheatley, certainly claimed that she had been "improved in Service" to him and his family. After he turned her out of doors to live in the birthplace of the Sons of Liberty as a legally free woman, Phillis Wheatley was unable to support a family on her wages.

[5]

THE SPIRIT OF MASTERY: SAMSON OCCOM, BENJAMIN FRANKLIN, AND MODERN HYPOCRISY

IN A WELL-KNOWN passage from *The Protestant Ethic and the Spirit of Capitalism*, Max Weber quotes at length from conduct literature that he takes to exemplify the capitalist spirit "in almost classical purity."[1] A voice drones the aphorisms of this "peculiar ethic": "Remember, that *time* is money. . . . Remember this saying, *The good paymaster is lord of another man's purse*. . . . [N]ever keep borrowed money an hour beyond the time you promised. . . . He that wastes idly a groat's worth of his time per day, one day with another, wastes the privilege of using one hundred pounds each day." When Weber resumes, he wittily reveals, "It is Benjamin Franklin that preaches to us in these sentences." Weber chose Franklin to exhort the doctrines of bourgeois morality.

It is Cotton Mather who preaches to us in the sentences below, from his 1696 conduct manual, *A Good Master Well Served*:

> The first thing that you owe to your *Servants*, is, *Work*. Let them have *Work* to do, and let their *Work* be well done; countenance them not in *any Idleness*, whereof there comes *no Goodness*. This is the Demand of God, in Col. 4.1. *Masters, give unto your Servants, that which is just and equal. . . . Bread* they should have; and so much *Meat*, and so much *Drink*, as may be reasonably Esteemed, *Enough*. Our Lord has told us, *The Labourer is Worthy of it*.

> Let your *Diligence* in the *Service* of your *Masters (and Mistresses)* be such as to render you *Profitable* and *Acceptable* Servants. There are many *slothful* Servants; and *Servants*, that would willingly *Sleep* away, or *Talk* away, if not *Play* away, all their Time: Will you now see the Brand of such a *Servant*? You shall see it, in Mat. 25. 16 *Thou Wicked and Slothful Servant. We are told, Cursed will he be who does the Work of the Lord Negligently*;

> and I will venture to say, *He who does his Masters Work Negligently, shall not be Blessed.*
>
> I do Vehemently *Warn* every one of you, to take heed of *Wronging* your *Masters* unto the Value of a Penny as long as you live. Never Give to *Others*, Never Take to *Your selves*, of your *Masters* Goods, without their Leave, unto the Value of a Farthing. Mark what I say; By every Act of *Dishonesty* towards your *Masters*, you do but entail *Everlasting Disasters* upon your own *Affayrs*. Probably your own *Affayrs* will afterwards be so unsuccessful that you shall see, you have Impoverished your selves a *Pound*, by every *Shilling*, whereof you have Rob'd your *Masters* in such Pranks of *Dishonesty*. (GM 10, 13–14, 40–41, and 44)

Industry, frugality, honesty—the virtues Weber associated with "the spirit of capitalism" were forged in the master-servant lived metaphors of vocation.[2] What spiritualized the dutiful labor of the Protestant ethic was the understanding that the things of the world (time, wealth, the body, and everything that sustained it) belonged properly to God, and particularly to his form as Master. To waste time was to waste a master's time. To steal, lie, cheat, or even just fail to understand the value of a farthing was to waste a master's money. To consume or desire more than is "reasonably Esteemed, Enough" was to waste a master's goods. In secular vocation, the individual internalizes a servant's obligations to a master, and the obligations of both master and servant to God, as an economic conscience: the "duty of the individual toward the increase of his capital . . . assumed as an end in itself." In Franklin's "The Way to Wealth," Father Abraham invokes Poor Richard's wisdom: "If you were a Servant, would you not be ashamed that a good Master should catch you idle? Are you then your own Master, *be ashamed to catch yourself idle*, as Poor Dick says."[3] The "spirit of capitalism" is the spirit of self-mastery.

It is also, as I have been arguing, the spirit of white mastery. Ideologies of self-mastery emerged from the work of spiritualizing white Christian mastery over racial others, as Mather's conduct manuals did. The racialization of traditional master-servant lived metaphors of Christian labor accommodated and spiritualized practices that had been denounced as hypocrisy, attempts to serve both God and mammon. The central type of racial vocation was a white Christian master who could be different kinds of master to white servants, black slaves, and Native Americans, and yet another to himself. He took himself to be serving God in all of these roles, whether or not he deemed his servants capable of doing so. These multiple shades of master and servant indexed the transformation of hypocrisy—the spiritual peril of serving the self—into virtuous self-mastery, New England's modern vocation.

Charges of hypocrisy have, of course, long been leveled against Franklin and his doctrines.[4] To some observers, Franklin's personality is a series of masks, and his morality an inch deep. His most impassioned detractor, D. H. Lawrence, turned Franklin's ideologies of service and mastery against him to expose capitalism as a force of bondage, not liberation. The "grandsons of the Pilgrim Fathers" have reduced God to a "heavenly storekeeper," Lawrence wrote, "the supreme servant of men who want to get on, to *produce*."[5] Lawrence satirizes "Ben's" aphoristic style: "'Henceforth be masterless,' retorts Ben. 'Be ye each one his own master unto himself, and don't let even the Lord put His spoke in.' 'Each man his own master' is but a puffing up of masterlessness."[6] To Franklin, "I am nothing but a servant of mankind—galley-slave I call it," Lawrence retorts.[7] Extolling his own counterdoctrine, "'That my soul is a dark forest,'" he deems Franklin's version of freedom a "barbed wire enclosure" in which "the liberator, cracking his whip," shouts, "'*Work, you free jewel,* WORK!'"[8] "Benjamin, I will not work," Lawrence declares. "I do not choose to be a free democrat. I am absolutely a servant of my own Holy Ghost." Weber offers his own version of Lawrence's wire fence in his concluding image of secular asceticism as an "iron cage": "The Puritan wanted to work in a calling; we are forced to do so."[9]

A century and a half before Lawrence and Weber, the Mohegan public intellectual, pantribal leader, and New Light minister Samson Occom made a calling of exposing the hypocrisies of market morality. Unlike Weber and Lawrence, Occom also explicitly denounced it as racial hypocrisy: a concept of political, economic, and individual liberty that spiritualized white mastery over nonwhite servants and slaves.[10] Like Franklin, Occom has been deemed a hypocrite, criticized in his time "for being too Indian or not Indian enough" and in ours for being too Christian to be Indian enough.[11] Occom turned charges of racial hypocrisy back on his accusers. Throughout his public and private writings, he mounted a sustained critique of white English Christians who, in purporting to serve both God and mammon, neglected their obligations to their heavenly Master. In one sermon, he chides Christians who have ignored their primary duty, being "Truely thankful to god," by acting as their own spiritual merchants, "Set[ting] price upon the Benefits" God grants them.[12] Such ingratitude perverts created nature: "the very Dumb Beasts of the Field, they Manifest a kind of Gratitude to their Benefactors or Masters, by a Certain Noise, or the Motion of their Bodies"; even

"Toads and Frogs and all the Venomous Kind, have their way of giving thanks to their Ma[ster]" (SO 222). "If all these Creatures give thanks and Praise to God," Occom concludes, "how ought Man who is Endow'd to give . . . thanks and Praise to the God of Heaven." God endows man with grace and with reason to allow them to serve him and each other, not to devise ever-more-elaborate ways to spiritualize serving themselves and enslaving others.

In a letter to Occom in February 1774, Phillis Wheatley invoked the dominant discourse of hypocrisy associated with this period, decrying "the strange Absurdity of their Conduct whose Words and Actions are so diametrically opposite. How well the Cry for Liberty, and the reverse Disposition for the Exercise of oppressive Power over others agree,—I humbly think it does not require the Penetration of a Philosopher to determine."[13] But racial slavery also produced forms of modern hypocrisy that have not been visible as such: ideological forms of mastery that emerged from the spiritual type of the eye-servant, including ideals of public service and of self-mastery rooted in the master's vocation; and the calling of Indian servants of the Lord, no longer mere Praying Indians, yet paid barely a servant's wage by white missionaries. Occom and Franklin craft concepts of public service with a canny understanding of what it means, both legally and spiritually, to live under the eye of multiple masters.

This chapter juxtaposes their creative approaches to master-servant personhood to illuminate the literary and cultural history of modern vocation, both the dominant form that has been associated with Franklin and equally modern alternatives to it. Both men reject a central tenet of orthodox vocation: that God called man to labor contentedly in a servant's place and to find spiritual fulfillment by remaining there. To them, this ideal of vocation was itself hypocrisy, spiritualized injustice. To counter it, they promote and embody liberal and republican ideals of service that emerged from a culture of racialized bound labor, not the formally free labor that has long been the premise of accounts of New England's modernizing economic culture.[14] Their common grounding in Protestant discourses of vocation and hypocrisy also provides a foundation for a postsecular approach to this history. Whether in a celebratory or critical vein, both men have been read as instrumentalizing Christianity for worldly purposes, but such readings slight the dynamic relations between the temporal and the spiritual that shaped them and their world.[15]

The two men also understand the reading public as a master and authorship as a calling in which the power to command is diffused into multiple forms, including the power to serve. They employ irony as a form of virtuous hypocrisy, a way to say one thing and mean another as a moral good—which allows them to negotiate the dance of authority and willing submission in the author-reader relationship. For Franklin, irony is a way of aligning the interests and self-conception of his narrating self with those of a canny self-governing reader-citizen, of creating the impression of candor—a virtue shared by republican citizens and moral merchants. For Occom, irony is a strategy of virtuous resistance to the equation of mastery and public service.[16] Master-servant personhood did not just determine Occom's horizon of socioeconomic possibility; it also shaped his literary and political imagination as he struggled to expand that horizon, for himself and his native communities, beyond the jurisdiction of white mastery.

"That Which Is Just and Equal"

"Self-mastery" might seem to us synonymous with the moral independence and self-discipline of the liberal subject and "service" might appear to be a generic signifier of the republican citizen's disinterested labor, but for Franklin and Occom these ideologies remained attached to legal and scriptural master-servant personhood. Occom was never bound by contract to any master. Yet in his native southern New England, indentured servitude was so common for Native Americans that, by David Silverman's reckoning, "nearly all . . . were affected in some way" by it.[17] Given the pervasiveness of bound labor as an experience of native youth and Occom's dedication to educating them; his work reading and writing English legal documents for members of Native American communities; and, as I will discuss later, his effort to apprentice his own son, Aaron, it seems likely that he was very familiar with the mandates of indenture contracts (and perhaps had even served as a legal witness to them), and justifiably wary of how those terms could be exploited. So, from a different perspective, was Franklin, the "most famous American apprentice," as one historian has declared, and the quintessential apprentice made good.[18] He was also a master of white apprentices and enslaved Africans, and his approach to contracts as both a master and businessman was shaped by his experience as a servant with a keen awareness of how to exploit any loophole. Together, the free Occom and the bound Franklin exemplify the eighteenth-century world that David Waldstreicher has termed "runaway America," where "even those who never served or ran away were touched by the remarkable extremes of freedom and unfreedom that characterized the Atlantic littoral."[19]

Contracts of apprenticeship legislated the most intimate and routine aspects of daily life: during the term of service, food, lodging, clothing, sex, work, and leisure were domains of moral obligation between servant and master. Because these mandates were largely standardized across regions and over time, we can take the 1756 contract that bound Isaiah Thomas to the Boston printer Zachariah Fowle to be representative (indeed, by the time of Thomas's apprenticeship, Boston masters were using boilerplate printed contracts with blank spaces for names, dates, type of trade, and any bonus to be given upon completion of the term).[20] Thomas was to labor faithfully and obediently, to keep the "Secrets" of his master's trade, and abide by a host of "shall nots": "waste the Goods of his said Master . . . nor lend them unlawfully to any"; play "Cards, Dice, or any other unlawful Game or Games"; commit fornication or contract marriage; haunt or frequent "Taverns, Ale-Houses, or Places of Gaming"; or absent himself from the service of His Master "by Day or Night." Futhermore, "in all Things and at all Times, he shall carry and behave him self towards his said Master &c. and all theirs as a good and faithful Apprentice ought to do to his utmost ability during all the time or term aforesaid." Fowle, the master, was also bound by the contract. In addition to teaching Thomas the "art and mystery" of the trade and also how to "read, write and Cypher," he "shall and will, well and truly find, allow unto, and provide for the said Apprentice sufficient and wholesome Meat and Drink, with washing, Lodging, and Apparrall and other Necesaries meet and convenient for such an Apprentice, during all the Time or Term aforesaid." At the end of the term, Fowle was to provide Thomas with "two good suits of apparrell for all parts of his Body one for the Lords days the other for working days Suitable to his Degree."[21] Although Thomas's did not, some contracts also stipulated wages.

Although these contracts did not explicitly refer to religious education, their mandates were rooted in the shared concepts of master-servant personhood in scripture and English common law. Their guidelines closely follow those of Puritan master-servant conduct manuals, with the civil law taking the place of God the Master as moral authority.[22] A particular scripture provided the spiritual foundation for these contractual terms: "Masters, give unto your servants that which is just and equal; knowing that ye also have a Master in heaven" (Colossians 4:1). Mather's exegesis in *A Good Master Well Served* instructs masters that as God provides his servants with all they need to serve him faithfully, so masters should fulfill their obligations to their earthly servants: "Let them not want their *Food*, nor any of that *Physick*, or that *Cloathing*" (GM 13). The meaning of "what is just and equal" is quantities of "*Bread*" and "*Meat*" and "*Drink*, as may be reasonably Esteemed, *Enough*" (14); medical care when servants are ill, for the "Neglect of them *in* their Sickness, will be a sort of *Murder*, in the Account of God" (14); moderate corporal punishment, which involves being "a *Master*, . . . not a *Tyrant*: Let not your *Servants* have their *Lives* Embittered, their *Healths* Impaired, their *Bodies* Macerated, by your Tyranny" (12); and contractual wages, since "it will be a *Crying Sin* to Withold those *Wages*"(15). Spiritually, tyranny is hypocrisy: a master's failure to treat a servant as his heavenly Master treats him. In a hierarchical society, justice and equality constitute a doctrine of virtuous mastery. Good masters exhibit their self-mastery by not acting as tyrants to their servants.

Servants can also demonstrate self-mastery by regulating their bodies and spirits to conform to the will of their masters. They should be sure to govern their tongues: "*Servants* that will speak *Nothing*, when modest *Answers* are Expected from them, and *Servants* that will speak *Too much* with a malapert *Answering again*, giving it may be, Two Words for One . . . these are too *Irregular Things* to be Endured!" (GM 38). Indeed, servants should hold their tongues even before masters whose wages may not be "just and equal": "*John* said unto *Servants*, *Be content with your Wages*; and *Paul* said, unto the Servants of the Lord Jesus Christ; *Be content with such things as you have*. Whatever may be your *Portion* here, prove your *Godliness*, by your *Contentment* with your *Portion*. If your Carnal Appetites are not in all things gratified, Meditate, *Servants must not be Choosers; My Glorious Master, sees it not fit for me to have these Little Things; and why should I murmur*?" (29). A servant's "Contentment with [his] Portion" exemplifies asceticism, a tenet of secular and spiritual vocation. Of course, Mather also deems it a master's prerogative to determine what counts as "enough," which "Carnal Appetites" are immoderate, and what needs are only "Little Things." Servants must keep themselves from murmuring when they think they might be better fit to tell the difference.

As I discussed in the previous chapter, Mather's manuals racialized these mandates, pressing them toward their secularized contractual forms —which also seem to encode racial distinctions. Margaret Ellen Newell's survey of Rhode Island contracts suggests that Native American apprenticeships were de facto indenture contracts that "more commonly omitted the masters' obligations for food, clothing, and education and instead focused on the apprentice's duties and limitations," and that also less often included "freedom dues."[23] At least some Massachusetts contracts did include these provisions for Indian apprentices; but regardless of the apprentice's race, contracts could be subject to dispute if either party violated them.[24] Whether or not they successfully fulfilled these daily obligations to each other, masters and servants formed each other's economic consciences, for their duties to each other also constituted a material code of civic obedience and authority, the lived experience of abstract moral principles like justice, equality, liberty, and tyranny.

These ideals translate into a discourse of public morality in the concept of serviceability, the concept of shunning self-interest to do good for others that encompasses Christian vocation and republican virtue. Vocation defines the other as a master: an earthly master and God the Master. Republican disinterestedness defines the other as the public. Mather helps us see how master-servant personhood defined serviceability, seeing it as the primary virtue that servants should learn in their callings—whether they serve an earthly master, God, or the public.[25] Mather urges servants to "*Contrive* continually, how you may be *Serviceable* unto the Lord Jesus Christ; and how you may do *Service* for Him, with all that you *are*, & all that you *have*, and all that you *can* do; *and Glorifie him with your Spirits and your Bodies, which are the Lords*" (GM 29). Servants learn how to be serviceable to God by cultivating serviceability to their earthly masters: "Let it be your Study to be *Serviceable* unto your *Masters* (and *Mistresses*) Really, Thoroughly, Universally *Serviceable*. . . . [Do] all the *Friendly Offices* that you can possibly do for your Masters, in all their *Many Interests*" (45). By instructing servants to "Study" how to be serviceable to their masters, he encourages them to cultivate the virtue of putting another's good above their own.

In *Bonifacius*, a tract Mather published in 1710 that Franklin explicitly cites as an influence in his *Autobiography*, serviceability emerges from master-servant personhood as an ideology of mastery, transferring the power to command from the household to the state in the form of public service. What it means for men to do good by serving others is to act as good masters to them, and the liberty to do so derives from the ability to be a good master to themselves. The first Boston edition of the tract was published with an appendix titled "Concerning the Essays that are made, for the Propagation of Religion among the Indians, in the Massachusetts Province of New England."[26] Mather touts the fact that Indian churches "have *pastors* and *elders* of their own; ordained, sometimes by the hands of *English* ministers; and sometimes by the hands of the *Indian* ministers, in the presence of the English; all after the solemn English manner."[27] Christian natives had the capacity to do good and serve God, but only "by the hands" and "in the presence" of Englishmen. Yet some made it difficult for Englishmen to do good. "There has been *something done* to *Christianize* the *Mohegans*, and other Indians, in the Colony of *Connecticut*; but *Lord, who has believed*!" Mather exclaims. "They have been obstinate in their paganism; however their obstinacy has not put an end unto our endeavours."[28]

Occom, a Connecticut Mohegan, and Franklin both understood the public as a domain of white mastery. As Christopher Tomlins has observed, the American republic "was founded as a property-based democracy by and for household masters."[29] Public debates about the legality and morality of African slavery invested the public with the authority of white mastery, even for those who opposed slavery and did not own slaves. Runaway slave advertisements, in newspapers like Franklin's, extended the public authority of mastery through an intercolonial, and later national, print public sphere.[30]

Franklin scholarship has treated the public as a secular form of the eye of God, but not the eye of a master in particular. Mitchell Robert Breitwieser argues that the "displacement from the eye of God to the eye of the community" is a key vector of the transition from Mather to Franklin, noting that this displacement was "already at work in Mather's thought" but that for Franklin, "the thought of the omniscient eye was a manufactured construct useful, perhaps, for those who lacked rational interior government, but obstructive for those who have it."[31] Michael Warner observes that in republican print culture, "social authority . . . is located not in the virtuous citizen nor in God nor in the king, but in the light of day, in the supervision of publicity itself. Thus print—not speech—is the ideal and idealized guardian of civic liberty."[32] Likening print to a "guardian of civic liberty" charged with the "supervision of publicity," Warner suggests that print is invested with the authority of mastery—both the master's eye and his command over his servant's speech.

Breitwieser's and Warner's arguments about Franklin's modernity also provide a context for Occom's economic personhood. In racial vocation, concepts like the "omniscient eye" and "those who lacked rational interior government"—and those who suppose themselves to have it—were embodied as white masters and black and Indian servants. In her discussion of the projects of white missionary schools like Eleazar Wheelock's Moor's Indian Charity School, Hilary Wyss observes that they were grounded on the premise "that the English must control and supervise Indians at all times, even the Indian missionaries and teachers his school produced."[33] For Wheelock and his peers, as well as their pupils, the meaning and forms of "control and supervise" derived from the callings of Christian masters and servants. Young native men training to serve the Lord and their native communities were, like legal servants, meant to internalize white men's mastery over them. Wheelock's son Ralph would make this logic explicit, chiding one missionary that his Native American mentor was no father: "He is no more than my father's servant, as so are all those ministers and schoolmasters he sends here."[34] By training their pupils to serve two masters, men like Eleazar Wheelock made the office of the Indian missionary into a secular vocation. But men like Occom made use of their servants' places to forge their own callings.

Servants and Sons

Though Occom was never legally bound, the pervasiveness of indentured service as an experience for native children forged his experience of economic injustice and racial hypocrisy. He explicitly likened his relationship to white authority—particularly but not exclusively that of his teacher, mentor, and fictive father, Eleazar Wheelock—to servitude. Scholars have followed his lead, describing the relationship of Occom and other pupils to Wheelock through metaphors of master and servant.[35] They have also illuminated Occom's critique of market morality, showing how he draws from both New Light antimaterialism and Native American cultures.[36] Yet New England's culture of racialized servitude has not been treated as the context for Occom's self-making or his sustained critique of white economic culture.

In his 1768 "A Short Narrative of My Life," Occom makes fairly quick work of the overtly spiritual elements of his conversion to Christianity, reporting that at age seventeen, he "found Serenity and Pleasure of Soul, in Serving god" (SO 54). He immediately turns to his longing to make service to his "poor Kindred" his particular calling, and his awareness that literacy is essential to that calling: he must be able to "read the Word of god" to "Instruct poor Children in Reading." Wheelock, a Congregationalist minister, was educating "a Number of English youth" in nearby Lebanon, Connecticut, and Occom felt a "great Inclination to . . . be with him for a week or a Fortnight." His mother, Sarah, helps him fulfill this desire, asking if Wheelock would "Instruct me in Readings." The minister, Occom reports, "received me With kindness and Compassion," and his stay in Lebanon extended from a few weeks to four years.

Occom deliberately presents his voluntary enrollment at Wheelock's school and his mother's willing disposal of her son to a white male guardian who would teach him to read as a counternarrative to the fate of so many native children in southern New England: being bound out as a servant to a white master. Because indenture contracts usually stipulated that masters must instruct their servants in Christianity and the English language, many eighteenth-century Native American children learned Christian precepts and English after they had been bound out, often because their parents had fallen into debt to white creditors.[37] The English encroached on native land and traditional lifeways, compelling them to buy food on credit that they would in the past have grown or hunted themselves. Native Americans who could not pay their debts to English merchants would be sued and bound out—or would bind their children out—to make restitution for the debt.[38] Silverman suggests that "by frugally managing their scant resources," some New England natives avoided becoming enmeshed in this "cycle of debt and indenture."[39]

This context illuminates Occom's depiction of his family's "Heathenism," their ability to "[depend] upon Hunting Fishing & Fowling for their Living" and resist commerce with the English except for "Small Trifles" (SO 52). As his parents, Sarah and Joshua Occom, would have known all too well, parents compelled to traffic with whites for the necessities of life made themselves and their children vulnerable to forced bondage. Samson Occom does not sentimentalize the poverty of his childhood, yet what he calls his parents' "heathenism"—their adherence to a Mohegan tradition of subsistence—testifies to their ability to elude that cycle. From this perspective, his parents embody a modern native asceticism rooted in their awareness that debt was, as Franklin would later put it, a "Species of Slavery" (BF 90).

To Occom, the creditor-debtor relationship was both legally and spiritually a master-servant relationship. Spiritual discourses of redemption defined freedom as liberty from Adam's debt of slavery to Satan and sin, and that freedom had been paid for by Christ's sacrifice—the price of redemption—which granted man the ability to serve God. Occom's parents kept him legally free to pursue a life of service. Yet his lifelong formal freedom could not protect him from the jurisdiction of white mastery. Wheelock may not have been Occom's legal master, but he was his creditor. Occom wondered whether the amount of his debt equaled the difference between what he was paid for his services and a just wage, to a farthing.

In his preface to "A Short Narrative of My Life," Occom explains that he felt compelled to write it to "do Justice to my Self" (SO 52). In Joanna Brooks's account, he wrote as a "defense against what had stretched into an almost five-year period of public scrutiny and disputation of his character."[40] Partly to resist the privileging of the "Short Narrative" in scholarly and classroom approaches to Occom, Brooks cautions against reading it "as a voluntary or creative record of his personhood," framing it instead as "an attempt to intervene decisively in the growing body of discourse about his identity and reputation," including his role in the Mason Land Case, the Mohegan tribe's legal battle to reclaim its land from the Connecticut government.[41] Occom accomplishes both ends, and the lived metaphors of hypocrisy and vocation provide material for both his "creative record of his personhood" and his rejoinder to his critics: his model of "do[ing] Justice" to himself and others, particularly native boys.

Discourses of racialized service shape Occom's account of his vulnerability to economic injustice, perpetuated by Wheelock and missionary institutions more broadly. He depicts the missionaries as masters who have violated the obligations of Christian mastery, turning the presumptions of white mastery against his guardians and supervisors. If they expect Native Americans to be their servants, he asks, should they not at least fulfill the obligations of Christian masters?

Occom governs his tongue in his account of his four years as Wheelock's pupil, using strategic silence to allude to Wheelock's neglect of his obligations. Occom provides no concrete details about how Wheelock actually educated him. Instead, he depicts Wheelock publicizing his "Intentions of Educating" Occom and his "Circumstances" to others: "good People" who provide "Some old and Some New Cloaths" and the Boston Commissioners of the Society for Propagating the Gospel, who "allowed him 60£ in old Tenor, which was about 6£ Sterling, and they Continu'd it 2 or 3: years, I Cant tell exactly" (SO 54). Occom's ability to calculate precisely the exchange rate between old tender and sterling, combined with his vagueness about the length of this support, creates irony in this passage, a sense that he knows more than he says about Wheelock's hypocrisy.

Occom does not directly criticize Wheelock for failing to direct these resources to his vocational training, but what he does say is perhaps even more damning: "While I was at Mr. Wheelocks, I was very Weakly and my Health much Empard, and at the End of 4 Years, I over Straind my Eyes to Degree, I Coud not persue my Studies any Longer; and out off these 4 years I Lost Just about one year;—And was obligd to quit my Studies" (SO 54). Occom's impaired health and strained eyesight testify to his diligence as well as bodily weakness, but they also suggest Wheelock's neglect of his servant in sickness. After Occom is "obliged to quit," he finds employment as a teacher among the Montaukett on Long Island. In contrast to his experience with Wheelock, Occom describes the terms of his employment with the Montaukett as just and equal: "I agreed to keep a School with them Half a Year, and left it with them to give me what they Pleasd; and they took turns to Provide Food for me" (55).

Occom's method of educating Montaukett boys offers a model of authority that counters Wheelock's premise of teachers as white masters and supervisors. Occom pointedly contrasts his own method of educating Native Americans to that of Jonathan Barber, the white minister he encountered when he was ten years old: "there was a man who went about among the Indian Wigwams, and where ever he Coud find the Indian Children, woud make them read—but the Children Usd to take Care to keep out of his way;—and he Us'd to Catch me Some times and make me Say over my Letters; and I believe I learnt Some of them" (SO 53). Occom's description—"he Us'd to Catch me"—likens Barber's methods to forced bondage, a way to instill the rote legalism suggested by "mak[ing] me Say over my Letters" and obedience to a white man's authority.

Occom contrasts this coercive method with his own playful method of teaching literacy to Native American children. He tailors his approach to "Some Children, who were Some what Dull," whose "Eyes can't Distinguish the Letters," (SO 56) by gluing letters on cedar chips and putting them in order on a bench. Then, he explains, "I order the Child to fetch me the Letter from ye Bench if it Brings the Letter, it is well, if not it must go again and again till he brings ye right Letter. When they Can bring any Letters, this way, then I Just Jumble them together, and bid them to Set them in Alphabetical order, and it is a Pleasure to them; and they soon Learn their Letters this way." Like all pupils, Occom's students are learning obedience along with literacy, as he "order[s] the Child to fetch" the letter and "bid[s]" them to set the letters "in Alphabetical order." But he teaches them the "Pleasure" of willingly obeying authority that is not embodied by a white man, "jumbling" the equation of whiteness with mastery that defined education and literacy.

This scrambling of a white master's authority to command as schoolmaster also defines Occom's method in what he calls "Religious matters" (SO 56). He notes that the departure of his predecessor, Azariah Horton, coincided with "a remarkable revival of religion among these Indians and many were hopefully converted to the Saving knowledge of God" by Occom, whose intimate knowledge of "the Dispositions of the Indians" leads him to take "a mild way to reclaim them." He describes his methods: "I opposd them not openly" but waited for "an opportunity" to "read Such passages of the Scriptures, as I thought woud confound their Notions." Then, he continues, "I woud come to them with all Authority, Saying, thus Saith the Lord, and by this means, the Lord was pleased to Bless my poor Endeavours, and they were reclaimd." His "mild way" spiritualizes his vocation as a native preacher, as resistance both to the methods of the white minister and to the equation of authority with mastery or ownership over those he converts.

After marrying one of his students, Mary Fowler, and starting his own family, Occom asks Wheelock for support, noting that the "Commissioners were so good as to grant £15 per An. Sterling" (SO 55). Yet Occom immediately raises the question of whether this or any charitable "grant" fulfills a good master's mandate to provide just wages. Lamenting what Reginald Dyck calls systematic "wage theft,"[42] Occom seems to accuse the commissioners of what Mather denounced as a "crying sin" (GM 15). "I kept on in my Service as usual, Yea I had additional Service," Occom reports. "I kept School as I did before and Caried on the Religious Meetings as often as ever, and attended the Sick and their Funerals, and did what Writings they wanted, and often Sat as a Judge"—the sentence can barely contain all of his labor—"And was fetchd often from my Tribe and from others to see into their Affairs Both Religious [and] Temporal,—Besides my Domestick Concerns" (SO 55). In his calling, Occom is not his own master but has multiple masters, providing "Service" and "additional Service" for his brethren in their "Affairs Both Religious, Temporal." He works for love, not for earthly or heavenly rewards, yet this is not exactly the vaunted asceticism of the work ethic.

Occom's bleak description of the poverty of his adulthood adds the element of dependency on a white economy to the poverty of his childhood. He carefully accounts for the labor and costs of maintaining his household: "I got my Ground Plow'd every year, which Cost me about 12 S[hillings] an acre; and I kept a Cow and a Horse, for which I paid 21 S every year York currency, and went 18 Miles to Mill for every Dust of Meal we Usd in my family" (SO 57). "I planted my own Corn, Potatoes, and Beans," hoeing the corn before and after teaching, and he "was alowed to keep 5 Swine." He fished, hunted fowl, and paid for his "Powder & Shott with Feathers." He rebound old books and made pails, churns, ladles, and spoons. He had miserable luck with horses: the loss of five of them increased his debts. In these dire straits, Occom appeals for help to friends who ask the Commissioners for 15 pounds, but as one informs him, they "blamed [him] for being Extravagant."

These missionary societies and their commissioners racialize what counts as a just wage. "I Cant Conceive how these gentlemen would have me Live," Occom reports. "I believe it can be provd to the world, that these Same Gentlemen, gave a young Missionary, a Single man, *one Hundred Pounds* for one year, and fifty Pounds for an Interpreter, and thirty Pounds for an Introducer; so it Cost them one Hundred & Eighty Pounds in one Single Year" (SO 57–58). This inequity was not just prejudice toward Occom, but policy. Wheelock touted as a benefit of his model the fact that "an Indian Missionary may be supported with less than half the Expense, that will be necessary to support an Englishman."[43] The economic culture of Occom's New England was founded on racialized types of master and servant, both earthly and spiritual. These forms of personhood provided the contractual basis of ministerial employment. Apparently working without a contract, Occom found that the logic of racialized servitude defined his calling to serve the Lord.

The narrative's conclusion locates Occom's vocation within the cycle of debt and servitude that New England whites imposed on natives. He appeals to the public's sense of justice: "See what difference they made between me and other Missionaries; they gave me 180 Pounds for 12 years Service, which they gave for one years Service in another Mission" (SO 58). He humbly asserts the value of his labors in teaching the English tongue: "In my Service (I speak like a fool, but I am Constraind) I was my own Interpreter. I was both a School master, and Minister to the Indians, yea I was their Ear, Eye & Hand, as Well [as] Mouth." He appeals to the "World, as wicked as it is, to Judge whether I ought not to have had half as much, they gave a young man Just mentiond which would have been but £50 a year." If the commissioners "ought to have given me that, I am not under obligations to them, I owe them nothing at all; what can be the Reason?" Occom's rhetorical question targets racial inferiority as a discourse of instrumental reason, for only the logic of racial vocation accounts for the differential wages paid for Occom's services and those of the "young man." By Occom's careful reckoning, he is no debtor: "I owe them nothing at all." Occom refuses to spiritualize the fact that he serves for unjust wages. To him, all mastery except God's is tyranny.

Occom responds to his rhetorical question with a parable of master and servant adapted to a culture of racial vocation: "I Cant think of any thing, but this as a Poor Indian Boy Said, Who was Bound out to an English Family, and he Usd to Drive [a] Plow for a young man, and he Whipt and Beat him allmost every Day, and the young man found fault with him, and Complaind of him to his master, and the poor Boy was Calld to answere for himself before his master" (SO 58). "Called" by earthly masters to answer why "he was So Complained of and beat almost every Day," the boy replies, "he did not know, but he Supposd it was because he could not drive any better; but says he, I Drive as well as I know how; and at other Times he Beats me, because he is mind to beat me, but Says he, I believe he Beats me for most of the Time, because I am an Indian."

Like Occom, the child understands and articulates the reason very clearly: white men violate God's command to masters, "Let not your Servants have their *Lives* Embittered, their *Healths* Impaired, their *Bodies* Macerated, by your Tyranny" (GM 12). Occom's "Indian Boy" is not a child, in the same sense as the "Negro-children" (NC 44) in Mather's 1706 tract are not children: they have masters instead of fathers. In a 1788 letter to Philadelphia Quakers, Occom expressed gratitude to "the Little Masters who have Collected for our Little Boys in the Wilderness" (SO 129). In a culture of racialized service, "boy" does not just signify a male child who will develop into an adult but a child who, if he is English, can develop into a master who has "boys"—as Franklin did.[44] If the "boy" is a child of color, he was most likely being trained to remain a "boy"—a man meant, like Occom, to obey white mastery, whether or not he is legally free. Both the "Indian Boy" and Occom serve white masters who violate principles of Christian mastery.

In the parable's turn, Occom makes himself into the bound-out child he never was, merging the Indian servant of the Lord with the Indian boy servant: "So I am ready to Say, they have used me thus, because I Cant Instruct the Indians so well as other missionaries, but I can asure *them* I have endeavourd to teach them as well as I how—but I must Say, I believe it is because I am [a] poor Indian. I Can't help that God has made me So; I did not make my self So" (SO 58). Occom has been called to serve his people, to "endeavor to teach them as well as I know how," but he finds that men have "made" him a servant. Occom's "poor Indian" plays with the hypocrisy of racialized mastery and its relation to modernity. The "Poor Indian Boy" and the "poor Indian" are servants whose masters have forgotten their Master in heaven. Occom depicts Wheelock and the commissioners as masters who steal from their servant and thereby cheat God of Occom's services—and those of his people who will remain unconverted because of Occom's poverty.

"Your ~~Humble~~ Worthless Servant"

Racialized exchanges between sonship and servitude, and fatherhood and mastery, also circulate in Occom and Wheelock's correspondence. Wheelock expected his pupils to "call themselves his 'sons,'" but Occom "also acceded to the deferential epistolary conventions of the time," which included signing letters as the recipient's servant.[45] Occom's self-consciousness about these closings reveal how charged these conventions were and provide poignant evidence of the lived experience of racial vocation.

In four extant letters to Wheelock that Occom wrote on missionary travels between January 1760 and May 1762, Occom variously signs himself "your unworthy Servant," "*Your Most Obedient Indian Son*," "*Your Indian Son*," and "with Sincere obediance . . . from your true tho' unworthy Servant" (SO 66–69). The content of the letters themselves provide no clear evidence of the emotions, motives, moods, or situations that prompted his choice of particular closings—why he positioned himself as Wheelock's "Indian Son" or his "unworthy Servant," or why he chose "true tho' unworthy Servant" instead of "humble Servant"—but the variations are meaningful in themselves.

Scholars have illuminated the significance of the fictive social relations expressed by these epistolary conventions, but they also signified spiritual relations.[46] When Occom distinguishes between the obedience of sons and that of servants, he alludes to the covenant dialectic in which a child's willingness to serve his Father was evangelical obedience, while a servant's labors were legal or moral obedience, and thus mere hypocrisy.[47] Whether addressing Wheelock as a father or a master, Occom was meant to internalize mastery: "Indian Son" would signify a child's willingness to serve his father, while versions of "servant" would insist that Wheelock was, in a spiritual as well as social sense, no father to Occom. By signing himself as Wheelock's servant, then, Occom charges him with hypocrisy.

Occom closes all extant letters written after 1764 as a "servant," though with some meaningful variations, thus entwining his dependency on Wheelock with his growing critique of Wheelock's economic morality. Occom closes a February 1764 letter to Wheelock arranging a meeting with George Whitefield, "This, with sincere service is in utmost haste, from your ~~humble~~ worthless servant" (SO 70). While the closing is not in Occom's hand, the decision to substitute "worthless" for "humble" likely reflects his intent: that summer, he penned a letter with the same closing, "With Sincere Service I Subscribe your worthless Servant" (72). Unlike the more conventional "humble servant," "worthless servant" functions both as a conventional expression of deference and as a critique of white power to determine the "worth"—and economic value—of Native Americans and their labor. In both closings Occom separates his "sincere service," a phrase suggesting the willing obedience of vocation, from the degraded social position of "worthless Servant." Perhaps he no longer wished to consider himself Wheelock's "Indian Son" or perhaps, unlike the prodigal son, he realized that his "father" was content to employ him as a hired servant.

Occom's missionary travels created additional hardships for his family, and he appealed to Wheelock to honor his promise to help Mary keep home and family together in Occom's absence. In an August 1764 letter, he notes his determination to persist in a mission despite the lack of financial support, "tho' no White Missionary wou'd go in Such Circumstances" (SO 72). Occom was building a house for his family at Mohegan, and he trusted Wheelock to pay for its construction as he had said he would. "I leave my House and other Business to be done upon your Credit," Occom says, including the hiring of "Hands" to be paid "at any Marchents who will except [accept] and trust to your obligation," a phrase that suggests that Wheelock's own credit might have been extended. He also appeals to Wheelock to provide what is just and equal, describing his family's need of "Cloathing" and "provission" and reporting, "I have lately heard there is Salt meat enough at the Landing to be Sold" (72–73). "In a word," he concludes, "I leave my Poor Wife and Children at your feet and if they hunger starve and die let them Die there" (73). Occom closes the letter "with Sincere Obedience" from "Your Good for Nothing Indian Sarvant." Michael Elliott reads Occom's rhetorical "posture of servitude" as part of his larger economic critique, describing Occom's closing as a "parodic flourish" that is nevertheless "at some level true."[48] The corresponding posture of Wheelock as a master is also "true," both spiritually and socially, to Occom's denunciation of economic injustice. In effect, the letter translates Wheelock's oral promises into an informal written contract, ratified with humility and a reminder that their common Master in heaven has witnessed it.

David Murray reads these closings as exemplifying Occom's irony: "when this humility is accompanied by a sense of grievance, as it quite often is in the case of Samson Occom, the same gesture of abasement can carry a sting in the tail."[49] But it is harder to read a "sting in the tail" in a letter written the following fall that was signed "your Unworthy Servant" (SO 73). Wheelock was a master of African slaves, and Occom asked to "borrow" one of Wheelock's "Negroes and a Yoke of oxen," pleading that "my Business is Crouding, and I want to dispatch it as fast as I can,—pray let me have a yoke of oxen, if you cant Spare a Negroe." Occom would later preach abolition and advocate policies that excluded Afro-Natives from pantribal communities.[50] In all these positions, Occom embodies the complexity of racial hypocrisy. He likely sought to avoid incurring additional debt to pay wage laborers. Wheelock's "Negroe" and oxen represented a kind of free labor to Occom, a way to borrow his mastery instead of borrowing against his credit to enable his "Business"—which was, like Franklin's, continually "Crouding."

Occom's parents protected him from servitude, but Samson and Mary asked for Wheelock's help in binding out their own "Wild Son" (SO 79) Aaron. In April 1766, Wheelock wrote to Occom in London. Addressing him as "My dear Son Occom," he reproached Occom for pride, chiding him by saying, "I hope God has made you more humble than you have commonly been—and if So he will exalt & lift you up."[51] Perhaps to humble his "Son," Wheelock critiques Occom's performance as a father, reporting Joshua Occom's assessment that his grandson Aaron "is not a good Boy, runs abroad and [is] not so Obedient to his Mother as he should be. I advised to put him out to a good Master, and Supply her Some other way." Aaron's disobedience might also have been charged to Wheelock; the Occoms had sent him to the Moor's Indian Charity School at the age of seven, but he left after a year. Wheelock proposed that Mary Fowler Occom bind out her son to a "good Master" to make him more "obedient," acknowledging that the labor the thirteen-year-old provided his own kin would need to be "supplied some other way"—by hired labor that Occom could not afford, and that would be charged against his account with Wheelock (Aaron's sonship, however vexed, could not, of course, be supplied by alternative means).

Occom's poignant response laments the damage his calling did to his family, particularly his neglect of his children: "Whilest I am a Teacher to others, I have neglected my own Children . . . and now my Children are growing up, and are growing Wild; and the Devil has been Angry . . . and if he can, he will Drag all my Children into all Manner Sins and Down to Hell" (SO 79). Occom responds favorably to Wheelock's advice to bind out Aaron, writing, "I am Glad, and am thankful that you have taken my Wild Son, if you Can make any thing of him, I shall be happy in him." If Aaron takes after his father and "Inclines to Book Learning," Occom directs Wheelock, "give him [a] Good English Education, but if not let him go to some Good Master, to Learn Joiners Trade, he Inclines to that." He specifies that Aaron not be disposed of to just any master, but to a "Good" one who will allow him to follow his inclinations. "If that won't do," Occom directs Wheelock, "Send him over to me, and I will give him a Way to Some gentleman here." Aaron did not go to some "Good Master." After writing to Occom but before receiving his response, Wheelock and Mary reenrolled Aaron in the school, but he ran away to sea. He returned to Mohegan and married in 1771, at the age of eighteen. He died in the same year, leaving a son, also named Aaron.

Dead Services: The Execution of Moses Paul

Occom's most famous sermon was addressed to another prodigal son, Moses Paul. A Wampanoag man who had been bound out to a white master at the age of five, Paul was sentenced to death for killing a white man outside a tavern. He asked Occom to address him on September 2, 1772, the day he would go to the gallows, where one or another invisible master was poised to reclaim him.

Occom concludes the printed version of *A Sermon, Preached at the Execution of Moses Paul, An Indian*—a best seller that went through multiple editions—with a brief biography of Paul. He says that he included the biographical sketch to serve the desires of "*the inquisitive Public*," but it suits his themes and doctrines. Together with the preface, it frames the sermon as a vocational tract for a culture of racialized service. For sixteen years, Occom reports, Paul served John Manning, who taught him to read and write and instructed him in religion. At the end of his indenture, Paul embarked upon other kinds of service, enlisting in the provincial army before taking to the sea, in "ships of war" and also the "Merchants service," where he "got confirmed in those evil Habits which he too easily imbibed in the Army"—this alludes to abuse of alcohol. These habits "almost entirely eradicated from his Mind those good Principles in which he had been instructed" by Manning, who had apparently fulfilled his duties to educate his servant in the English tongue (SO 194). Paul, in other words, was no heathen but a backslider who succumbed to the pull of sin while in the "service" of white men and despite having had a good white master. Occom's inclusion of Paul's history as an indentured servant thus offers a tacit critique of servitude to white masters and service to white mastery as a model of Native American moral and spiritual education.

Paul's execution is one form of public white mastery, and Occom uses the occasion to make equally visible the pervasive, systemic economic injustice that is also an urgent matter of life and death. He observes that "a dead man, in a natural sense, is unactive, and is of no service to the living" (SO 183). Instead of focusing on the public criminal, Occom's auditors should question whether they are among the spiritually dead, "unholy, rotten hypocrites" whose "prayers and religious exercises were cold, dead, and abominable services to God," and for whom the Bible "is like an old almanack to them, a dead book."

Occom makes sure that the dual spectacles of a Native American on the gallows and in the pulpit are not the dead services of hypocrisy but means by which fresh doctrines of cross-racial and pan-Indian service might live.[52] Occom roots his economic critique in white men's usurpation of the authority of God the Master. No less than Franklin's *Autobiography*, the Moses Paul sermon provides lessons in how to perform morality in the public eye. Franklin is often positioned as the original voice of American modernity, but Occom also crafts an exceptional version of modern vocation: his particular calling as a public native serving a native public.[53]

In the preface, Occom valorizes his authorship and publicity as racialized serviceability and demonstrates that he uses print to embody a kind of public service not rooted in mastery over others and a public of people who are not white masters. He uses a conventional rhetoric of humility to depict his authorship as genuine service, not an exercise of pride. "I am ready to say with my self, what folly and madness is it in me to suffer any thing of mine to appear in print, to expose my ignorance to the world?" he explains (SO 177). "It seems altogether unlikely that my performance will do any manner of service in the world," yet he is "willing to suffer my broken hints to appear" in a marketplace of "books that . . . are written in very high and refined language" and "sermons that . . . are in a very high and lofty stile, so that the common people understand but little of them." Racial vocation spiritualizes a white master's inevitably futile efforts to convert African slaves and natives, but Occom depicts the difficulty of "the common people" to "understand" as a failure of an elite ministry whose members seek to master rather than serve the common people. In contrast, he presents himself as a faithful servant of servants: the people "can't help understanding my talk; it is common, plain, every-day talk—little children may understand it; and poor Negroes may plainly and fully understand my meaning; and it may be of service to them. Again, it may in a particular manner be serviceable to my poor kindred the Indians." He presents service to, rather than mastery of, children and racial others as a basis for moral authorship and the spiritualized public labor of serviceability.

As in the "Short Narrative," Occom structures the print version of the Moses Paul sermon by identifying his calling to serve the Lord with the place of an indentured servant. He links his own embodied calling as a native preacher to Paul's embodiment of the common figure of the "drunken Indian."[54] Occom uses the same phrase that he used in the preface to characterize his own impulse to publicity—"folly and madness"—to describe Paul, "the poor miserable object who is to be executed this day before your eyes, for the due reward of his folly and madness" (SO 177). Adopting the "sane," rational gaze of the audience, especially those who "look upon [them]selves [as] christians," Occom ironically criminalizes his own public service as a Native American and spiritualizes Paul's public criminality.

Occom also links himself to Paul by playing with the dual typology of Moses Paul's name: Moses is the lawgiver of the Old Testament, and Paul is the gospel's most tireless servant of the Lord. If Occom is also Moses Paul, both are Paul of Tarsus—Occom the apostle, and Moses the (God willing) instant convert. Paul of Tarsus epitomizes willing service to God: "It is his meat and drink, yea, more than his meat and drink, to do the will of his heavenly Father. It is his delight, his happiness, and pleasure to serve God. He does not drag himself to his duties now, but he does them out of choice, and with alacrity of soul" (SO 186). Unlike Occom's employers, Paul's heavenly Father is also a good Master, giving his servant what is just and equal: "his meat and drink, yea, more than his meat and drink."

Occom's text is Romans 6:23, "For the wages of sin is death; but the gift of God is eternal life through Jesus Christ our Lord." Occom's exegesis addresses the spiritual paradoxes of the Christian gothic (of sin as living death, and eternal life through Christ's death) to questions of economic justice. Noting that George Whitefield also cited this text "to criticize British and colonial American consumer society," Sandra Gustafson argues that Occom presents a version of grace that "function[s] like a gift economy," offering "Occom's Indian audience an escape from the destructive effects of market exchange."[55] I concur with her estimation of Occom's skill at radicalizing and racializing Christian tropes, but I would add that his choice also exemplifies the broader importance of service and mastery to economic applications of redemption. His exegesis trades in the imagery of verses 16–22, including, "For when ye were the servants of sin, ye were free from righteousness. . . . But now being made free from sin, and become servants to God, ye have your fruit until holiness, and the end everlasting life." The "servants of sin" are Satan's servants but also masters of themselves: "sin" encompasses the unconverted and those resting in the works of righteousness, or the pride of the hypocrite who does not credit his heavenly Master. Puritan sermons commonly collated Romans 6:22–23 with proof-texts of adoption, and Occom follows this tradition, lamenting that "the pure religion of Jesus Christ is turned out of doors, and is dying without; or, in other words, the Lord Jesus Christ is turned out of doors by men in general, and even by his professed people" (SO 179). In the metaphors of orthodox adoption, the servant is turned out of doors while the son abideth ever. In its hypocritical version, even "his professed people," so-called children of God, have treated Christ as their servant instead of the Son of God and their Lord and Master.

Occom points out that God does not confer spiritual liberty as a privilege for elites. Grace, he says, is "offered upon free terms. He that hath no money may come . . . the call is to poor undone sinners; the call is not to the righteous, but sinners, calling them to repentance" (SO 189). White men might have the authority to convict and execute Moses Paul, but "Christ alone has a right to call sinners to himself." This insistence undermines a premise of racial vocation, the blurring of God's power to call men to serve him with white men's authority over nonwhites and their sense of self-mastery. Referring to this power as a "right" puts it into the political context and insists that the spiritual calling align with earthly justice. Occom underscores this point later in the sermon, closely paraphrasing the injunction against eye-service in Ephesians 6:5–6 and then citing Ephesians 6:10, which activates the entire context of verses 5–10 (191). In verse 9, Paul reminds earthly masters that they too must avoid hypocrisy as servants of God, "knowing that your Master also is in heaven; neither is there respect of persons with him." Ministers who serve their white congregants and themselves while mastering their nonwhite congregants do not obey their heavenly Master, with whom there is no "respect of persons."

Occom enjoins "the Indians, my brethren and kindred according to the flesh" (SO 192) to respect themselves as God respects them, warning that a particular sin deadens their ability to do good: "when a person is drunk, he is just good for nothing in the world; he is of no service to himself, to his family, to his neighbours, or his country; and how much more unfit is he to serve God; yet he is just fit for the service of the devil" (193). If drunkenness made both the victim Moses and the killer Moses susceptible to violence, it also made natives vulnerable to economic violence, being "cheated over and over again" and also pressed into bondage: forced to be servants instead of being free to serve.[56] Drunkenness thus cheats God of his due service and threatens native sovereignty, the ability of a man to be "of service . . . to his neighbours, or his country"—which is unjust both economically and spiritually.

Occom continued to develop the themes and rhetoric of the Moses

Paul sermon in his later sermons and public writings, particularly the petitions he wrote to state and federal governments on behalf of Indian communities. In the sermon "When He Drowned His Reason," Occom reprises, in nearly identical phrasing, his denunciation of drunkenness as imperiling a man's ability to be of "Service" and consigning him to "Serve the Devil" (SO 226). In the white man's version of racial vocation, God calls natives to be drunk; in Occom's version, they must forswear alcohol so they can use their reason to do good, to serve each other and God.

Racial Serviceability

In his public callings as minister and pantribal advocate, Occom frequently turned to the tropes of white hypocrisy and promoted a modern doctrine of native vocation: doing good to themselves and each other and being free from the domination of white masters, including representatives of the new American republic. In a 1787 sermon on Luke 10:26–7, "Thou Shalt Love Thy Neighbor as Thyself," Occom denounces Christian "Monopolizers" who "When they have Horded up What they can then they will set an Extravagant Price upon their Commodities" (SO 202). He entwines the histories of Native American servitude and slavery, the African slave trade, and the racialization of credit and debt to expose the hypocrisy at the heart of New England's economic culture. The sermon echoes John Winthrop's "Model of Christian Charity"[57] in presenting love as a medium of economic justice in a community. However, while Winthrop celebrates the bonds of mutual obligation between rich and poor in a hierarchical community, Occom promotes a more egalitarian model of neighborliness and touts "Savage Indians, as they are so calld" (SO 206) as its exemplars.

The "Indian Heathen in this great Continent . . . are very Compassionate one to another" and properly expand the category of "Neighbors" to include "Strangers" (SO 203):

> When there is Scarsity of Food amongst them, they will yet Divide what little they have if there is but a mouth full a Piece, and When any of kills any Creature, they will equally divide it amongst them all and when they have Plenty especially what they got in Hunting & Fishing,—and when anyone is destitude of a Blanket, he that has two, will freely give him one, and they are very kind to one another in Sickness, and they Weep with them that Weep—This I take to be a Human Love or Being Neighbourly, according to our Text. (SO 203–4)

In contrast, Occom denounces white Christians who "have no regard for the happiness of your Neighbour," who "have no pity and Compassion upon the Poor and distrest" (SO 202). He looks into the hearts of such "Monopolizers": "you do not Love God, if you think you Love god, you are deceiving yourselves" (202). Occom predicts (alluding to Malachi 2.3) that "the Lord . . . will cast all [these hypocrites'] Prayers in their Faces as Dung" (203).

Occom proceeds to read the golden rule as an abolitionist text, denouncing Christian slave-holding as hypocrisy. "You that are Slavekeepers, do you Love God, and do you Love your Neighbour, your Neighbour Negroe as Yourself, are you willing to be Slaves yourselves, and your Children to be Slaves too?" he demands (SO 206). Mather spiritualized the calling of white Christian masters to African slaves, but Occom bluntly insists that those who own slaves cannot be Christians: "if you can prove it from the Bible that Negroes are not the Race of Adam, then you may keep them as Slaves, Otherwise you have no more right to keep them as slaves as they have to keep you as Slaves." Those who "will keep Slaves and plead for it, are not Neighbours to anyone, and Consequently they are not Lovers of God, They are no Christians."

Occom denounces the hypocrisy of slave-holding ministers in particular. Such servants of the Lord are slaves to "fashion": "it has been very fashionable for them to keep Negroe Slaves, Which I think is Inconsistant with their Character and Function, if I understand the gospel a wright, I think it is a Dispention of Freedom and Liberty, both Temporal and Spiritual" (SO 206). Slave-holding ministers necessarily secularize their callings by separating "Temporal" morality from "Spiritual" matters. "If Ministers are True Liberty men," Occom asserts in his vocational jeremiad, "let them preach Liberty for poor Negroes fervently with great Zeal, and them Ministers Who have Negroes set an Example before their People, by Freeing their Negroes, let them show their Faith by their Works" (207). He reports that a minister "preachd a Liberty Sermon for the Poor Negroes" that prompted five men to set their slaves free. Slavery, Occom insists, cannot be spiritualized.

Occom's public vocation also included political advocacy. In petitions to state and federal governments written on behalf of tribes and pantribal communities, he promoted native service in contrast to servitude, "the common pot" in contrast to a public defined by mastery over racial others and a concept of liberty and property rooted in rational economic individualism.[58] A 1778 document written in Occom's hand on behalf of the Mohegan tribe about how to distribute rent money notes that the tribe "agreed Unanimously . . . that we Shall look upon one another as one Family" and that "the Money does belong to the Whole Tribe, and it shall be dispos'd of accordingly for the Benefit of the Whole" (SO 147). This was no call to return to subsistence. The values of neighborliness and mutuality were modern accommodations to the reality of a money economy, not a capitulation to them.[59] Occom understood that economic independence from whites required natives to determine for themselves "that which is just and equal."

These petitions powerfully convey Occom's perceptiveness about how heavily the past and present of white hypocrisy would weigh on any native future.[60] In two documents he uses a chiasmus that ironically uses "serving and being served" as ideals to condemn racial injustice. In a 1785 petition from the Montaukett tribe, Occom cites the history of "Shameful agreements" that cheated and impoverished them, challenging the "gentlemen" he addresses with rhetorical questions: "don't this Show, that the English took advantage of the Ignorance of our Fore Fathers[?] Woud they be Willing to be Servd so by us? Were we Cabable to use them?" (SO 151). This accusation also appears in a letter he wrote in 1788 on behalf of John Dantuckquechen, who was being sued for a debt he purported to know nothing about: "if . . . any man draw upon account against his Neighbour Without any Dealings with him,—and Sue him, get Judgment against him,—Do you Serve one another So? if not, Why Should we be Serv'd So" (128). If there is no redress "for the Indians, by the Rulers," Occom declares, "I had rather be amongst the most Wild and uncultivated Indians, in the Western Wilderness."

Occom worked with other native leaders to establish and promote self-governing communities based on ideals of service. As Hilary Wyss and David Silverman have described, these ideals were not realized in the Brotherton and Stockbridge communities, where Occom was a divisive figure who became increasingly disillusioned and depressed about the prospect of native sovereignty.[61] In his later writings, his hopes for the future have a decidedly conditional cast, shaded by experience. In a December 1791 letter to his "Dear Brethren" at New Stockbridge, where he had just moved his family, Occom offers as a blessing the hope that "we Shall be profitable to one another as long as we Shall Live" (SO 135). "Let us, then go on in Serving the Lord our God and let us help one another in all our Concerns," he continues, "May we be found to build up one another both in our Temporal and in our Religious Life, and let us try to do all the good that we are Capable of unto all men, and if it be possible let us Live in Peace with all men" (135). Occom here offers a version of being "profitable to one another" and of "doing all the good that we are Capable of unto all men" that does not equate "men" with masters. Occom wants freedom to serve his fellow natives and to have them serve each other, not to be white men's servants—or, as he put it in a 1783 account of the "Remarkable and Strange Situation and Appearance of Indian Tribes in this Great Continent," merely "good Servants to themselves" (59).

Boy Masters

Like Occom, in his *Autobiography* Franklin wrote a role for a poor servant boy who is the narrator's uncanny double. Franklin's representation of himself as a "Boy" in part 1 of the *Autobiography* might be one of his least convincing characters: the child Franklin seems to present itself to the imagination as merely a short version of the shiny-pated or beaver-hatted older man of the famous portraits. This is undoubtedly at least in part because those images are so iconic, but we can also attribute it to Franklin's narrative point of view, the eye of a master. As Anna Mae Duane observes, "apprenticeship . . . casts the child-Franklin as an agent and master of his future destiny, even as he is placed in a dependent position."[62] Even Franklin's gesture of addressing the memoir to his "Dear Son" William is a feint of public fatherhood addressed to a child who is, like his father, part of a community of public masters (BF 9). Occom and Franklin offer two versions of "the poor Boy" as a lived metaphor of racial vocation: the boy who will always be a servant, even if he becomes a minister; and an exceptionally precocious child who serves who is a very quick study in the arts of self-mastery.

Franklin depicts two governors, William Burnet of New York and William Keith of Pennsylvania, affirming that the "poor Boy" was a master to be. Burnet, "the second Governor who had done me the Honor to take Notice of me," seeks Franklin out for "Conversation about Books and Authors," which, he observes, "to a poor Boy like me was very pleasing" (BF 35). The first governor, Keith, prompts Franklin to use a different meaning of "poor." Keith promises to help establish him in the Philadelphia printing business, to "procure me the public Business, and do me every other Service in his Power" (32). The governor writes to Josiah Franklin, Benjamin's father, explaining this plan, but Josiah finds it ill-advised, opining that Keith "must be of small Discretion, to think of setting a Boy up in Business who wanted yet 3 Years of being at Man's Estate" (33). In Josiah's "Opinion," Benjamin was "too young to be trusted with the Management of a Business so important; and for which the

Preparation must be so expensive." But it was Keith who was not to be trusted. Franklin relives the moment when he arrived in England and found that Keith had not written letters of introduction as promised: "But what shall we think of a Governor's playing such pitiful Tricks, and imposing so grossly on a poor ignorant Boy!" (42).

In these passages, the character of the "poor Boy" not entirely successfully sentimentalizes this posture of humility, and Franklin knows it. He uses irony when asking for sympathy and chooses reason instead of feeling as the force that bridges the distance between reader and text, and between the "poor Boy" protagonist and the wealthy narrator who has mastered his experience and can be trusted to manage his own business. He wants the reader to observe both Keith's dishonesty and his invulnerability to it. The "poor Boy's" ability to rightly command and obey himself makes him superior to Keith—who will, soon enough, be restored to his rightful place, walking the streets as a common citizen.

Before encountering these governors, Franklin is a "boy" longing to free himself from his apprenticeship to his brother James, devising his own course of self-mastery—which included developing a serviceable prose style. Critics have associated Franklin's acquisition of literary mastery with his relationship to patriarchal authority, focusing on the fatherly strand of that authority.[63] Yet Franklin masters language while being legally bound to an earthly master, imagining the prospect of becoming a master printer. Teaching himself how to write by imitating items published in the *Spectator*, Franklin reveals his sense of writing as craft, not art: "without looking at the Book," he labors to "[express] each hinted Sentiment at length and as fully as it had been express'd before, in any suitable Words that should come to hand" (BF 20). The words "come to hand," not to mind—a phrase evoking the printer's apprentice reaching into the case to set type. Franklin deems himself capable of identifying his own "Faults" when comparing the two versions, yet he finds that he remains unable to correct them to his satisfaction because he lacked "a Stock of Words or a Readiness in recollecting and using them," which he attributes to his abandonment of "making Verses." The constraint of obeying the rules of meter and rhyme, he explains, requires "a constant Necessity of searching for Variety," and that training would "have tended to fix that Variety in my Mind, and make me Master of it." Franklin's method of teaching himself to write is not just a "literary apprenticeship," but also a version of the contractual mandates of moral mastery. For Franklin, successful self-education culminates in being a master printer with an ample "Stock of Words."

The triangular relationship between Benjamin Franklin, his father, and his brother is a kind of transitional formation between the early modern household and the kinship model.[64] Instead of the traditional master-father, Franklin serves a master-brother, a calling that adapts household obedience to a public of citizens, not subjects, by investing masterly authority in a male relative who is more a peer than a father. Benjamin represents his relationship to his brother as a competition between two masters, a model of relations between unequal citizens in the public sphere.

The fiction of a brother-master creates friction between James and Benjamin, who explains: "tho' a Brother, he considered himself as my Master, and me as his Apprentice; and accordingly expected the same Services from me as he would from another; while I thought he demean'd me too much in some he requir'd of me, who from a Brother expected more Indulgence" (BF 24). James might "consider himself" his brother's master, but Franklin insists on the brother status. Meanwhile, Josiah Franklin, having bound out one son to another, is free to act as "affectionate" father, even in his role as "Judge": "Our Disputes were often brought before our Father, and I fancy I was either generally in the right, or else a better Pleader, because the Judgment was generally in my favor." Josiah mediates a dispute between his two sons, not between a master and his apprentice. When it comes to resolving conflicts between the apprentice-brother and the master-brother, Benjamin Franklin legitimates his contractual violations as servant protest, or secularized Christian liberty.

"Sufficient Meat" and "Bread Enough"

While Occom exposed the hypocrisy of white men who act as masters to their legally free dependents, Franklin focuses on the hypocrisy of men who are masters by contract but incapable of fulfilling the mandates of good mastery. The historian W. J. Rorabaugh has noted that, unlike English trades, American apprenticeship was not regulated by guilds, and one effect of this was that "anyone could call himself a master artisan and any such artisan could take an apprentice."[65] Rorabaugh does not intend the pun involved in his use of "call," but the notion that masters could "call themselves" to their vocation is essential to Franklin's depiction of his earthly masters. Like Occom, Franklin embarks on a creative path of self-making against the resistance of hypocritical masters: those who lack self-mastery, in the case of his brother; or those who lack both mastery and self-mastery, in the case of Samuel Keimer, who was "by Agreement" obligated to teach his hands presswork and bookbinding, "tho' he knew neither one nor t'other" (BF 51).

Franklin observes of his term of service to his brother that he had thought it "very tedious" and "was continually wishing for some Opportunity of shortening it" (BF 24). He ultimately seizes the "Opportunity" presented when James was ordered to cease publishing the *New England Courant* after running articles critical of local governors; to get around this order, James cancels his brother's indenture so the paper could be run in Benjamin's name instead. To Benjamin, this gesture exposes what was a legal fiction anyway, and he asserts his natural mastery by running away. But another example of how he mines contractual loopholes to create "opportunities" is one that he does not narrate as such: his famous foray into vegetarianism, inspired by Thomas Tryon's 1691 *The Way to Health*. While hardly as dramatic a gesture as the cancelled indenture, his vegetarian diet demonstrates Franklin's view of the contract as a source of innovative personhood, at least for artisans of English descent.[66]

As noted above, apprentice contracts stipulated that masters provide servants not just with food, but with "sufficient meat." Indeed, "meat" was one of the fixed mandates in boilerplate printed apprentice contracts. As a contractual expression of the moral obligation of masters to servants, then, "meat" was nonnegotiable. However, Franklin revels in the productive friction it generates between him and two of his masters, a friction that exposes their failures of mastery and liberates his inner master. Noting that Tryon was both an advocate of vegetarianism and a staunch critic of systemic slavery who nevertheless "called upon owners to treat their slaves in a Christian manner and predicted obedience by the slaves in return," Waldstreicher observes that "Tryon's advice, in short, was for masters, not servants."[67] Franklin's version of vegetarianism was intended as advice for both.

Franklin's master was not yet a father or a husband and so he "did not keep House but boarded himself and his Apprentices in another Family," where, Franklin observes, "My refusing to eat Flesh occasioned an Inconveniency, and I was frequently chid [chided] for my singularity" (BF 20). One can imagine the brothers quarreling at communal meals as the other members of this nonkin "Family" tucked into their portions of "Flesh," wondering at the dietarily perverse adolescent at their table. The "Inconveniency" was also a technical breach of contract, which the apprentice negotiates into a new verbal agreement. To avoid the frequent chidings, Franklin offers new terms for his board: if his brother "would give me Weekly half the Money he paid for my Board, I would board myself. He instantly agreed to it, and I presently found that I could save half what he paid me. This was an additional Fund for buying Books" and also bought him time alone to read them, since he did not join the others for meals (21). Even if, by custom, the contractual "meat" served as a metonym for "food," Franklin demonstrates his self-mastery not just in his asceticism and frugality but also in his virtuous disobedience of contractual servitude to a paper master.

This liberty also applies to his relation to his inner master. After explaining how the smell of fried cod tempted him to abandon his vegetarianism, and how the realization that the cod itself eats little fish licenses him to eat it, Franklin crafts one of his most famous aphorisms: "So convenient a thing it is to be a *reasonable Creature*, since it enables one to find or make a Reason for everything one has a mind to do" (BF 37). This expression of instrumental reason combines a master's control over his servant's diet with his ability to transform an unruly inclination into useful wit.

Unlike his younger brother, James Franklin proves incapable of mastering himself. The conduct manuals' insistence that a master resist acting as a tyrant to his servant legitimates Benjamin's desertion of his brother's service as an instance of Christian liberty. James cannot resist delivering "the Blows his Passion too often urg'd him to bestow upon me" (BF 25). In a note, Franklin adds, "I fancy his harsh and tyrannical Treatment of me, might be a means of impressing me with that Aversion to arbitrary Power that has stuck to me thro' my whole life" (24). His moment of self-reflection projects their dispute into the future, and also into the world of politics and a marketplace in goods and labor whose shared premise is rationally moderated competition between masters.

After leaving Boston and his brother's service, Franklin gave up vegetarianism, but he adopts it again, in even more mischievous forms, to reveal Keimer's lack of self-mastery. Noting his aversion to Keimer's practice of wearing a long beard and keeping "the seventh-day Sabbath," Franklin explains that he nevertheless "agreed to admit them upon Condition of his adopting the Doctrine of using no animal Food" (BF 37). Keimer "was usually a great Glutton," he explains, "and I promis'd myself some Diversion in half-starving him. He agreed to try the Practice if I would keep him Company," which they did together for three months (38). "I went on pleasantly," Franklin reports, "but Poor Keimer suffer'd grievously, tir'd of the Project, long'd for the Flesh Pots of Egypt," and "could not resist the Temptation" to consume an entire roast pig intended to feed four. Keimer's "Gluttony" demonstrates his inability to master not just his servant, but also himself: he consumes more than "sufficient meat," a lived metaphor for the asceticism of the bourgeois ethic and the republican ideal of a competence. To internalize the obligations of a good master was to measure properly what is "sufficient" to live comfortably and what is properly left over for saving, investing, and giving to those in need.

Franklin draws on the parable of the prodigal son to depict the consumer marketplace as such a benevolent master. Mather collates Luke 15:17 with Colossians 4:1 to emphasize the master's obligation to provide his servants with adequate sustenance (GM 13). Recall that the prodigal's turn toward repentance happens when his foreign master commands him to feed swine. In verse 17, this prompts him to reflect on his father as a master whose servants "have bread enough and to spare" and to express his repentance as willingness to be his father's servant. The fact that this aspect of the parable was part of Franklin's literary imagination is clear in his depiction of George Webb, the Oxford scholar who became a "bought Servant" to Keimer: Webb had "spent his Guineas . . . grew necessitous . . . and wanted Bread" and so bound himself "to serve in America," which occupies the role of the "foreign master" in Franklin's parable (BF 52). "Wanting bread" allegorizes the wages of sin as servitude to tyrannical masters, and "bread enough and to spare" as just wages due from good masters to willing servants.

Franklin's engagement with the "bread enough" imagery of the parable shapes one of the most famous scenes in the narrative: his entry into Philadelphia and the allegory of the Puffy Rolls.[68] When Franklin enters the "foreign land" of Philadelphia, he finds the marketplace to be a master that provides "bread enough and to spare." Hungry and cash-strapped, Franklin goes to a bakery and asks for Boston bread—"Biscuit" or a "three-penny Loaf"—neither of which are for sale (BF 28). So, "not considering or knowing the Difference of Money," he asks for "three pennyworth of any sort" of bread and receives in return "three great Puffy Rolls," walking away "with a Roll under each Arm, and eating the other" (28–29). In this posture, he sees not his father but his future wife, Deborah Read, standing at her father's door—giving him a glimpse of himself as a future father and husband (Franklin frequently addressed Deborah, who capably managed his business and household during his years-long absences, as "Dear Child" in their correspondence). Though famished, Franklin determines that one roll is bread enough, and gives "the other two to a Woman and her Child" he knows from the boat he had arrived on (29). The "spare" bread gives Franklin an opportunity for self-mastery, eating only until he is full. But it also provides him with the opportunity to do good, to act as a benevolent public master providing nonkin dependents with "bread enough." When he arrives at Keimer's shop a couple of paragraphs later, then, Franklin has already amply demonstrated his internalized mastery of serviceability.

Consuming an entire pig is not the only way Keimer violates the good master's calling; his contracts also violate the just wage mandate of Christian mastery. He contracts "at extreme low Wages" with a motley crew of unlikely "Hands," luring them with the promise that it would be "rais'd a Shilling every 3 Months, as they would deserve by improving in their Business" (BF 51). At the same time, he employs Franklin at suspiciously high wages: "I soon perceiv'd that the Intention of engaging me at Wages so much higher than he had been us'd to give, was to have these raw cheap Hands form'd thro' me, and as soon as I had instructed them, then, they being all articled to him, he should be able to do without me." Franklin persists "very cheerfully," despite his awareness of Keimer's scheme and of the fact that not even Franklin can make most of these men into master printers. He can, however, teach them how to serve as their own economic consciences, "to mind their Business and do it better." He reconfigures his servitude to Keimer and surrogate mastery of the "Hands" as a kind of public service, lamenting that "however serviceable I might be, I found that my Services became every Day of less Importance, as the other Hands improv'd in the Business" (52–53). When Franklin rebuffs Keimer's attempt to reduce his wages, Keimer "grew by degrees less civil, put on more of the Master, frequently found Fault, was captious and seemed ready for an Out-breaking" (53). Keimer can only "put on more of the Master," but this putting on is either a bad performance of good mastery or a good performance of bad mastery.

Thus, as with his desertion of his brother's service, Franklin narrates his break with Keimer as legitimate disobedience of an unjust master. It happens over a "Trifle": hearing a noise in the street, Franklin looks out, and when Keimer looks up and sees Franklin at the window, he berates him "in a loud Voice and angry Tone to mind my Business, adding some reproachful Words, that nettled me the more for their Publicity, all the Neighbors who were looking out on the same Occasion being Witnesses how I was treated" (BF 53). Franklin, of course, has been minding Keimer's business. Having privately treated Franklin as a master, Keimer publicly treats him as a servant. When the "Quarrel" continues inside, Franklin releases his master from his contractual obligation of a "Quarter's Warning." "Taking my Hat," he recalls, "I walk'd out of Doors" and quit Keimer's service for good. As when he left his brother's service, Franklin is not "some runaway," but rather a master turning himself out of doors.

After leaving Keimer, he pauses dramatically on the threshold of the narrative before "enter[ing] upon my public Appearance in Business" (55). It won't be long before his labor will be seen, and given due credit, by an admiring public.

The Work of the Master's Eye

In a passage from "The Way to Wealth," Franklin crafts an aphorism of modern vocation from the concept of eye-service:

> With our Industry, we must . . . oversee our own Affairs *with our own Eyes*, and not trust too much to others. . . .
>
> He that by the Plough would thrive,
> *Himself must either hold or drive.*
>
> And again, *The Eye of a Master will do more Work than both his Hands.*[69]

Franklin's memoirs are more playful than Father Abraham's prescriptions, but the equation of "our own Eyes" with the "Eye of a Master" is a central precept of his economic personhood. The phrase "minding my business" itself expresses an ideological form of the eye of the master, with economic conscience taking the form of self-mastery. Franklin's famous doctrine of visible industry is a version of eye-service in which he serves two masters: one internalized as an economic conscience, and the other the public. The public performance of morality that has led Franklin's critics to charge him with hypocrisy thus derives from one of the primary lived metaphors of spiritual hypocrisy, the traditional countertype of vocation's willing service.

Franklin writes his own eyewitness account of the "Industry visible to our Neighbors" that "began to give us Character and Credit" (BF 58). "Us" refers to his partnership with Hugh Meredith, but only one of the partners is industrious. In fact, Meredith is visibly dissolute, "often seen drunk in the Streets, and playing at low Games in Alehouses, much to our Discredit" (62). The "general Opinion" is that the venture will fail (58), but one Doctor Baird testifies to the contrary: "the Industry of that Franklin, says he, is superior to anything I ever saw of the kind: I see him still at work when I go home from Club; and he is at Work again before his Neighbors are out of bed" (59). Franklin scripts Baird's "first-person" account; shared mastery collapses his authorial point of view into that of the public eye.

Franklin is a faithful eye-servant to himself. He may work only when in his master's sight, but like an omniscient God, his inner master keeps constant watch. He confesses to private virtue, not private sin. "In order to secure my Credit and Character as a Tradesman," he recounts, "I took care not only to be in *Reality* Industrious and frugal, but to avoid all *Appearances* of the Contrary. I dressed plainly; I was seen at no Places of idle Diversion; I never went out a-fishing or shooting" (BF 64). He adds primly that "a Book, indeed, sometimes debauch'd me from my Work; but that was seldom, snug, and gave no Scandal." The iconic image of Franklin's visible industry is the performance of a master acting as his own apprentice: to "show that I was not above my Business, I sometimes brought home the Paper I purchas'd at the Stores, thro' the Streets on a Wheelbarrow." Franklin is no boy but a credit-worthy, "industrious thriving young man," who "pay[s] duly for what I bought" and is "esteem'd" as such. He serves two masters: himself and the public. He that by the wheelbarrow must thrive, himself must either hold or drive.

The eye of the master also does its work in Franklin's "bold and arduous Project of arriving at moral Perfection"—a "Task," as he wryly concedes, "of more Difficulty than I had imagined" (BF 78). Franklin is invested in not just cultivating the virtues, but also making them visible. "I made a little Book in which I allotted a Page for each of the Virtues," creating a record of his successes and failures that he can actually see (81). "I rul'd each Page with red Ink," he notes of his examination book. "I rul'd" might suggest self-tyranny, but Franklin's method firmly distinguishes tyrant from master as a godly master should. "I should have (I hoped) the encouraging Pleasure of seeing on my Pages the Progress I made in Virtue, by clearing successively my Lines of their Spots, till in the End by a Number of Courses, I should be happy in viewing a clean Book" (81). The virtues might be defined in the imperative, but success in achieving them is always conditional. He replaces the paper version with "the Ivory leaves of a Memorandum Book," which allows him to "easily wipe out" his faults "with a wet Sponge" and to "always carr[y] my little Book with me" (84). The examination book allows him to literally "see himself" as a master reviewing his apprentice's progress, and as God the Master reviews the activities of all his servants in their callings. "I was surprise'd to find myself so much fuller of Faults than I had imagined," he reports, "but I had the Satisfaction of seeing them diminish." The "Faults" diminish rather than disappear, but the traces that remain prompt continual exercise. Franklin included in his *Autobiography* a visual representation of a sample page, providing the example of "Temperance," blots and all, so the reader can also "see them"—to emulate but also to invent their own methods of self-mastery. The eye of a master will do more work than both his hands.

Commanding Virtues

Franklin's "Method" inculcates "Dependence" on "a steady uniform Rectitude of Conduct" instead of on a social superior (or chain of them) who embodies God the Master: that is, it teaches self-mastery (BF 79). It is an elaborate version of the prodigal's petition, "make me as one of thy hired servants," which Franklin addresses to multiple master-fathers: himself, the public, and God. Rather than trying to "acquire the *Habitude* of all these Virtues" at once, Franklin explains, he "judg'd it would be well . . . to fix it on one of them at a time, and when I should be Master of that, then to proceed to another, and so on till I should have gone thro' the thirteen" (80). Critics have followed Franklin's own metaphor in describing his quest in part 2 of the *Autobiography* as "mastery."[70] But to Franklin, "mastery" is not just a synonym for self-discipline. What Franklin means by being "Master" is shaped by specific mandates of scriptural and contractual master-servant personhood, especially the secularized versions that undergird racial vocation. He embodies two kinds of good white master to himself: one content to have a moral servant who strives to please him, and perhaps also God; and one whose struggle to govern his intractably disobedient servant spiritualizes his self-mastery.

Franklin describes his approach to defining each "Virtue": "I propos'd to myself, for the sake of Clearness, to use rather more Names with fewer Ideas annex'd to each, than a few names with more Ideas" (BF 79). The self-reflexivity of "propos'd to myself" has been taken to characterize Franklin's modern individualism. Warner observes of Franklin's concept of rational selfhood: "He can carry out actions of which he is both subject and object, and in which neither God nor anyone else participates. So his reason seems to be pure individuality."[71] For Franklin, master and servant are the lived metaphors of subject and object, and God participates in collapsing the distinction between them. The traditional ideal of spiritual labor, the child willing to serve his Father, is preserved in Franklin's version of virtuous self-mastery. "Prefix'd to my Tables of Examination, for daily Use," Franklin explains, is a prayer that addresses God as "bountiful Father! merciful Guide!" and asking him to "Accept my kind Offices to thy other Children, as the only return in my Power for thy continual Favors to me" (BF 83). This is the thankful obedience of the child who serves, who has internalized God as both Master and Father, the mixture of rational and affective consent that confers the subject's liberty to call God Father.

When such a child is called as a master, he can resist acting as a tyrant to his servants, and Franklin is such a master—both to his own inner servant and in his public callings. Breitwieser has observed that Franklin "must demonstrate that service to the self is not onerous in the way that service to the father is," but nothing is more onerous than the commands of a bad master.[72] Franklin both gives and obeys his commands, but he is a good master to himself. The "Ideas" that define each virtue are phrased as commands but without the threat of damnation or promise of salvation "annex'd" to them. "Something that pretended to be Reason was every now and then suggesting to me . . . that a perfect Character might be attended with the Inconvenience of being envied and hated," Franklin muses, "and that a benevolent Man should allow a few Faults in himself, to keep his Friends in Countenance" (BF 86). It is not just an act of instrumental reason to "allow a few Faults in himself": its desirability is suggested by "Something that pretended to be Reason," perhaps the father's love mixed with the master's command. Franklin seems willing to be respected rather than loved or feared, but being "envied and hated" would hinder his ability to be serviceable in his public capacity as a "benevolent Man," the embodiment of civic virtue.

The virtues are forms of master-servant obedience. "Resolution" exemplifies how Franklin transforms the mutual obligations of masters and servants into a sense of duty to the self: "Resolve to perform what you ought. Perform without fail what you resolve" (BF 79). The self's sense of "ought" is an internalized God as Master, particularly as he deputizes masters and servants to act as each other's eyewitnesses and moral and economic consciences. Justice resonates with the obligation of a just wage: "Wrong none, by doing Injuries or omitting the Benefits that are your duty" (80). Sincerity, silence, and humility are all versions of governance of the tongue, embodied by the servant who resists answering back to a master's lawful commands. Temperance and frugality are versions of a master's duty to provide "sufficient" food and drink, neither too much nor too little, and a servant's duty not to waste a master's goods, even to the value of a farthing. Moderation, with the idea of not "resenting injuries so much as you think they deserve," resonates with a master's obligation to "moderate his corporal punishment of servants, as James Franklin had failed to do. Chastity resonates with the stock contractual admonition to apprentices: "Fornication he shall not commit: Matrimony during the said term he shall not contract." Industry derives from masters' owing their servants work, and thus mandating the diligence that will preserve them from the sin of idleness; and servants' owing good masters their faithful service. "Lose no time," Franklin commands himself. "Be always employ'd in something useful. Cut off all unnecessary Actions" (79).

Franklin treats the virtues as his servants, not as his masters; and even when they disobey, as Franklin's experience tells him they inevitably will, they can still spiritualize their master's labor—including his authorial labor. Earthly mastery sometimes impedes self-mastery, as Franklin rather proudly notes when explaining why "Order" gives him the most trouble: "tho' it might be practicable where a Man's Business was such as to leave him the Disposition of his Time, that of a Journeyman Printer for instance, it was not possible to be exactly observ'd by a Master, who must mix with the World, and often receive People of Business at their own Hours" (BF 84). Rather than "content myself with a faulty Character" with respect to order, Franklin makes a virtue of his struggles with order by crafting an analogy from his family's history of being "bred" as smiths that concludes with the aphorism, "a speckled Axe was best."

Lawrence's Franklin would insist that the smith keep joylessly turning the wheel until the axe gleamed to perfection—that is, forever. But the Franklin of the *Autobiography* makes virtues of his speckles. By confessing his failures to perfectly master himself, Franklin demonstrates his successful avoidance of self-tyranny: "[on] the whole, tho' I never arrived at the Perfection I had been so ambitious of obtaining, but fell far short of it, yet I was by the Endeavour made a better and happier Man than I otherwise should have been, if I had not attempted it" (BF 86). Franklin's version of self-mastery is the "bold and arduous Project" of separating God the Master from the moral law he embodied, a gesture that both secularizes morality and spiritualizes alternative models of obedience and authority.

The Uses of Humiliation

Franklin's much much-discussed thirteenth virtue, humility, plays a particularly vital role in the rhetorical economy of serviceability. I concur with William Huntting Howell's recent claim that Franklin's concept alludes to the Protestant imitatio Christi, but I would add that it does so through the master-servant imagery of the doctrine of humiliation.[73] As I discuss in chapter 1, in the Puritan imitatio Christi, humiliation was associated with Christ's willingness to take human form as a servant. The ceaseless spiritual labor of shunning pride was preached as labor discipline, the duty of finding contentment in serving the Lord in God's appointed place, however lowly. In his letter urging Franklin to continue writing his memoir (inserted into the text itself according to Franklin's wishes), Benjamin Vaughan praises "modesty" and "disinterestedness" as essential features of his moral model: without them, he explains, Franklin "never could have waited for your advancement . . . which is a strong lesson to show the poverty of glory, and the importance of regulating our minds" (BF 72). What orthodox humiliation would valorize as "the glory of poverty" exemplified by Christ's servant form becomes to Vaughan the "poverty of glory," a doctrine of self-mastery, a means of teaching young readers in particular to regulate their minds, not their souls.

They should also learn to regulate their tongues. As I discuss in the case of the "demoniac" Elizabeth Knapp, the exercise of shunning pride in humiliation was particularly associated with the capacity to govern one's tongue, as in Titus 2:9, and not answering back to a master's lawful commands—especially commands to perform homely services. Defined by the mandate to "Imitate Jesus and Socrates" (BF 80), Franklin's version of humility, like Puritan humiliation, trades in the imagery of pride and self-regulated speech. Franklin confides that his list originally had only twelve virtues, but that he added humility after "a Quaker Friend" told him that his "Pride show'd itself frequently in Conversation" (87). Franklin concludes his discussion of the virtues and part 2 of his *Autobiography* with the image of his continued bedevilment by a trickster pride that cannot be subdued: "Disguise it, struggle with it, beat it down, stifle it, mortify it as much as one pleases, it is still alive, and will every now and then peep out and show itself. You will see it perhaps often in this History. For even if I could conceive that I had completely overcome it, I should probably be proud of my Humility" (88). The paradox "proud of my Humility" exemplifies Franklin's secularization of humiliation. He rhetorically accepts that he can never overcome pride not by confessing in fierce repentance, but by admitting it, in the tone of jovial irony that defines Franklinian candor.

Franklin's imitation of Socrates is also a method of mastering his tongue and making pride serviceable, one of the "natural Passions" (BF 88), not a sin. Franklin's knowledge of public service as an arena of public mastery shapes his approach to civic rhetoric. To be effective, a republican leader cannot act as a master to a public composed of masters. The public servant converts the master's power to command his servants' obedience into the power to persuade the public, the Power of doing Good (114).[74] Franklin's approach to civic rhetoric demonstrates his lack of pretense that the power to do good is, in fact, power.

Spiritual and legal master-servant personhood shapes Franklin's view of conversational power dynamics. We can see this when he charges James with tyranny but then—describing himself with the conventional adjective attached to verbally unruly servants—concedes that "he was otherwise not an ill-natur'd Man: Perhaps I was too saucy and provoking" (BF 25). Franklin's version of the Socratic method works because it transforms a master's command into a public servant's persuasiveness. Finding that his mode of "abrupt Contradiction and positive Argumentation" is not consistently useful, even when he won his debates, Franklin learns to "put on the humble Enquirer and Doubter" (21); he finds in this approach both "Delight" in "embarrassing" even those with "superior Knowledge" and the pleasure of "obtaining Victories that neither myself nor my Cause always deserved" (21–22). Though a course of self-denial, he converts the pleasure of humbling his social superiors into serviceability, by making a "Habit of expressing myself in Terms of modest Diffidence," which "has been of great Advantage to me, when I have had occasion to inculcate my Opinions and persuade Men into Measures that I have been from time to time engag'd in promoting" (22). The pragmatic Franklin comments, "I wish well-meaning sensible Men would not lessen their Power of doing Good by a Positive assuming Manner that seldom fails to disgust, tends to create Opposition and to defeat every one of those Purposes for which Speech was given us."

He repeats this lesson in his discussion of humility, explaining that though he cannot "boast of much Success in acquiring the *Reality* of this Virtue," he "had a good deal with regard to the *Appearance* of it" (BF 87–88). Rather than chiding servants that their tongues belong to their masters, as Mather had, Franklin devises both "a Rule to forbear all direct Contradiction to the Sentiments of others, and all positive Assertion of my own" and "Laws of our Junto" that forbid "the Use of every Word or Expression in the Language that imported a fix'd Opinion" (88). He concludes that "this Mode, which I at first put on, with some violence to natural Inclination, became at length so easy and so habitual to me, that perhaps for these Fifty Years past no one has ever heard a dogmatical Expression escape me"—there are no runaways among his saucy thoughts. He credits this "Habit" for his "Weight with my Fellow Citizens" and "Influence in public Councils when I became a Member. For I was but a bad Speaker, never eloquent . . . and yet I generally carried my Points" (88). His newspaper's policy of "exclud[ing] all Libelling and Personal Abuse" (92) is one example of how Franklin extends his rules of self-mastered speech into the print public sphere, to preserve an aura of disinterest and to serve the "Interests" of master printers.

The *Autobiography* itself, I would suggest, is another. The memoir, as the letters from Abel James and Benjamin Vaughan that bridge parts 1 and 2 insist, was an apt genre to use in inculcating in its readers emerging forms of mastery and service, including "management."[75] Both letters suggest that the memoir can fulfill the traditional role of a master to provide moral guidance for youth. The master's authority to command obedience from his servants in the conduct manuals becomes the memoirist's subtle influence on "the Minds of Youth," which "almost insensibly leads the Youth into the Resolution of endeavouring to become as good and as eminent" as the writer (BF 69). The author's relationship to his reader and, Vaughan suggests, to his own life experience are both forms of mastery. He twice refers to the authorship of memoir as "management" of lived experience (70, 71). Vaughan conflates "management" with being a "master": "it is not likely that any one besides yourself can be sufficiently master of the facts of your life, or the intentions of your mind" (73). Sympathetic identification across the master-servant boundary makes the genre a "very useful" and "particularly serviceable" moral instrument, a way of shaping a public of masters. Franklin wants to "inspire" morality, to persuade his readers to serve willingly, not just to command moral obedience (77). Franklin's acquisition of self-mastery coincided with his acquisition of servants. By transforming a master's power to command into an author's power—his moral duty—to persuade, delight, and instruct his readers, Franklin offers literary means by which readers can imagine themselves as future self-masters and masters of others.

The Power to Serve

Like Michael Zuckerman and others, I read Franklin's concept of public service as sincere, not just a discourse of benevolence that justifies a doctrine of acquisitiveness.[76] But not every person can become "well qualified" (BF 90) enough to even attempt to act "in Public Affairs . . . with a View to the Good of Mankind" (88). Franklin deems himself qualified to determine who is capable of serving, and who is worthy of being served. Occom also defined liberty as the ability to serve God by doing good to man, but he had a different idea of who merited the benefit and dignity of serving instead of being the object of someone else's good deeds. Franklin's views on slavery, women, and Native Americans were complex; he may not have thought that God called Africans to be slaves, Native Americans to be drunk, and women to bear children and be silent. He viewed them all as capable of contributing productively to the public good—but not in public callings, which were only for white men, and in fact only for white men who proved they could master themselves.

In the benevolent institutions that undergird Franklinian public service, "good and Wise Rules," not the commands of "good Masters," compel willing obedience. Recounting his plan for a "united Party for Virtue," he observes that "good and wise Men may probably be more unanimous in their Obedience to" such "Rules" for moral conduct "than common People are to common Laws" (BF 89–90). At the heart of this plan are the "virtues" that inculcate obedience to the inner master; a "creed" that spiritualizes it; and an economic morality that defines liberty as freedom "from the Dominion of Vice" and "from Debt, which exposes a Man to Confinement and a Species of Slavery to his Creditors" (90). "Whoever attempts this aright, and is well qualified," Franklin affirms, "cannot fail of pleasing God, and of meeting with Success." But not everybody is "qualified." Like Occom's, Franklin's economic personhood was shaped by the racialization and secularization of credit and debt. Slavery denotes an incapacity to make the virtues a habit, to be your own master. In Franklin's world, white men who fail to be their own masters and fall into debt, like Deborah Read's first husband and Samuel Keimer, are exiled to the West Indies; a death sentence for New England's native prisoners of war and enslaved Africans becomes a fate of figurative slavery for those who cannot master themselves.[77] To Franklin, economic justice lies in benevolent self-mastery and mastery over others.

Franklin also trades in spiritual discourses of credit, debt, and hypocrisy, as in his representation of Whitefield. Like Occom, though in a very different register, Franklin juxtaposes his service to that of hypocritical ministers who compete with him in the moral marketplace. Franklin admires Whitefield's "Eloquence," which gives him such "wonderful Power over the Hearts and Purses of his Hearers," including Franklin himself (BF 100–101). Attending one of Whitefield's sermons, Franklin decides to increase the amount of his contribution and finally "emptied my Pocket wholly into the Collector's Dish, Gold and all" (101). Franklin awards Whitefield the highest praise one might give a moral merchant: "he was in all his Conduct, a perfectly *honest Man*" (101). Yet he teases Whitefield for relying on the rhetoric of heavenly rewards to negotiate balances of social obligation in his favor. Franklin offers to host the minister during a stay in Philadelphia: "He replied, that if I made that kind Offer for

Christ's sake, I should not miss of a Reward.—And I return'd, *Don't let me be mistaken; it was not for Christ's sake, but for your sake.* One of our common Acquaintance jocosely remark'd that knowing it to be the Custom of the Saints, when they receiv'd any favor, to shift the Burden of the Obligation from off their own Shoulders, and place it in Heaven, I had contriv'd to fix it on Earth" (102). Franklin's reply suggests that the minister uses Christ to deflect earthly obligations, playfully turning his spiritualized discourse into a kind of hypocrisy. Whitefield wants to occupy the place of the creditor, but he is actually a debtor. The price of redemption becomes the crutch of a servant of God who, from an earthly perspective, is a debtor to a virtuous public man.

In a world of hypocrites, the public calls its own visibly godly servant, someone who makes a religion of serving them. Franklin repeatedly asserts that he does not seek "Offices" but is rather "chosen" by the public, another way in which the public is invested with the power of invisible mastery. When told that he would face competition in the next election as clerk of the Pennsylvania Assembly and advised to resign rather than lose the seat, Franklin responds, "I shall never *ask*, never *refuse*, nor ever *resign* an Office. . . . I will not by giving it up, lose my Right of some time or other making Reprisals on my Adversaries" (BF 106). Of course, he retains the office: "I was chosen again, unanimously as usual, at the next Election." The pun on "Election" is irresistible: God elects the saints, and those chosen remain so. Occom highlights the hypocrisy of a white public that assumes God's power to put his servants in their places. Franklin celebrates the fact that "the Public" calls him, a disinterested "Man of Leisure" (113), to occupations that allow him to "enlarge my Power of doing Good" (113–14). But he does not subordinate the public's judgment to his own. "The Officers of the Companies composing the Philadelphia Regiment . . . chose me for their Colonel," he explains, "but conceiving myself unfit, I declin'd that Station" (105). Instead, he helps keep a night watch, and "among the rest I regularly took my Turn of Duty there as a common Soldier." This is not just strategic humility; Franklin asserts a master's prerogative to determine his proper place.

Franklin's "Rules" do not explicitly deny anyone access to the power to do good, but he anecdotally restricts it to white men, even poor ones like his former self. He recounts that a poor older woman inspired his public-spirited imagination by sweeping clean a London street. Franklin sent "my Servant to examine it, who reported that the whole Street was swept perfectly clean" (BF 119). The woman's virtuous labor prompts the thought that "a strong active Man might have done it in half the time" (120). He proposes that "several Watchmen be contracted with" to keep the streets clean and "furnish'd with Brooms and other proper Instruments . . . ready to furnish the poor People they may employ in the Service." These "poor People" are English, the kind of poor man whose street-sweeping prowess can become contractual and qualify as public "Service."

For Franklin, comedy is the appropriate register for depicting Native American and black public service. He treats the possibility of black governance as a joke between white public masters. He and Governor Robert Hunter Morris were adversaries in the Assembly, "but he was so good-natur'd a Man, that . . . we often din'd together" (125). "In gay Conversation over our Wine after Supper," one night, Morris jokes "that he much admir'd the Idea of Sancho Panza, who when it was propos'd to give him a Government, requested it might be a Government of *Blacks*, as then, if he could not agree with his People he might sell them." When a friend of Morris turns and asks, "'Franklin, why do you continue to side with these damn'd Quakers? had you not better sell them? the Proprietor would give you a good Price,'" Franklin replies: "The Governor . . . had not yet *black'd* them enough. He had indeed labour'd hard to blacken the Assembly in all his Messages, but they wip'd off his Coloring as fast as he laid it on, and plac'd it in return thick upon his own Face; so that finding he was likely to be negrified himself, he . . . grew tir'd of the Contest, and quitted the Government." Occom's image of how God treats hypocritical prayers suggests an appropriate "Coloring" medium for this scene. Franklin may have become an abolitionist who believed that freed slaves could, after a period of apprenticeship, come to govern themselves; but black public service was imagined as a minstrel show.[78]

Like Occom, Franklin suggests that Native Americans' self-governance was thwarted by drunkenness and holds whites morally accountable for it. Occom sought to reform his brethren so they could govern themselves, and Franklin depicts Meredith as a public drunk capable of reforming and making himself serviceable. But in a scene from his history as a diplomat, Franklin treats alcoholism as a trait that permanently excludes Native Americans from the power of being useful. As a public servant, he is sent to make a treaty with natives seeking English help to defend them against the French: "As those People are extremely apt to get drunk, and when so are very quarrelsome and disorderly, we strictly forbad the selling any Liquor to them; and when they complain'd of this Restriction, we told them that if they would continue sober during the Treaty, we would give them Plenty of Rum when Business was over" (BF 114). Sure enough, after the treaty is concluded, "they were all drunk, Men and Women, quarreling and fighting." "Half-naked . . . running and beating one another with Firebrands," they "form'd a Scene the most resembling our Ideas of Hell that could well be imagined" (114–15). Franklin quotes one of their "old Counsellors" sent to apologize: "'The great Spirit who made all things made everything for some Use, and whatever Use he design'd anything for, that Use it should always be put to; Now, when he made Rum, he said, LET THIS BE FOR INDIANS TO GET DRUNK WITH. And it must be so'" (115). Franklin's own uses of instrumental reason demonstrate his capacity for self-mastery and public service, but in the "Counsellor's" speech it demonstrates his uselessness to his people or anyone else. Franklin extends this critique to "these Savages" more broadly, adding, however ruefully: "And indeed if it be the Desire of Providence to extirpate these Savages in order to make room for Cultivators of the Earth, it seems not improbable that Rum may be the appointed Means. It has already annihilated all the Tribes who formerly inhabited the Seacoast." In "Remarks Concerning the Savages of North America," Franklin notes approvingly that natives are capable of obeying their own "Rules" and correctly understand white men's attempts to "civilize" them as a way "to contrive the *cheating of Indians in the Price of Beaver*."[79] Franklin has a Mohawk tell a joke at the expense of whites, but "the Price of Beaver" is an inadequate metaphor for native losses. Dana Nelson has perceived Occom's "consciousness of the systematic robbery of Indian selfhood."[80] By Occom's reckoning, the whites of Franklin's native New England cheated its "Savages" of the price of redemption and of the liberty to serve.

Prodigals and Servants

In part 3 of the *Autobiography*, Franklin recounts a "very cordial and affectionate" visit to his brother's printing house in Newport, Rhode Island. The visit is the long-deferred resolution of the earlier scene where Franklin writes of himself as the prodigal, returning to James's printing house "better dress'd than ever while in his Service," his "Pockets lin'd with near Five Pounds Sterling in Silver," a performance of prosperity that his elder brother greets with a "grum and sullen" expression (as, in the parable, the elder brother scowls) (BF 33). Ten years later, his health "fast declining," James asks Benjamin "that in case of his Death which he apprehended not far distant, I would take home his Son, then but 10 Year of Age, and bring him up to the Printing Business. This I accordingly perform'd, sending him a few Years to School before I took him into the

Office" (95). Franklin adds, "thus it was that I made my Brother ample Amends for the Service I had depriv'd him of by leaving him so early" (96). Franklin tells the story to his advantage, of course, but it is also worth noting that he grants his brother a bit of grace, lending him a capacity for forgiveness that the original parable gives only to the father. In Franklin's version, the form of the older brother's forgiveness is apprenticing his son to his prodigal brother, a master who has "bread enough and to spare." Franklin sought to be such a master to New England apprentices even after his death.

"I was born in Boston, New England," Franklin wrote in a 1789 codicil to his will intended to express his "gratitude" to his native "State of Massachusetts."[81] He explains the simple premise of a bequest of "one thousand pounds sterling" to the city: that "among artisans, good apprentices are most likely to make good citizens." This is also a premise of his memoir. Both the codicil and the *Autobiography* are methods of being "useful, even after my death, if possible, in forming and advancing other young men, that may be serviceable to their country."[82] The sum he leaves to Boston, he specifies, is to be

> managed under the direction of the selectmen, united with the ministers of the oldest Episcopalian, Congregational, and Presbyterian churches who are to let out the sum upon interest, at five per cent. per annum, to such young married artificers, under the age of twenty-five years, as have served an apprenticeship in the said town, and faithfully fulfilled the duties required in their indentures, so as to obtain a good moral character from at least two respectable citizens, who are willing to become their sureties, in a bond with the applicants, for the repayment of the moneys so lent, with interest.[83]

These creditworthy young artisans will pay it forward, with the help of various "managers" and capitalism itself ("as the capital increases by the accumulated interest," he remarks, the loans "will be more ample"). To "serve as many as possible in their turn, as well as to make the repayment of the principle borrowed more easy," Franklin specifies, "each borrower shall be obliged to pay, with the yearly interest, one tenth part of the principal, which sums of principal and interest, so paid in, shall be again let out to fresh borrowers." In Franklin's plan, these apprentice borrowers do not just become master creditors; they become citizens, cultivating self-mastery by fulfilling their "obligation to pay" their debts and experiencing the virtue of serving others in a republic based on a credit economy that needs a steady supply of "fresh borrowers." Franklin the prodigal thus repaid Boston some of the portion that he did not inherit but earned, allowing future moral white men access to the liberty of public service.

Occom also sought to build earthly institutions that would enable future generations to be serviceable to their communities, as several of his petitions to white governments reveal. These petitions register a kind of servant protest, formal appeals to a hypocritical master to fulfill his moral duty to provide what is just and equal. Like blacks' petitions to Massachusetts for emancipation in the 1780s, several of them call for racial justice by employing the rhetoric of political slavery used by American rebels to legitimate their independence from Britain.[84] Their rhetorical power lies in juxtaposing the sweeping rhetoric of America's triumph over tyranny with the community's requests for humble means of subsistence, bare freedom from "pinching Necessity" (SO 150).[85] For example, a petition to New York (tentatively dated 1785) opens with the Montauk proclaiming themselves "glad . . . that you have at last got your Freedom Liberty and Independence . . . by Your Steadiness, Boldness, and Great Courage, you have broke the Yoke and the Chain of Slavery" (SO 150), and then requesting "150 head of Cattle and some [Sheep] and a few more Hogs" (152). A petition from the Brotherton tribe to Congress begins by congratulating the legislators for breaking the "Slavish Chains and the galling Yoke" and then asks for a grist mill, a saw mill, "Husbandry Tools," and some books "for a little Liberary [*sic*], for we would have our Children have some Learning,—our Young People are much inclined to Learn" (150). To follow their inclinations to learn, as Occom and Franklin had, native "Young People" needed books. Yet as Occom's experience had taught him, even granted such meager access to cultural capital, they might never have the liberty of Franklin's apprentices: to be "borrowers" instead of "debtors," to be children and mothers and fathers, not America's hired servants.

CODA: SERVING THE PLOT

CHILDREN WHO SERVE, eye-servants, servants turned out of doors, prodigals, tyrants, self-masters, and public servants: these saints, sinners, and hypocrites were familiar characters in Puritan and post-Puritan narratives about the relationship between spiritual and earthly profits. The varieties of obedience and authority they embodied were the currency of New England's economy of service. In the New England setting of God's plot, these lived metaphors connected every soul and body, and mind and heart, to the earthly business of households, churches, courts, and markets in a network that extended as far as the heavenly Master could see, across space and time.

New England's antebellum literary culture offers vibrant evidence of the ongoing life of these secular and sacred types, as writers confronted a world devoted to the service of mammon. They shaped Ralph Waldo Emerson's ideal of self-reliance as they had shaped Benjamin Franklin's model of self-discipline, though more enigmatically: "Who has more obedience than I masters me, though he should not raise his finger. Round him I must revolve by the gravitation of spirits."[1] To counter the moral and spiritual blight she deemed the "servility of individuals," Margaret Fuller offered a vision of the prodigal as a "radiant apparition of genius and love," who "feels himself called to understand and aid nature, that she may, through his intelligence, be raised and interpreted; to be a student of, and servant to, the universe-spirit."[2] William Apess narrated his conversion from a Pequot child bound out to multiple abusive white masters to "Son of the Forest" and servant of the Lord, a Methodist preaching "in my proper element, just harnessed for the work, with the fire of divine love burning on my heart."[3]

These figures also served fictional plots and shaped the novel form.

Catharine Maria Sedgwick helped invent a curious genre, the Puritan romance. She narrates *Hope Leslie* as a historian "confined not to the actual, but the possible," one who claims an imaginative relationship to the past in the spirit of moral reform. Sedgwick celebrates her Puritan ancestors as protorepublicans who "sacrificed all that gratifies them, to the cause of God and of man—the cause of liberty and religion," but the novel is hardly an uncomplicated filiopietistic exercise.[4] Sedgwick sets her novel in the aftermath of the Pequot War and Antinomian Controversy. If the spirit of liberty belongs to the realm of the Puritan "actual," so does their denial of it to the Native Americans whose lives they destroyed and the women whose submission they demanded.

The narrative follows the path of its heroine, a child who serves the novel's plot and themes by disobeying the laws of men. Hope Leslie embodies a kind of gendered mastery, the magical power to bend men to her will even as she virtuously disobeys their authority. A prodigal daughter, she is bound out to John Winthrop's household after she frees from prison Nelema, a Native American woman sentenced to be executed for witchcraft, but Hope's spirit remains untamed; she later breaks Magawisca out of prison, too. The other heroines have less liberty than Hope, but they are also romantic types of the child who serves. Magawisca—daughter of the Pequot sachem Mononotto and his wife, Monoca—is bound out as a servant to the Fletcher household after the war. She refuses to submit to the authority of white men and their laws but also refuses to serve her father's revenge plot, sacrificing her arm to save the life of Everell Fletcher, the young man all of the women love. Esther Downing provides the fourth point in the novel's romantic quadrangle. She is too tightly bound by duty and scripture and tends toward a servant's legalism, but she redeems herself as a child who serves by sacrificing romantic love for a republican ideal of disinterested service to God and mankind, becoming a spinster who serves. Another child who serves is Rosa: seduced by the novel's rake, she travels with him to Boston in disguise (quite unconvincingly) as his boy page. Like Magawisca and Esther, Rosa martyrs herself to serve the marriage plot, disobeying her master's command to assist in Hope's kidnapping. Martyrdom and vocation are mirror versions of willing obedience in one's place. These characters are not just versions of each other, but of Sedgwick herself as author.

Yet the female character that most reveals Sedgwick's hopes and fears about her authorial vocation is one who has received almost no critical attention. Though the novel features a mustache-twirling rake and a vengeful Pequot sachem whose minions dash an infant's head against a doorstep, the character whom Sedgwick deems the novel's "evil genius" is Jennet, a servant who will not govern her tongue.[5] Nearly all of the characters tell her at some point to shut up, a chorus of shared mastery in which the reader is meant to participate. In particular, Jennet is the novel's shrillest voice of race prejudice (unlike the more anxious and affective version expressed by Hope). Sedgwick displaces unapologetic prejudice onto a female servant to inspire her middle-class readers to reform their own prejudices—hoping to convince them that such racism is for servants, not ladies. Jennet has an eye-servant's hypocritical, unromantic approach to religion that emphasizes scripture and duty rather than spirit. Mistakenly kidnapped in place of Hope in a plot she helped set in motion, Jennet dies with a bag over her head in a ship explosion (so much for being "confined . . . to the possible"). The bag remains intact when her body is eventually taken out of the harbor.

Sedgwick's treatment of Jennet is quite sadistic, even by the standards of divine justice with its will to fit the punishment to the crime. Jennet is a ritual sacrifice to Sedgwick's romanticized Puritanism and her gendered vocation. Sedgwick displaces onto Jennet the intractable hypocrisy and race prejudice of "actual" Puritans who enslaved and slaughtered so-called savages, not the romanticized liberty-loving progenitors of patriots. For all the novel's desire to transcend the prejudices of the earlier age and its own, it ultimately remains tethered, as does its spirited heroine, to the actual. If Esther in particular projects an idealized version of Sedgwick's authorial calling as public service, Jennet projects an anxious one: the unimaginative, unromantic, literal-minded woman who will not hold her tongue in public—no artist but merely, to paraphrase Nathaniel Hawthorne's notorious comment, a scribbler.[6]

In Hawthorne's *The House of the Seven Gables*, Phoebe Pyncheon exemplifies the cheerful child who serves, the countertype of the prideful Alice Pyncheon in the sketch he writes under Holgrave's name in chapter 13. While the supernatural elements in the novel as a whole are only a tease, this chapter overtly gothicizes Puritan hypocrisy, depicting a wizard's power to possess a woman's soul as analogous to an author's power to captivate a reader (or, in this case, put her to sleep). But Holgrave has internalized the moral of his own story and resists mastering Phoebe; instead he will marry her, with her consent, in a happy ending that seems, in truth, more congenial to Holgrave's implied readers than to Hawthorne's. But if Hawthorne satirizes Holgrave's tale, he also borrows the daguerreotypist's romantic artistry: the power to harness nature to expose the scowl of hypocrisy beneath the benignant smile of the esteemed public servant Jaffrey Pyncheon, whose "swarthy whiteness" is so evocative of Paul Bayne's eye-servant chameleon, the prototype of racial vocation's many-shaded white master.[7]

Types of racial vocation spiritualized abolitionist authorship. When Frederick Douglass published his life story in 1845, brilliantly making his readers imaginative eyewitnesses in the case against slavery, William Lloyd Garrison and Wendell Phillips supplied their own versions of New England eye-mastery: prefatory testimonies that legitimated Douglass as the author of his own life. In his preface to the 1845 narrative, Garrison touts his own "endeavor[s] to instill hope and courage" into Douglass, to inspire him to promote "the anti-slavery enterprise"—which Garrison calls "a vocation so anomalous and responsible for a person in his situation."[8] Douglass's own account of pursuing his vocation differs from Garrison's. While "attending an anti-slavery convention at Nantucket," he explains, "I felt strongly moved to speak" but also "felt myself a slave, and the idea of speaking to white people weighed me down." After just "a few moments," however, "I felt a degree of freedom, and said what I desired with considerable ease."[9] Douglass here enacts his own vocation, claiming his freedom to speak his mind before a white public whose members he refuses to consider his masters. In the "Appendix" that immediately follows, he calls himself to testify against hypocrisy—a national sin, not just a southern one. "Between the Christianity of this land, and the Christianity of Christ, I recognize the widest possible difference," he explains. "I love the pure, peaceable, and impartial Christianity of Christ: I therefore hate the corrupt, slave-holding, women-whipping, cradle-plundering, partial and hypocritical Christianity of this land."[10] Douglass was willing to die to resist the unjust authority of white mastery. His authorship, like the dramatic resistance of his overseer Covey that restores his manhood, is racialized Christian liberty. In neither form of resistance did Douglass require a white man to give him hope and courage or teach him the meaning of freedom.

Harriet Beecher Stowe built a novel on Douglass's premise, offering a sweeping condemnation of slavery as national sin. *Uncle Tom's Cabin*'s panorama of hypocrites includes Ophelia St. Clare, Augustine's "cousin Vermont." Like many New England ladies, Ophelia is no child who serves; rather, she is "the absolute bond-slave of the '*ought*,'" embodying the chilly heart of the Protestant ethic.[11] Ophelia's opposition to slavery is merely moral and rational, so Stowe turns her out of doors, sending her south for a stay at Augustine's New Orleans plantation. Stowe subjects the unsympathetic woman to a moral dressing-down by her louche cousin, who challenges her: "If we emancipate, are you willing to educate?"[12] He has provided her with an opportunity to convert his rhetorical question into a genuine one, giving her an enslaved girl, Topsy, who confirms Samuel Sewall's premise that "Negroes are generally Eye-Servants, great Thieves, much addicted to Stealing, Lying and Purloining."[13]

The moralist Ophelia and the licentious child Topsy allegorize a racialized and gendered dialectic of obedience. Spiritually, Ophelia is the servant who must learn to serve from love, and Topsy is the unredeemed prodigal who must internalize the moral law. Through the spiritual medium of their love for Little Eva, they reform each other: fulfilling their mutual obligations, Ophelia does become "Miss Feely," while Topsy imbibes the spirit of Christian self-mastery. In serving Stowe's redemption plot, both transform eye-service into an abolitionist calling. Unlike the eternal child Eva, Topsy becomes a woman and a Christian under Ophelia's "efficient" guidance, showing "so much intelligence, activity, and zeal, and desire to do good in the world" that she becomes "recommended and approved" to be an African missionary. The narrator proudly reports, "the same activity and ingenuity which, when a child, made her so multiform and restless in her developments, is now employed, in a safer and wholesomer manner, in teaching the children of her own country."[14] Stowe credited God with writing the novel; here she celebrates his power to convert even the most incorrigible slave girl into a child who serves—in this case, one who serves other children. When Stowe calls Africa Topsy's "own country," however, she reveals the limits of God's political imagination. As Topsy eloquently explains, she "never was born . . . never had no father nor mother . . . was raised by a speculator."[15] She is in this sense a daughter of American slavery. Stowe allows that Christianity can make anyone profitable, but former slaves like Topsy and the Harris family, however virtuous, can best serve the United States by willingly turning themselves out of its doors.

These writers used types of master and servant to imaginatively connect past and present, and we might follow their lead when we try to understand the relationships between how things were and how they are, and to express our hopes and fears about what they will become. The boundary between private and public is continually adjusted by technologies that multiply ways to be watched, watch others, and monitor ourselves. But these technologies can also occlude or distract us from what we may not want to see: the world's women and children, servants and slaves, who make so many of its cultural goods far from the places where many of us buy them. To some people, "service economy" is a euphemism for employment conditions that serve shareholders at the expense of workers who do not have living wages, populated by "wage slaves" and gig laborers who can be beckoned by the swipe of a phone. Others tout the flexibility that economy offers to those so-called independent contractors, who might set their own schedules if not their wages. And what might it mean to those who shop on e-commerce sites for tote bags and aprons embossed with "I am an unprofitable servant" (Luke 17:10)? Public service, as a description of political office, seems to many the domain of self-interested careerists at the call of lobbyists. But others invest their hopes in what they call the "real Americans who manage to achieve high office," who "realize that they are servants of the people, meant to use their position for the public good."[16] White women and people of color can occupy these positions, but those who do might have their legitimacy challenged, be hectored to produce proof of citizenship, or be admonished by their colleagues to hold their tongues.

The motto of Portland State University, where I have worked for almost twenty years, is *doctrina urbi serviat* (let knowledge serve the city). The English translation, in gold letters, adorns a sky bridge that connects two buildings on opposite sides of Broadway, the major street that runs through our downtown campus. My long acquaintance with Elizabeth Knapp may have made me more likely than most people to think these words mean something and to wonder how they connect to my actual work. Who issues this injunction, and in whose name? What kind of servant is "knowledge"? What kind of master is "the city"? Whom, what, and how do I serve? The answers change depending on whether I am in the classroom with my amazing students or grading their papers; engaging with exciting work in my field or finally grasping that "research" is also a budget line item and the humanities do not count; working through tricky curricular issues with thoughtful colleagues or poring over spreadsheets and reports to prepare for committee meetings. Not all of this is work for love, but I never forget how lucky I am to have my job and the professional autonomy that is, like the Puritan covenant's liberty to serve, both the condition of tenure and its ongoing obligation. Discourses of service continue to shape the stories we tell about the meaning and value of all kinds of work. So if the Devil did in fact have the power to show Knapp the whole world and used it to transport her here, she might well find it as astonishingly different and strangely familiar as we find hers.

NOTES

Introduction

1. Matt. 25:14–30, Authorized (King James) Version. All quotations from the Bible are from this version.

2. John Winthrop, "Particular Considerations," in *The Puritan Tradition in America, 1630–1720*, ed. Alden Vaughan (Columbia: University of South Carolina Press, 1972), 33.

3. John Winthrop, "A Model of Christian Charity," in *The Puritans in America: A Narrative Anthology*, ed. Alan Heimert and Andrew Delbanco (Cambridge, MA: Harvard University Press, 1985), 89.

4. Ibid., 91–92.

5. Matt. 6:24.

6. C. S. Manegold, *Ten Hills Farm: The Forgotten History of Slavery in the North* (Princeton, NJ: Princeton University Press, 2010), 26. Manegold takes Winthrop's estate as a metonym for the "forgotten history" of racial slavery in colonial New England, establishing a network that extended throughout the British Atlantic and across several generations of elite families. See also Margaret Ellen Newell, *Brethren by Nature: New England Indians, Colonists, and the Origins of American Slavery* (Ithaca, NY: Cornell University Press, 2015).

7. John Winthrop, *Winthrop's Journal "History of New England, 1630–1649,"* ed. James Kendall Hosmer (New York: Scribner, 1908), 1:272. On the Bay Colony's economic policies in this decade, see Stephen Innes, *Creating the Commonwealth: The Economic Culture of Puritan New England* (New York: Norton, 1995), 175–79.

8. There has been only one monograph dedicated to legal and institutional servitude in early New England, Lawrence Towner's unrevised 1955 dissertation. It was published posthumously as *A Good Master Well Served: Masters and Servants in Colonial Massachusetts, 1620–1750* (New York: Garland Publishing, 1998). Otherwise, New England servants have played relatively small roles in studies of transatlantic migration, labor markets, and the household. On migration, see David Cressy, *Coming Over: Migration and Communication between England and New England in the Seventeenth Century* (Cambridge: Cambridge University Press, 1987); Alison Games, *Migration and the Origins of the English Atlantic World* (Cambridge, MA: Harvard University Press, 1999). Household studies include Edmund Morgan, *The Puritan Family: Religion and Domestic Relations in Seventeenth-Century New England*, rev. ed. (New York: Harper and Row, 1966); Helena Wall, *Fierce Communion: Family and Community in Early America* (Cambridge, MA: Harvard University Press, 1990); Gloria L. Main, *Peoples of a Spacious Land: Families and Cultures in Colonial New*

England (Cambridge, MA: Harvard University Press, 2001); M. Michelle Jarrett Morris, *Under Household Government: Sex and Family in Puritan Massachusetts* (Cambridge, MA: Harvard University Press, 2013). Many of these studies also associate servants with deviance. Indeed, one of the richest narrative sources on New England servants is a collection of execution sermons: Daniel E. Williams, ed., *Pillars of Salt: An Anthology of Early American Criminal Narratives* (Lanham, MD: Rowman and Littlefield, 1994). Works on service are common in early modern to eighteenth-century English literary and cultural studies; but despite the insights of Atlanticism, no scholars of early Anglo-America have taken up the topic (indeed, scholars of early American literature have ceded the topic of labor to historians). Two book-length studies of servants in American literature, Barbara Ryan's *Love, Wages, Slavery: The Literature of Servitude in the United States* (Urbana: University of Illinois Press, 2006) and Veronica C. Hendrick's *Servants, Slaves, and Savages: Reflections of Law in American Literature* (Durham, NC: Carolina Academic Press, 2011), focus on the nineteenth century. I distinguish these books within the scholarship on slavery and labor in American literature, which is vast.

9. Cotton Mather, *A Good Master Well Served* (Boston, 1696), 21.

10. As Edmund Morgan pointed out long ago, "most of the inhabitants of seventeenth-century New England either were or had been 'servants'" (*The Puritan Family*, 109). As Morgan's quote marks suggest, the word "servant" covered a broad range of legal and employment statuses. David D. Hall limns the significance of "the everyday experience of accepting the authority of those above you" for understanding the political culture of first-generation New Englanders, noting that "no one was spared this experience, not even the Stuart kings, who repeatedly were told (and sometimes said themselves) that they were God's servants" (*A Reforming People: Puritanism and the Transformation of Public Life in New England* [New York: Knopf, 2011], 9). The ambiguity of the word "servant" in seventeenth-century England sparked a spirited debate between Peter Laslett and C. B. MacPherson about the Levellers' enfranchisement policy. Ann Kussmaul deems that debate to have produced more heat than light and offers some useful clarifications (*Servants in Husbandry in Early Modern England* [Cambridge: Cambridge University Press, 1981], 135).

11. Approaches to lived metaphor have revolved around Perry Miller's enduring tropes of covenant and errand. See his *Errand into the Wilderness* (1956; repr., Cambridge, MA: Belknap Press of Harvard University Press, 1984) and *The New England Mind: The Seventeenth Century* (1939; repr., Boston: Beacon Press, 1961), chapters 13–15. Sacvan Bercovitch recasts Miller's trope as "New England's errand into free enterprise" in *The Rites of Assent: Transformations in the Symbolic Construction of America* (New York: Routledge, 1993), 30. For other notable revisions of these foundational metaphors, see Elizabeth Maddock Dillon, *The Gender of Freedom: Fictions of Liberalism and the Literary Public Sphere* (Stanford, CA: Stanford University Press, 2004); Jonathan Beecher Field, *Errands into the Metropolis: New England Dissidents in Revolutionary London* (Hanover, NH: Dartmouth College Press, 2009). The only scholarly book entirely devoted to the subject of servitude in covenant theology, Michael S. Horton's *Lord and Servant: A Covenant Christology* (Louisville, KY: Westminster John Knox Press, 2005), is geared toward a very specialized readership

of theologians (for example, chapter 1 is subtitled "A Covenantal Prolegomenon"). Scholars examining how the contractual metaphor affected the lived experience of covenant often cite passages about servants or use their own metaphors of service. See, for example, David Zaret, *The Heavenly Contract: Ideology and Organization in Pre-Revolutionary Puritanism* (Chicago, IL: University of Chicago Press, 1985), 160–61; Andrew Delbanco, *The Puritan Ordeal* (Cambridge, MA: Harvard University Press, 1989), 61–62. Miller's discussion of "errand's" etymology also ties it to service (*Errand into the Wilderness*, 3).

12. Sarah Rivett, "Early American Religion in a Postsecular Age, *PMLA* 128, no. 4 (2013): 990.

13. Robert Steinfeld, *The Invention of Free Labor: The Employment Relation in English and American Law and Culture, 1350–1870* (Chapel Hill: University of North Carolina Press, 1991); Christopher Tomlins, *Freedom Bound: Law, Labor, and Civic Identity in Colonizing English America, 1580–1865* (New York: Cambridge University Press, 2010), 328–31.

14. David Roediger and Elizabeth D. Esch, *The Production of Difference: Race and the Management of Labor in U.S. History* (New York: Oxford University Press, 2013); Caitlin Rosenthal, "Slavery's Scientific Management: Masters and Managers," in *Slavery's Capitalism: A New History of American Economic Development*, ed. Sven Beckert and Seth Rockman (Philadelphia: University of Pennsylvania Press, 2016), 62–86. The quotes around "new" appear in Seth Rockman's useful overview of the field, "What Makes the Study of Capitalism Newsworthy?" *Journal of the Early Republic* 34, no. 3 (2014): 441.

15. Bethany Moreton, *To Serve God and Wal-Mart: The Making of Christian Free Enterprise* (Cambridge, MA: Harvard University Press, 2009), 125 and 101.

16. Innes, *Creating the Commonwealth*, 125. Louise Breen critiques Innes's "Weberian" approach in *Transgressing the Bounds: Subversive Enterprises among the Puritan Elite, 1630–1692* (New York: Oxford University Press, 2001), 52.

17. Richard Archer, *Fissures in the Rock: New England in the Seventeenth Century* (Hanover, NH: University of New Hampshire Press, 2001), 126–28; Tomlins, *Freedom Bound*, 54–56.

18. As John Wood Sweet has observed, "the presence of even a small number of enslaved Africans would transform the ways all New Englanders lived, how they thought about themselves, and the character of their body politic" (*Bodies Politic: Negotiating Race in the American North, 1730–1830* [2003; repr., Philadelphia: University of Pennsylvania Press, 2006], 63). See also Wendy Warren, *New England Bound: Slavery and Colonization in Early America* (New York: Norton, 2016); Newell, *Brethren by Nature*; Manegold, *Ten Hills Farm*; M. Morris, *Under Household Government*; Allegra di Bonaventura, *For Adam's Sake: A Family Saga in Colonial New England* (New York: Liveright, 2013); Eric Kimball, "'What Have We to Do with Slavery?': New Englanders and the Slave Economies of the West Indies," in *Slavery's Capitalism*, 181–94; Ann Marie Plane, *Colonial Intimacies: Indian Marriage in Early New England* (Ithaca, NY: Cornell University Press, 2000); Elise Lemire, *Black Walden: Slavery and Its Aftermath in Concord, Massachusetts* (Philadelphia: University of Pennsylvania Press, 2009). On New England's role in trade among British colonies, see Gregory E.

O'Malley, *Final Passages: The Intercolonial Slave Trade of British America, 1619–1807* (Chapel Hill: University of North Carolina Press, 2014). These studies, in turn, build upon Lorenzo Greene's pioneering work, *The Negro in Colonial New England, 1620–1776* (1942; repr., New York: Atheneum, 1968); and two 1998 books that revived attention to slavery in colonial New England: Joanne Pope Melish, *Disowning Slavery: Gradual Emancipation and "Race" in New England, 1780–1860* (Ithaca, NY: Cornell University Press, 1998); and Ira Berlin, *Many Thousands Gone: The First Two Centuries of Slavery in North America* (Cambridge, MA: Harvard University Press, 1998).

19. On the blurriness of freedom and unfreedom as the defining feature of Atlantic labor culture, see Tomlins, *Freedom Bound.* On the literary implications of viewing the New England economy from an Atlantic perspective, see Michelle Burnham, *Folded Selves: Colonial New England Writing in the World System* (Hanover, NH: Dartmouth College, 2007).

20. Warren, *New England Bound*, 14.

21. Bercovitch prefaced his own 1993 contribution to this conversation by expressing the hope that his "view of the Puritan errand will not overstrain the worn links between Protestantism and the rise of capitalism" (*The Rites of Assent*, 30). For a summary of these debates, see Mark Valeri, *Heavenly Merchandize: How Religion Shaped Commerce in Puritan America* (Princeton, NJ: Princeton University Press, 2010), 7–9. For a fascinating recent re-reading of Max Weber's concept of "spirit" as it relates to contemporary economic culture, see Arjun Appadurai, *Banking on Words: The Failure of Language in the Age of Derivative Finance* (Chicago, IL: University of Chicago Press, 2016), 39–40. Richard A. Bailey does consider the relationship between Puritan theology and New England slavery, examining the racialization of spiritual liberty in *Race and Redemption in Puritan New England* (New York: Oxford University Press, 2011); I consider Christian liberty as part of a broader discourse of service. Although they do not focus on New England Puritanism, there are several fine recent studies of Christianity and Atlantic slavery: see, for example, Rebecca Anne Goetz, *The Baptism of Early America: How Christianity Created Race* (Baltimore, MD: Johns Hopkins University Press, 2012); Travis Glasson, *Mastering Christianity: Missionary Anglicanism and Slavery in the Atlantic World* (New York: Oxford University Press, 2012); Colin Kidd, *The Forging of Races: Race and Scripture in the Protestant Atlantic World, 1600–2000* (Cambridge: Cambridge University Press, 2006).

22. Bercovitch puts it particularly baldly (*The Rites of Assent* 32), but his phrase exemplifies the critical tendency that Valeri decries, of treating "religious language . . . merely as an ex post facto legitimization of commercial expansion and justification for economic elites" (*Heavenly Merchandize*, 5).

23. Valeri, *Heavenly Merchandize*; Innes, *Creating the Commonwealth*; Mark Peterson, *The Price of Redemption: The Spiritual Economy of Puritan New England* (Stanford, CA: Stanford University Press, 1997); Charles Lloyd Cohen, *God's Caress: The Psychology of Puritan Religious Experience* (New York: Oxford University Press, 1986). Literary criticism in this vein includes Burnham, *Folded Selves*; Jennifer Jordan Baker, *Securing the Commonwealth: Debt, Speculation, and Writing in the Making of Early America* (Baltimore, MD: Johns Hopkins University Press, 2005); and Nan

Goodman, "Robert Keayne's Nails, or a Mercantilist's Version of Christian Charity," in *The Turn Around Religion in America: Literature, Culture, and the Work of Sacvan Bercovitch*, ed. Nan Goodman and Michael P. Kramer (Farnham, UK: Ashgate Publishing, 2011), 223–35. The merchant Robert Keayne, who was admonished for price gouging, is a common object of analysis in these studies.

24. Valeri, *Heavenly Merchandize*, 6.

25. Tomlins, *Freedom Bound*, 386–87. See also Lisa Wilson, *Ye Heart of a Man: The Domestic Life of Men in Colonial New England* (New Haven, CT: Yale University Press, 1999), 36. David Leverenz has observed that histories of secular individualism and the work ethic have overlooked the "central family and community thrust of the American Puritan emigration" and in particular "the power of a language of voluntary dependence" (*The Language of Puritan Feeling: An Exploration in Literature, Psychology, and Social History* [New Brunswick, NJ: Rutgers University Press, 1980], 137).

26. As William K. B. Stoever explains, "Puritans characteristically defined the 'new being' of the regenerate as the capacity willingly to obey, and therein to seek the incarnation of, God's will in all aspects of earthly life" (*"A Faire and Easie Way to Heaven": Covenant Theology and Antinomianism in Early Massachusetts* [Middletown, CT: Wesleyan University Press, 1978], 18).

27. Max Weber's paradigmatic account of the "Protestant ethic" is rooted in this fine distinction: "however useless good works might be as a means of attaining salvation, for even the elect remain beings of the flesh, and everything they do falls infinitely short of divine standards, nevertheless, they are indispensable as a sign of election. They are the technical means, not of purchasing salvation, but of getting rid of the fear of damnation" (*The Protestant Ethic and the Spirit of Capitalism*, trans. Talcott Parsons [1930; repr., London: Routledge Classics, 2002], 69). For important correctives to Weber's understanding of covenant theology, see Innes, *Creating the Commonwealth*, 128–31; Cohen, *God's Caress*, 111–19.

28. Luke 17:5–10.

29. Jean Calvin, *A Harmony of the Gospels: Matthew, Mark and Luke*, trans. A. W. Morrison, ed. David W. Torrance and Thomas F. Torrance (Grand Rapids, MI: William B. Eerdmans, 1975), 2:123.

30. John Cotton, *Treatise of the Covenant of Grace* (London, 1659), 94, 116, and 184; Thomas Shepard, *The Sincere Convert*, in Thomas Shepard, *The Works of Thomas Shepard*, ed. John A. Albro (New York: AMS Press, 1967), 1:98. Shepard's exegesis is closer to that of the influential Puritan divine William Ames, who insisted that "in respect of God, our very soules are to be subjected, and wee ought to acknowledge our selves not only unprofitable servants, Luke 17:10 but nothing . . . and to be abhorred" (*Conscience with the Power and Cases Thereof* [London, 1643], book 5, 151).

31. Samuel Sewall, *The Diary of Samuel Sewall 1674–1729*, ed. M. Halsey Thomas (New York: Farrar, Straus and Giroux, 1973), 1:605. To Sewall, Hobart was not just an "excellent" preacher, but the former master of two of his sons. See Judith S. Graham, *Puritan Family Life: The Diary of Samuel Sewall* (Boston: Northeastern University Press, 2000), 112–13. Graham provides a table of all the Sewall children who had been "sent out" and takes their experiences as case studies in the meaning of binding out in Puritan culture and the historiography of Puritan child rearing (ibid., 144–66).

32. Samuel Sewall, "The Selling of Joseph," in Samuel Sewall, *The Selling of Joseph: A Memorial*, ed. Sidney Kaplan (Amherst: University of Massachusetts Press, 1969), 14; Greene, *The Negro in Colonial New England*, 28. Greene also refers to Belcher's son as the "slave-trading Governor of Massachusetts" (ibid., 56). A year and a half after they attended Hobart's lecture, Sewall vociferously opposed Belcher's plan to sell six thousand bushels of wheat to Caribbean buyers after a drought made it scarce and unaffordable for New Englanders (Valeri, *Heavenly Merchandize*, 170–71).

33. Joanna Brooks, "'This Indian World': An Introduction to the Writings of Samson Occom," in Samson Occom, *The Collected Writings of Samson Occom, Mohegan: Leadership and Literature in Eighteenth-Century Native America*, ed. Joanna Brooks (New York: Oxford University Press, 2006), 21–22.

34. Occom, *The Collected Writings of Samson Occom*, 82. Occom wrote the letter in September 1768, the same month he wrote his well-known autobiography. He does not cite Luke 17:10 but alludes to it in his famous sermon, *The Execution of Moses Paul*, affirming the goodness of God's sovereignty: "we have nothing to give unto God if we essay to give all the service that we are capable of, we should give him nothing but what was his own, and when we give ourselves unto God, both soul and body, we give him nothing; for we were his before; he had a right to do with us as he pleased, either to throw us into hell or to save us" (ibid., 107).

35. In a 1783 letter to John Bailey, Occom complained bitterly that Wheelock's schools "are become altogether unprofitable to the poor Indians—In short he has done little or no good to the Indians with all that Money we Collected in England," adding, "all that money has done, is, it has made the Doctor's Family very grand in the World" (ibid., 119). He repeats the charge in a 1784 letter to Bailey (ibid., 121). Wheelock had died in 1779, but his son was leading the institution.

36. David Graeber, *Debt: The First 5,000 Years*, updated ed. (Brooklyn, New York: Melville House, 2014), 87.

37. Weber, *The Protestant Ethic*, 108 and 114. His prominent interlocutor R. H. Tawney also refers to scriptural masters and servants to explain capitalism as a system in which "a man can serve two masters, for—so happily is the world disposed—he may be paid by one, while he works for the other" (*Religion and the Rise of Capitalism: A Historical Study* [Gloucester, MA: Peter Smith, 1962], 247).

38. William Perkins, *A Treatise of the Vocations or Callings of Men*, in William Perkins, *The Work of William Perkins*, ed. Ian Breward (Abingdon, UK: Sutton Courtenay Press, 1970), 451 and 457.

39. Alan Heimert and Andrew Delbanco, introduction to *The Puritans in America*, 15.

40. Innes, *Creating the Commonwealth*, 122; Miller, *The New England Mind*, 42–43.

41. John Cotton, *The Way of Life* (London, 1641), 442.

42. Ibid., 443.

43. Ibid., 449.

44. Sarah Rivett offers a compelling alternative account of how hypocrisy relates to secular and sacred forms of Puritan modernity, spotlighting the "social problem of hypocrisy" as the "religious version of philosophical doubt," a consequence of the

quest for evidence of grace (*The Science of the Soul in Colonial New England* [Chapel Hill: University of North Carolina Press, 2011], 11 and 31).

45. Benjamin Franklin, *Autobiography*, in Benjamin Franklin, *Benjamin Franklin's Autobiography: An Authoritative Text, Contexts, Criticism*, ed. Joyce E. Chaplin (New York: Norton, 2012), 86.

46. Ibid., 77 and 90.

47. Tracy Fessenden, *Culture and Redemption: Religion, the Secular, and American Literature* (Princeton, NJ: Princeton University Press, 2007), 6.

48. Abigail Adams, *The Book of Abigail and John: Selected Letters of the Adams Family, 1763–1784*, ed. with an introduction by L. H. Butterfield, Marc Friedlaender, and Mary-Jo Kline, and with a new foreword by David McCullough (Boston: Northeastern University Press, 2002), 121. Her husband returns the banter, calling Abigail "saucy" and mockingly protesting, "We have only the Name of Masters, and rather than give up this, which would completely subject Us to the Despotism of the Peticoat, I hope General Washington and all our brave Heroes would fight" (ibid., 123.

49. Occom, *The Collected Writings of Samson Occom*, 191.

50. Daniel Vickers, *Farmers and Fishermen: Two Centuries of Work in Essex County, Massachusetts, 1630–1850* (Chapel Hill: University of North Carolina Press, 1994), 220. Vickers also refers to "by parental command" (ibid., 221).

51. Tomlins, *Freedom Bound*, 258; Wall, *Fierce Communion*, 86–125. See also Melvin Yazawa, *From Colonies to Commonwealth: Familial Ideology and the Beginnings of the American Republic* (Baltimore, MD: Johns Hopkins University Press, 1985), 19–27; M. Morris, *Under Household Government*, 209–10.

52. Gal. 4:22–24. See also William Ames, *The Marrow of Theology*, ed. and trans. John Dykstra Eusden (Durham, NC: Labyrinth Press, 1983), 219–20.

53. John Cotton, *The Covenant of God's Free Grace* (London, 1645), 12.

54. This is one root of the bourgeois ideology of work for love, which often involves lower monetary compensation and generally connotes professional labor that is referred to as service. Marc Bousquet discusses the implications of faculty labor conceived in these terms in "We Work," *Minnesota Review* 71–72 (winter–spring 2009): 145–52.

55. Valeri, *Heavenly Merchandize*, especially 1–5 and 152–60.

56. Jackson Lears, *Something for Nothing: Luck in America* (New York: Penguin, 2003), 75.

Chapter 1: The Child Who Serves

1. Thomas Shepard, *Parable of the Ten Virgins*, in Thomas Shepard, *The Works of Thomas Shepard*, ed. John A. Albro (New York: AMS Press, 1967), 2:93. All further references to this work will be cited parenthetically as PTV.

2. John Cotton, *The Way of Life* (London, 1641), 316. All further references to this work will be cited parenthetically as WL.

3. On the iconicity and ubiquity of the parable, see Alan R. Young, *The English Prodigal Son Plays: A Theatrical Fashion of the Sixteenth and Seventeenth Centuries* (Salzburg, Austria: Institute for English and American Studies, 1979). On Protestant visual rhetoric, see William Dyrness, *Reformed Theology and Visual Culture: The*

Protestant Imagination from Calvin to Edwards (Cambridge: Cambridge University Press, 2004); Gregory S. Jackson, *The Word and Its Witness: The Spiritualization of American Realism* (Chicago, IL: University of Chicago Press, 2009).

4. J. Albert Harrill argues that the Greek word translated as "hiring out" to denote the prodigal's service to the citizen refers to a Hellenistic institution akin to indentured labor ("The Indentured Labor of the Prodigal Son [Luke 15:15]," *Journal of Biblical Literature* 115, no. 4 [1996]: 717).

5. Christopher Tomlins, *Freedom Bound: Law, Labor, and Civic Identity in Colonizing English America, 1580–1865* (New York: Cambridge University Press, 2010), 258. Alison Games estimates that "as much as 61 percent" of the dependent children who migrated to New England in the earliest cohort may have been in service (*Migration and the Origins of the English Atlantic World* [Cambridge, MA: Harvard University Press, 1999], 49). On the significance of the correlation in household governance, see Helena M. Wall, *Fierce Communion: Family and Community in Early America* (Cambridge, MA: Harvard University Press, 1990), 86–125; Gloria L. Main, *Peoples of a Spacious Land: Families and Cultures in Colonial New England* (Cambridge, MA: Harvard University Press, 2001), 146–51; Melvin Yazawa, *From Colonies to Commonwealth: Familial Ideology and the Beginnings of the American Republic* (Baltimore, MD: Johns Hopkins University Press, 1985), 19–27; M. Michelle Jarrett Morris, *Under Household Government: Sex and Family in Puritan Massachusetts* (Cambridge, MA: Harvard University Press, 2013), 209–10. Mary Beth Norton refers to servants as "fictive children" in *Founding Mothers and Fathers: Gendered Power and the Forming of American Society* (New York: Vintage, 1997), 100 and 132. Children can also be read as fictive servants. Norton claims that patriarchal political theorists did not consider servants, and that servants on their own were "seldom treated at any length by the writers of prescriptive familial tracts" (ibid., 100). Puritan familial tracts, at least, did treat the particular callings of servants at some length and commonly defined childhood and servanthood as analogous conditions. Norton's epigram from Thomas Hobbes and a passage she cites from Robert Filmer refer to "children and servants" when describing the power of the father, so patriarchal political theorists did "consider servants" this way (ibid., 96 and 98).

6. John Cotton lists the "vices" that occur in "every family," and "eye-service" takes pride of place: "1. Eye-service; children and servants are more carefull to approve themselves to their Parents and Masters then [*sic*] to God" (*The Covenant of God's Free Grace* [London, 1645], 4). On laws, see Tomlins, *Freedom Bound*, 255. Douglas Hay observes that in Elizabethan master-servant law, labor was "forced into service" and that the "economic purposes" of doing so "were inextricably mixed with issues of governance, in particular of the young and disorderly" ("England, 1562–1875: The Law and Its Uses," in *Masters, Servants, and Magistrates in Britain and the Empire, 1562–1955*, ed. Douglas Hay and Paul Craven [Chapel Hill: University of North Carolina Press, 2004], 63 and 64). See also Carla Gardina Pestana, *The English Atlantic in an Age of Revolution, 1640–1661* (Cambridge, MA: Harvard University Press, 2004), 204.

7. Historians have debated how extensive the practice of putting out actually was and whether it was driven primarily by economic necessity or ideology, but most of

them agree that it provided discipline for children across social ranks, either keeping or bringing them under the yoke of a Puritan master-father and providing training for adulthood. For a summary of the debates, see Judith Graham, *Puritan Family Life: The Diary of Samuel Sewall* (Boston: Northeastern University Press, 2000), 144–57. In addition to the works cited by Graham, see C. Dallett Hemphill, *Bowing to Necessities: A History of Manners in America, 1620–1860* (New York: Oxford University Press, 1999), 45.

8. William Bradford, *Of Plymouth Plantation, 1620–1647* (New York: Modern Library, 1981), 355–56; John Winthrop, *Winthrop's Journal "History of New England," 1630–1649*, ed. James Kendall Hosmer (New York: Scribner, 1908), 1:42.

9. Charles Lloyd Cohen engages briefly but insightfully with this imagery, affirming sonship as the preferred status (*God's Caress: The Psychology of Puritan Religious Experience* [New York: Oxford University Press, 1986], 70). See also Janice Knight, *Orthodoxies in Massachusetts: Rereading American Puritanism* (Cambridge, MA: Harvard University Press, 1994), 34; Michael W. Kaufmann, *Institutional Individualism: Conversion, Exile, and Nostalgia in Puritan New England* (Hanover, NH: Wesleyan University Press, 1998), 8.

10. John Coolidge contrasts Conformist views of Christian liberty with that of Elizabethan Puritans, explaining that "the Puritan thinks of Christian liberty less as a permission than as a command" (*The Pauline Renaissance in England: Puritanism and the Bible* [London: Oxford University Press, 1970], 26). I concur with Kauffman's sense of the complexity of submission to and dependence on authority in Puritan New England in the "development and strengthening of a desirable identity," one he calls "institutional individualism" (*Institutional Individualism*, 3). On Paul's definition of Christian liberty in a Puritan context, see Coolidge, *The Pauline Renaissance*, 23–54. Sarah Rivett discusses how Luther's and Calvin's versions of Christian liberty relate to Christian epistemology in *The Science of the Soul in Colonial New England* (Chapel Hill: University of North Carolina Press, 2011), 32–33.

11. Holly Brewer, *By Birth or Consent: Children, Law, and the Anglo-American Revolution in Authority* (Chapel Hill: University of North Carolina Press, 2005), 2. Studies that consider colonial Anglo-Americans, including Puritans, as children include Gillian Brown, *The Consent of the Governed: The Lockean Legacy in Early American Culture* (Cambridge, MA: Harvard University Press, 2001); Jay Fliegelman, *Prodigals and Pilgrims: The American Revolution Against Patriarchal Authority, 1750–1800* (Cambridge: Cambridge University Press, 1982); Jackson, *The Word and Its Witness*; Carol Singley, *Adopting America: Childhood, Kinship, and National Identity in Literature* (New York: Oxford University Press, 2011); David Leverenz, *The Language of Puritan Feeling: An Exploration in Literature, Psychology, and Social History* (New Brunswick, NJ: Rutgers University Press, 1980); Philip Greven, *The Protestant Temperament: Patterns of Child-Rearing, Religious Experience, and the Self in Early America* (Chicago, IL: University of Chicago Press, 1988); Anna Mae Duane, *Suffering Childhood in Early America: Violence, Race, and the Making of the Child Victim* (Athens: University of Georgia Press, 2010). There has been no extended study of Puritans as metaphorical servants; even the scholarship on actual servants is relatively slight.

12. Cohen critiques Weber's emphasis on vocation as the defining doctrine of Puritan labor (*God's Caress*, 117), instead associating it—as others have done—with "preparationism" (ibid., 123). Cohen points out that the prodigal "epitomized the person in preparation" by "prepar[ing] to submit to his father's (i.e., God the Father's will)," but does not discuss how critical servitude is to the prodigal's preparatory work (ibid., 78 and 79). My reading of the servant-son dialectic extends Cohen's insightful connection between humiliation and work discipline.

13. Cathy Matson, "Economic History at a Crossroads: Reconsidering Methods, Spaces, and Peoples," *Journal of the Early Republic* 36, no. 4 (2016): 605.

14. The literature on the transition from Filmer to John Locke is extensive, but Kaufmann provides a lucid summary of it (*Institutional Individualism*, 19–24). Among those cited above, for parent-child relationships, see Brewer, *By Birth or Consent*; Brown, *The Consent of the Governed*; Fliegelman, *Prodigals and Pilgrims*; Norton, *Founding Mothers and Fathers*. For husband-wife relationships, see ibid.; Carole Pateman, *The Sexual Contract* (Stanford, CA: Stanford University Press, 1988); Elizabeth Maddock Dillon, *The Gender of Freedom: Fictions of Liberalism and the Literary Public Sphere* (Stanford, CA: Stanford University Press, 2004).

15. Quoted in Michael S. Horton, *Lord and Servant: A Covenant Christology* (Louisville, KY: Westminster John Knox Press, 2005), 175.

16. William Ames, *The Marrow of Theology*, ed. and trans. John Dykstra Eusden (Durham, NC: Labyrinth Press, 1968), 135. Ames reads Christ's humiliation as modeling "legal obedience" only (ibid., 139); William K. B. Stoever follows him (*"A Faire and Easie Way to Heaven": Covenant Theology and Antinomianism in Early Massachusetts* [Middletown, CT: Wesleyan University Press, 1978], 93–96). Cotton's emphasis on the fluidity of Christ's moves from son to servant and back again in these passages suggests the activity of both kinds of obedience in his version of humiliation.

17. Thomas Hooker, *The Soules Humiliation* (London, 1637), 109. All further references to this work will be cited parenthetically as SH.

18. On Christ's obedience as central to the Reformed version of the imitatio Christi, which focused on experience rather than miracles, see Sacvan Bercovitch, *The Puritan Origins of the American Self* (New Haven, CT: Yale University Press, 1975), 9–10. On the prevalence of humiliation in Puritan culture, see Perry Miller's witty exposition in *The New England Mind: From Colony to Province* (1953; repr., Cambridge, MA: Belknap Press of Harvard University Press, 1981), 19–20; Charles E. Hambrick-Stowe, *The Practice of Piety: Puritan Devotional Disciplines in Seventeenth-Century New England* (Chapel Hill: University of North Carolina Press, 1982), 166–75.

19. Theodore Dwight Bozeman, *The Precisianist Strain: Disciplinary Religion and Antinomian Backlash in Puritanism to 1638* (Chapel Hill: University of North Carolina Press, 2004), 266.

20. Ames, *The Marrow of Theology*, 164. "The first fruit of adoption," Ames explains, "is that Christian liberty by which all believers are freed from the bondage of the law, sin, and the world. John 8:32–36, *If the Son shall set you free, you shall be free indeed*; Rom. 6:22, *Being freed from sin we were made servants to God*" (ibid., 167). Translated into lived metaphors, the difference between Adam's and Christ's sonship (which Ames characterized as the difference between metaphorical and nat-

ural sonship) becomes the difference between servitude and sonship. Thus, the "natural" children of the covenant (the Jews) become only "metaphorical," and Puritan saints become God's "natural children."

21. Cohen, *God's Caress*, 70. On the relationship between the spiritual and social dimensions of adoption, see Singley, *Adopting America*, 29–39. Singley considers the asymmetry between theories of spiritual sonship and practices of church membership and compares adoption to "putting out," but she does not consider how the son-servant covenant dialectic shaped adoption. Fliegelman discusses Jonathan Edwards's rendering of adoption in *A History of the Work of Redemption*, reading the servant as a figure of disavowal (*Prodigals and Pilgrims*, 173).

22. Thomas Shepard, *The Sincere Convert*, in Shepard, *The Works of Thomas Shepard*, 1:100. On finding a middle way between the extremes of legalism and libertinism as the essence of Puritan theology, see John von Rohr, *The Covenant of Grace in Puritan Thought* (Atlanta, GA: Scholars Press, 1986), 111.

23. John Cotton, *Treatise of the Covenant of Grace* (London, 1659), 156–7. All further references to this work will be cited parenthetically as TCG. I concur with Cohen's sense that these passages in Cotton's work complicate readings that suggest he refuted preparationism outright. See Cohen, *God's Caress*, 84–85, note 25.

24. Rom. 8:14–17 contrasts the "spirit of bondage" to "the spirit of adoption."

25. William Perkins, *A Treatise of the Vocations or Callings of Men*, in William Perkins, *The Work of William Perkins*, ed. Ian Breward (Abingdon, UK: Sutton Courtenay Press, 1970), 453. All further references to this work will be cited parenthetically as WP.

26. Tomlins, *Freedom Bound*, 386. An exception in the scholarship of early New England is Lisa Wilson, *Ye Heart of a Man: The Domestic Life of Men in Colonial New England* (New Haven, CT: Yale University Press, 1999).

27. On the significance of the household master, see Christopher Hill, *Society and Puritanism in Pre-Revolutionary England* (New York: Schocken Books, 1964), 443–81.

28. Ames, *The Marrow of Theology*, 311.

29. The power of the husband is also defined in relation to mastery; the husband may not treat his wife as a servant. Perkins defines the duty of a husband as to "honour his wife . . . as his companion or yokefellow. For this cause, the woman when she was created was not taken out of the man's head, because she was not made to rule over him: nor out of his feet, because God did not make her subject to him as a servant: but out of his side, to the end that man should take her as his mate" (WP 428).

30. William Ames, *Conscience with the Power and Cases Thereof* (London, 1643), book 5, 159.

31. Ibid., 159 and 160.

32. Perkins's instructions to masters cited Eph. 6:5–7 and Col. 3:22, the duty to avoid eye-service that also defined the servant's calling (WP 432).

33. Ames, *The Marrow of Theology*, 311.

34. M. Morris, *Under Household Government*, 6.

35. Brewer, *By Birth or Consent*, 59.

36. The issue of the child's growing into his or her ability to "consent" to the terms of visible sainthood versus the legalist parent's mere "willing[ness]" to baptize his or

her children would be an issue during the debates about baptism and church membership that culminated in the Halfway Covenant in the 1660s. On Halfway Covenant baptism, see Mark Peterson, *The Price of Redemption: The Spiritual Economy of Puritan New England* (Stanford, CA: Stanford University Press, 1997), 35. I take up the relationship between Halfway Covenant evangelism and the imagery and practice of putting out in chapter 2.

37. Ames, *The Marrow of Theology*, 312. These proof-texts are found in instructions to servants; and instructions to masters cite Eph. 6:9, which reminds them that verse 5 applies to them as God's servants. See, for example, Ames, *Conscience with the Power and Cases Thereof*, book 5, 160–61.

38. Darren Staloff, *The Making of an American Thinking Class: Intellectuals and Intelligentsia in Puritan Massachusetts* (New York: Oxford University Press, 1998), 16–20.

39. "The Body of Liberties," in *The Colonial Laws of Massachusetts, Reprinted from the Edition of 1660* (1889; repr., Littleton, CO: Fred B. Rothman, 1995), 51–53.

40. Ames, *Conscience with the Power and Cases Thereof*, book 5, 161.

41. Ibid., 162.

42. William Perkins, *The Arte of Prophecying* (London, 1607), 115–16.

43. Ibid., 116.

44. Ames, *Conscience with the Power and Cases Thereof*, book 5, 51–52.

45. As Lisa Gordis and Janice Knight have observed, Hooker is loose about "openings": the prodigal is a crucial figure in the sermon and provides the foundation for its doctrines and applications, but Hooker does not systematically "open" the parable. See Lisa Gordis, *Opening Scripture: Bible Reading and Interpretive Authority in Puritan New England* (Chicago, IL: University of Chicago Press, 2003), 77–96; J. Knight, *Orthodoxies in Massachusetts*, 174.

46. On preparationism, see Norman Pettit, *The Heart Prepared: Grace and Conversion in Puritan Spiritual Life* (New Haven, CT: Yale University Press, 1966). Pettit observes that preparationism required a shift in reformed theology from a focus on God's work in effectual calling to the human response to that calling (ibid., 27–29). On the aesthetic dimensions of preparationism, see Alfred Habegger, "Preparing the Soul for Christ: The Contrasting Sermon Forms of John Cotton and Thomas Hooker," *American Literature* 41, no. 3 (1969): 342–354. Cotton has been located on the "absolutist" side of the preparationist divide, in contrast to Shepard and Hooker, who emphasized conditions and submission to ministerial authority, but Bozeman argues that Cotton preached preparationism in England, offering a "later modification" of it in New England (*The Precisianist Strain*, 213). Janice Knight avers that literary sensibilities account for stylistic differences between Cotton and preparationists but also attributes them to the doctrine (*Orthodoxies in Massachusetts*, 173).

47. On Cotton as a "constant brake" and exception to Weber's paradigm, see Larzer Ziff, *The Career of John Cotton: Puritanism and the American Experience* (Princeton, NJ: Princeton University Press, 1962), 154. On preparationism and the work ethic, see Cohen, *God's Caress*, 123; J. Knight, *Orthodoxies in Massachusetts*, 98 and 104; Jennifer Jordan Baker, *Securing the Commonwealth: Debt, Speculation, and Writing in the Making of Early America* (Baltimore, MD: Johns Hopkins University Press, 2005), 32. Louise Breen laments this commonplace, pointing out that

Puritan merchants often "chafed" against orthodoxy as they "developed transatlantic markets" (*Transgressing the Bounds: Subversive Enterprises among the Puritan Elite in Massachusetts, 1630–1692* [New York: Oxford University Press, 2001], 53).

48. Cotton notes that the Holy Spirit will dwell in even in "a poor kitchin-boy [*sic*]" whose spirit is properly humbled (TCG 175). These "kitchen boys" are perhaps Puritan versions of literary rogues, picaresque figures. Bruce Robbins points out that "picaro" originally meant "kitchen boy" (*The Servant's Hand: English Fiction from Below* [1986; repr., Durham, NC: Duke University Press, 1993), 82.

49. Staloff, *The Making of an American Thinking Class*, 15.

50. Quoted in Hambrick-Stowe, *The Practice of Piety*, 163. On meditation as essential exercise of Puritan devotion, see ibid., 175.

51. Winthrop, *Winthrop's Journal*, 1:120–21. Winthrop tells the story in the third person and does not identify Deane, but Hambrick-Stowe deduces that the story is about Deane (*Practice of Piety*, 85).

52. Jonathan Beecher Field, "The Antinomian Controversy Did Not Take Place," *Early American Studies* 6, no. 2 (2008): 449.

53. Ibid., 450 and 463.

54. Abram Van Engen, *Sympathetic Puritans: Calvinist Fellow Feeling in Early New England* (New York: Oxford University Press, 2015), 102.

55. Michael Winship, *Making Heretics: Militant Protestants and Free Grace in Massachusetts, 1636–1641* (Princeton, NJ: Princeton University Press, 2002), 1. Winship offers the most comprehensive and compelling recent account of this heavily studied event.

56. Dillon, *The Gender of Freedom*, 58.

57. Thomas Shepard, "Journal," in Thomas Shepard, *God's Plot: The Paradoxes of Puritan Piety, Being the Autobiography and Journal of Thomas Shepard*, ed. with an introduction by Michael McGiffert (Amherst: University of Massachusetts Press, 1972), 158–59.

58. Winship, *Making Heretics*, 117.

59. David D. Hall, ed., *The Antinomian Controversy, 1636–1638: A Documentary History* (Durham, NC: Duke University Press, 1990), 27. All further references to this work will be cited parenthetically as AC. Hall retains the spelling and punctuation of the original manuscripts; to make them more readable, I have modernized them throughout.

60. This exchange dovetails with Van Engen's nice against-the-grain reading of Cotton versus the elders: "the elders feared that Cotton's doctrine of assurance canceled what comfort weak Christians had already cobbled together and replaced it" with something unattainable (*Sympathetic Puritans*, 81).

61. Winthrop, *Winthrop's Journal*, 1:204.

62. Quoted in Winship, *Making Heretics*, 112.

63. On the fates of three legal servants who were part of the Hutchinson faction, see Games, *Migration*, 147–9.

64. Winship, *Making Heretics*, 128.

65. Winthrop seems to have appreciated that she had gotten the better of him. In the version of the exchange published later as *A Short Story*, he omitted this lame re-

joinder, saying "we cannot stand to dispute causes with you now" and then changing the subject (AC 267).

66. For references to "humiliation," see AC 373, 378, 383, and 387. On Cotton's recuperation, see Winship, *Making Heretics*, 149–65.

67. For a complementary reading of how Hutchinson embodies an emerging type of modern economic personhood that focuses on commercial practices and imagery, see Michelle Burnham, *Folded Selves: Colonial New England Writing in the World System* (Hanover, NH: Dartmouth College Press, 2007), 95–114.

68. Janice Knight suggests that Shepard's series of sermons, preached in the period 1636–40, "might be a record of the changes wrought upon Shepard" by the Antinomian Controversy (*Orthodoxies in Massachusetts*, 180–81).

69. For examples of this commonplace, see WP 453; PTV 441–42.

70. Nancy Armstrong and Leonard Tennenhouse observe that "the puritan family was not infused with the qualities of personal life but was a miniature version of the aristocratic state" (*The Imaginary Puritan: Literature, Intellectual Labor, and the Origins of Personal Life* [Berkeley: University of California Press, 1992], 165).

71. Ivy Schweitzer, *The Work of Self-Representation: Lyric Poetry in Colonial New England* (Chapel Hill: University of North Carolina Press, 1991), 23.

72. Cotton, *The Covenant of God's Free Grace*, 2.

73. Everett Emerson and Edmund Morgan read this passage as being preached to the unregenerate only, but it applies to the regenerate as well. See Everett Emerson, *John Cotton*, rev. ed. (Boston: G. K. Hall, 1990), 78; Edmund Morgan, *The Puritan Family: Religion and Domestic Relations in Seventeenth-Century New England* (rev. ed., New York: Harper and Row, 1966), 180–81. Morgan also takes this passage to suggest that Cotton, unlike John Davenport, was open to extending church membership to the servants of church members, but Morgan concedes that "there is no evidence that servants received any ecclesiastical privileges because of their master's connection with a church" (ibid., 136). Perry Miller stresses the spiritual metaphor, describing its depiction of covenant conditions as an "apprenticeship in learning the trade of godliness" (*Errand into the Wilderness* [1955; repr., Cambridge, MA: Belknap Press of Harvard University Press,1984], 85).

74. Cotton, *The Covenant of God's Free Grace*, 20.

75. Ibid., 18.

76. Winship observes that Cotton's sermons after the trials show that he "retreated from his previous emphases" and instead emphasized conditions as a source of assurance (*Making Heretics*, 218).

77. Margaret Ellen Newell, *Brethren by Nature: New England Indians, Colonists, and the Origins of American Slavery* (Ithaca, NY: Cornell University Press, 2015), 35.

78. Thomas Shepard, *The Sound Believer*, in Shepard, *The Works of Thomas Shepard*, 1:255.

79. For a discussion of the "Puritan-Pequot" households created by these practices, see Newell, *Brethren by Nature*, 60–84.

80. Ibid., 36–37.

81. Roger Williams, *A Key into the Language of America*, ed. John Teunissen and Evelyn J. Hinz (Detroit, MI: Wayne State University Press, 1973), 116.

82. Ibid., 124.

83. Ibid., 129.

84. Jonathan Beecher Field, *Errands into the Metropolis: New England Dissidents in Revolutionary London* (Hanover, NH: Dartmouth College Press, 2009), 27.

85. Ibid., 36.

86. *New England's First Fruits* (London, 1643).

87. Ibid., 3.

88. Ibid.,13.

89. Ibid., 15.

90. Fliegelman, *Prodigals and Pilgrims*, 177. The tale of the prodigal son serves as a metonym for the complexity of patriarchal authority in Fliegelman's paradigmatic cultural history of early America, but he discusses the actual parable only briefly (ibid., 68–69). Although he does not linger on the racialization of servant and son, he alludes to the fact that not all servants became sons in his discussion of revolutionary-era engravings and mezzotints that represent the son standing rather than kneeling (ibid., 114).

91. Gordon Wood tracks the history of "patriarchal dependence" in the racialized distinctions between sonship, servitude, and slavery in eighteenth-century America (*The Radicalism of the American Revolution* [New York: Knopf, 1992], 43–56). David Roediger tracks the racialization of these legal and social distinctions in his "prehistory of the white worker" (*The Wages of Whiteness: Race and the Making of the American Working Class*, rev. ed. [London: Verso, 1999], 19–40). Holly Brewer follows the implications of the slave-child and woman-child analogies for understanding the racialization and gendering of Enlightenment consent (*By Birth or Consent*, 352–65).

92. Shepard, *The Sound Believer*, 1:252.

93. Thomas Shepard, *Thomas Shepard's Confessions*, ed. George Selement and Bruce C. Woolley (Boston: Colonial Society of Massachusetts, 1981), 185–86. I discuss the gender friction of this imagery at greater length in chapters 2 and 3. Schweitzer has read the gendering of adoption in relation to marriage imagery: "In the logic of conversion, all saints pass through the feminizing process. Brides become sons and heirs and are thus remasculinized, but they remain on the feminine side of the gender/power divide" (*The Work of Self-Representation*, 28).

94. Dillon, *The Gender of Freedom*, 57.

95. John Woodbridge, "Epistle to the Reader," in Anne Bradstreet, *The Works of Anne Bradstreet*, ed. Jeannine Hensley (Cambridge, MA: Belknap Press of Harvard University Press, 1967), 3.

96. Anne Bradstreet, "The Author to Her Book," in Bradstreet, *The Works*, 221.

Chapter 2: Answering Back

1. "How Puritans Turned Capitalist," *Idea of the Day* (blog), *New York Times*, August 10, 2010, accessed October 1, 2017, ideas.blogs.nytimes.com/2010/08/10/how-puritans-turned-capitalist/?_r=0.

2. Mark Valeri, *Heavenly Merchandize: How Religion Shaped Commerce in Puritan America* (Princeton, NJ: Princeton University Press, 2010), 104 and 160.

3. Samuel Willard, "A Brief Account of a Strange and Unusual Providence of God Befallen to Elizabeth Knapp of Groton," in *Remarkable Providences: Readings on Early American History*, ed. John Demos, rev. ed. (Boston: Northeastern University Press, 1991), 423. All further references to this work will be cited parenthetically as BA. Knapp owes her enduring fame to Demos, whose edition of Willard's narrative has made her experience readily available to teachers and scholars of early New England. He has also reinforced Knapp's association with Salem. Instead of placing Willard's narrative in the section on "The Supernatural," he might, for example, have included it under "Family and Household," which includes the subheading "Dependents: Young People and Servants."

4. John Demos, *Entertaining Satan: Witchcraft and the Culture of Early New England* (New York: Oxford University Press, 1982), 99.

5. Samuel Green, *Groton During the Witchcraft Times* (Cambridge, MA, 1883), 22. On Brattle's praise of Willard's skepticism, see Mary Beth Norton, *In the Devil's Snare: The Salem Witchcraft Crisis of 1692* (New York: Vintage, 2003), 283.

6. Stephen Foster, *The Long Argument: English Puritanism and the Shaping of New England Culture, 1570–1700* (Chapel Hill: University of North Carolina Press, 1991), 267. On the politics of Willard's rôle in Salem and his relationship to Increase Mather, see ibid., 254–67.

7. For example, Demos lists the fact that Knapp was a servant last among the five "genetic" causes of her affliction (*Entertaining Satan*, 127). Nancy Ruttenburg refers repeatedly to Knapp as Willard's "maidservant" (*Democratic Personality: Popular Voice and the Trials of American Authorship* [Stanford, CA: Stanford University Press, 1998], 121–24), an epithet that helps valorize Knapp as an early example of the "voice of the people" (ibid. 120)—whose history Ruttenburg traces in "the symbolic economy of American Puritanism as it was enacted by common and anonymous persons rather than a cultural elite" (ibid., 18).

8. Jane Kamensky observes that Puritanism entailed "a fundamental redefinition of both the spiritual and social meanings of speaking . . . propounding at once new freedoms for the tongue and new demands for its government" (*Governing the Tongue: The Politics of Speech in Early New England* [New York: Oxford University Press, 1997], 29). Books that consider questions of voice and authority in early American cultural history include Ruttenburg, *Democratic Personality*; Jay Fliegelman, *Declaring Independence: Jefferson, Natural Language, and the Culture of Performance* (Stanford, CA: Stanford University Press, 1993); Christopher Looby, *Voicing America: Language, Literary Form, and the Origins of the United States* (Chicago, IL: University of Chicago Press, 1996); and Sandra Gustafson, *Eloquence Is Power: Oratory and Performance in Early America* (Chapel Hill: University of North Carolina Press, 2000).

9. Leigh Eric Schmidt, *Hearing Things: Religion, Illusion, and the American Enlightenment* (Cambridge, MA: Harvard University Press, 2000), 35.

10. Bruce Robbins, *The Servant's Hand: English Fiction from Below* (1986; repr., Durham, NC: Duke University Press, 1993), 60.

11. Jeffrey Richards, *Theater Enough: American Culture and the Metaphor of the World Stage, 1607–1789* (Durham, NC: Duke University Press, 1991), 101–26. Demos locates Knapp "at the center of the local stage," noting that the "metaphor of

theater suggests itself quite naturally" (*Entertaining Satan*, 117). The theatrical metaphor is not "meant to imply literal 'staging' on Elizabeth's part" (ibid., 118): he doesn't read her as acting but rather as "acting out" her narcissistic rage (ibid., 122). Knapp and Willard share this flair for the dramatic.

12. On those others in the New England workforce, see, for example, Wendy Warren, *New England Bound: Slavery and Colonization in Early America* (New York: Norton, 2016); Margaret Ellen Newell, *Brethren by Nature: New England Indians, Colonists, and the Origins of American Slavery* (Ithaca, NY: Cornell University Press, 2015); Richard Archer, *Fissures in the Rock: New England in the Seventeenth Century* (Hanover, NH: University of New Hampshire Press, 2001); Marsha L. Hamilton, *Social and Economic Networks in Early Massachusetts: Atlantic Connections* (University Park: Pennsylvania State University Press, 2009).

13. For a powerful feminist reading of Knapp's possession, see Carol Karlsen, *The Devil in the Shape of a Woman: Witchcraft in Colonial New England* (New York: Norton, 1987), chapter 7. Her experience can also be located in the prehistory of what Gillian Brown has called "domestic individualism" in her account of the "feminization of selfhood in service to an individualism most available to (white) men" (*Domestic Individualism: Imagining Self in Nineteenth-Century America* [Berkeley: University of California Press, 1990], 7).

14. William Perkins, *Christian Oeconomy*, in William Perkins, *The Work of William Perkins*, ed. Ian Breward (Abingdon, UK: Sutton Courtenay Press, 1970), 433–34.

15. Thomas Hooker, *The Faithful Covenanter* (London, 1644), 26.

16. *The Laws and Liberties of Massachusetts, Reprinted from the Copy of the 1648 Edition in the Henry E. Huntington Library* (Cambridge, MA: Harvard University Press, 1929), 11. Laws regarding servants also appeared in two other categories, "Bond-slavery" and "Masters, Servants, Labourers," where master and servant as particular callings seem to be more clearly legislated (wages are a special concern).

17. Ibid.

18. Ibid.

19. Ibid. E. Jennifer Monaghan notes that this law derived from English Poor Laws, which were primarily driven by economic motives; the educational provisions in the New England laws suggest the primacy of piety as a motive. Monaghan queries how important reading ability was to training in a trade (*Learning to Read and Write in Colonial America* [Amherst: University of Massachusetts Press, 2005], 34–35). I would suggest that what binds the aspects of the law together is their reinforcement of a relationship to the law of the master across domains of family, church, and state.

20. *The Laws and Liberties of Massachusetts*, 11.

21. Kamensky notes of John Porter Jr. that he was removed to the House of Correction: "Because the younger Porter had so clearly outstripped his father's ability to govern his son's tongue, the court assigned him another 'keeper and master'" (*Governing the Tongue*, 109).

22. "Records of Town Proceedings," in *Watertown [Mass.] Records* (Watertown, MA, 1894), 104. This appears to have been part of a larger concerted effort on the part of selectmen to make sure the law was being enforced. Town records list the birth on July 23, 1657, of Elizabeth Knapp, daughter of William and Margaret Knapp

("Births, Marriages and Deaths," in ibid., 20). William and Margaret Knapp's daughter Judy would have been eighteen, so the daughter mentioned in the text must be Elizabeth, a cousin to the possessed servant.

23. Ibid., 109. Monaghan surmises that the Watertown Elizabeth Knapp had been bound out to Smyth (*Learning to Read*, 36).

24. *Early Records of Groton, Massachusetts, 1662–1707*, ed. Samuel A. Green (Groton, MA, 1880), 30. James Knapp was again chosen selectman in December 1671 (ibid., 39–40), during his daughter's possession. He was one of the original proprietors of Groton, and Demos explains that his "economic position was above average" though below that of the wealthiest few like the Willards. Demos uncovered Knapp's publicly sordid past, including being brought up on charges of adultery when he resided in Watertown in the 1650s; but in Groton, Knapp was able to recover his reputation through "extensive public service" (*Entertaining Satan*, 112). Town records suggest that his manual labor underwrote his public service. In 1666, he was hired to make two doors and a set of stairs, and to lay the upper floor of the new meetinghouse (*Early Records of Groton*, 16).

25. The following year, Samuel Willard's wealthy and powerful father, Simon, moved to Groton and served alongside James Knapp as a selectman (*Early Records of Groton*, 42). Public service smoothed over differences of rank between Puritan men.

26. He was originally hired at a rate of 40 pounds in 1663, which was raised to 50 in 1665 and rose again to 60 after he signed his covenant (ibid., 9, 12–13, and 17).

27. The law concerning the education of children elides the issue of the child's consent to be bound. On the changing concepts of consent reflected in the labor contracts of children, see Holly Brewer, *By Birth or Consent: Children, Law, and the Anglo-American Revolution in Authority* (Chapel Hill: University of North Carolina Press, 2005), 271–80.

28. *Early Records of Groton*, 39.

29. Kamensky explains that "public *concern* with the rhetoric of filial duty (or its absence) reached something of a fever pitch in New England's third decade. . . . Beginning in the late 1640s, legislatures throughout the Puritan colonies enacted laws making actions *or speech* against one's parents a capital offense" (*Governing the Tongue*, 102; italics in original).

30. Ibid., 168.

31. Kamensky describes the case of John Porter Jr., "the only child ever to face the gallows for such crimes" (ibid., 112).

32. According to the online edition of the *Oxford English Dictionary*, accessed August 19, 2017, www.oed.com (subscription required).

33. Willard's alacrity in making "visitations" was a notable aspect of his ministerial service at the Third Church. See Mark Peterson, *The Price of Redemption: The Spiritual Economy of Puritan New England* (Stanford, CA: Stanford University Press, 1997), 126–27.

34. The making of the narrative might thus complicate the usual modern division between menial and intellectual labor. Hannah Arendt has observed that "by itself, thinking never materializes into any objects. Whenever the intellectual worker wishes to manifest his thoughts, he must use his hands and acquire manual skills just like

any other worker. . . . [T]he thinker who wants the world to know the 'content' of his thoughts must first of all stop thinking and remember his thoughts. . . . The specific work quality of intellectual work is no less due to the 'work of our hands' than any other kind of work" (*The Human Condition* [Chicago, IL: University of Chicago Press, 1958], 90–91). One might add that the manual laborer who wants the world to know the content of his or her thoughts must change the nature of his or her labor, which is precisely what Knapp does by transforming earthly service into spiritual service.

35. Kamensky, *Governing the Tongue*, 167. E. Brooks Holifield has linked Willard's skepticism to the ministerial vocation via the significance of reason and "method" in pastoral care (*A History of Pastoral Care in America: From Salvation to Self-Realization* [Nashville, TN: Abingdon Press, 1983], 44).

36. Bruce Robbins says that it is "power rather than reason that is decisive" when masters fail to register a servant's will as anything other than "interference," especially when the message that the servant bears is a threat of violence (*The Servant's Hand*, 77). I would say that in this instance, it is the master's power in the guise of reason, and that Knapp turns the threat of violence against masters on herself.

37. Ibid., 65. Demos reads her "speechlessness" as "a signal instance of compromise between unconscious aims and defenses" (*Entertaining Satan*, 122), while Kamensky perceives the comic note in the "demoniac's inability to speak (and to listen)," which "must have sounded like a spiteful joke, a satiric twist on the notion that women should hold their tongues in public" (*Governing the Tongue*, 165).

38. According to Raymond Williams, "signification, the social creation of meanings through the use of formal signs, is then a practical material activity; it is indeed, literally, a means of production" (*Marxism and Literature* [Oxford: Oxford University Press, 1977], 38).

39. For Demos's interpretation of Knapp's tongue, see *Entertaining Satan*, 122. For a different view, see Michael Clark, "'Like Images Made Black with the Lightning': Discourse and the Body in Colonial Witchcraft," *Eighteenth Century* 34, no. 3 (1993): 214.

40. Robbins, *The Servant's Hand*, 82.

41. Ibid., 53–90.

42. Willard's generation of Harvard graduates was the first to insist upon such written contracts between minister and congregation as a way of "coping with insecurity of employment" in a labor market marked by a shortage of pulpits. See David D. Hall, *The Faithful Shepherd: A History of the New England Ministry in the Seventeenth Century* (Chapel Hill: University of North Carolina Press, 1972), 190. Hall also links the covenant as contract to the strain of legalism in Willard's doctrine, noting that he "made the term 'covenant' synonymous with contract, in the sense, as he explained, that 'the very notion of a Covenant implies a dependent Condition to which the Privileges of it refer'" (ibid., 258–59).

43. *The Colonial Laws of Massachusetts, Reprinted from the Edition of 1660* (1889; repr., Littleton, CO: Fred B. Rothman, 1995), 175.

44. Willard's contract stipulated that if he voluntarily vacated his post "before the seven years be expired," he would "leave these [*sic*] whole accommodation to the

town . . . the house and land [are] to remain the town's" (*Early Records of Groton*, 15). Only in the event of Willard's death before the expiration of the contract would the property revert to his heirs: "But if it shall please god to take him by death then the house and land . . . to his eayers [heirs] freely for ever" (ibid., 16). At the time of Satan's possession of Knapp, Willard was in the final year of his contract.

45. Ibid., 17.

46. Robert Steinfeld equates "master" with "employer" and "servant" with "employee" in tracking the emergence of modern labor law from master-servant law (*The Invention of Free Labor: The Employment Relation in English and American Law and Culture, 1350–1870* [Chapel Hill: University of North Carolina Press, 1991]).

47. *Early Records of Groton*, 27.

48. Ibid., 31.

49. Ibid., 39.

50. Robbins, *The Servant's Hand*, 75.

51. Demos, *Entertaining Satan*, 118.

52. Valeri, *Heavenly Merchandize*, 165.

53. Ibid.

54. Ibid., 90.

55. In another instance, Willard uses the noun form, "applied myself in council" (BA 430).

56. Samuel Willard, *Useful Instructions for a Professing People in a Time of Great Security and Degeneracy* (Cambridge, MA: 1673), 58. All further references to this work will be cited parenthetically as UI.

57. *Early Records of Groton*, 40.

58. Demos, *Entertaining Satan*, 118.

59. C. Dallett Hemphill points out that deference was a form of "self-mastery," an important theme in ministerial conduct manuals: "The need to appear meek grew even stronger for the high status 'second generation' of ministers in the late seventeenth century, who mounted a conscious campaign of 'imagebuilding'" (*Bowing to Necessities: A History of Manners in America, 1620–1860* [New York: Oxford University Press, 1999], 23).

60. Demos, *Entertaining Satan*, 114. She was about at the median age at which women in the Third Church participated in the ritual of owning their parents' covenant to become "children of the church" in the 1670s. See Robert G. Pope, *The Half-Way Covenant: Church Membership in Puritan New England* (Princeton, NJ: Princeton University Press, 1969), 282.

61. I am indebted to Rayna Kalas for this insight.

62. Valeri, *Heavenly Merchandize*, 103.

63. Ibid.

64. The central innovation of the New England way was the requirement of conversion testimonies for full church membership. Following two decades of debate about whether the visibly godly who had not given this public testimony required for full membership could present their children for baptism, the Synod of 1662 answered this question in the affirmative, recommending that "baptismal privileges [be] extended to all lineal descendants of full members, not just the children but future generations,"

whether or not those children or grandchildren ever attained full membership status (Peterson, *The Price of Redemption*, 35). Janice Knight locates the Halfway Covenant in a broader history of conflict within Puritan orthodoxy, in *Orthodoxies in Massachusetts: Rereading American Puritanism* (Cambridge, MA: Harvard University Press, 1994), 184–97; her pithy summary of the historiographical debate is on page 185. On the implications of the Halfway Covenant for understandings of consent, see Brewer, *By Birth or Consent*, 62–64; Darren Staloff, *The Making of an American Thinking Class: Intellectuals and Intelligentsia in Puritan Massachusetts* (New York: Oxford University Press, 1998), 138–42.

65. For example, Willard warns Groton's children that they "may be the natural Children of godly Parents, and yet the spiritual Children of the Devil": do not "trust to your Parents Covenant" or "rest upon their godliness" or "upon your Parents Prayers" (UI 39). I would speculate that Willard's position on the synod's recommendations could be the reason why several townspeople voted against his initial hire. Later church records indicate that the Groton church abided by Halfway Covenant measures. A June 1814 list of "Members Admitted to Full Communion and of Those that own The Covenant" ends with the following wry notation: "The church unanimously voted to discontinue the practice of admitting persons on the half covenant (so called)" (*Early Church Records of Groton, Massachusetts 1761–1830* [Groton, MA, 1896], 78).

66. Peterson, *The Price of Redemption*, 35.

67. Samuel Willard, *The Duty of a People that have Renewed their Covenant with God* (Boston, 1680), 8.

68. Willard was credited with sparking a minirevival early in 1680 (Peterson, *The Price of Redemption*, 48). Robert Pope observes that Willard's success in that revival contributed to normalizing halfway membership as a "permanent status" in the Third Church. By 1690, "the number of half-way members probably equaled the number of full communicants and within the next few years they should have achieved a sizable majority" (*The Half-Way Covenant*, 222–23).

69. Willard, *The Duty of a People*, 10.

70. Ibid., 8.

71. Ibid., 10–11.

72. Ibid., 10.

73. Samuel Willard, *Covenant-Keeping: The Way to Blessedness* (Boston, 1682), 121.

74. Samuel Willard, *Reformation the Great Duty of an Afflicted People* (Boston, 1694), 74.

75. Ibid., 74–75.

76. Ibid., 75.

77. Samuel Willard, *The Child's Portion: Or the Unseen Glory of the Children of God* (Boston, 1684), 43.

78. Ibid., n.p.

79. Willard, *Reformation the Great Duty*, 73. On spiritual deafness, see also 21, 30, and 33.

80. Ibid., 36.

81. Willard, *Covenant-Keeping*, 82–83. Kamensky notes that the events at Salem prompted Cotton Mather to cite this injunction in *Ornaments for the Daughters of Zion* (1692) (*Governing the Tongue*, 150 and 263, note 1).

82. Samuel Willard, *Heavenly Merchandize* (Boston, 1686), 126.

83. Ibid., 129–30.

84. Ibid., 14.

85. On how Willard exemplified this partnership between ministers and merchants, see Valeri, *Heavenly Merchandize*, 155-57.

86. Peterson, *The Price of Redemption*, 124.

87. Quoted in ibid.

88. Ibid., 125.

89. Ebenezer Pemberton, "The Author's Character," in Samuel Willard, *A Compleat Body of Divinity* (Boston, 1726), 3. At Groton, Willard had asked his auditors to "consider why hath God lately taken away so many of his precious Servants in the Ministry, it is not to their damage or wrong, they are gone to their rest . . . they were despised here, and they are now received to honour and glory: and this may call us to solemn consideration" (UI 77).

90. Peterson, *The Price of Redemption*, 90. David Waldstreicher observes that James Franklin's master in the printing trade, the London printer Benjamin Harris, "printed work for Samuel Willard, the pastor of Old South Church—a connection that father Josiah certainly appreciated and probably had relied upon" (*Runaway America: Benjamin Franklin, Slavery, and the American Revolution* [New York: Hill and Wang, 2004], 37).

91. Kathryn Zabelle Derounian, "The Publication, Promotion, and Distribution of Mary Rowlandson's Indian Captivity Narrative in the Seventeenth Century," *Early American Literature* 23, no. 3 (1988): 244.

92. Jill Lepore observes that Rowlandson's manuscript was "'captivated,' and put into God's service" (*The Name of War: King Philip's War and the Origins of American Identity* [New York: Vintage, 1999], 131).

Chapter 3: Servant to a Christian

1. Mary Rowlandson, *The Sovereignty and Goodness of God*, in Mary Rowlandson, *The Sovereignty and Goodness of God, with Related Documents*, ed. with an introduction by Neal Salisbury (Boston: Bedford Books, 1997), 88. All further references to this work will be cited parenthetically as SG.

2. The discourse of service also translates the experience of captivity and its moral and spiritual lessons for readers across the Atlantic, who were removed from actual Native Americans and likely to remain that way. On reading Rowlandson in a transatlantic context, see Kathryn Zabelle Derounian, "The Publication, Promotion, and Distribution of Mary Rowlandson's Indian Captivity Narrative in the Seventeenth Century," *Early American Literature* 23, no. 3 (1988): 255–57; Michelle Burnham, *Captivity and Sentiment: Cultural Exchange in American Literature, 1682–1861* (Hanover, NH: Dartmouth College Press, 1997), 41–49; Eve Tavor Bannet, *Transatlantic Stories and the History of Reading, 1720–1810: Migrant Fictions* (Cambridge: Cambridge University Press, 2011), 60–64.

3. Neal Salisbury, "Introduction: Mary Rowlandson and Her Removes," in Mary Rowlandson, *The Sovereignty and Goodness of God, with Related Documents*, ed. with an introduction by Neal Salisbury (Boston: Bedford Books, 1997), 29 and 31.

4. Mitchell Robert Breitwieser, *American Puritanism and the Defense of Mourning: Religion, Grief and Ethnology in Mary White Rowlandson's Captivity Narrative* (Madison: University of Wisconsin Press, 1990), 19 (italics in original).

5. 1 Cor. 7:21. Rowlandson scholarship frequently registers the significance of her rhetoric of servant and master as it illuminates how her captivity relates to Puritan status and gender assumptions, but has not connected it to spiritual discourses of service. In addition to the works cited in this chapter, see, for example, Margaret H. Davis, "Mary White Rowlandson's Self-Fashioning as Puritan Goodwife," *Early American Literature* 27, no. 1 (1992): 49–60.

6. Increase Mather [Ter Amicum, pseud.], "Preface to the Reader," in Mary Rowlandson, *The Sovereignty and Goodness of God, with Related Documents*, ed. with an introduction by Neal Salisbury (Boston: Bedford Books, 1997), 65.

7. Breitwieser, *American Puritanism*, 176.

8. Tara Fitzpatrick gives Rowlandson a particularly heavy load in her influential essay, "The Figure of Captivity: The Cultural Work of the Puritan Captivity Narrative," *American Literary History* 3, no. 1 (1991): 1–26 (see especially 20–21). Bryce Traister offers a nuanced postsecular account of Rowlandson's relationship to modernity in "Mary Rowlandson and the Invention of the Secular," *Early American Literature* 42, no. 2 (2007): 323–54.

9. Rowlandson's ambivalent relationship to Puritan orthodoxy is a staple of recent criticism. In Susan Howe's terse and powerful formulation, "Mary Rowlandson saw what she did not see [and] said what she did not say" (*The Birth-Mark: Unsettling the Wilderness in American Literary History* [Middletown, CT: Wesleyan University Press, 1993], 128). For a less enigmatic expression, see Christopher Castiglia, *Bound and Determined: Captivity, Culture-Crossing, and White Womanhood from Mary Rowlandson to Patty Hearst* (Chicago, IL: University of Chicago Press, 1996), 80–82. Though Breitwieser reads Rowlandson as upholding orthodoxy, he argues that her work of mourning "breaks through or outdistances her own and her culture's dominant means of representation" (*American Puritanism*, 10). By foregrounding what servitude might have meant to Rowlandson and her contemporaries, my method hews to Gary Ebersole's preferred mode of trying to "reconstruct the world of the text and the reading practices brought to bear on it" (*Captured by Texts: Puritan to Postmodern Images of Indian Captivity* [Charlottesville: University Press of Virginia, 1995], 43). However, I am less inclined than he is to characterize as "presumptuous" (ibid., 281, note 21) and anachronistic such sensitive and sophisticated readings as Breitwieser's, which help us continue to make vibrant connections between our critical reading practices (and those of our students) and those of Rowlandson and her contemporary audience.

10. Traister's witty rhetorical question sums up the line of scholarship that has identified a tension between the captive's "empirical narrative" and the author's "rhetorical narrative": "did Mary Rowlandson or Increase Mather insert all those Bible references?" ("Mary Rowlandson," 334).

11. Margaret Ellen Newell documents a cycle of debt, crime, and bondage that she calls "judicial enslavement," the legal apparatus of servitude and mastery that would define postwar Native-Anglo relations ("The Changing Nature of Indian Slavery in New England, 1670–1720," in *Reinterpreting New England Indians and the Colonial Experience*, ed. Colin Calloway and Neal Salisbury [Boston: Colonial Society of Massachusetts, 2003], 106–36). This concept gets less play in her book, *Brethren by Nature: New England Indians, Colonists, and the Origins of American Slavery* (Ithaca, NY: Cornell University Press, 2015), but chapters 6–8 of that work are essential reading on the role of Indian servitude during the war and the fate of Indians after it. On the diaspora of war captives sold into slavery and the creation of a newly defined Anglo master class, see especially 168–88.

12. Jill Lepore, *The Name of War: King Philip's War and the Origins of American Identity* (New York: Vintage, 1999), 126.

13. Ann Marie Plane, *Colonial Intimacies: Indian Marriage in Early New England* (Ithaca, NY: Cornell University Press, 2000), 102. See also Newell, *Brethren by Nature*, 89; Lepore, *The Name of War*, 166.

14. Rowlandson's text was literally bound together with public discourses of humiliation that exemplified the jeremiad (Salisbury, "Introduction," 45). Joseph Rowlandson's final sermon was preached on November 21, 1678, "a Day of FAST and HUMILIATION" (Joseph Rowlandson, "The Possibility of God's Forsaking a People," in Mary Rowlandson, *The Sovereignty and Goodness of God, with Related Documents*, ed. with an introduction by Neal Salisbury [Boston: Bedford Books, 1997], 150), and it was published with the earliest editions of his wife's captivity narrative. Teresa Toulouse considers the cultural work of humiliation embodied by women captives but not its relation to servitude (*The Captive's Position: Female Narrative, Male Identity, and Royal Authority in Colonial New England* [Philadelphia: University of Pennsylvania Press, 2006], especially chapter 4). My argument bears the influence of Toulouse's attention to Samuel Willard's *Mercy Magnified on a Penitent Prodigal* (Boston, 1684) (all further references to this work will be cited parenthetically as MM) and her focus on issues of "fatherly authority" (Toulouse, *The Captive's Position*, 17), a term whose self-evidence she productively questions.

15. Michelle Burnham usefully summarizes the recent scholarship on the rhetoric of spiritual declension as a discourse of economic morality (*Folded Selves: Colonial New England Writing in the World System* [Hanover, NH: Dartmouth College Press, 2007], 8–13). To the works she discusses, I would add Mark Valeri, *Heavenly Merchandize: How Religion Shaped Commerce in Puritan America* (Princeton, NJ: Princeton University Press, 2010).

16. Rowlandson's use of the prodigal has attracted little sustained attention, but Toulouse and Breitwieser are compelling exceptions: both read the passage as a rich instance of Rowlandson's resistance to the orthodox interpretation of her experience and focus on the disparity between infraction and punishment. See Toulouse, *The Captive's Position*, 62–63; Breitwieser, *American Puritanism*, 118.

17. For a discussion of lip service and hypocritical confessions, see chapter 2.

18. Willard accounts for the omission of the petition after the confession in verse 21, observing that among "diverse reasons" for the omission, the "most probable, is that his

father's kind carriage, and abundant expression of his love, had left him no room for it, because he now found himself accepted in quality of a son" (MM, 319–20).

19. Mark Peterson, *The Price of Redemption: The Spiritual Economy of Puritan New England* (Stanford, CA: Stanford University Press, 1997), 168.

20. See note 9.

21. MM, 260. As in these passages, Willard's exegesis of the prodigal alludes to Rowlandson's captivity strongly enough to suggest not just that they shared dominant understandings of the parable but also that his interpretation was shaped by Rowlandson's experience—or, perhaps, pursuing what Traister calls the "composite authorship question," that Willard had an authorial hand in Rowlandson's narrative ("Mary Rowlandson," 335).

22. Virginia DeJohn Anderson, "King Philip's Herds: Indians, Colonists, and the Problem of Livestock in Early New England," *William and Mary Quarterly* 51, no. 4 (1994): 601–24.

23. Derounian deems Rowlandson's narrative "public service" ("The Publication," 240).

24. On Rowlandson as homemaker, see Abram Van Engen, *Sympathetic Puritans: Calvinist Fellow Feeling in Early New England* (New York: Oxford University Press, 2015), chapter 6; Lisa Logan, "Mary Rowlandson's Captivity and the 'Place' of the Woman Subject," *Early American Literature* 28, no. 3 (1993): 255–77; Bridget Bennett, "The Crisis of Restoration: Mary Rowlandson's Lost Home," *Early American Literature* 49, no. 2 (2014): 327–56. On exchanges between Algonquian and English concepts of the household, see Plane, *Colonial Intimacies*; Ann M. Little, *Abraham in Arms: War and Gender in Colonial New England* (Philadelphia: University of Pennsylvania, 2007), chapter 3. Relocating the generic origins of the "English novel" to Puritan New England, Nancy Armstrong and Leonard Tennenhouse have read Richardson's *Pamela* as a captivity narrative in *The Imaginary Puritan: Literature, Intellectual Labor, and the Origins of Personal Life* (Berkeley: University of California Press, 1992). Their reading depends for its force on an analogy between Pamela's domestic entrapment by Mr. B (first as his servant and later as his wife) and Rowlandson's wilderness servitude to Quinnopin and Weetamoo. Their argument can move convincingly between seventeenth-century New England and eighteenth-century England, and between a historical woman and the fictional creation of a male author, because of the structural equality of Rowlandson's captivity and Pamela's domestic service—not just as conditions of household labor, class status, or susceptibility to violence, but as authorial positions: the place of the gendered "writing subject" (ibid., 202). On the Rowlandson-Richardson analogy, see especially 203–14.

25. Burnham, *Captivity and Sentiment*, 27.

26. Laurel Thatcher Ulrich, *Good Wives: Image and Reality in the Lives of Women in Northern New England, 1650–1750* (New York: Knopf, 1982), 228. See also Teresa Toulouse, "'My Own Credit': Strategies of (E)valuation in Mary Rowlandson's Captivity," *American Literature* 64, no. 4 (1992): 658. Tiffany Potter suggests that the exchanges between motherhood and servitude are dialectical, not just a reversal, when she observes that "it is Rowlandson's knowable role as a mother to which she clings while she struggles concurrently to create and negate her identity as a captive

slave" ("Writing Indigenous Femininity: Mary Rowlandson's Narrative of Captivity," *Eighteenth-Century Studies* 36, no. 2 [2003]: 158). The wife, mother, and mistress was also, of course, a dependent of the household master; in Puritan household conduct, the role of wife was defined in contrast to that of servant. For example, William Perkins presents Adam and Eve as the prototype of husband and wife, explaining that though the husband has authority over the wife, "God did not make her subject to him as a servant: but out of his side, to the end that man should take her as his mate" (*Christian Oeconomy*, in William Perkins, *The Work of William Perkins*, ed. Ian Breward [Abingdon, UK: Sutton Courtenay Press, 1970], 428). The wife is not a servant but must obey her husband's lawful commands. This distinction between being a servant and serving the husband would define the wife's role in companionate marriage. Elizabeth Maddock Dillon observes that "the companionate marriage, while it bespeaks a sense of contractual agency on the part of the wife, works much like the conversion narrative to weld the woman to a particular nonvolitional status relation" (*The Gender of Freedom: Fictions of Liberalism and the Literary Public Sphere* [Stanford, CA: Stanford University Press, 2004], 113).

27. Van Engen, *Sympathetic Puritans*, 173–74.

28. Abigail Adams, *The Book of Abigail and John: Selected Letters of the Adams Family, 1763–1784*, ed. with an introduction by L. H. Butterfield, Marc Friedlaender, and Mary-Jo Kline, with a new foreword by David McCullough (Boston: Northeastern University Press, 2002), 121–23.

29. Richard Slotkin reads such moments that describe the violent separation of parents from children as an allegory of the "trauma of emigration" from England to New England (*Regeneration through Violence: The Mythology of the American Frontier, 1600–1860* [1973; repr., Norman: University of Oklahoma Press, 2000], 108). See also Van Engen, *Sympathetic Puritans*, 179.

30. Pamela Lougheed, "'Then Began He to Rant and Threaten': Indian Malice and Individual Liberty in Mary Rowlandson's Captivity Narrative," *American Literature* 74, no. 2 (2002): 287–313.

31. Lawrence Towner, *A Good Master Well Served: Masters and Servants in Colonial Massachusetts, 1620–1750* (New York: Garland Publishing, 1998), 51–76.

32. Increase Mather, *Renewal of Covenant the Great Duty Incumbent on Decaying or Distressed Churches* (Boston, 1677), A3.

33. Ibid., 19.

34. Ibid.

35. Though he emphasizes the exemplary aspects of contract, Increase Mather also presents the threat of hypocritical service and rebellion (*Renewal*, 13). The rebellious child was a spiritual and earthly criminal, and the magistracy and the ministry spoke as one to discipline her: "When the magistrates passed a series of laws in November 1675 to reform the sins that had caused God to send the Indians upon them, they specifically targeted youth, appending 'especially amongst the younger sort' to nearly every declaration" (Jenny Hale Pulsipher, *Subjects unto the Same King: Indians, English, and the Contest for Authority in Colonial New England* [Philadelphia: University of Pennsylvania Press, 2005], 150).

36. Matthew Brown opens his discussion of fasting and humiliation with a reading

of Joseph Rowlandson's final sermon but does not connect it explicitly to Mary Rowlandson's starvation (*The Pilgrim and the Bee: Reading Rituals and Book Culture in Early New England* [Philadelphia: University of Pennsylvania Press, 2007], 107–10). Jordan Alexander Stein has offered a provocative reading of Rowlandson's hunger, arguing that it expands the kinds of evidence that can be included in the archive of early modern sexuality ("Mary Rowlandson's Hunger and the Historiography of Sexuality," *American Literature* 81, no. 3 [2009]: 469–95).

37. Lawrence Towner, "'A Fondness for Freedom': Servant Protest in Puritan Society," *William and Mary Quarterly* 19, no. 2 (1962): 201–19.

38. Ibid., 213–14. On Native Americans' unequal access to justice under English law, see Yasuhide Kawashima, *Puritan Justice and the Indian: White Man's Law in Massachusetts, 1630–1763* (Middletown, CT: Wesleyan University Press, 1986).

39. William Ames, *The Marrow of Theology*, ed. and trans. John Dykstra Eusden (Durham, NC: Labyrinth Press, 1968), 312.

40. Ibid., 134–35.

41. Towner discusses the 1644 case of a master who was executed when his apprentice died from mistreatment (*A Good Master*, 165).

42. Kristina Bross points out that while famous English missionaries like John Eliot and Thomas Mayhew positioned the natives as bondslaves to Satan, native converts themselves tended to not to use this trope to apply to their spiritual histories (*Dry Bones and Indian Sermons: Praying Indians in Colonial America* [Ithaca, NY: Cornell University Press, 2004], 148–53).

43. Hilary Wyss offers a compelling account of their roles, and those of other Christian natives during the war, reading against the grain of Anglo depictions (*Writing Indians: Literacy, Christianity, and Native Community in Early America* [Amherst: University of Massachusetts Press, 2000], chapter 1).

44. Toulouse, *The Captive's Position*, chapter 2. Potter observes that Rowlandson uses the "language of the English mistress-servant relationship" to depict Weetamoo as a "failure of indigenous femininity," against which "Rowlandson can affirm her own privileged status and identity" ("Writing Indigenous Femininity," 159).

45. Burnham, *Captivity and Sentiment*, 29 and 31.

46. Ibid., 33.

47. Nan Goodman, "'Money Answers All Things': Rethinking Economic and Cultural Exchange in the Captivity Narrative of Mary Rowlandson," *American Literary History* 22, no. 1 (2010): 11.

48. Salisbury's edition of Rowlandson's narrative includes Cotton Mather's 1699 account of Dustan's captivity in *Decennium Luctousum* (SG 164–68).

49. Goodman, "'Money Answers All Things,'" 11–12. As David Graeber argues, the idea that capitalism emerged from a barter economy is essentially a cherished myth of liberal capitalist economic theory and history, for there is no evidence that such an economy ever existed. Graeber brilliantly challenges that narrative in *Debt: The First 5,000 Years*, updated ed. (Brooklyn, NY: Melville House, 2014).

50. Towner, *A Good Master*, 195–217.

51. William Ames, *Conscience with the Power and Cases Thereof* (London, 1643), book 5, 160.

52. Toulouse reads Rowlandson's "testing" of martyrdom as a way of conferring value upon female submission in particular ("'My Own Credit,'" 661). See also ibid., 658–63.

53. Steven Neuwirth, "Her Master's Voice: Gender, Speech, and Gendered Speech in the Narrative of the Captivity of Mary White Rowlandson," in *Sex and Sexuality in Early America*, ed. Merril D. Smith (New York: New York University Press, 1998), 69.

54. Shepard was only two years older than Rowlandson (he was born in 1635, she in 1637).

55. Breitwieser, *American Puritanism*, 176. Among other astute readings of Rowlandson's phrase, see Goodman, "'Money Answers All Things,'" 5–6; Logan, "Mary Rowlandson's Captivity," 267–68.

56. Breitwieser suggests this aspect of vocation in his observation that "puritan identity is rigorously generic. One would of course differ in the extrinsic traits collected under the term *particular calling*, the talents one used as the vehicle or body for practical and expressive devotion" (*American Puritanism*, 54). By presenting the "particular calling" as the expression of variation within the type, he implies that servant is the "generic" Puritan identity: according to the general calling, all humans are God's servants. See also Logan, "Mary Rowlandson's Captivity," 255.

57. Lepore, *The Name of War*, 150–70.

58. Newell, *Brethren by Nature*, chapters 7 and 9. As David Silverman explains, after the war, "most colonists abandoned expectations of making Indians like themselves and instead used enhanced power to relegate Natives to landlessness, debt peonage, and political impotency" (*Red Brethren: The Brothertown and Stockbridge Indians and the Problem of Race in Early America* [Ithaca, NY: Cornell University Press, 2010], 24).

59. Plane, *Colonial Intimacies*, 102. Daniel Richter identifies a strong legalist strain even within the conversion efforts of John Eliot at Natick (*Facing East from Indian Country: A Native History of Early America* [Cambridge, MA: Harvard University Press, 2001], 120–25).

60. Daniel Gookin, "A Memorandum of Indian Children put Forth into Service to the English," in Mary Rowlandson, *The Sovereignty and Goodness of God, with Related Documents*, ed. with an introduction by Neal Salisbury (Boston: Bedford Books, 1997), 142).

61. Ibid., 144.

62. Ibid., 143.

63. Salisbury suggests that Rowlandson "sought to participate in the debates among those who were interpreting the war's history in print," noting that her treatment of the Praying Indians explicitly countered the sympathetic view expressed by Gookin ("Introduction," 41). In this, Salisbury explains, she also differed from the accounts of Increase Mather and William Hubbard.

64. Quoted in Pulsipher, *Subjects unto the Same King*, 150.

65. David Waldstreicher, *Runaway America: Benjamin Franklin, Slavery, and the American Revolution* (New York: Hill and Wang, 2004).

66. David L. Greene, "New Light on Mary Rowlandson," *Early American Literature* 20, no. 1 (1985): 24–38.

67. By concluding my discussion of Rowlandson with this court case, I follow in the footsteps of Breitwieser (*American Puritanism*, 192–94) and Goodman ("'Money Answers All Things,'" 19–20).

68. Quoted in George H. Moore, *Notes on the History of Slavery in Massachusetts* (New York: D. Appleton, 1866), 36.

Chapter 4: Racial Vocation

1. Samuel Sewall, *The Diary of Samuel Sewall 1674–1729*, ed. M. Halsey Thomas (New York: Farrar, Straus and Giroux, 1973), 1:432–33.

2. Paul Bayne, *An Entire Commentary upon the Whole Epistle of the Apostle Paul to the Ephesians* (London, 1643), 695.

3. Sewall, *The Diary of Samuel Sewall*, 1:433.

4. Albert J. Von Frank, "John Saffin: Slavery and Racism in Colonial Massachusetts," *Early American Literature* 29, no. 3 (1994): 266. Von Frank complicates this assumption, as does Mark Peterson, who positions "The Selling of Joseph" not as "the first salvo in a concerted antislavery movement but [as] an early statement in a complex conversation in which slavery took its place among a host of social and ideological issues animating the Protestant world" ("The Selling of Joseph: Bostonians, Antislavery, and the Protestant International," *Massachusetts Historical Review* 4 [2002]: 14).

5. Bayne, *An Entire Commentary*, 695; William Ames, *Conscience with the Power and Cases Thereof* (London, 1643), book 5, 159–60.

6. Cotton Mather, *A Good Master Well Served* (Boston, 1696), 22. All further references to this work will be cited parenthetically as GM.

7. See the introduction, note 18.

8. William Pettigrew, *Freedom's Debt: The Royal African Company and the Politics of the Atlantic Slave Trade, 1672–1752* (Chapel Hill: University of North Carolina Press, 2013), 8. In *Race and Redemption in Puritan New England* (New York: Oxford University Press, 2011), Richard A. Bailey shows how race interacted with Puritan ideals of spiritual liberty in New England.

9. Eric Kimball, "'What Have We to Do with Slavery?': New Englanders and the Slave Economies of the West Indies," in *Slavery's Capitalism: A New History of American Economic Development*, ed. Sven Beckert and Seth Rockman (Philadelphia: University of Pennsylvania Press, 2016), 182.

10. Samuel Sewall, "The Selling of Joseph," in Samuel Sewall, *The Selling of Joseph: A Memorial*, ed. Sidney Kaplan (Amherst: University of Massachusetts Press, 1969), 7.

11. Robert C. Twombly and Richard H. Moore, "Black Puritan: The Negro in Seventeenth-Century Massachusetts," *William and Mary Quarterly* 24, no. 2 (1967): 238–39.

12. For an example of each of these kinds of "servant" law passed during the same 1698 legislative session, see *Acts and Resolves Public and Private of the Province of the Massachusetts Bay* (Boston: Wright and Potter, 1869), 1:324–25. Cautioning against taking a monolithic view of "the 'New England' experience of race," Ann Marie Plane notes that during the last quarter of the seventeenth century, "the institution of servitude . . . was being stretched in new directions to accommodate African and Indian servants," creating "increasing links between servitude and *any*

non-European ancestry" (*Colonial Intimacies: Indian Marriage in Early New England* [Ithaca, NY: Cornell University Press, 2000], 122–23, italics in original).

13. Cotton Mather, *The Negro Christianized* (Boston, 1706). All further references to this work will be cited parenthetically as NC.

14. Ames, *Conscience with the Power and Cases Thereof*, book 5, 160.

15. Bayne, *An Entire Commentary*, 699–700.

16. Ames, *Conscience with the Power and Cases Thereof*, book 5, 161.

17. Bayne, *An Entire Commentary*, 707 and 709.

18. Ibid., 709.

19. Ibid.

20. Ibid., 700. Though he somewhat privileges Michel Foucault over Puritan writers when framing his understanding of what is specifically Puritan about New England slavery, Dominik Nagl aptly observes that hypocrisy was important to it ("The Governmentality of Slavery in Colonial Boston, 1690–1760," *Amerikastuden* 58, no. 1 [2013]: 17).

21. Philip Gould suggests the useful term "commercial jeremiad" for a "cultural narrative against slave trading" that emerged from the "long-standing use by antislavery writers of Protestant discourses about human sin, Christian morality, and divine judgment." This genre "represents the gradual process of secularization of these Protestant discourses in antislavery writing—the use of traditional languages and rhetorical conventions in formulating modern commercial ideologies" (*Barbaric Traffic: Commerce and Antislavery in the Eighteenth-Century Atlantic World* [Cambridge, MA: Harvard University Press, 2003], 13–14). Mather's sermons suggest that Protestant proslavery texts also fit Gould's category.

22. See David Goldenberg, *The Curse of Ham: Race and Slavery in Early Judaism, Christianity, and Islam* (Princeton, NJ: Princeton University Press, 2005).

23. Rebecca Anne Goetz finds in Anglo-Virginia "a budding idea of hereditary heathenism—the notion that Indians and Africans could never become Christian" that provided "the foundations for an emergent idea of race and an ideology of racism" (*The Baptism of Early America: How Christianity Created Race* [Baltimore, MD: Johns Hopkins University Press, 2012], 3). Evidently this strain was also present even in the New England texts that staunchly advocated for the conversion of black slaves.

24. Mark Valeri, *Heavenly Merchandize: How Religion Shaped Commerce in Puritan America* (Princeton, NJ: Princeton University Press, 2010), 160.

25. Cotton Mather, *A Christian at His Calling* (Boston, 1701), 68.

26. Ibid., 46 and 69.

27. Ibid., 5.

28. Ibid., 16.

29. Ibid., 16–17.

30. Ibid., 64.

31. Cotton Mather, *Lex Mercatoria* (Boston, 1705), 13.

32. Ibid., 20.

33. A passage in which Mather likens a crooked merchant to a servant who has stolen from his master also illustrates how the master-servant dyad overlaps conceptually with the buyer-seller dyad (ibid., 38).

34. Sargent Bush Jr., introduction to Sarah Kemble Knight, "The Journal of Madam Knight," ed. with an introduction by Sargent Bush Jr., in *Journeys in New Worlds: Early American Women's Narratives*, ed. William L. Andrews, Sargent Bush Jr., Annette Kolodny, Amy Schrager Lang, and Daniel B. Shea (Madison: University of Wisconsin Press, 1990), 72. See also Julia Stern, "To Relish and to Spew: Disgust as Cultural Critique in *The Journal of Madam Knight*," *Legacy* 14, no. 1 (1997): 1–2; Scott Michaelsen, "Narrative and Class in a Culture of Consumption: The Significance of Stories in Sarah Kemble Knight's 'Journal,'" *College English* 21, no. 2 (1994): 33–46. Scholarship on Knight remains relatively sparse, but for an insightful recent discussion, see Laura Laffrado, *Uncommon Women: Gender and Representation in Nineteenth-Century U.S. Women's Writing* (Columbus: Ohio State Press, 2009), chapter 1.

35. Valeri, *Heavenly Merchandize*, 82–83.

36. Julia Stern observes that Knight's complaints about her aches, pains, and bad food "suggests by contrast that Knight is not accustomed to the physical strain of the traveler's life, that she is, under ordinary circumstances, sedentary, domestic, and the frequent object of attentive service" ("To Relish and to Spew," 3).

37. Sarah Kemble Knight, "The Journal of Madam Knight," ed. with an introduction by Sargent Bush Jr., in *Journeys in New Worlds: Early American Women's Narratives*, ed. William L. Andrews, Sargent Bush Jr., Annette Kolodny, Amy Schrager Lang, and Daniel B. Shea (Madison: University of Wisconsin Press, 1990), 103.

38. Ibid., 105.

39. Ibid.

40. Ibid., 106.

41. Ibid., 104–5.

42. Ibid., 105.

43. It is possible that Knight comments obliquely here on a case described to her by one of the few people who offered her shelter from the wilds of incivility, the Reverend Gurdon Saltonstall. During the same year that Saltonstall played gracious host to the weary Knight, he participated in the legal struggle of a slave named Abda who sued for his freedom. Lorenzo Greene discusses the case, describing it as "extremely important because it set a legal precedent for holding mulattoes in bondage" (*The Negro in Colonial New England, 1620–1776* [1942; repr., New York: Atheneum, 1968], 182–83).

44. S. Knight, "The Journal of Madam Knight," 116.

45. Laffrado, *Uncommon Women*, 42; Michaelsen, "Narrative and Class in a Culture of Consumption," 36.

46. S. Knight, "The Journal of Madam Knight," 116. Sargent Bush Jr. notes the Sewall-Saffin debate (described below) when he provides "historical context" for Knight's journey, but he does not explicitly analyze the connections between them (introduction, 70).

47. Adam was legally an indentured servant, not a slave. See Von Frank, "John Saffin," 257–61. The case and attendant pamphlet war between Sewall and Saffin is a staple in histories of New England slavery. For a comprehensive recent account, see Wendy Warren, *New England Bound: Slavery and Colonization in Early America* (New York: Norton, 2016), 220–45.

48. *Acts and Resolves Public and Private of the Province of Massachusetts Bay*, vol. 8 (Boston: Wright and Potter, 1895), 266.

49. Ibid.

50. Ibid., 268.

51. Ibid., 267.

52. John Saffin, "A Brief and Candid Reply," in George H. Moore, *Notes on the History of Slavery in Massachusetts* (New York: D. Appleton, 1866), 251–56.

53. Sewall, "The Selling of Joseph," 11.

54. Ibid., 12 and 14.

55. Saffin, "A Brief and Candid Reply," 256.

56. Ibid.

57. Sewall, "The Selling of Joseph," 10.

58. Ibid., 16.

59. Ibid., 10.

60. Saffin, "A Brief and Candid Reply," 252.

61. Ibid., 253.

62. Sewall would continue to argue in print that black slaves' inability to serve willingly made them unprofitable servants. In a June 1706 issue of the *Boston News-Letter*, Sewall published a "Computation that the Importation of Negroes is not so profitable as that of White Servants," which Moore reproduces in its entirety (Moore, *Notes on the History of Slavery in Massachusetts*, 107). It is unsigned, but Moore is "inclined to attribute" authorship to Sewall (ibid., 106). As part of his case, Sewall wrote, "Negroes are generally Eye-Servants, great Thieves, much addicted to Stealing, Lying and Purloining" (ibid., 107). "An Act to Encourage the Importation of White Servants" was passed in 1708–9 (*Acts and Resolves*, vol. 1, 634).

63. Plane discusses the Sewall-Saffin debate in the context of her discussion of race, servitude, and household ideology in the aftermath of King Philip's War, but she does not consider spiritual household discourses (*Colonial Intimacies*, 118–19).

64. Sewall, "The Selling of Joseph," 10–11.

65. Ames, *Conscience with the Power and Cases Thereof*, book 5, 159.

66. Ibid., 160.

67. Saffin, "A Brief and Candid Reply," 255.

68. John Saffin, *The Note Book of John Saffin 1665–1708*, ed. with an introduction by Caroline Hazard (New York: Harbor Press, 1928), 146.

69. Twombly and Moore, "Black Puritan," 238, note 30.

70. Moore, *Notes*, 61.

71. *Acts and Resolves*, vol. 8, 271.

72. For the context, see David Levin, *Cotton Mather: The Young Life of the Lord's Remembrancer, 1664–1703* (Cambridge, MA: Harvard University Press, 1978), 296–97.

73. Sewall, *The Diary of Samuel Sewall*, 1:454–55. The entry suggests that Saffin might not have been far off the mark when he commented that Sewall "would deem himself much neglected, if we should show him no more Defference [*sic*] than to an ordinary Porter" (quoted in Moore, *Notes*, 256). John Wood Sweet cites this entry as evidence that "enslaved Africans were, on the one hand, excluded from social recogni-

tion and, on the other, a constant point of reference" (*Bodies Politic: Negotiating Race in the American North, 1730–1830* [2003; repr., Philadelphia: University of Pennsylvania Press, 2006, 63).

74. Cotton Mather, *A Family Well Ordered* (Boston, 1699), 8.

75. Ibid., 8–9.

76. Ibid., 22.

77. Ibid., 22–23.

78. Ibid., 26.

79. Ibid., 4.

80. Lisa Wilson, *Ye Heart of a Man: The Domestic Life of Men in Colonial New England* (New Haven, CT: Yale University Press, 1999), 15–22.

81. C. Mather, *A Christian at His Calling*, 30.

82. Cotton Mather, *Youth under a Good Conduct. A Short Essay to Render Young People Happy* (Boston, 1704), 19.

83. Ibid., 21.

84. Valeri, *Heavenly Merchandize*, 160. Kathryn S. Koo has observed that "Mather's practical experiment in Christianized slaveholding does represent a significant case study by which to examine the paradox of slavery as a form of 'kinship' in New England" ("Strangers in the House of God: Cotton Mather, Onesimus, and an Experiment in Christian Slaveholding," *Proceedings of the American Antiquarian Society* 117, part 1 [2007]: 151).

85. Mather's fatalistic rhetoric of "casting" can be viewed in light of Jackson Lears's argument about how a managerial "ethic of mastery" emerges as a defense against the arbitrariness of grace as "spiritual luck," expressed as a disdain for "gambling as indiscipline and the culture of chance as superstition" (*Something for Nothing: Luck in America* [New York: Penguin, 2003], 75). As this passage exemplifies, this "ethic of mastery" emerges not just in broader discourses of providence, but also more narrowly in discourses of providential mastery over other humans.

86. Dana D. Nelson shows that Mather uses race to align the spiritual and economic rewards for masters who labor to convert their slaves, characterizing his "plan" as "a scheme of cosmic capitalism" (*The Word in Black and White: Reading "Race" in American Literature, 1638–1867* [New York: Oxford University Press, 1992], 28).

87. Quoted in Koo, "Strangers in the House of God," 156.

88. Nelson presents Mather's *The Negro Christianized* and *Bonifacius* as two examples of Mather's urging Christians to capitalize on opportunities to "Do Good" (*The Word in Black and White*, 24).

89. For a perceptive extended discussion of Mather and smallpox, see Cristobal Silva, *Miraculous Plagues: An Epidemiology of Early New England Narrative* (New York: Oxford University Press, 2011), 142–79.

90. Discussing Wheatley's interactions with Benjamin Franklin, David Waldstreicher notes that she targeted "the hypocrisy of the patriot cause" and that "English reviewers of her volume used it as another opportunity to condemn the hypocrisy of colonists like the Wheatleys for keeping such persons in bondage" (*Runaway America: Benjamin Franklin, Slavery, and the American Revolution* [New York: Hill and Wang, 2004], 203). Paula Bennett discusses "Wheatley's project of poetic self-redemption—

that is, her legitimation of her right to practice her vocation" ("Phillis Wheatley's Vocation and the Paradox of the 'Afric Muse,'" *PMLA* 113, no. 1 (1998): 66.

91. Phillis Wheatley, "On Being Brought from Africa to America," in Phillis Wheatley, *The Collected Works of Phillis Wheatley*, ed. John C. Shields (New York: Oxford University Press, 1988), 18.

Chapter 5: The Spirit of Mastery

1. Max Weber, *The Protestant Ethic and the Spirit of Capitalism*, trans. Talcott Parsons (1930; repr., London: Routledge Classics, 2002), 14. The other passages quoted in the text, from Benjamin Franklin's "Advice to a Young Tradesman" (1748) and "Necessary Hints to Those That Would Be Rich" (1736), are on pages 14–16. On the origins and criticism of Weber's concept, see Gordon Marshall, *In Search of the Spirit of Capitalism: An Essay on Max Weber's Protestant Ethic Thesis* (New York: Columbia University Press, 1982), 17–68.

2. Weber implies this himself, citing the parable of the talents to illustrate the "ethic of ascetic Protestantism" (*The Protestant Ethic*, 114–15).

3. Benjamin Franklin, "The Way to Wealth," in Benjamin Franklin, *Autobiography and Other Writings*, ed. Ormond Seavey (Oxford: Oxford University Press, 1993), 267.

4. Karl Weintraub summed up the charges at that time in "The Puritan Ethic and Benjamin Franklin," *Journal of Religion* 56, no. 3 (1976): 231.

5. D. H. Lawrence, *Studies in Classic American Literature* (1923; repr., New York: Viking Press, 1968), 10.

6. Ibid., 13.

7. Ibid., 19.

8. Ibid., 16 and 19.

9. Weber, *The Protestant Ethic*, 123.

10. Reginald Dyck discusses Occom's critique of the "contradictory principles of New England capitalism and Christianity" but does not consider hypocrisy as a spiritual discourse ("The Economic Education of Samson Occom," *Studies in American Indian Literature* 24, no. 3 [2012]: 16).

11. Keely McCarthy, "Conversion, Identity, and the Indian Missionary," *Early American Literature* 36, no. 3 (2001): 355.

12. Samson Occom, "'Giving Thanks Always for all Things unto God,' Ephesians 5:20," in Samson Occom, *The Collected Writings of Samson Occom, Mohegan: Leadership and Literature in Eighteenth-Century Native America*, ed. Joanna Brooks (New York: Oxford University Press, 2006), 221. All further references to Occom's writings will cite this edition parenthetically as SO. Brooks includes symbols indicating interlineations on the original manuscripts, which I have omitted here. Where she brackets unclear, incomplete, or missing words, I have used her proposed language.

13. Phillis Wheatley, "Letter to Samson Occom," in Phillis Wheatley, *The Collected Works of Phillis Wheatley*, ed. John C. Shields (New York: Oxford University Press, 1988), 177.

14. For different comparative approaches to Franklin's and Occom's economic personhood, see Drew Lopenzina, "Compromised Currencies: Why Samson Occom Is

Not Pictured on the One Hundred Dollar Bill," in *Sovereignty, Separatism, and Survivance: Ideological Encounters in the Literature of Native North America*, ed. Benjamin D. Carson (Newcastle-upon-Tyne, UK: Cambridge Scholars Publishing, 2009), 15–51; Dana D. Nelson, "'(I Speak Like a Fool, but I Am Constrained)': Samson Occom's *Short Narrative* and Economies of the Racial Self," in *Early Native American Writing: New Critical Essays*, ed. Helen Jaskoski and A. LaVonne Brown Ruoff (New York: Cambridge University Press, 1996), 62.

15. Weber asserts that the capitalist spirit was "the content of the Puritan worldly asceticism, only without the religious basis, which by Franklin's time had died away" (*The Protestant Ethic*, 123). David Waldstreicher contends that Franklin "sought at first to abandon religion" but found that "Christianity, however various in the Anglo-American world, remained the common coin in which a public man had to trade" (*Runaway America: Benjamin Franklin, Slavery, and the American Revolution* [New York: Hill and Wang, 2004], 56–57). Even those scholars who read Christianity as a powerful source of moral, political, and rhetorical strength for Occom feel the need to say explicitly that that they have no reason to doubt the sincerity of his faith. See, for example, Lopenzina, "Compromised Currencies," 30.

16. I share Jace Weaver's sense of Occom as an ironist of "clearly subversive" intent (*That the People Might Live: Native American Literatures and Native American Community* [New York: Oxford University Press, 1997], 53).

17. David Silverman, "The Impact of Indentured Servitude on the Society and Culture of Southern New England Indians, 1680–1810," *New England Quarterly* 74, no. 4 (2001), 623.

18. W. J. Rorabaugh, *The Craft Apprentice: From Franklin to the Machine Age in America* (New York: Oxford University Press, 1986), 3. Franklin was also famous among servants, as John Adams observed, noting Franklin's "universal" appeal with a combination of scorn and envy: "there was scarcely a peasant or a citizen, a *valet de chambre*, coachman or footman, a lady's chambermaid or a scullion in a kitchen, . . . who did not consider him as a friend to human kind" ("On Franklin, May 15, 1811," in Benjamin Franklin, *Benjamin Franklin's Autobiography: An Authoritative Text, Contexts, Criticism*, ed. Joyce Chaplin [New York: Norton, 2012], 285).

19. Waldstreicher, *Runaway America*, 6. Waldstreicher demonstrates the influence of Puritan Boston's culture of servitude on Franklin (ibid., 27–54), showing how it illuminates the congruity of capitalist self-making, republican nation making, and slavery in his "philosophy, his politics, and his practice" (ibid., 89). Other works that contextualize Franklin's apprenticeship are Rorabaugh, *The Craft Apprentice*, and Ralph Frasca, *Benjamin Franklin's Printing Network: Disseminating Virtue in Early America* (Columbia: University of Missouri Press, 2006).

20. A comparison between the 1756 Thomas-Fowle contract and one binding William Mathews to Thomas Windover in New York in 1718, the same year that Franklin was indentured to his brother, reveals only minor differences. The Mathews contract is quoted in Richard Morris, *Government and Labor in Early America* (New York: Columbia University Press, 1946), 366–67.

21. "Contract binding Isaiah Thomas to Zachariah Fowle, Boston 1756," Indenture Collection, American Antiquarian Society, Worcester, MA. Thomas became a

master printer and revolutionary who published the *Massachusetts Spy* and founded the American Antiquarian Society. His *History of American Printing* (1810) discusses Franklin's career, and the two men briefly corresponded in 1787–88.

22. The ideals of master-servant personhood that Mather promoted in *A Good Master Well Served* and *The Negro Christianized* were not exclusive to New England, but part of a transatlantic culture of service. Franklin explicitly praises the novels of Samuel Richardson and Daniel Defoe. See Benjamin Franklin, *Autobiography*, in *Benjamin Franklin's Autobiography: An Authoritative Text, Contexts, Criticism*, ed. Joyce Chaplin (New York: Norton, 2012), 26. All further references to this work will be cited parenthetically as BF. Although it is beyond the scope of this chapter to pursue the point, I would also suggest that Franklin was influenced by their conduct tracts. See Samuel Richardson, *The Apprentice's Vade Mecum* (1734; repr., Los Angeles: Augustan Reprint Society for the University of California, Los Angeles, 1975); Daniel Defoe, *The Complete English Tradesman* (London, 1726). In particular, Franklin seems to have accepted the challenge Richardson lays down in a passage in which he dares "Scepticks" to devise their own systems of morality (*The Apprentice's Vade Mecum*, 66–83).

23. Margaret Ellen Newell, *Brethren by Nature: New England Indians, Colonists, and the Origins of American Slavery* (Ithaca, NY: Cornell University Press, 2015), 232.

24. The terms of a 1716 indenture contract between "an Indian Lad" named James Bryant and Thomas Hathaway seem to have been the source of some dispute. Five years later, two men were called to attest that they had witnessed the original indenture and "do perfectly remember" its terms, including providing "sufficient meat drink Lodging, etc." during the contract and to "dismiss him with" a suit of new clothes, and to give Bryant's mother, Abigail, "twenty shillings in money and a good fat sheep." Abigail likely claimed that Hathaway had not paid her the money, for the witnesses specifically attest that "the payment of the twenty shillings we were Eye witnesses of." The witnesses, Samuel Spooner and John Jonne Jr., signed with marks. "Witness to an indenture, 9 October 1721," Miscellaneous Manuscripts, Massachusetts Historical Society, Boston.

25. In a passage that may have influenced Franklin, who retired early from printing, Mather observes: "There are *Gentlemen*, 'tis true, who Live upon their *Means*; and some in their *Age* retire to eat the pleasant Fruit of the *Labour*, which they underwent in their *Youth*. But yet it well becomes the best *Gentlemen*, to Study some way of being *Serviceable* in the world, and Employ themselves in some good *Business*" (Cotton Mather, *A Christian at his Calling* [Boston, 1701], 42).

26. Cotton Mather, *Bonifacius: An Essay upon the Good*, ed. with an introduction by David Levin (Cambridge, MA: Belknap Press of Harvard University Press, 1966), 153.

27. Ibid., 155.

28. Ibid., 157.

29. Christopher Tomlins, *Freedom Bound: Law, Labor, and Civic Identity in Colonizing English America, 1580–1865* (New York: Cambridge University Press, 2010), 399.

30. David Waldstreicher, "Reading the Runaways: Self-Fashioning Print Culture,

and Confidence in Slavery in the Eighteenth-Century Mid-Atlantic," *William and Mary Quarterly* 56, no. 2 (1999): 243–72.

31. Mitchell Robert Breitwieser, *Cotton Mather and Benjamin Franklin: The Price of Representative Personality* (Cambridge: Cambridge University Press, 1984), 177–78. Jennifer Jordan Baker also notes the "alignment of visibility and public spiritedness" that allows Franklin to function as an embodied voucher for public credit in parts 3 and 4 of the *Autobiography* (*Securing the Commonwealth: Debt, Speculation, and Writing in Early America* [Baltimore, MD: Johns Hopkins University Press, 2005], 91).

32. Michael Warner, *Letters of the Republic: Publication and the Public Sphere in Eighteenth-Century America* (Cambridge, MA: Harvard University Press, 1990), 82.

33. Hilary Wyss, *English Letters and Indian Literacies: Reading, Writing, and New England Missionary Schools, 1750–1830* (Philadelphia: University of Pennsylvania Press, 2012), 37.

34. Quoted in W. DeLoss Love, *Samson Occom and the Christian Indians of New England* (1899; repr., Syracuse, NY: Syracuse University Press, 2000), 161.

35. The most developed analysis along these lines is in Laura Murray, "'Pray Sir, Consider a Little': Rituals of Subordination and Strategies of Resistance in the Letters of Hezekiah Calvin and David Fowler to Eleazar Wheelock, 1764–1768," *Studies in American Indian Literature* 4, nos. 2–3 (1992): 48–74. Peter L. Bayers cites Silverman's essay, "The Impact of Indentured Servitude," as context, noting that Occom's "personal history took a different path" than indentured youths, but Bayers does not pursue the significance of servitude to Occom's self-conception ("'We Unman Ourselves': Colonial and Mohegan Manhood in the Writings of Samson Occom," *MELUS* 39, no. 1 [2014]: 174).

36. Dyck, "The Economic Education of Samson Occom," 4.

37. Wyss, *English Letters and Indian Literacies*, 15; Silverman, "The Impact of Indentured Servitude," 657.

38. Silverman, "The Impact of Indentured Servitude," 625–26. Newell adds that the legal and culture pressures that made such servitude into "de facto" slavery weighed most heavily on women and children (*Brethren by Nature*, 229). See chapter 9, especially 229–32.

39. Silverman, "The Impact of Indentured Servitude," 647.

40. Joanna Brooks, "'This Indian World': An Introduction to the Writings of Samson Occom," in Samson Occom, *The Collected Writings of Samson Occom, Mohegan: Leadership and Literature in Eighteenth-Century Native America*, ed. Joanna Brooks (New York: Oxford University Press, 2006), 20.

41. Ibid., 20 and 21. Lisa Brooks insists on the centrality of the Mason-Mohegan case as a context for understanding Occom's life and work, particularly as a corrective to the outsized role scholars have attributed to his relationship to Wheelock and white society more broadly (*The Common Pot: The Recovery of Native Space in the Northeast* [Minneapolis: University of Minnesota Press, 2008], 51–105).

42. Dyck, "The Economic Education of Samson Occom," 11.

43. Quoted in Lopenzina, "Compromised Currencies," 37.

44. Waldstreicher draws attention to Franklin's own "negro boy," Joseph (*Runa-*

way America, 26). For an interpretation of what "boy" signified in Mohegan norms of masculinity, see Bayers, "We Unman Ourselves," 184–85. Reading norms of masculinity in relation to republican harangues against the effeminacy of luxury, Anne S. Lombard observes: "So long as boys were effeminate, they would remain dependent and have to submit to the authority of a superior. Rational self-mastery, however was manly." (*Making Manhood: Growing Up Male in Colonial New England* [Cambridge, MA: Harvard University Press, 2003], 164).

45. Joanna Brooks, "Letters," in Samson Occom, *The Collected Writings of Samson Occom, Mohegan: Leadership and Literature in Eighteenth-Century Native America*, ed. Joanna Brooks (New York: Oxford University Press, 2006), 62. She comments that "silences and gaps in correspondence mark spaces where Wheelock affirmed his authority by withdrawing his affection, as well as spaces where Wheelock's students refused to allow his surveillance" (ibid.).

46. Laura Murray exposes how the "mutually-agreed upon fiction of the father-son relationship" between Wheelock and his pupils masks a creditor-debtor relationship that more closely resembles a master-servant relationship ("'Pray Sir,'" 60). She does so via an analogy to Pierre Bourdieu's study of the Algerian *khammes*, which focuses on household mastery, but she does not consider New England's own culture of servitude.

47. The distinction between the two kinds of obedience corresponds to Wyss's insightful distinction between two types of Indian personhood that New England missionary schools sought to produce: the passive "Readerly Indian," who was moral and submissive to white men's governance; and the more active "Writerly Indian," who would speak for him or herself and other Native Americans. Wheelock sought to produce readerly Indians (*English Letters and Indian Literacies*, 35), but Occom became a writerly Indian, especially after his return from London. In contrast, in his Stockbridge, Massachusetts, mission, Jonathan Edwards advocates for writerly Indians but still assumes that "he authorizes Indian voices," and thus, Wyss concludes, "the Writerly Indian remains a phantasm" (ibid., 56).

48. Michael Elliott, "'This Indian Bait': Samson Occom and the Voice of Liminality," *Early American Literature* 29, no. 3 (1994): 243.

49. David Murray, *Forked Tongues: Speech, Writing, and Representation in North American Indian Texts* (Bloomington: University of Indiana Press, 1991), 53.

50. David Silverman, *Red Brethren: The Brothertown and Stockbridge Indians and the Problem of Race in Early America* (Ithaca, NY: Cornell University Press, 2010), 101–5 and 138.

51. Quoted in Wyss, *English Letters and Indian Literacies*, 66–67. Wyss notes that Mary Fowler Occom signs herself "your most obedient and very humble serv't" in letters to Wheelock asking for his support, but she adds, "The remarkable range of individuals who in fact do come to Mary's aid—wives, daughters, accountants, and other associates—reveals that however much Wheelock longs to revel in his mastery over Occom, his wife, and Indians in general, the situation is far more complex than he is willing to admit" (ibid., 72).

52. Occom's promotion and embodiment of a specifically Native American version of "service" jibes with Weaver's concept of "communitism," a combination of "com-

munity" and "activism" that is a strategy for "participat[ing] in the healing of the grief and sense of exile felt by native communities and the pained individuals in them" (*That the People Might Live*, 43).

53. For an illuminating discussion of Occom's "radical intercultural adaptation of evangelicalism" and invention and embodiment of "a potent new figure of native American spiritual eloquence and power," see Sandra Gustafson, *Eloquence Is Power: Oratory and Performance in Early America* (Chapel Hill: University of North Carolina Press, 2000), 90.

54. Occom had grappled with alcoholism himself. DeLoss Love discusses Occom's self-recriminations and others' charges against him as a context for the Moses Paul sermon, "the greatest temperance sermon ever delivered to the Indian race" (*Samson Occom and the Christian Indians of New England*, 167). See also ibid., 162–67.

55. Gustafson, *Eloquence Is Power*, 98–99.

56. Silverman, "The Impact of Indentured Servitude," 630.

57. John Winthrop, "A Model of Christian Charity," in *The Puritans in America: A Narrative Anthology*, ed. Alan Heimert and Andrew Delbanco (Cambridge, MA: Harvard University Press, 1985), 82–92.

58. Lisa Brooks brilliantly illuminates the complexity of this trope for the shared material, emotional, and spiritual resources of extended intertribal networks and local communities within "Native space" (*The Common Pot*, xxvii).

59. Lopenzina, "Compromised Currencies," 45; Dyck, "The Economic Education of Samson Occom," 18.

60. On how Occom's petitions both served and enacted Indian sovereignty, see Caroline Wigginton, "Extending Root and Branch: Community Regeneration in the Petitions of Samson Occom," *Studies in American Indian Literature* 20, no. 4 (2008): 24–55.

61. Hilary Wyss, *Writing Indians: Literacy, Christianity, and Native Community in Early America* (Amherst: University of Massachusetts Press, 2000), chapter 4; Silverman, *Red Brethren*, chapter 6.

62. Anna Mae Duane, *Suffering Childhood in Early America: Violence, Race, and the Making of the Child Victim* (Athens: University of Georgia Press, 2010), 147.

63. Jay Fliegelman writes that the lesson of Lockean epistemology is that "as early as we may be victims of language, so may we be its masters when we have succeeded in learning" (*Prodigals and Pilgrims: The American Revolution Against Patriarchal Authority, 1750–1800* [Cambridge: Cambridge University Press, 1982], 111). Christopher Looby notes of Franklin's quest to become a "master" of language by submitting to language that "Franklin's desire . . . was for an evacuation of selfhood. Still, some kind of mastery is what he paradoxically expected to achieve by this means" (*Voicing America: Language, Literary Form, and the Origins of the United States* [Chicago, IL: University of Chicago Press, 1996], 117). As a printer's apprentice, though, Franklin would have seen the method of becoming a master by submitting to the will of a master as a routine developmental model, not as a paradox. "Apprenticeship" functions almost entirely metaphorically for Albert Furtwangler ("Franklin's Apprenticeship and the *Spectator*," *New England Quarterly* 52, no. 3 [1979]: 377–96).

64. Fliegelman reads James's dual status as brother and master as evidence that

"the hierarchical patriarchal relationship had not yet given way to the affectional one" (*Prodigals and Pilgrims*, 108). For a different interpretation of the dispersal of patriarchal authority among several men in the Franklin family, see Looby, *Voicing America*, 105–12.

65. Rorabaugh, *The Craft Apprentice*, 4.

66. Franklin insisted that these contractual mandates applied firmly, not playfully, to slaves. See his 1770 letter in the *Public Advertiser*, quoted in David Roediger, *The Wages of Whiteness: Race and the Making of the American Working Class*, rev. ed. (London: Verso, 1999), 29.

67. In a nice moment of productive overreading, Waldstreicher concludes that when Franklin returns to eating meat, he also gives up "any hope of a world without slavery" (*Runaway America*, 67). On Franklin's vegetarianism and bodily discipline, see Betsy Erkkila, "Franklin and the Revolutionary Body," *ELH* 67, no. 3 (2000): 720–21.

68. Fliegelman's extended reading of Franklin's creative relation to the parable in the *Autobiography*, which Fliegelman deems to be "the optimistic report of a prodigal," remains one of the common paradigms used to understand "antipatriarchalism" in early national American culture (*Prodigals and Pilgrims*, 111). Breitwieser subtly characterizes Franklin as rejecting the Puritan model of the prodigal as "the only alternative to filiopious remembrance" in favor of a model that "combines the independence of the prodigal with the orderliness of the remembrancer—self-fathering" (*Cotton Mather and Benjamin Franklin*, 235). To my knowledge, the Puffy Rolls episode has not been linked to the parable, though Steven Shapiro connects it to Franklin's modernity, "the onset of deinstitutionalized, laissez-faire capitalism and its new breed of masterless bourgeois men, like Benjamin, the runaway apprentice breaking free from the standing order of status hierarchy" (*The Culture and Commerce of the Early American Novel: Reading the Atlantic World-System* [University Park: Pennsylvania State University Press, 2008], 174).

69. Franklin, "The Way to Wealth," 268 (italics in original).

70. Erkkila provides a representative example, arguing that part 2 focuses on "the need to achieve control and mastery of the body" ("Franklin and the Revolutionary Body," 726). The coexistence of master and servant and ideologies of mastery and service might be read as an example of the "residual and emergent modes of social organization in colonial America" that Grantland Rice observes in Franklin's depictions of "certain sets of relationships between writers, readers, and texts" (*The Transformation of Authorship in America* [Chicago, IL: University of Chicago Press, 1997], 51).

71. Warner, *Letters of the Republic*, 80.

72. Breitwieser, *Cotton Mather and Benjamin Franklin*, 193.

73. William Huntting Howell, *Against Self-Reliance: The Arts of Dependence in the Early United States* (Philadelphia: University of Pennsylvania, 2015), 22–26.

74. Michael Zuckerman ties Franklin's "persuasiveness" to his self-mastery, arguing that "Franklin had to persuade people because he could not command them" ("Doing Good While Doing Well: Benevolence and Self-Interest in Franklin's Autobiography," in *Reappraising Benjamin Franklin: A Bicentennial Perspective*, ed. J. A. Leo Lemay [Newark: University of Delaware Press, 1993], 442). In a patronage society, he

adds, Franklin had "to master or mask his aggression in order to achieve advancement and influence" (ibid., 443).

75. Shapiro views the making of "managerial authority" as essential to Franklin's project in the *Autobiography*, arguing that Franklin "sees the power of management in a postabsolutist world as emanating from the gentle art of persuasion and the securing of volunteerist personal assent through the organization of a mass public's consent" (*Culture and Commerce*, 176–77).

76. Zuckerman, "Doing Good While Doing Well," 445. See also William Pencak, "Benjamin Franklin's Autobiography, Cotton Mather, and a Puritan God," *Pennsylvania History* 53, no. 1 (1986): 9.

77. Franklin fails to mention that Keimer "eventually triumphed over [his former apprentice David] Harry and reestablished himself as a master and entrepreneur of letters" (Waldstreicher, *Runaway America*, 76).

78. His gradualist antislavery position was "compromised and compromising" (ibid., 244). Franklin's satirical premise might seem to have played out in the culture of resistance to Barack Obama's presidency, which created the conditions for the election of America's first reality-TV president, the man who issued some of the loudest calls to see Obama's birth certificate. But Donald Trump is no Benjamin Franklin.

79. Benjamin Franklin, "Remarks Concerning the Savages of North America," in Benjamin Franklin, *Autobiography and Other Writings*, ed. Ormond Seavey (Oxford. Oxford University Press, 1993), 318.

80. Nelson, "'(I Speak Like a Fool, but I Am Constrained),'" 52.

81. Benjamin Franklin, "Last Will and Testament, 1788, and Codicil, 1789," in Benjamin Franklin, *Benjamin Franklin's Autobiography: An Authoritative Text, Contexts, Criticism*, ed. Joyce Chaplin (New York: Norton, 2012), 249.

82. Ibid., 249-50.

83. Ibid., 250.

84. For a discussion of the black petitions and the problem of slavery as a political discourse of American liberty and an aesthetic discourse of neoclassical imitation, see Eric Slauter, "Neoclassical Culture in a Society with Slaves: Race and Rights in the Age of Wheatley," *Early American Studies* 2, no. 1 (2004): 81–122.

85. As Wigginton observes, the "mundane necessity of these requests . . . shatters the vanishing Indian image" by asserting Native Americans' "continuing presence and a community with commonplace needs" ("Extending Root and Branch," 50).

Coda: Serving the Plot

1. Ralph Waldo Emerson, "Self-Reliance," in Ralph Waldo Emerson, *Selected Writings of Emerson*, ed. Donald McQuade (New York: Modern Library, 1981), 142.

2. Margaret Fuller, *Woman in the Nineteenth Century* (New York: Norton, 1971), 25 and 15–16.

3. William Apess, *A Son of the Forest: The Experience of William Apess, A Native of the Forest*, in William Apess, *On Our Own Ground: The Complete Writings of William Apess, a Pequot*, ed. with an introduction by Barry O'Connell (Amherst: University of Massachusetts Press, 1992), 41.

4. Catharine Maria Sedgwick, *Hope Leslie; or, Early Times in the Massachusetts* (New York: Penguin, 1998), 4 and 10.

5. Ibid., 345.

6. Hawthorne's comment is quoted in Michael Winship, "Hawthorne and the 'Scribbling Women': Publishing *The Scarlet Letter* in the Nineteenth-Century," *Studies in American Fiction* 29, no. 1 (2001): 3.

7. Nathaniel Hawthorne, *The House of the Seven Gables* (Mineola, NY: Dover, 1999), 192.

8. William Lloyd Garrison, preface to Frederick Douglass, *Narrative of the Life of Frederick Douglass, an American Slave*, in *The Classic Slave Narratives*, ed. Henry Louis Gates Jr. (New York: Signet Classics, 2002), 327.

9. Frederick Douglass, *Narrative of the Life of Frederick Douglass*, in *The Classic Slave Narratives*, ed. Henry Louis Gates Jr. (New York: Signet Classics, 2002), 429.

10. Ibid., 430.

11. Harriet Beecher Stowe, *Uncle Tom's Cabin; or, Life Among the Lowly* (New York: Signet Classics, 1981), 175.

12. Ibid., 338.

13. Samuel Sewall, "Computation that the Importation of Negroes is not so profitable as that of White Servants." In George H. Moore, *Notes on the History of Slavery in Massachusetts* (New York: D. Appleton, 1866), 107.

14. Stowe, *Uncle Tom's Cabin*, 463.

15. Ibid., 262.

16. Paul Krugman, "When the President Is Un-American," *New York Times*, August 14, 2017, accessed October 8, 2017, https://www.nytimes.com/2017/08/14/opinion/when-the-president-is-un-american.html.

BIBLIOGRAPHY

Abbreviations

BA	Samuel Willard, "A Brief Account of a Strange and Unusual Providence"
BF	Benjamin Franklin, *Benjamin Franklin's Autobiography*
GM	Cotton Mather, *A Good Master Well Served*
MM	Samuel Willard, *Mercy Magnified*
NC	Cotton Mather, *The Negro Christianized*
PTV	Thomas Shepard, *Parable of the Ten Virgins*
SG	Mary Rowlandson, *The Sovereignty and Goodness of God*
SH	Thomas Hooker, *The Soules Humiliation*
SO	Samson Occom, *The Collected Writings of Samson Occom*
TCG	John Cotton, *Treatise of the Covenant of Grace*
UI	Samuel Willard, *Useful Instructions*
WL	John Cotton, *The Way of Life*
WP	William Perkins, *The Work of William Perkins*

Acts and Resolves Public and Private of the Province of the Massachusetts Bay. Vol. 1. Boston: Wright and Potter, 1869.

Acts and Resolves Public and Private of the Province of Massachusetts Bay. Vol. 8. Boston: Wright and Potter, 1895.

Adams, Abigail. *The Book of Abigail and John: Selected Letters of the Adams Family, 1763–1784*. Edited with an introduction by L. H. Butterfield, Marc Friedlaender, and Mary-Jo Kline. With a new foreword by David McCullough. Boston: Northeastern University Press, 2002.

Adams, Henry. *The Education of Henry Adams*. New York: Modern Library, 1999.

Adams, John. "On Franklin, May 15, 1811." In Benjamin Franklin, *Benjamin Franklin's Autobiography: An Authoritative Text, Contexts, Criticism*, edited by Joyce Chaplin, 284–88. New York: Norton, 2012.

Ames, William. *Conscience with the Power and Cases Thereof*. London, 1643.

———. *The Marrow of Theology*. Edited and translated by John Dykstra Eusden. Durham, NC: Labyrinth Press, 1983.

Anderson, Virginia DeJohn. "King Philip's Herds: Indians, Colonists, and the Problem of Livestock in Early New England." *William and Mary Quarterly* 51, no. 4 (1994): 601–624.

Apess, William. *A Son of the Forest: The Experience of William Apess, A Native of the Forest*. In William Apess, *On Our Own Ground: The Complete Writings of*

William Apess, a Pequot, edited with an introduction by Barry O'Connell, 3–97. Amherst: University of Massachusetts Press, 1992.

Appadurai, Arjun. *Banking on Words: The Failure of Language in the Age of Derivative Finance*. Chicago, IL: University of Chicago Press, 2016.

Archer, Richard. *Fissures in the Rock: New England in the Seventeenth Century*. Hanover, NH: University of New Hampshire Press, 2001.

Arendt, Hannah. *The Human Condition*. Chicago, IL: University of Chicago Press, 1958.

Armstrong, Nancy, and Leonard Tennenhouse. *The Imaginary Puritan: Literature, Intellectual Labor, and the Origins of Personal Life*. Berkeley: University of California Press, 1992.

Bailey, Richard A. *Race and Redemption in Puritan New England*. New York: Oxford University Press, 2011.

Baker, Jennifer Jordan. *Securing the Commonwealth: Debt, Speculation, and Writing in the Making of Early America*. Baltimore, MD: Johns Hopkins University Press, 2005.

Bannet, Eve Tavor. *Transatlantic Stories and the History of Reading, 1720–1810: Migrant Fictions*. Cambridge: Cambridge University Press, 2011.

Bayers, Peter L. "'We Unman Ourselves': Colonial and Mohegan Manhood in the Writings of Samson Occom." *MELUS* 39, no. 1 (2014): 173–91.

Bayne, Paul. *An Entire Commentary upon the Whole Epistle of the Apostle Paul to the Ephesians*. London, 1643.

Bennett, Bridget. "The Crisis of Restoration: Mary Rowlandson's Lost Home." *Early American Literature* 49, no. 2 (2014): 327–56.

Bennett, Paula. "Phillis Wheatley's Vocation and the Paradox of the 'Afric Muse.'" *PMLA* 113, no. 1 (1998): 64–76.

Bercovitch, Sacvan. *The Puritan Origins of the American Self*. New Haven, CT: Yale University Press, 1975.

———. *The Rites of Assent: Transformations in the Symbolic Construction of America*. New York: Routledge, 1993.

Berlin, Ira. *Many Thousands Gone: The First Two Centuries of Slavery in North America*. Cambridge, MA: Harvard University Press, 1998.

Bousquet, Marc. "We Work." *Minnesota Review* 71–72 (winter–spring 2009): 145–52.

Bozeman, Theodore Dwight. *The Precisianist Strain: Disciplinary Religion and Antinomian Backlash in Puritanism to 1638*. Chapel Hill: University of North Carolina Press, 2004.

Bradford, William. *Of Plymouth Plantation, 1620–1647*. New York: Modern Library, 1981.

Bradstreet, Anne. "The Author to Her Book." In Anne Bradstreet, *The Works of Anne Bradstreet*, edited by Jeannine Hensley, 221. Cambridge, MA: Belknap Press of Harvard University Press, 1967.

Breen, Louise. *Transgressing the Bounds: Subversive Enterprises among the Puritan Elite, 1630–1692*. New York: Oxford University Press, 2001.

Breitwieser, Mitchell Robert. *American Puritanism and the Defense of Mourning:*

Religion, Grief and Ethnology in Mary White Rowlandson's Captivity Narrative. Madison: University of Wisconsin Press, 1990.

———. *Cotton Mather and Benjamin Franklin: The Price of Representative Personality.* Cambridge: Cambridge University Press, 1984.

Brewer, Holly. *By Birth or Consent: Children, Law, and the Anglo-American Revolution in Authority.* Chapel Hill: University of North Carolina Press, 2005.

Brooks, Joanna. "Letters." In Samson Occom, *The Collected Writings of Samson Occom, Mohegan: Leadership and Literature in Eighteenth-Century Native America*, edited by Joanna Brooks, 61–64. New York: Oxford University Press, 2006.

———. "'This Indian World': An Introduction to the Writings of Samson Occom." In Samson Occom, *The Collected Writings of Samson Occom, Mohegan: Leadership and Literature in Eighteenth-Century Native America*, edited by Joanna Brooks, 3–39. New York: Oxford University Press, 2006.

Brooks, Lisa. *The Common Pot: The Recovery of Native Space in the Northeast.* Minneapolis: University of Minnesota Press, 2008.

Bross, Kristina. *Dry Bones and Indian Sermons: Praying Indians in Colonial America.* Ithaca, NY: Cornell University Press, 2004.

Brown, Gillian. *The Consent of the Governed: The Lockean Legacy in Early American Culture.* Cambridge, MA: Harvard University Press, 2001.

———. *Domestic Individualism: Imagining Self in Nineteenth-Century America.* Berkeley: University of California Press, 1990.

Brown, Matthew. *The Pilgrim and the Bee: Reading Rituals and Book Culture in Early New England.* Philadelphia: University of Pennsylvania Press, 2007.

Burnham, Michelle. *Captivity and Sentiment: Cultural Exchange in American Literature, 1682–1861* Hanover, NH: Dartmouth College Press, 1997.

———. *Folded Selves: Colonial New England Writing in the World System.* Hanover, NH: Dartmouth College Press, 2007.

Bush, Sargent, Jr. Introduction to Sarah Kemble Knight, "The Journal of Madam Knight," edited with an introduction by Sargent Bush Jr., in *Journeys in New Worlds: Early American Women's Narratives*, edited by William L. Andrews, Sargent Bush Jr., Annette Kolodny, Amy Schrager Lang, and Daniel B. Shea, 69–83. Madison: University of Wisconsin Press, 1990.

Calvin, Jean. *A Harmony of the Gospels: Matthew, Mark and Luke.* Translated by A. W. Morrison. Edited by David W. Torrance and Thomas F. Torrance. Grand Rapids, MI: William B. Eerdmans, 1975.

Castiglia, Christopher. *Bound and Determined: Captivity, Culture-Crossing, and White Womanhood from Mary Rowlandson to Patty Hearst.* Chicago, IL: University of Chicago Press, 1996.

Clark, Michael. "'Like Images Made Black with the Lightning': Discourse and the Body in Colonial Witchcraft." *Eighteenth Century* 34, no. 3 (1993): 199–220.

Cohen, Charles Lloyd. *God's Caress: The Psychology of Puritan Religious Experience.* New York: Oxford University Press, 1986.

The Colonial Laws of Massachusetts, Reprinted from the Edition of 1660. Boston, 1889. Reprint, Littleton, CO: Fred B. Rothman, 1995.

Coolidge, John. *The Pauline Renaissance in England: Puritanism and the Bible.* London: Oxford University Press, 1970.

Cotton, John. *The Covenant of God's Free Grace.* London, 1645.

———. *Treatise of the Covenant of Grace.* London, 1659.

———. *The Way of Life.* London, 1641.

Cressy, David. *Coming Over: Migration and Communication between England and New England in the Seventeenth Century.* Cambridge: Cambridge University Press, 1987.

Davis, Margaret H. "Mary White Rowlandson's Self-Fashioning as Puritan Goodwife." *Early American Literature* 27, no. 1 (1992): 49–60.

Delbanco, Andrew. *The Puritan Ordeal.* Cambridge, MA: Harvard University Press, 1989.

Demos, John. *Entertaining Satan: Witchcraft and the Culture of Early New England.* New York: Oxford University Press, 1982.

Derounian, Kathryn Zabelle. "The Publication, Promotion, and Distribution of Mary Rowlandson's Indian Captivity Narrative in the Seventeenth Century." *Early American Literature* 23, no. 3 (1988): 239–61.

Di Bonaventura, Allegra. *For Adam's Sake: A Family Saga in Colonial New England.* New York: Liveright, 2013.

Dillon, Elizabeth Maddock. *The Gender of Freedom: Fictions of Liberalism and the Literary Public Sphere.* Stanford, CA: Stanford University Press, 2004.

Douglass, Frederick. *Narrative of the Life of Frederick Douglass.* In *The Classic Slave Narratives*, edited by Henry Louis Gates Jr., 339–436. New York: Signet Classics, 2002.

Duane, Anna Mae. *Suffering Childhood in Early America: Violence, Race, and the Making of the Child Victim.* Athens: University of Georgia Press, 2010.

Dyck, Reginald. "The Economic Education of Samson Occom." *Studies in American Indian Literature* 24, no. 3 (2012): 3–25.

Dyrness, William. *Reformed Theology and Visual Culture: The Protestant Imagination from Calvin to Edwards.* Cambridge: Cambridge University Press, 2004.

Early Church Records of Groton, Massachusetts 1761–1830. Groton, MA, 1896.

Early Records of Groton, Massachusetts, 1662–1707. Edited by Samuel A. Green. Groton, MA, 1880.

Ebersole, Gary. *Captured by Texts: Puritan to Postmodern Images of Indian Captivity.* Charlottesville: University Press of Virginia, 1995.

Elliott, Michael. "'This Indian Bait': Samson Occom and the Voice of Liminality." *Early American Literature* 29, no. 3 (1994): 233–53.

Emerson, Everett. *John Cotton.* Rev. ed. Boston: G. K. Hall, 1990.

Emerson, Ralph Waldo. "Self-Reliance." In Ralph Waldo Emerson, *Selected Writings of Emerson*, edited by Donald McQuade, 129–53. New York: Modern Library, 1981.

Erkkila, Betsy. "Franklin and the Revolutionary Body." *ELH* 67, no. 3 (2000): 717–41.

Fessenden, Tracy. *Culture and Redemption: Religion, the Secular, and American Literature*. Princeton, NJ: Princeton University Press, 2007.

Field, Jonathan Beecher. "The Antinomian Controversy Did Not Take Place." *Early American Studies* 6, no. 2 (2008): 448–63.

———. *Errands into the Metropolis: New England Dissidents in Revolutionary London*. Hanover, NH: Dartmouth College Press, 2009.

Fitzpatrick, Tara. "The Figure of Captivity: The Cultural Work of the Puritan Captivity Narrative." *American Literary History* 3, no. 1 (1991): 1–26.

Fliegelman, Jay. *Declaring Independence: Jefferson, Natural Language, and the Culture of Performance*. Stanford, CA: Stanford University Press, 1993.

———. *Prodigals and Pilgrims: The American Revolution Against Patriarchal Authority, 1750–1800*. Cambridge: Cambridge University Press, 1982.

Foster, Stephen. *The Long Argument: English Puritanism and the Shaping of New England Culture, 1570–1700*. Chapel Hill: University of North Carolina Press, 1991.

Franklin, Benjamin. *Autobiography*. In Benjamin Franklin, *Benjamin Franklin's Autobiography: An Authoritative Text, Contexts, Criticism*, edited by Joyce E. Chaplin, 9–160. New York: Norton, 2012.

———. "Last Will and Testament, 1788, and Codicil, 1789." In Benjamin Franklin, *Benjamin Franklin's Autobiography: An Authoritative Text, Contexts, Criticism*, edited by Joyce E. Chaplin, 243–54. New York: Norton, 2012.

———. "Remarks Concerning the Savages of North America." In Benjamin Franklin, *Autobiography and Other Writings*, edited by Ormond Seavey, 311–18. Oxford: Oxford University Press, 1993.

———. "The Way to Wealth." In Benjamin Franklin, *Autobiography and Other Writings*, edited by Ormond Seavey, 264–74. Oxford: Oxford University Press, 1993.

Frasca, Ralph. *Benjamin Franklin's Printing Network: Disseminating Virtue in Early America*. Columbia, MO: University of Missouri Press, 2006.

Fuller, Margaret. *Woman in the Nineteenth Century*. New York: Norton, 1971.

Furtwangler, Albert. "Franklin's Apprenticeship and the *Spectator*." *New England Quarterly* 52, no. 3 (1979): 377–96.

Games, Alison. *Migration and the Origins of the English Atlantic World*. Cambridge, MA: Harvard University Press, 1999.

Garrison, William Lloyd. Preface to Frederick Douglass, *Narrative of the Life of Frederick Douglass, an American Slave*. In *The Classic Slave Narratives*, edited by Henry Louis Gates Jr., 325–34. New York: Signet Classics, 2002.

Glasson, Travis. *Mastering Christianity: Missionary Anglicanism and Slavery in the Atlantic World*. New York: Oxford University Press, 2012.

Goetz, Rebecca Anne. *The Baptism of Early America: How Christianity Created Race*. Baltimore, MD: Johns Hopkins University Press, 2012.

Goldenberg, David. *The Curse of Ham: Race and Slavery in Early Judaism, Christianity, and Islam*. Princeton, NJ: Princeton University Press, 2005.

Goodman, Nan. "'Money Answers All Things': Rethinking Economic and Cultural

Exchange in the Captivity Narrative of Mary Rowlandson." *American Literary History* 22, no. 1 (2010): 1–25.

———. "Robert Keayne's Nails, or a Mercantilist's Version of Christian Charity." In *The Turn Around Religion in America: Literature, Culture, and the Work of Sacvan Bercovitch*, edited by Nan Goodman and Michael P. Kramer, 223–35. Farnham, UK: Ashgate Publishing, 2011.

Gookin, Daniel. "A Memorandum of Indian Children put Forth into Service to the English." In Mary Rowlandson, *The Sovereignty and Goodness of God, with Related Documents*, edited with an introduction by Neal Salisbury, 141–44. Boston: Bedford Books, 1997.

Gordis, Lisa. *Opening Scripture: Bible Reading and Interpretive Authority in Puritan New England*. Chicago, IL: University of Chicago Press, 2003.

Gould, Philip. *Barbaric Traffic: Commerce and Antislavery in the Eighteenth-Century Atlantic World*. Cambridge, MA: Harvard University Press, 2003.

Graeber, David. *Debt: The First 5,000 Years*. Updated ed. Brooklyn, New York: Melville House, 2014.

Graham, Judith S. *Puritan Family Life: The Diary of Samuel Sewall*. Boston: Northeastern University Press, 2000.

Green, Samuel. *Groton During the Witchcraft Times*. Cambridge, MA, 1883.

Greene, David L. "New Light on Mary Rowlandson." *Early American Literature* 20, no. 1 (1985): 24–38.

Greene, Lorenzo. *The Negro in Colonial New England, 1620–1776*. 1942. Reprint, New York: Atheneum, 1968.

Greven, Philip. *The Protestant Temperament: Patterns of Child-Rearing, Religious Experience, and the Self in Early America*. Chicago, IL: University of Chicago Press, 1988.

Gustafson, Sandra. *Eloquence Is Power: Oratory and Performance in Early America*. Chapel Hill: University of North Carolina Press, 2000.

Habegger, Alfred. "Preparing the Soul for Christ: The Contrasting Sermon Forms of John Cotton and Thomas Hooker." *American Literature* 41, no. 3 (1969): 342–54.

Hall, David D. ed. *The Antinomian Controversy, 1636–1638: A Documentary History*. Durham, NC: Duke University Press, 1990.

———. *The Faithful Shepherd: A History of the New England Ministry in the Seventeenth Century*. Chapel Hill: University of North Carolina Press, 1972.

———. *A Reforming People: Puritanism and the Transformation of Public Life in New England*. New York: Knopf, 2011.

Hambrick-Stowe, Charles E. *The Practice of Piety: Puritan Devotional Disciplines in Seventeenth-Century New England*. Chapel Hill: University of North Carolina Press, 1982.

Hamilton, Marsha L. *Social and Economic Networks in Early Massachusetts: Atlantic Connections*. University Park: Pennsylvania State University Press, 2009.

Harrill, J. Albert. "The Indentured Labor of the Prodigal Son (Luke 15:15)." *Journal of Biblical Literature* 115, no. 4 (1996): 714–17.

Hawthorne, Nathaniel. *The House of the Seven Gables*. Mineola, NY: Dover, 1999.

Hay, Douglas. "England, 1562–1875: The Law and Its Uses." In *Masters, Servants, and Magistrates in Britain and the Empire, 1562–1955*, edited by Douglas Hay and Paul Craven, 59–116. Chapel Hill: University of North Carolina Press, 2004.

Heimert, Alan, and Andrew Delbanco, Introduction to *The Puritans in America: A Narrative Anthology*, edited by Alan Heimert and Andrew Delbanco, 1–15. Cambridge, MA: Harvard University Press, 1985.

Hemphill, C. Dallett. *Bowing to Necessities: A History of Manners in America, 1620–1860*. New York: Oxford University Press, 1999.

Hendrick, Veronica C. *Servants, Slaves, and Savages: Reflections of Law in American Literature*. Durham, NC: Carolina Academic Press, 2011.

Herbert, George. "The Collar." Poetry Foundation. Accessed October 20, 2017. https://www.poetryfoundation.org/poems/44360/the-collar.

Hill, Christopher. *Society and Puritanism in Pre-Revolutionary England*. New York: Schocken Books, 1964.

Holifield, E. Brooks. *A History of Pastoral Care in America: From Salvation to Self-Realization*. Nashville, TN: Abingdon Press, 1983.

Hooker, Thomas. *The Faithful Covenanter*. London, 1644.

———. *The Soules Humiliation*. London, 1637.

Horton, Michael S. *Lord and Servant: A Covenant Christology*. Louisville, KY: Westminster John Knox Press, 2005.

"How Puritans Turned Capitalist." *Idea of the Day* (blog), *New York Times*, August 10, 2010. Accessed October 1, 2017. ideas.blogs.nytimes.com/2010/08/10/how-puritans-turned-capitalist/?_r=0.

Howe, Susan. *The Birth-Mark: Unsettling the Wilderness in American Literary History*. Middletown, CT: Wesleyan University Press, 1993.

Howell, William Huntting. *Against Self-Reliance: The Arts of Dependence in the Early United States*. Philadelphia: University of Pennsylvania, 2015.

Innes, Stephen. *Creating the Commonwealth: The Economic Culture of Puritan New England*. New York: Norton, 1995.

Jackson, Gregory S. *The Word and Its Witness: The Spiritualization of American Realism*. Chicago, IL: University of Chicago Press, 2009.

Kamensky, Jane. *Governing the Tongue: The Politics of Speech in Early New England*. New York: Oxford University Press, 1997.

Karlsen, Carol. *The Devil in the Shape of a Woman: Witchcraft in Colonial New England*. New York: Norton, 1987.

Kaufmann, Michael W. *Institutional Individualism: Conversion, Exile, and Nostalgia in Puritan New England*. Hanover, NH: Wesleyan University Press, 1998.

Kawashima, Yasuhide. *Puritan Justice and the Indian: White Man's Law in Massachusetts, 1630–1763*. Middletown, CT: Wesleyan University Press, 1986.

Kidd, Colin. *The Forging of Races: Race and Scripture in the Protestant Atlantic World, 1600–2000*. Cambridge: Cambridge University Press, 2006.

Kimball, Eric. "'What Have We to Do with Slavery?': New Englanders and the Slave Economies of the West Indies." In *Slavery's Capitalism: A New History of American Economic Development*, edited by Sven Beckert and Seth Rockman, 181–94. Philadelphia: University of Pennsylvania Press, 2016.

Knight, Janice. *Orthodoxies in Massachusetts: Rereading American Puritanism.* Cambridge, MA: Harvard University Press, 1994.

Knight, Sarah Kemble. "Journal of Madam Knight," edited with an introduction by Sargent Bush Jr. In *Journeys in New Worlds: Early American Women's Narratives*, edited by William L. Andrews, Sargent Bush Jr., Annette Kolodny, Amy Schrager Lang, and Daniel B. Shea, 85–116. Madison: University of Wisconsin Press, 1990.

Koo, Kathryn S. "Strangers in the House of God: Cotton Mather, Onesimus, and an Experiment in Christian Slaveholding." *Proceedings of the American Antiquarian Society* 117, part 1 (2007): 143–76.

Krugman, Paul. "When the President Is Un-American." *New York Times*, August 14, 2017. Accessed October 8, 2017. https://www.nytimes.com/2017/08/14/opinion/when-the-president-is-un-american.html.

Kussmaul, Ann. *Servants in Husbandry in Early Modern England.* Cambridge: Cambridge University Press, 1981.

Laffrado, Laura. *Uncommon Women: Gender and Representation in Nineteenth-Century U.S. Women's Writing.* Columbus: Ohio State Press, 2009.

Larcom, Lucy. *A New England Girlhood.* New York; Corinth Books, 1961. Reprint, Gloucester, MA: Peter Smith, 1973.

Lawrence, D. H. *Studies in Classic American Literature.* 1923. Reprint, New York: Viking Press, 1968.

The Laws and Liberties of Massachusetts, Reprinted from the Copy of the 1648 Edition in the Henry E. Huntington Library. Cambridge, MA: Harvard University Press, 1929.

Lears, Jackson. *Something for Nothing: Luck in America.* New York: Penguin, 2003.

Lemire, Elise. *Black Walden: Slavery and Its Aftermath in Concord, Massachusetts.* Philadelphia: University of Pennsylvania Press, 2009.

Lepore, Jill. *The Name of War: King Philip's War and the Origins of American Identity.* New York: Vintage, 1999.

Leverenz, David. *The Language of Puritan Feeling: An Exploration in Literature, Psychology, and Social History.* New Brunswick, NJ: Rutgers University Press, 1980.

Levin, David. *Cotton Mather: The Young Life of the Lord's Remembrancer, 1664–1703.* Cambridge, MA: Harvard University Press, 1978.

Little, Ann M. *Abraham in Arms: War and Gender in Colonial New England.* Philadelphia: University of Pennsylvania, 2007.

Logan, Lisa. "Mary Rowlandson's Captivity and the 'Place' of the Woman Subject." *Early American Literature* 28, no. 3 (1993): 255–77.

Lombard, Anne S. *Making Manhood: Growing Up Male in Colonial New England.* Cambridge, MA: Harvard University Press, 2003.

Looby, Christopher. *Voicing America: Language, Literary Form, and the Origins of the United States.* Chicago, IL: University of Chicago Press, 1996.

Lopenzina, Drew. "Compromised Currencies: Why Samson Occom Is Not Pictured on the One Hundred Dollar Bill." In *Sovereignty, Separatism, and Survivance: Ideological Encounters in the Literature of Native North America*, edited by Benjamin D. Carson, 15–51. Newcastle-upon-Tyne, UK: Cambridge Scholars Publishing, 2009.

Lougheed, Pamela. "'Then Began He to Rant and Threaten': Indian Malice and Individual Liberty in Mary Rowlandson's Captivity Narrative." *American Literature* 74, no. 2 (2002): 287–313.

Love, W. DeLoss. *Samson Occom and the Christian Indians of New England.* 1899. Reprint, Syracuse, NY: Syracuse University Press, 2000.

Main, Gloria L. *Peoples of a Spacious Land: Families and Cultures in Colonial New England.* Cambridge, MA: Harvard University Press, 2001.

Manegold, C. S. *Ten Hills Farm: The Forgotten History of Slavery in the North.* Princeton, NJ: Princeton University Press, 2010.

Marshall, Gordon. *In Search of the Spirit of Capitalism: An Essay on Max Weber's Protestant Ethic Thesis.* New York: Columbia University Press, 1982.

Mather, Cotton. *Bonifacius: An Essay upon the Good.* Edited with an introduction by David Levin. Cambridge, MA: Belknap Press of Harvard University Press, 1966.

———. *A Christian at His Calling.* Boston, 1701.

———. *A Family Well Ordered.* Boston, 1699.

———. *A Good Master Well Served.* Boston, 1696.

———. *Lex Mercatoria.* Boston, 1705.

———. *The Negro Christianized.* Boston, 1706.

———. *Youth under a Good Conduct. A Short Essay to Render Young People Happy.* Boston, 1704.

Mather, Increase. *Renewal of Covenant the Great Duty Incumbent on Decaying or Distressed Churches.* Boston, 1677.

———. [Ter Amicum, pseud.]. "Preface to the Reader." In Mary Rowlandson, *The Sovereignty and Goodness of God, with Related Documents*, edited with an introduction by Neal Salisbury, 63–68. Boston: Bedford Books, 1997.

Matson, Cathy. "Economic History at a Crossroads: Reconsidering Methods, Spaces, and Peoples." *Journal of the Early Republic* 36, no. 4 (2016): 601–12.

McCarthy, Keely. "Conversion, Identity, and the Indian Missionary." *Early American Literature* 36, no. 3 (2001): 353–69.

Melish, Joanne Pope. *Disowning Slavery: Gradual Emancipation and "Race" in New England, 1780–1860.* Ithaca, NY: Cornell University Press, 1998.

Michaelsen, Scott. "Narrative and Class in a Culture of Consumption: The Significance of Stories in Sarah Kemble Knight's 'Journal.'" *College English* 21, no. 2 (1994): 33–46.

Miller, Perry. *Errand into the Wilderness.* 1956. Reprint, Cambridge, MA: Belknap Press of Harvard University Press, 1984.

———. *The New England Mind: From Colony to Province.* 1953. Reprint, Cambridge, MA: Belknap Press of Harvard University Press, 1981.

———. *The New England Mind: The Seventeenth Century.* 1939. Reprint, Boston: Beacon Press, 1961.

Monaghan, E. Jennifer. *Learning to Read and Write in Colonial America.* Amherst: University of Massachusetts Press, 2005.

Moore, George H. *Notes on the History of Slavery in Massachusetts.* New York, D. Appleton, 1866.

Moreton, Bethany. *To Serve God and Wal-Mart: The Making of Christian Free Enterprise*. Cambridge, MA: Harvard University Press, 2009.

Morgan, Edmund. *The Puritan Family: Religion and Domestic Relations in Seventeenth-Century New England*. Rev. ed. New York: Harper and Row, 1966.

Morris, M. Michelle Jarrett. *Under Household Government: Sex and Family in Puritan Massachusetts*. Cambridge, MA: Harvard University Press, 2013.

Morris, Richard. *Government and Labor in Early America*. New York: Columbia University Press, 1946.

Murray, David. *Forked Tongues: Speech, Writing, and Representation in North American Indian Texts*. Bloomington: University of Indiana Press, 1991.

Murray, Laura. "'Pray Sir, Consider a Little': Rituals of Subordination and Strategies of Resistance in the Letters of Hezekiah Calvin and David Fowler to Eleazar Wheelock, 1764–1768." *Studies in American Indian Literature* 4, nos. 2–3 (1992): 48–74.

Nagl, Dominik. "The Governmentality of Slavery in Colonial Boston, 1690–1760." *Amerikastuden* 58, no. 1 (2013): 5–26.

Nelson, Dana D. "'(I Speak Like a Fool, but I Am Constrained)': Samson Occom's *Short Narrative* and Economies of the Racial Self." In *Early Native American Writing: New Critical Essays*, edited by Helen Jaskoski and A. LaVonne Brown Ruoff, 42–82. New York: Cambridge University Press, 1996.

———. *The Word in Black and White: Reading "Race" in American Literature, 1638–1867*. New York: Oxford University Press, 1992.

Neuwirth, Steven. "Her Master's Voice: Gender, Speech, and Gendered Speech in the Narrative of the Captivity of Mary White Rowlandson." In *Sex and Sexuality in Early America*, edited by Merril D. Smith, 55–86. New York: New York University Press, 1998.

New England's First Fruits. London, 1643.

Newell, Margaret Ellen. *Brethren by Nature: New England Indians, Colonists, and the Origins of American Slavery*. Ithaca, NY: Cornell University Press, 2015.

———. "The Changing Nature of Indian Slavery in New England, 1670–1720." In *Reinterpreting New England Indians and the Colonial Experience*, edited by Colin Calloway and Neal Salisbury, 106–36. Boston: Colonial Society of Massachusetts, 2003.

Norton, Mary Beth. *Founding Mothers and Fathers: Gendered Power and the Forming of American Society*. New York: Vintage, 1997.

———. *In the Devil's Snare: The Salem Witchcraft Crisis of 1692*. New York: Vintage, 2003.

Occom, Samson. *The Collected Writings of Samson Occom, Mohegan: Leadership and Literature in Eighteenth-Century Native America*, edited by Joanna Brooks. New York: Oxford University Press, 2006.

O'Malley, Gregory E. *Final Passages: The Intercolonial Slave Trade of British America, 1619–1807*. Chapel Hill: University of North Carolina Press, 2014.

Pateman, Carole. *The Sexual Contract*. Stanford, CA: Stanford University Press, 1988.

Pemberton, Ebenezer. "The Author's Character." In Samuel Willard, *A Compleat Body of Divinity*, 1–3. Boston, 1726.

Pencak, William. "Benjamin Franklin's Autobiography, Cotton Mather, and a Puritan God." *Pennsylvania History* 53, no. 1 (1986): 1–25.

Perkins, William. *The Arte of Prophecying*. London, 1607.

———. *Christian Oeconomy*. In William Perkins, *The Work of William Perkins*, edited by Ian Breward, 416–39. Abingdon, UK: Sutton Courtenay Press, 1970.

———. *A Treatise of the Vocations or Callings of Men*. In William Perkins, *The Work of William Perkins*, edited by Ian Breward, 446–76. Abingdon, UK: Sutton Courtenay Press, 1970.

Pestana, Carla Gardina. *The English Atlantic in an Age of Revolution, 1640–1661*. Cambridge, MA: Harvard University Press, 2004.

Peterson, Mark. *The Price of Redemption: The Spiritual Economy of Puritan New England*. Stanford, CA: Stanford University Press, 1997.

———. "The Selling of Joseph: Bostonians, Antislavery, and the Protestant International." *Massachusetts Historical Review* 4 (2002): 1–22.

Pettigrew, William. *Freedom's Debt: The Royal African Company and the Politics of the Atlantic Slave Trade, 1672–1752*. Chapel Hill: University of North Carolina Press, 2013.

Pettit, Norman. *The Heart Prepared: Grace and Conversion in Puritan Spiritual Life*. New Haven, CT: Yale University Press, 1966.

Plane, Ann Marie. *Colonial Intimacies: Indian Marriage in Early New England*. Ithaca, NY: Cornell University Press, 2000.

Pope, Robert G. *The Half-Way Covenant: Church Membership in Puritan New England*. Princeton, NJ: Princeton University Press, 1969.

Potter, Tiffany. "Writing Indigenous Femininity: Mary Rowlandson's Narrative of Captivity." *Eighteenth-Century Studies* 36, no. 2 (2003): 153–67.

Pulsipher, Jenny Hale. *Subjects unto the Same King: Indians, English, and the Contest for Authority in Colonial New England*. Philadelphia: University of Pennsylvania Press, 2005.

Rice, Grantland. *The Transformation of Authorship in America*. Chicago, IL: University of Chicago Press, 1997.

Richards, Jeffrey. *Theater Enough: American Culture and the Metaphor of the World Stage, 1607–1789*. Durham, NC: Duke University Press, 1991.

Richardson, Samuel. *The Apprentice's Vade Mecum*. 1734. Reprint, Los Angeles: Augustan Reprint Society for the University of California, Los Angeles, 1975.

Richter, Daniel. *Facing East from Indian Country: A Native History of Early America*. Cambridge, MA: Harvard University Press, 2001.

Rivett, Sarah. "Early American Religion in a Postsecular Age." *PMLA* 128, no. 4 (2013): 989–96.

———. *The Science of the Soul in Colonial New England*. Chapel Hill: University of North Carolina Press, 2011.

Robbins, Bruce. *The Servant's Hand: English Fiction from Below*. 1986. Reprint, Durham, NC: Duke University Press, 1993.

Rockman, Seth. "What Makes the Study of Capitalism Newsworthy?" *Journal of the Early Republic* 34, no. 3 (2014): 439–66.

Roediger, David. *The Wages of Whiteness: Race and the Making of the American Working Class*. Rev. ed. London: Verso, 1999.

——— and Elizabeth D. Esch. *The Production of Difference: Race and the Management of Labor in U.S. History*. New York: Oxford University Press, 2013.

Rorabaugh, W. J. *The Craft Apprentice: From Franklin to the Machine Age in America*. New York: Oxford University Press, 1986.

Rosenthal, Caitlin. "Slavery's Scientific Management: Masters and Managers." In *Slavery's Capitalism: A New History of American Economic Development*, edited by Sven Beckert and Seth Rockman, 62–86. Philadelphia: University of Pennsylvania Press, 2016.

Rowlandson, Joseph. "The Possibility of God's Forsaking a People." In Mary Rowlandson, *The Sovereignty and Goodness of God, with Related Documents*, edited with an introduction by Neal Salisbury, 149–64. Boston: Bedford Books, 1997.

Rowlandson, Mary. *The Sovereignty and Goodness of God*. In Mary Rowlandson, *The Sovereignty and Goodness of God, with Related Documents*, edited with an introduction by Neal Salisbury, 63–112. Boston: Bedford Books, 1997.

Ruttenburg, Nancy. *Democratic Personality: Popular Voice and the Trials of American Authorship*. Stanford, CA: Stanford University Press, 1998.

Ryan, Barbara. *Love, Wages, Slavery: The Literature of Servitude in the United States*. Urbana: University of Illinois Press, 2006.

Saffin, John. "A Brief and Candid Reply." In George H. Moore, *Notes on the History of Slavery in Massachusetts*, 251–56. New York: D. Appleton, 1866.

———. *The Note Book of John Saffin 1665–1708*, edited with an introduction by Caroline Hazard. New York: Harbor Press, 1928.

Salisbury, Neal. "Introduction: Mary Rowlandson and Her Removes." In Mary Rowlandson, *The Sovereignty and Goodness of God, with Related Documents*, edited with an introduction by Neal Salisbury, 1–55. Boston: Bedford Books, 1997.

Schmidt, Leigh Eric. *Hearing Things: Religion, Illusion, and the American Enlightenment*. Cambridge, MA: Harvard University Press, 2000.

Schweitzer, Ivy. *The Work of Self-Representation: Lyric Poetry in Colonial New England*. Chapel Hill: University of North Carolina Press, 1991.

Sedgwick, Catharine Maria. *Hope Leslie; or, Early Times in the Massachusetts*. New York: Penguin, 1998.

Sewall, Samuel. "Computation that the Importation of Negroes is not so profitable as that of White Servants." In George H. Moore, *Notes on the History of Slavery in Massachusetts*, 107–8. New York: D. Appleton, 1866.

———. *The Diary of Samuel Sewall 1674–1729*, edited by M. Halsey Thomas. Vol. 1. New York: Farrar, Straus and Giroux, 1973.

———. "The Selling of Joseph." In Samuel Sewall, *The Selling of Joseph: A Memorial*, edited by Sidney Kaplan, 7–26. Amherst: University of Massachusetts Press, 1969.

Shapiro, Steven. *The Culture and Commerce of the Early American Novel: Reading the Atlantic World-System*. University Park: Penn State University Press, 2008.

Shepard, Thomas. "Journal." In Thomas Shepard, *God's Plot: The Paradoxes of Puritan Piety, Being the Autobiography and Journal of Thomas Shepard*, edited with an introduction by Michael McGiffert, 81–238. Amherst: University of Massachusetts Press, 1972.

———. *Parable of the Ten Virgins*. In Thomas Shepard, *The Works of Thomas Shepard*, edited by John A. Albro, 2:13–635. New York: AMS Press, 1967.

———. *The Sincere Convert*. In Thomas Shepard, *The Works of Thomas Shepard*, edited by John A. Albro, 1:9–109. New York: AMS Press, 1967.

———. *The Sound Believer*. In Thomas Shepard, *The Works of Thomas Shepard*, edited by John A. Albro, 1:115–284. New York: AMS Press, 1967.

———. *Thomas Shepard's Confessions*. Edited by George Selement and Bruce C. Woolley. Boston: Colonial Society of Massachusetts, 1981.

Silva, Cristobal. *Miraculous Plagues: An Epidemiology of Early New England Narrative*. New York: Oxford University Press, 2011.

Silverman, David. "The Impact of Indentured Servitude on the Society and Culture of Southern New England Indians, 1680–1810." *New England Quarterly* 74, no. 4 (2001): 622–66.

———. *Red Brethren: The Brothertown and Stockbridge Indians and the Problem of Race in Early America*. Ithaca, NY: Cornell University Press, 2010.

Singley, Carol. *Adopting America: Childhood, Kinship, and National Identity in Literature*. New York: Oxford University Press, 2011.

Slauter, Eric. "Neoclassical Culture in a Society with Slaves: Race and Rights in the Age of Wheatley." *Early American Studies* 2, no. 1 (2004): 81–122.

Slotkin, Richard. *Regeneration through Violence: The Mythology of the American Frontier, 1600–1860*. 1973. Reprint, Norman: University of Oklahoma Press, 2000.

Staloff, Darren. *The Making of an American Thinking Class: Intellectuals and Intelligentsia in Puritan Massachusetts*. New York: Oxford University Press, 1998.

Stein, Jordan Alexander. "Mary Rowlandson's Hunger and the Historiography of Sexuality." *American Literature* 81, no. 3 (2009): 469–95.

Steinfeld, Robert. *The Invention of Free Labor: The Employment Relation in English and American Law and Culture, 1350–1870*. Chapel Hill: University of North Carolina Press, 1991.

Stern, Julia. "To Relish and to Spew: Disgust as Cultural Critique in *The Journal of Madam Knight*." *Legacy* 14, no. 1 (1997): 1–12.

Stoever, William K. B. *"A Faire and Easie Way to Heaven": Covenant Theology and Antinomianism in Early Massachusetts*. Middletown, CT: Wesleyan University Press, 1978.

Stowe, Harriet Beecher. *Uncle Tom's Cabin; or, Life Among the Lowly*. New York: Signet Classics, 1981.

Sweet, John Wood. *Bodies Politic: Negotiating Race in the American North, 1730–1830*. 2003. Reprint, Philadelphia: University of Pennsylvania Press, 2006.

Tawney, R. H. *Religion and the Rise of Capitalism: A Historical Study*. Gloucester, MA: Peter Smith, 1962.

Tomlins, Christopher. *Freedom Bound: Law, Labor, and Civic Identity in Colonizing English America, 1580–1865*. New York: Cambridge University Press, 2010.

Toulouse, Teresa. *The Captive's Position: Female Narrative, Male Identity, and Royal Authority in Colonial New England*. Philadelphia: University of Pennsylvania Press, 2006.

———. "'My Own Credit': Strategies of (E)valuation in Mary Rowlandson's Captivity." *American Literature* 64, no. 4 (1992): 655–76.

Towner, Lawrence. "'A Fondness for Freedom': Servant Protest in Puritan Society." *William and Mary Quarterly* 19, no. 2 (1962): 201–19.

———. *A Good Master Well Served: Masters and Servants in Colonial Massachusetts, 1620–1750*. New York: Garland Publishing, 1998.

Traister, Bryce. "Mary Rowlandson and the Invention of the Secular." *Early American Literature* 42, no. 2 (2007): 323–54.

Twombly, Robert C., and Richard H. Moore. "Black Puritan: The Negro in Seventeenth-Century Massachusetts." *William and Mary Quarterly* 24, no. 2 (1967): 224–42.

Ulrich, Laurel Thatcher. *Good Wives: Image and Reality in the Lives of Women in Northern New England, 1650–1750*. New York: Knopf, 1982.

Valeri, Mark. *Heavenly Merchandize: How Religion Shaped Commerce in Puritan America*. Princeton, NJ: Princeton University Press, 2010.

Van Engen, Abram. *Sympathetic Puritans: Calvinist Fellow Feeling in Early New England*. NY: Oxford University Press, 2015.

Vickers, Daniel. *Farmers and Fishermen: Two Centuries of Work in Essex County, Massachusetts, 1630–1850*. Chapel Hill: University of North Carolina Press, 1994.

Von Frank, Albert J. "John Saffin: Slavery and Racism in Colonial Massachusetts." *Early American Literature* 29, no. 3 (1994): 254–72.

Von Rohr, John. *The Covenant of Grace in Puritan Thought*. Atlanta, GA: Scholars Press, 1986.

Waldstreicher, David. "Reading the Runaways: Self-Fashioning Print Culture, and Confidence in Slavery in the Eighteenth-Century Mid-Atlantic." *William and Mary Quarterly* 56, no. 2 (1999): 243–72.

———. *Runaway America: Benjamin Franklin, Slavery, and the American Revolution*. New York: Hill and Wang, 2004.

Wall, Helena. *Fierce Communion: Family and Community in Early America*. Cambridge, MA: Harvard University Press, 1990.

Warner, Michael. *Letters of the Republic: Publication and the Public Sphere in Eighteenth-Century America*. Cambridge, MA: Harvard University Press, 1990.

Warren, Wendy. *New England Bound: Slavery and Colonization in Early America*. New York: Norton, 2016.

Watertown [Mass.] Records. Watertown, MA, 1894.

Weaver, Jace. *That the People Might Live: Native American Literatures and Native American Community*. New York: Oxford University Press, 1997.

Weber, Max. *The Protestant Ethic and the Spirit of Capitalism*. Translated by Talcott Parsons. 1930. Reprint, London: Routledge Classics, 2002.

Weintraub, Karl. "The Puritan Ethic and Benjamin Franklin." *Journal of Religion* 56, no. 3 (1976): 223–37.

Wheatley, Phillis. "Letter to Samson Occom." In Phillis Wheatley, *The Collected Works of Phillis Wheatley*, edited by John C. Shields, 176–77. New York: Oxford University Press, 1988.

———. "On Being Brought from Africa to America." In Phillis Wheatley, *The Collected Works of Phillis Wheatley*, edited by John C. Shields, 18. New York: Oxford University Press, 1988.

Wigginton, Caroline. "Extending Root and Branch: Community Regeneration in the Petitions of Samson Occom." *Studies in American Indian Literature* 20, no. 4 (2008): 24–55.

Willard, Samuel. "A Brief Account of a Strange and Unusual Providence of God Befallen to Elizabeth Knapp of Groton." In *Remarkable Providences: Readings on Early American History*, edited by John Demos, 421–36. Rev. ed. Boston: Northeastern University Press, 1991.

———. *The Child's Portion: Or the Unseen Glory of the Children of God*. Boston, 1684.

———. *Covenant-Keeping: The Way to Blessedness*. Boston, 1682.

———. *The Duty of a People that have Renewed their Covenant with God*. Boston, 1680.

———. *Heavenly Merchandize*. Boston, 1686.

———. *Mercy Magnified on a Penitent Prodigal*. Boston, 1684.

———. *Reformation the Great Duty of an Afflicted People*. Boston, 1694.

———. *Useful Instructions for a Professing People in a Time of Great Security and Degeneracy*. Cambridge, MA, 1673.

Williams, Daniel E., ed. *Pillars of Salt: An Anthology of Early American Criminal Narratives*. Lanham, MD: Rowman and Littlefield, 1994.

Williams, Raymond. *Marxism and Literature*. Oxford: Oxford University Press, 1977.

Williams, Roger. *A Key into the Language of America*, edited by John Teunissen and Evelyn J. Hinz. Detroit, MI: Wayne State University Press, 1973.

Wilson, Lisa. *Ye Heart of a Man: The Domestic Life of Men in Colonial New England*. New Haven, CT: Yale University Press, 1999.

Winship, Michael B. "Hawthorne and the 'Scribbling Women': Publishing *The Scarlet Letter* in the Nineteenth-Century." *Studies in American Fiction* 29, no. 4 (2001): 3–11.

Winship, Michael P. *Making Heretics: Militant Protestants and Free Grace in Massachusetts, 1636–1641*. Princeton, NJ: Princeton University Press, 2002.

Winthrop, John. "A Model of Christian Charity." In *The Puritans in America: A Narrative Anthology*, edited by Alan Heimert and Andrew Delbanco, 82–92. Cambridge, MA: Harvard University Press, 1985.

———. "Particular Considerations." In *The Puritan Tradition in America, 1630–1720*, edited by Alden Vaughan, 33–35. Columbia: University of South Carolina Press, 1972.

———. *Winthrop's Journal "History of New England, 1630–1649."* Edited by James Kendall Hosmer. Vol. 1. New York: Scribner, 1908.

Wood, Gordon. *The Radicalism of the American Revolution*. New York: Knopf, 1992.

Woodbridge, John. "Epistle to the Reader." In Anne Bradstreet, *The Works of Anne Bradstreet*, edited by Jeannine Hensley, 3. Cambridge, MA: Belknap Press of Harvard University Press, 1967.

Wyss, Hilary. *English Letters and Indian Literacies: Reading, Writing, and New England Missionary Schools, 1750–1830*. Philadelphia: University of Pennsylvania Press, 2012.

———. *Writing Indians: Literacy, Christianity, and Native Community in Early America*. Amherst: University of Massachusetts Press, 2000.

Yazawa, Melvin. *From Colonies to Commonwealth: Familial Ideology and the Beginnings of the American Republic*. Baltimore, MD: Johns Hopkins University Press, 1985.

Young, Alan R. *The English Prodigal Son Plays: A Theatrical Fashion of the Sixteenth and Seventeenth Centuries*. Salzburg, Austria: Institute for English and American Studies, 1979.

Zaret, David. *The Heavenly Contract: Ideology and Organization in Pre-Revolutionary Puritanism*. Chicago, IL: University of Chicago Press, 1985.

Ziff, Larzer. *The Career of John Cotton: Puritanism and the American Experience*. Princeton, NJ: Princeton University Press, 1962.

Zuckerman, Michael. "Doing Good While Doing Well: Benevolence and Self-Interest in Franklin's Autobiography." In *Reappraising Benjamin Franklin: A Bicentennial Perspective*, edited by J. A. Leo Lemay, 441–51. Newark: University of Delaware Press, 1993.

INDEX